The Beginner's Guide to Android Game Development

James S. Cho

GLASNEVIN
PUBLISHING

Glasnevin Publishing, 2nd Floor,
13 Upper Baggot Street, Dublin 4, Ireland
www.glasnevinpublishing.com

This edition published in 2014 by Glasnevin Publishing

ISBN: 978-1-908689-26-9

A CIP catalogue record for this book is available from the British Library

Papers used by Glasnevin Publishing are from well managed forests and other responsible sources.

Glasnevin Publishing books are available at special quantity discounts for use in educational courses or for use in corporate training programs. For more information, please email info@glasnevinpublishing.com

Cover Design by Racheal Reeves: http://rachealreeves.com/

Android™ and Google Play™ are trademarks of Google Inc. The Android robot is reproduced or modified from work created and shared by Google and used according to terms described in the Creative Commons 3.0 Attribution License.

Java™ is a registered trademark of Oracle and/or its affiliates

CONTENTS

Unit 1: Java Basics

Unit 2: Java Game Development

Unit 3: Android Game Development

Unit 4: Finishing Touches

Introduction – You Need to Read This!

For a beginner who knows little or nothing about programming, beginning Android game development can feel like journeying across a strange, new galaxy. There is so much to try, so much to learn and, unfortunately, there are so many different ways to get hopelessly lost.

Perhaps a reason for this is because the term Android game development is misleadingly simple. It suggests that there is just one topic to learn and master, when in reality, Android game development encompasses a variety of different topics, some of which are listed below:

- Basic Programming
- Java Programming Language
- Object-Oriented Design Principles
- Game Development
- Code Optimization
- Android Application Development

If you don't know anything about these topics, don't panic! That is where this guide comes in. This book is written for beginners by someone who was once a beginner—someone who did not know where to even begin. This book will guide you through each step you need to take in order to build your own Android games. If that sounds like what you are looking for, you are reading the correct book!

This book does not make many assumptions about you, the reader. Of course, it assumes that you know some basic math and know how to install a program or application on your computer, but it does not assume that you have written programs before or that you have a degree in physics.

If you are beginning to code for the first time, you will inevitably run into some problems. That's okay! In fact, whenever you get stuck, visit the forum on the book's companion site and ask for guidance. Either the author, a Kilobolt employee, or a kind stranger will gladly help you get your questions answered and problems sorted out.

You will read and write a lot of code in this book. Some chapters will be devoted entirely to learning how to code and will discuss little about game development. The idea behind this is that if you can understand and write code outside of a game development environment, you can easily apply that knowledge when creating graphics and games.

You will get the most out of this book by reading it from start to finish. With that said, if you are very comfortable with a certain topic, you will find that it is okay to skip around. Periodic *checkpoints* allow you to download the latest version of the working project and start working in the middle of a unit or a chapter.

Above all, try to stay motivated! Your journey will not be as suspenseful as traveling across an unknown galaxy, but my hope is that it will be exciting just the same. With this book as your guide, you will be creating your own games in no time.

Although this book is written to be comprehensive, one book cannot do justice to the topic of Android game development. With that said, this book is designed to grow via its companion site. If you feel like coverage on a certain concept is insufficient, let us know at `jamescho7.com/book/feedback`. The author will be happy to explain vital concepts in more detail.

Acknowledgements

I would like to thank Dr. Helen McGrath at Glasnevin Publishing for giving me the opportunity to write this book. You have been immensely helpful throughout the entire process and this work would not have been possible without you.

Next, I would like to extend my deep gratitude to Dr. Bryan Mac Donald, Kyle Yu, Vignesh Sivashanmugam and all others who have tediously combed through my manuscripts, trying to make them as error-free as possible. Thanks to your efforts, this book will be a proper guide to those who want to learn Android game development.

Racheal Reeves, thank you for the amazing work you've done with the book's cover. I truly appreciate the hard work you've put in to make it as great as it is.

Finally, Ling Yang, thank you for your unending patience. Your loving support has motivated me to work through many sleepless nights to finish this book. I hope that you will get around to reading it one day!

WEB RESOURCES

The Java and Android code presented in this book, together with additional resources, are available from the books companion website: http://www.jamescho7.com

Additional information is also available at:
 http://www.glasnevinpublishing.com/books-1/books/the-beginner-s-guide-to-android-game-development

Comments, suggestions and corrections are welcome by email:
info@glasnevinpublishing.com

ABOUT THE AUTHOR

James has been making games for as long as he could draw a robot. He began his game development career on a spiral notebook and eventually founded Kilobolt, an indie game studio based in the United States. In addition, he has taught programming through a series of popular tutorials and served as a teaching assistant at Duke University, while studying Computer Science.

When James is not coding or reading about scientific discoveries, you will find him supporting Manchester United and exploring new types of foods.

UNIT 1

JAVA BASICS

CHAPTER 1: THE FUNDAMENTALS OF PROGRAMMING

Maybe you've picked up this book because you have a passion for building things, and you want to try your hand at developing your own game. Or perhaps locked inside your brain are the ideas for a brilliant game that will change the world as we know it.

In any case, you will not make it very far without becoming a programmer. This chapter will be dedicated to building much of the basic foundation you will need in order to grow into a thoughtful, successful Java programmer who can build great games while writing efficient code. As we will not be executing real programs until Chapter 2, you do not need your computer yet!

What is Programming?

At the basic level, to program is to instruct the computer to perform a series of tasks provided in the form of *code*. Let's have a look at some example code and see what kind of instructions programmers can provide. Don't worry about the meaning behind each symbol and line of code just yet. We will be revisiting these in detail throughout this book. For now, aim to understand the logic. Read the descriptive green text that precedes each line of code and try to follow the following code from top to bottom.

Listing 1.01   A Programmer's Instructions

```
01 // Instruct the computer to create two integer variables called a and
02 // b, and assign values 5 and 6, respectively.
03 int a = 5;
04 int b = 6;
05 // Create another integer variable called result using a + b.
06 int result = a + b;
07 // Print the result (Outputs the value of result to the Console).
08 print("The value of a + b is " + result);
```

Listing 1.01 shows what a programmer types into a text editor such as Notepad (Windows) or TextEdit (Mac). The output produced by the computer on the console display is shown below:

```
The value of a + b is 11
```

Okay, we looked at a small example of some Java code. Here are some key points that you should remember before we proceed further.

KEY POINTS

Basic rule of code execution:
Code is executed line by line from top to bottom. This is a simplification, but it will suit our purposes for now. We will be adding to this rule later.

Comments (//)
In Java, any line of code that follows two forward slashes is a comment. Comments are written specifically for humans (and in this case, as my way of describing code to you), and so comments will not be executed by the Java Virtual Machine (more on the JVM later).

Line numbers
We can refer to each line of code by its line number. You must count both comments and empty lines when determining line numbers! As an example, in listing 1.01, the following code appears on line 3:
```
int a = 5;
```

As demonstrated in listing 1.01, we can instruct the computer to store values (as variables), and we can perform arithmetic and concatenation (combining text with integers – see listing 1.01 line 08) operations with them. We can even display results of these operations to the console. This is just the tip of the iceberg. Before long, we will be drawing a video game character and animating its walk cycle as it moves across the screen, playing a footstep sound at each step. This may look something like this (remember that the following is ONLY an example. Several chapters into this book, you will be writing your own code like this):

Listing 1.02   Examples of More Complex Instructions

```
while (mainCharacter.isAlive()) {
    mainCharacter.updatePosition();
    mainCharacter.animate(time);
    if (mainCharacter.getFoot().collidesWith(ground)) {
        footstepSound.play(volume);
    }
    screen.render(mainCharacter);
}
```

Types of Data

Primitives

In the previous examples, we saw examples of *data types*. For instance, in listing 1.01, we worked with *integer values* 5 and 6, both examples of numerical data. Let's discuss some other types of data, starting with more numerical types.

- *Integers* can be represented using four types, each of which has a different size. In Java, we have the 8-bit `byte`, the 16-bit `short`, the 32-bit `int`, and the 64-bit `long`. Each of these four types can hold positive and negative integer values.
- *Decimal* values (such as 3.14159) can be represented in one of two types: the 32-bit `float` and the 64-bit `double`.
- We can represent a single *character* or *symbol* using `char`.
- To represent something being *true* or *false*, we use the `boolean` type.

These are the most basic data types in Java, and we refer to them as *primitive types*, or *primitives* for short. We will be seeing many of these primitives in action in the upcoming chapters.

Strings

The word *String* refers to a string of characters. As the name suggests, we can use a String to hold multiple *characters* together (the primitive type `char` can only hold one):

```
char firstInitial= 'J';
char lastInitial = 'C';
String name = "James";
```

Notice here that the word `String` is capitalized, while the primitive type `char` is not capitalized. This is because Strings belong to a category called *objects*, not primitives. We will spend a lot of time later discussing these objects, which play a huge role in Java programming. For the time being, however, we will treat Strings as if they were primitives.

Declaring and Initializing Variables

All primitives (and Strings) can be represented as variables. They are each declared (created) using the same basic syntax.

When creating a new variable, we must *always* declare two things: the variable's *data type* and the *variable name*. In most cases, we will also assign a starting value for the variable using the *assignment operator*, the equal sign (=). There are two ways to do this. The first way is to assign a *literal value*, such as 'J' as shown in Figure 1-1. The second way is to assign an *expression* that evaluates to a value, such as 35 + 52 also shown in Figure 1-1 (the expression is evaluated before the value is assigned).

3

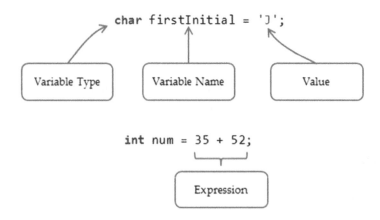

Figure 1-1   Examples of Variable Declarations

The assignment operator (=) does NOT declare equality. This is important. As the name suggests, we use the assignment operator to *assign* a value (on the right side of the equal sign) to a variable (on the left side of the equal sign). For example, consider the following two lines of code:

```
int a = 5;
a = a + 10;
```

In this case, you are not stating a contradictory equality of a and a + 10. You are simply assigning the value of a + 10 to an existing variable a. A common practice to help make this distinction is to read the equal sign as "gets." Figure 1-1 would then read "int num gets the result of the expression 35 + 52."

As an exercise, look through each of the six lines of code in the listing 1.03 and try to read aloud what each line says and what each line means. Remember to distinguish between *literal values* and *expressions* (look back to *Figure 1-1* if you do not remember what these are). Line 1 should be read as, "short num gets 15." Remember that this means, "Declare a new variable of type short called num and assign the *literal value* of 15."

Listing 1.03   Declaring Various Variable

```
1    short numberOfLives = 15;
2    long highScore = 21135315431 - 21542156; // uses an expression
3    float pi = 3.14159f;
4    char letter = 'J';
5    String J = "James";
6    boolean characterIsAlive = true;
```

Variable Names versus Literals

Note that when we describe characters and Strings, we use ' ' and " " to distinguish literal values from *variables* of the same name. As an example, in listing 1.03, the variable name J refers to "James" and the literal 'J' refers to itself.

To Initialize or Not Initialize

In each of the above examples, we *initialized* the variable with a starting value during *declaration*. However, as I've mentioned at the beginning of this section, initialization (assigning a starting value) at declaration of a variable is not *obligatory*, per se. We could, for example, do this:

```
int a, b, c;
a = 5;
b = 6;
c = 7;
```

The first line, above, declares three integers names a, b and c. No starting values are explicitly assigned. The next lines initialize the three integers with the values 5, 6 and 7, respectively.

Although this *is* allowed, we will typically declare variables and initialize them with values in one go, as we did previously in listing 1.03.

KEY POINTS

Declaring Variables:
When we create a new variable, we are storing a value into our computer's memory for later use. We can refer to this value by its variable name.

An analogy is to think of a variable as a box. When we type int a = 5 we are telling the *Java Virtual Machine* to create a box of an appropriate size and to fill it with our value.

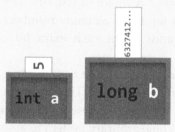

Referencing Variables
Once a variable is created, we should not state its type when referring to it. Providing the name of the variable will suffice.

<u>Copying Values</u>

Consider the following code:

```
int x = 5;  // declare a new integer called x
int z = x;  // assign the value of x to a new integer z
z = z + 5;  // increment z by 5
[End of Program]
```

Can you tell me what the values of x and z are at the end of the program? If you said 5 and 10, then you are correct!

If not, don't worry! Many beginners interpret the second line of this code incorrectly. In line 2 of this code, we are NOT saying that int x and int z refer to the same box (variable). Instead, we are creating a new box called int z giving it a copy of int x's contents.

What does this mean for us? It means that when we increment z by 5 in line 3, z becomes 10 but x remains 5.

It's All About the Bits (A Brief Discussion of Bits and Bytes)

Before we move further, it's worth elaborating on how exactly we store values inside variables. I previously mentioned that different primitives have different bit sizes. As an example, I told you that an int has 32-bits and that a long has 64-bits. You might be wondering, what are bits, exactly?

A *bit* simply refers to a binary digit. In other words, if you have a binary number that only has 0's and 1's, each digit is one bit. Take eight of those bits, e.g. (10101001), and you have a *byte*.

What you have to remember about bits is this: the more bits you have, the more numbers you can represent. To illustrate this, let me ask this question. How many numbers can you represent with one decimal digit? Ten, of course (0, 1, 2, 3, 4, 5, 6, 7, 8 and 9). What about two digits? A hundred (00, 01 ... 99). We see that each additional digit allows us to represent ten times as many numbers. This is the same with binary numbers, except that the addition of each extra bit only allows 2 times as many numbers.

Bits are important in computing because the machines we work with are made up of tiny circuits that can either be on or off. The challenge of data representation arises precisely from this. We can't *directly* represent something like the word "hello" using these circuits. We must use some arbitrary system to associate the word "hello" to some combination of on/off circuits.

In the context of variables, this is what you should know. By declaring a new variable, we are setting aside a specified number of bits in memory (based on the declared type), and storing a binary representation of some data that we want to keep for later use.

Converting between data types

It is possible in Java to convert from one data type to another. For example, we can take an int value and store it inside a long variable. This can happen because the long variable, which holds 64-bits, can easily fit all the data from the smaller type int (32-bit) without much trouble. But what happens if we try to take a 64 bit long number and try to stuff it into a 32-bit int "container"? We risk losing precision. 32 of those 64 bits must be removed before we can place the number into our int variable.

The takeaway is this: if you are converting from a smaller type to a larger type, you are safe. If you are converting from a larger type to a smaller type, you should be mindful so that you do not lose important data. We will see how exactly we can convert from one type to another later in this book.

Operations

We've previously seen that variables can be used to store values and that variables can also be used as operands in operations:

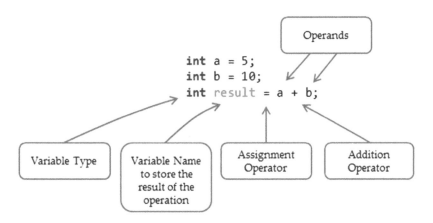

Figure 1-2   Variables can be used to both store values and be operands.

Arithmetic Operations

Below are the five arithmetic operators that you must know. As you look through the examples, keep these two rules in mind:

> ***Rule #1:***   An operation involving two integers will always yield an integer result (decimal values are not allowed on integer variables).

Rule #2:   An operation involving at least one float (decimal values) will always result in a float.

Operator	Description	Example(s) / Value
+ (addition)	Adds the two operands on either side of the plus sign.	`3 + 10 = 13` `4.0f + 10 = 14.0f`
- (subtraction)	Subtracts the second operand from the first operand	`16 - 256 = -240`
* (multiplication)	Multiplies the two operands on either side of the asterisk.	`4.0f * 3 = 12.0f`

/ (division)	Divides the first operand by the second operand.
	
	The aforementioned two rules are especially important here.
		`6/4 = 1`
		Remember Rule #1! We floor (round down) to the nearest integer.
		
		`6.0f/4 = 1.5f`
		Remember Rule #2!

% (remainder, modulus, mod)	Calculates the remainder of an analogous division operation.	`10 % 2 = 0`
		(Perform 10/2, then calculate remainder, which is zero).
		`7 % 4 = 3`

Figure 1-3   The five arithmetic operators that you must know.

Order of Operations

When performing operations, the standard order of operations apply. The computer will perform operations in the following order:

1.   Parentheses (or brackets)
2.   Exponents
3.   Multiplication/division/remainder
4.   Addition/subtraction

The following examples illustrate the importance of the order of operations:

```
print(2 + 5 % 3 * 4);          - Outputs "10"
print((2 + 5) % 3 * 4);        - Outputs "4"
```

Relational/Boolean Operations

We will now look at relational operators that are used to perform comparisons between two values. Note in the following examples that arithmetic operations are performed before relational operations are. All of the following operations yield a *true* or *false* value (boolean).

Operator	Description	Example(s) / Value

`== (equal to)`	Checks whether the two values on either side of the operator are equal.	`(3 + 10 == 13)`
		`= true`
		
		`(true == false)`
		`= false`

`!= (not equal to)`	Checks whether the two values on either side of the operator are NOT equal	`(6/4 != 6.0f/4)` `= true`
`> (greater than)`	Determines whether the first operand has a larger value than the second operand.	`6 > 5` `= true`
`< (less than)`	Determines whether the second operand has a larger value than the first operand.	`6 < 5` `= false`
`>= (greater than or equal to)`	Self-explanatory	`6 >= 6` `= true`
`<= (less than or equal to)`	Self-explanatory	`10 <= 9 + 1` `= true`

`! (inverse)`	Inverts a boolean value. This is a unary operator (you only need one operand).	`!true`
		`= false`
		
		`!false`
		`= true`

Figure 1-4   The relational operators are used to determine how values compare to one another.

KEY POINT

Assignment vs Comparison

Note that the == operator is not the same as the = operator. The former (==) is used for comparing two values and outputs a true or false value. The latter (=) is used to assign a value to a variable.

Listing 1.04 below shows some additional examples of these relational operators in action. I have labeled each of the print statements, so that you can see the corresponding output.

Listing 1.04   Relational Operators

```
01      print(1 == 2); // #1 (equal to)
02      print(!(1 == 2)); // #2 (inverse of print # 1)
03
04      int num = 5;
05      print(num < 5); // #3 (less than)
06
07      boolean hungry = true;
08      print(hungry); // #4
09      print(hungry == true); // #5 (equivalent to print #4)
10      print(hungry == false); // #6
11      print(!hungry); // #7 (equivalent to print #6)
```

The output from listing 1.04 is shown in the box below:

```
false
true
false
true
true
false
false
```

The next few sections will assume that you understand how relational operators work, so make sure you understand what is happening on each printed line. Have a careful look at the examples #5 and #6 from listing 1.04 and understand how we can omit the == operator.

Conditional Operators

The two primary conditional operators are the || (OR) and the && (AND) operators. The || (OR) operator will evaluate to true if the boolean values on EITHER side of the operator are true. The && (AND) operator will only evaluate to true if the boolean values on BOTH sides of the operator are true.

Let's say we want to determine if a given number is a positive even number. To do so, we must check two conditions. Firstly, we must make sure that the number is positive. Secondly, we must check whether the number is divisible by two. Listing 1.05 gives an example of some code we might write to do this:

Listing 1.05   Conditional Operators

```
1       // Remember to evaluate the RIGHT side of the = operator before
2       // assigning the result to the variable.
3       int number = 1353;
4       boolean isPositive = number > 0; // evaluates to true
5       boolean isEven = number % 2 == 0; // evaluates to false
6       print(isPositive && isEven); // prints false
7       print(isPositive || isEven); // prints true
```

Functions (better known in Java as 'Methods')

Let's combine everything that we have learned so far and discuss a very important aspect of programming: functions.

A function is a set of rules. Specifically, a function should accept a value and output a corresponding result. Take a mathematical function for example:

$$f(x) = 3x + 2 \quad : \qquad \text{The input is any number } x. \text{ The output is the result of } 3x + 2$$
$$\text{For example:} \quad f(1) = 3(1) + 2 = 5$$

We can define a very similar function in Java. The following function will accept a `float` input, assign the value to a variable x, and output the result of the operation: `3*x + 2`.

Listing 1.06   A Java Function

```
1       float firstFunction (float x) {
2               return 3*x + 2;
3       }
```

Now, let's take a closer look at how a Java function – also called a *method* for reasons we will discuss in the next chapter – is written. To write a Java function, you begin by declaring the data type of the returned value. You also give the function a name, such as `firstFunction`. Between the parentheses that follow the function's name, you list all the necessary inputs.

The opening and closing curly braces { } will denote where your function begins and where your function ends. If you have trouble visualizing this, it helps to imagine a rectangle around each function by using the curly braces as opposite corners, as shown in Figure 1-5. This helps you quickly determine where each function begins and ends.

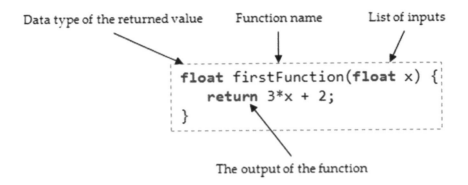

Data type of the returned value   Function name   List of inputs

```
float firstFunction(float x) {
    return 3*x + 2;
}
```

The output of the function

Figure 1-5   An in-depth look at how a function is written

Listing 1.07 shows how we can use functions inside our code. Note that we assume that the function named firstFunction is defined elsewhere in the code, and that it will behave exactly as described in listing 1.06.

Listing 1.07   Using a Function

```
1    // 1. declare a new float called input
2    float input = 3f;
3    // 2. declare a new float called result and initialize it with the
4    // value returned from firstFunction(input);
5    float result = firstFunction(input);
6    // 3. print the result
7    print(result);
```

Output from listing 1.07:

```
11.0
```

An Overview of Function Calls

There's some kind of magic going on in line 5 of listing 1.07. Let's discuss what exactly happens here. As always, we must evaluate the right side of the assignment operator first. Evaluating this expression involves calling the function defined in listing 1.06. When firstFunction is *called* (or invoked), our program will enter the function's definition in listing 1.06, passing in the argument input. In firstFunction, the value of input is accepted and copied into a temporary *local variable* called x, and the function returns the value of 3*x + 2 to the *caller* (line 5). This returned value can be stored as a variable, as we have done using result. The program then proceeds, printing the returned value.

More on Arguments

Functions may accept multiple inputs or even no inputs. In the function definition, you must list all the inputs that you would like your function to accept, by declaring a temporary *local variable* for each desired input. Each of these required inputs can be referred to as *parameters,* and examples are shown in listing 1.08.

Listing 1.08   Function Declarations

```
1       // Requires three integer inputs.
2       int getScore(int rawScore, int multiplier, int bonusScore) {
3           return rawScore * multiplier + bonusScore;
4       }
5
6       // Requires no inputs.
7       float getPi() {
8           return 3.141592f;
9       }
```

Whenever you call a function, you must pass in all the arguments that are listed in between the parentheses. The function `getScore` in listing 1.08, for example, requires three integer variables. You must pass in the appropriate values or your program will not run. Similarly, the function `getPi` will only work if you do not pass in *any* arguments.

As previously mentioned, when we pass in a variable as an argument for a function, only its *value* is made available to the function (the value is *copied*). This means that the following two listings 1.09 and 1.10 will both print the same value, `15700` (from the formula provided on line 3 of listing 1.08).

Listing 1.09   Calling getScore Using Variables

```
1       int num1 = 5000;
2       int num2 = 3;
3       int num3 = 700;
4       print(getScore(num1, num2, num3));
```

Listing 1.10   Calling getScore Using Hardcoded Literal Values

```
1       print(getScore(5000, 3, 700));
```

In listing 1.09 we call the `getScore` function using variables. Notice that since we pass arguments by value, variable names of our arguments do NOT matter. They do NOT have to match the names of the local variables inside the function definition. Listing 1.10 does not use variables and sends *hardcoded* values directly.

Of course, in most of the games that we write, arguments for functions such as getScore will change depending on the user's performance and play style, so we will typically refrain from *hardcoding* literal values.

Summary of Functions

To summarize, we must do two things to use a function: firstly, we must declare its definition (as in listing 1.06). Secondly, we must call the function (as in listing 1.07). When we want our function to have access to some outside value, we pass in an argument. The value returned by a function has a type, which must be explicitly stated when the function definition is declared, and we can store this value using the appropriate variable type and the assignment operator.

Let's have a look at one more function:

Listing 1.11   Still Alive?

```
1       boolean isAlive (int characterHealth) {
2               return characterHealth > 0;
3       }
```

As an exercise, please try and answer the following questions (the answers are at the bottom of this page):

Q1:   The name of the function in listing 1.11 is _____.
Q2:   The function in listing 1.11 returns a value of what type? _____.
Q3:   How many inputs does the function in listing 1.11 take? _____.
Q4:   List the names of all the inputs to the function: _____.
Q5:   Does isAlive(5) evaualte to True or False? _____.
Q6   Does isAlive(-5) evaluate to True or False? _____.
Q7:   Does isAlive(0) evaluate to True or False? _____.

If you are feeling lost, do not despair! Functions can take a while to understand fully. If functions aren't fully clear yet, they will make much more sense as you see more examples in this chapter and begin to write your own functions in Chapter 2.

The answers to the questions above are: Q1: isAlive, Q2: boolean, Q3: one, Q4: characterHealth, Q5: true, Q6: false and Q7: false.

Control Flow Part 1 – If and Else statements

We will now turn our attention to *control flow* (also known as "flow control"), which refers to the order in which our lines of code will execute. Recall the *basic rule of code execution*, which says that code is executed from top to bottom. In the simplest programs, our code will indeed execute from top to bottom in a linear fashion. In any useful program however, we will likely see lines of code that are skipped or even repeated based on some condition. Let's have a look at some examples.

If-Else Blocks

If-else blocks are used to create branches, or multiple paths in our code. We can check conditions such as `characterLevel > 10` to determine a character's title, for example, as shown in Figure 1-6. Depending on the value of `characterLevel`, our game will execute a different instruction. You can see the three paths in Figure 1-6 below.

```
if-else block

if (characterLevel > 10) {
    characterTitle = "King";
} else if (characterLevel > 5) {
    characterTitle = "Knight";
} else {
    characterTitle = "Noob";
}
```

Figure 1-6   An if-else block comprising an if statement, an else-if statement and an else statement

We can create if-else blocks with more or fewer branches than the one in the example above. In fact, we can even nest if statements inside other if statements to allow "inner" branching.

If, Else-if and Else

Whenever you write the word `if`, you are beginning a new if-else block, as shown in the example in Figure 1-6. You could write an if block without any else-if or else statements. That is perfectly okay.

After you begin a new if-else block, each additional `else-if` indicates a new branch. The `else` statement is your "I give up" branch and will handle all remaining cases for you.

You may only take one branch in a given if-else block. In Figure 1-6, notice that if a character's level is 11, conditions in both the `if` *and* `else-if` statements appear be satisfied. You might think that this would result in the `characterTitle` becoming "King" then quickly changing to "Knight." This, however, does not happen, because your code can only take one branch inside an if-else block, as shown in Figure 1-7.

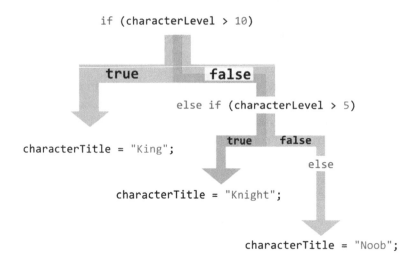

Figure 1-7   An if-else block comprising an if statement, an else-if statement and an else statement

Functions and If-Else Blocks

Functions are back! It turns out that we can make our functions more powerful by using if-else blocks. If-else blocks will work just as they did before, but now that we are wrapping them inside functions, that means we have more curly braces to worry about. See if you can look at the example functions below and determine which opening curly brace corresponds to which closing curly brace. The first one has been done for you!

Example 1
```
String theUltimateAnswer(boolean inBinary) {
   String prefix = "The answer to life the universe and everything:";
   if (inBinary) {
     return prefix + 101010;
   } else {
     return prefix + 42;
   }
}
```

Example 2
```
boolean isLessThanTen(int num) {
    if (num < 10) {
        return true;
    } else {
        return false;
    }
}
```

Example 3
```
boolean isEven(int num) {
    if (num % 2 == 0) {
        return true;
    } else {
        return false;
    }
}
```

Example 4
```
String desertSecurity(boolean hasGun, boolean hasRobots) {
    if (hasGun) {
        return "I've got a bad feeling about this.";
    } else if (hasRobots) {
        return "These are NOT the droids we are looking for."
    } else {
        return "Move along."
    }
}
```

Nested If-Else blocks

Now that we have mastered reading curly braces to determine where each block of code begins and ends, let's take this a step further. Suppose that we want to write a function that will tell us if a person can watch a restricted movie (we will return *true* or *false* depending on eligibility). We will set the following conditions:

- If a person has a fake ID, he or she will be able to watch the movie (regardless of age).
- If a person has an accompanying parent, he or she will be able to watch the movie (regardless of age).
- If a person does not have a fake ID or an accompanying parent:
    - If the person is over the minimum age requirement, he or she will be able to watch the movie.
    - If the person is below the minimum age requirement, he or she will NOT be able to watch the movie.

As you can tell, we are going to have to *nest* if-else statements inside a more general condition in order to handle the person who does not have a fake ID or an accompanying parent. Let's see this in code, starting with the three main branches:

Listing 1.12   Can I watch the movie? (Incomplete)

```
1 boolean canWatch(int age, int minimumAge, boolean fakeID, boolean withParent) {
2       if (fakeID) {
3           return true;
4       } else if (withParent) {
5           return true;
6       } else {
7           // Nested if statements go here.
8       }
9 }
```

Now let's add code for the two specific cases inside our 3rd branch (the else statement).

Listing 1.13   Inner Branches

```
if (age >= minimumAge) {
    return true;
} else {
    return false;
}
```

Now, we can put listing 1.12 and listing 1.13 together to give listing 1.14 (note that I have color-coded the curly braces to make it easier to tell where each block begins and ends):

Listing 1.14   Can I watch this movie? (Complete)

```
01 boolean canWatch(int age, int minimumAge, boolean fakeID, boolean withParent) {
02       if (fakeID) {
03           return true;
04       } else if (withParent) {
05           return true;
06       } else {
07           if (age >= minimumAge) {
08               return true;
09           } else {
10               return false;
11           }
12       }
13 }
```

Simplifying boolean statements

Although the code in listing 1.14 runs perfectly fine, we can clean it up a little bit as shown in listing 1.15.

Listing 1.15   Can I watch this movie? (Simplified #1)

```
01 boolean canWatch(int age, int minimumAge, boolean fakeID, boolean withParent) {
02      if (fakeID || withParent) {   // Two cases were combined into one if statement.
03          return true;
04      } else {
05          if (age >= minimumAge) {
06              return true;
07          } else {
08              return false;
09          }
10      }
11 }
```

Note that in listing 1.15 we have combined two of the cases into one if statement on line 02 using the "OR" operator ||. We can continue to simplify our function by grouping all of the "true" cases together, as shown in listing 1.16

Listing 1.16   Can I watch this movie? (Simplified #2)

```
01 boolean canWatch(int age, int minimumAge, boolean fakeID, boolean withParent) {
02      if (fakeID || withParent || age >= minimumAge) {
03          return true;
04      } else {
05          return false;
06      }
07 }
```

Believe it or not, we can simplify this even further by getting rid of the if-else block completely and just returning the value of (fakeID || withParent || age >= minimumAge) as shown in listing 1.17.

Listing 1.17   Can I watch this movie? (Simplified #3)

```
1 boolean canWatch(int age, int minimumAge, boolean fakeID, boolean withParent) {
2      return (fakeID || withParent || age >= minimumAge);
3 }
```

Writing clean code like this allows you (and your collaborators) to work more efficiently without working complicated logic such as that used in listing 1.14. We will look at more techniques for writing clean code throughout this book.

Control Flow Part 2 – While and For loops

In the previous section, we talked about using if and else blocks to branch our code. We will now be examining two types of loops: the *while loop* and the *for loop*. Loops allow us to perform repetitive tasks. Loops are especially important for us because games can't run without them!

While Loops

Suppose that we want to write a function that will print all positive integers up to a given input *n*. The strategy (algorithm) to solving this problem is as follows:

1. Create a new integer and initialize it at 1.
2. If this integer is less than or equal to the given input n, print its value.
3. Increment the integer by 1.
4. Repeat steps 2 and 3.

We've already learned how to perform the first three steps of this algorithm already. Let's write down what we already know:

Listing 1.18   The Counter (Incomplete)

```
1 ????? countToN(int n) {
2    int counter = 1; // 1. Create a new integer, initialize it at 0.
3    if (counter <= n) { // 2. If this integer is less than or equal to the input
4        print(counter); // Print the value
5        counter = counter + 1; // 3. Increment the integer by 1
6    }
7 }
```

We must address two issues with our code. Firstly, what should be our function's return type (indicated by the question marks on line 1 of listing 1.18)? Should it be an int? Actually, in our case, we do not even have a return statement; this function does not yield any *result* that we could use. When we do not return any value, as in the previous function, we say the return type is void.

Secondly, how can we make this code repeat steps 2 and 3? It's actually pretty simple. We use a *while* loop – a loop that runs as long as a certain condition is satisfied. In our case, all we need to do is replace the word "if" with the word "while." The completed function is shown in listing 1.19 (changed code is highlighted):

Listing 1.19   The Counter (Complete)

```
1 void countToN(int n) {
2    int counter = 1; // 1. Create a new integer, initialize it at 0.
3    while (counter <= n) { // 2. If this integer is less than or equal to the input
4        print(counter); // Print the value
```

```
5        counter = counter + 1; // 3. Increment the integer by 1
6    }
7 }
```

Let's have a look at our function (listing 1.19) line-by-line:
- Line 1 declares our function return type (void), name (countToN) and input (n)
- Line 2 declares a new integer named counter and assigns it a value of 1.
- Line 3 begins a while loop which runs as long as the condition (counter <= n) is satisfied.
- Line 4 prints the current value of the counter variable
- Line 5 increments the counter by 1.

When we reach the end of line 5 (the curly brace on line 6 denotes the end of our loop), our code will execute line 3 again! This repeats until counter becomes greater than n, at which point we break out of our while loop. To see this at work, let's call this function from elsewhere in the code.

```
print("Initiate counting!");
countToN(5); // Call our countToN() function with the argument of 5.
print("Counting finished!");
```

The corresponding output is shown in the box below:

```
Initiate counting!
1
2
3
4
5
Counting finished!
```

That's all there is to a while loop! Just take an if statement and throw the word "while" in there, and your code will repeat a task!

KEY POINT

While Loops

While loops will continue to iterate as long as the given condition evaluates to true. If we have a condition that is always true, such as while (5 > 3) ... , our while loop will never terminate. This is called an *infinite loop*.

For Loops

The counting logic described in listing 1.19 is so frequently used that there's a loop designed just for this purpose. It is called the *for loop*. The for loop syntax allows you to save lines of code, allowing for cleaner solutions to various problems. Here's what it looks like:

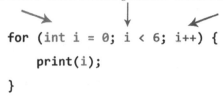

```
for (int i = 0; i < 6; i++) {
    print(i);
}
```

Figure 1-8   The for loop has three main components: initialization, termination and incrementation.

The for loop requires three things. You must *initialize* the counter variable, set a *terminating* condition then define an *increment* expression. The loop will continue to iterate (repeat) until the terminating condition evaluates to false (in the example above, this is until i is greater than 6). After each iteration, i is incremented using the rule given in the increment expression.

Using a for loop the counter in listing 1.19 can be re-written as shown in listing 1.20.

Listing 1.20   The Counter (for loop version)

```
1 void countToN(int n) {
2    for (int i=1; i<=n; i++) {
3       print(i);
4    }
5 }
```

Once you get the syntax down, the for loop is much faster to write than the while loop. The for loop will soon become an invaluable tool for us and will be used in everything from moving sprites to rendering animations.

The Training Wheels Are Now Off!

If you've made it this far, congratulations! You've taken an important first step into the beautiful, complex and occasionally frustrating world of programming. But you can't call yourself a Java programmer until you have written some Java code, so grab your computer and join me in Chapter 2, where we will build some Java programs.

CHAPTER 2: BEGINNING JAVA

Chapter 1 was all about preparing you to become a Java programmer. In this chapter, you will write your first Java programs (including a simple game) and learn about how we can represent our games' characters, power-ups and other entities as *Java objects*.

Object-Oriented Programming

Java is an object-oriented programming language. In an object-oriented paradigm, we represent data in the form of objects in order to help us conceptualize and communicate ideas. For example, when building a video-sharing web application, we might represent each user account (and all its data, such as username, password, uploaded videos and etc.) by creating a **User** object. Each uploaded video may be represented using a **Video** object, many of which can be grouped together inside a **Playlist** object.

Object-oriented programming allows us to organize relevant data together, allowing for clean, robust code that is easier to read and understand. To start exploring this idea, we will write our first Java program.

KEY POINT

Visit the book's companion site
All of the code examples in this book, documentation on errata, and additional bonus content are available at this book's companion site: **jamescho7.com**

Java installation can be a bit tricky. If at any point in this chapter you get lost, please visit the companion site. There are video guides to help you get through the initial Java setup.

Setting Up the Development Machine

Before we can write simple Java programs and build exciting games, we must install some software on our machine. Unfortunately, this is a bit tedious and time consuming, but it will all be worth it once we have our first program running!

Installing Eclipse

We will be making use of an integrated development environment (IDE) for writing Java/Android applications. An IDE is just a fancy name for a tool that helps you write, build, and run programs with ease.

The IDE that we will be using is called *Eclipse* and is a powerful open source software. Rather than installing the pure Eclipse, however, we will be downloading Google's modified version: the Android Developer Tools (ADT) Bundle. Let me explain what all of these terms mean.

In order to build Android applications, you must install the Android SDK (software development kit). Typically you need to download this separately from Eclipse and integrate it using a plug-in (an add-on that provides additional features to Eclipse); however, Google has made this much easier by allowing you to download a bundle that includes Eclipse and the Android SDK – the ADT Bundle.

Follow these steps to get your machine ready for Java/Android development.

1. To download the ADT Bundle, please visit the following site:

    `http://developer.android.com/sdk/index.html`

2. You should see a page similar to that shown in Figure 2-1.

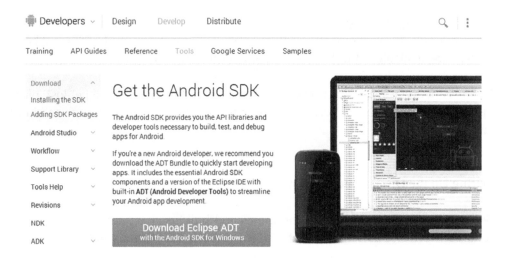

Figure 2-1   Android SDK Download Page

Once you are at this page, click the "Download Eclipse ADT" button. The site will automatically detect your operating system so that you can download the correct version.

3. You will then be presented with the following screen.

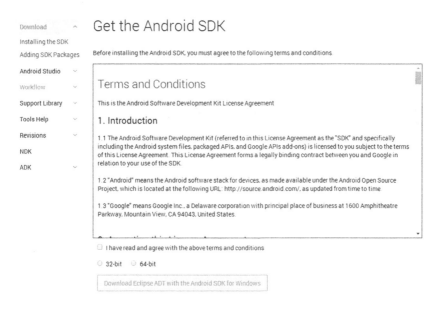

Figure 2-2   32 bit or 64 bit?

You will be downloading the 32-bit or 64-bit version depending on your OS type. Not sure what version you have? Here is how you can find out.

Checking Operating System Type on Windows
On Windows, right click on **My Computer** and click **Properties**. Alternatively, you could navigate to **Control Panel** and search for **System**. You will see a window as shown in Figure 2-3.
If your machine is 32-bit, you will see **32-bit Operating System** or **x86-based processor**. Otherwise, you should see **64-bit Operating System**. Take note of this version and download the appropriate version of ADT.

Checking Operating System Type on Mac OS X
To check whether you have a 32-bit or 64-bit OS, you must check which type of processor you have. The page linked below will tell you how to determine and interpret this information.

http://support.apple.com/kb/HT3696

Take note of your OS version and download the appropriate version of ADT.

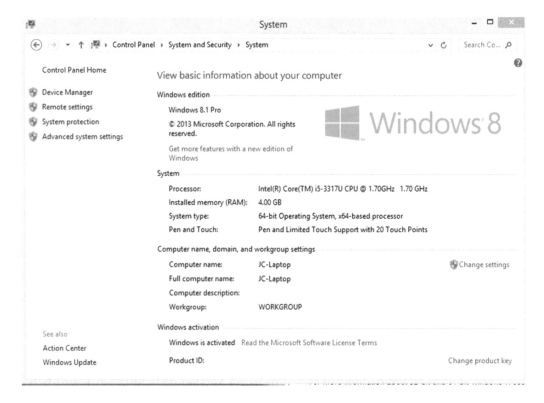

Figure 2-3   Windows System Information

4. The download will be pretty large .zip file (approximately 350 MB at the time of writing). You will simply be extracting the file into a folder that is most convenient for you. You do not have to install it.

Upon extracting, you should see two folders and a file called SDK Manager. You only have to worry about the **eclipse** folder for now, as we will not be working with Android until the later chapters.

Installing the Java Development Kit

Eclipse is built using Java. This means that you need to install a Java Runtime Environment (JRE) on your computer in order to run it on your machine. As we will be running Java programs AND developing Java programs, we will be installing the JDK (Java Development Kit), which bundles a JRE and developer tools.

1. To install the JDK, navigate to the following page.

    ```
    http://www.oracle.com/technetwork/java/javase/downloads/index.html
    ```

    As of this writing, the latest version of the JDK is JDK 8. We will be using **JDK 7** for compatibility reasons so that we do not run into issues with Android development.

    Scroll down until you see **Java SE 7uNN**, where NN will be the latest 2-digit update number for Java 7. In Figure 2-4 shown below, the current version is **Java SE 7u55**. The latest version will vary depending on when you are reading this book.

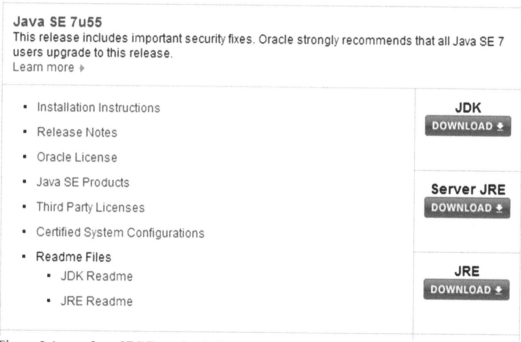

Figure 2-4   Java SE 7 Downloads Box

2. Click the **DOWNLOAD** button below *JDK*. You should be directed to the box shown in Figure 2-5.

Java SE Development Kit 7u55

You must accept the Oracle Binary Code License Agreement for Java SE to download this software.

○ Accept License Agreement   ◉ Decline License Agreement

Product / File Description	File Size	Download
Linux x86	115.67 MB	⬇ jdk-7u55-linux-i586.rpm
Linux x86	133 MB	⬇ jdk-7u55-linux-i586.tar.gz
Linux x64	116.97 MB	⬇ jdk-7u55-linux-x64.rpm
Linux x64	131.82 MB	⬇ jdk-7u55-linux-x64.tar.gz
Mac OS X x64	179.56 MB	⬇ jdk-7u55-macosx-x64.dmg
Solaris x86 (SVR4 package)	138.86 MB	⬇ jdk-7u55-solaris-i586.tar.Z
Solaris x86	95.14 MB	⬇ jdk-7u55-solaris-i586.tar.gz
Solaris x64 (SVR4 package)	24.55 MB	⬇ jdk-7u55-solaris-x64.tar.Z
Solaris x64	16.25 MB	⬇ jdk-7u55-solaris-x64.tar.gz
Solaris SPARC (SVR4 package)	138.23 MB	⬇ jdk-7u55-solaris-sparc.tar.Z
Solaris SPARC	98.18 MB	⬇ jdk-7u55-solaris-sparc.tar.gz
Solaris SPARC 64-bit (SVR4 package)	24 MB	⬇ jdk-7u55-solaris-sparcv9.tar.Z
Solaris SPARC 64-bit	18.34 MB	⬇ jdk-7u55-solaris-sparcv9.tar.gz
Windows x86	123.67 MB	⬇ jdk-7u55-windows-i586.exe
Windows x64	125.49 MB	⬇ jdk-7u55-windows-x64.exe

Figure 2-5   JDK 7 Download Page

3. Check "**Accept License Agreement**" and download the corresponding version of the JDK for your operating system. Here, x86 refers to 32-bit, and x64 refers to 64-bit. If you have forgotten this information, please refer to step 3 in the previous section.
4. Once the download is complete, install the file using the default settings.

Opening Eclipse

Now that we have downloaded all the necessary files, navigate to the extracted **ADT Bundle** folder and open the **eclipse** folder. Once inside the, start up the **eclipse** application (called eclipse.exe on Windows).

If you see an error regarding an undefined PATH variable, this means that Eclipse is unable to find the JRE. To resolve this issue, visit the following page:

```
http://docs.oracle.com/javase/tutorial/essential/environment/paths.html
```

If you have no errors, then you should see the dialog box shown in Figure 2-6 upon opening Eclipse.

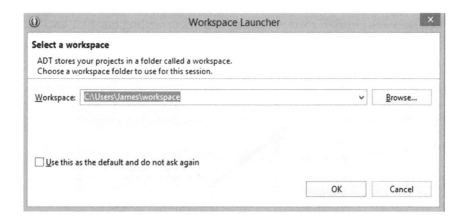

Figure 2-6   ADT Workspace Launcher

Figure 2-6 shows the dialog box asking you to set a workspace – the folder where you will create your Java projects. You can choose or create any folder you wish here, and Eclipse will use it to manage your Java projects.

Writing Your First Program

Upon choosing your workspace, eclipse will open up and you will see the welcome screen shown in Figure 2-7.

Figure 2-7   Android IDE Welcome Screen

Now that we have our IDE ready to go, we can begin writing our first Java program. As we will not be building any Android applications just yet, we can safely exit out of this tab.

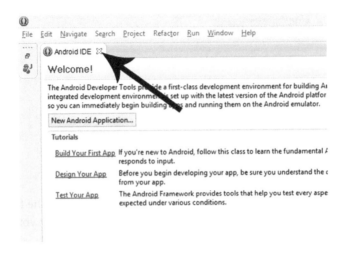

Figure 2-8   Exiting the Welcome Screen

When you have done so, we will gain access to a several different views. For now, you only have to worry about two of them: the Package Explorer and the Editor Window.

Figure 2-9   The Package Explorer and Editor Window

Creating a New Java Project

We can finally get started with our first Java program. Java programs in Eclipse are organized into Projects. To create a new Project, right click (Control + click on Mac) on the Package Explorer, click New, then Java Project, as shown in Figure 2-10.

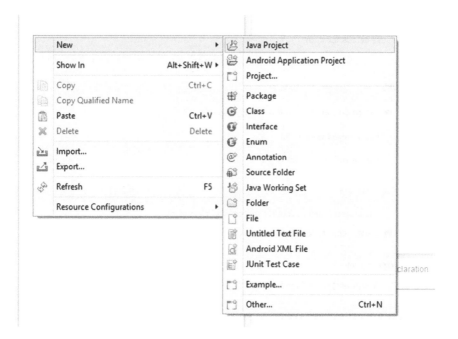

Figure 2-10   Creating a new Java Project

The dialog box shown in Figure 2-11 will now open, asking you to assign a Project name. Let's call the project "Beginning Java". You can leave the other boxes as they are.

Each Java project created in Eclipse will have two important components, as shown in the close-up in Figure 2-12:
1) The **src** folder is where we will place all of our source code (our Java classes). All the code that we will write will be placed inside the **src** folder.
2) The second component, the **JRE System Library**, contains all of the important Java libraries that we can make use of in our own Java code.

After assigning the Project name, click **Finish**.

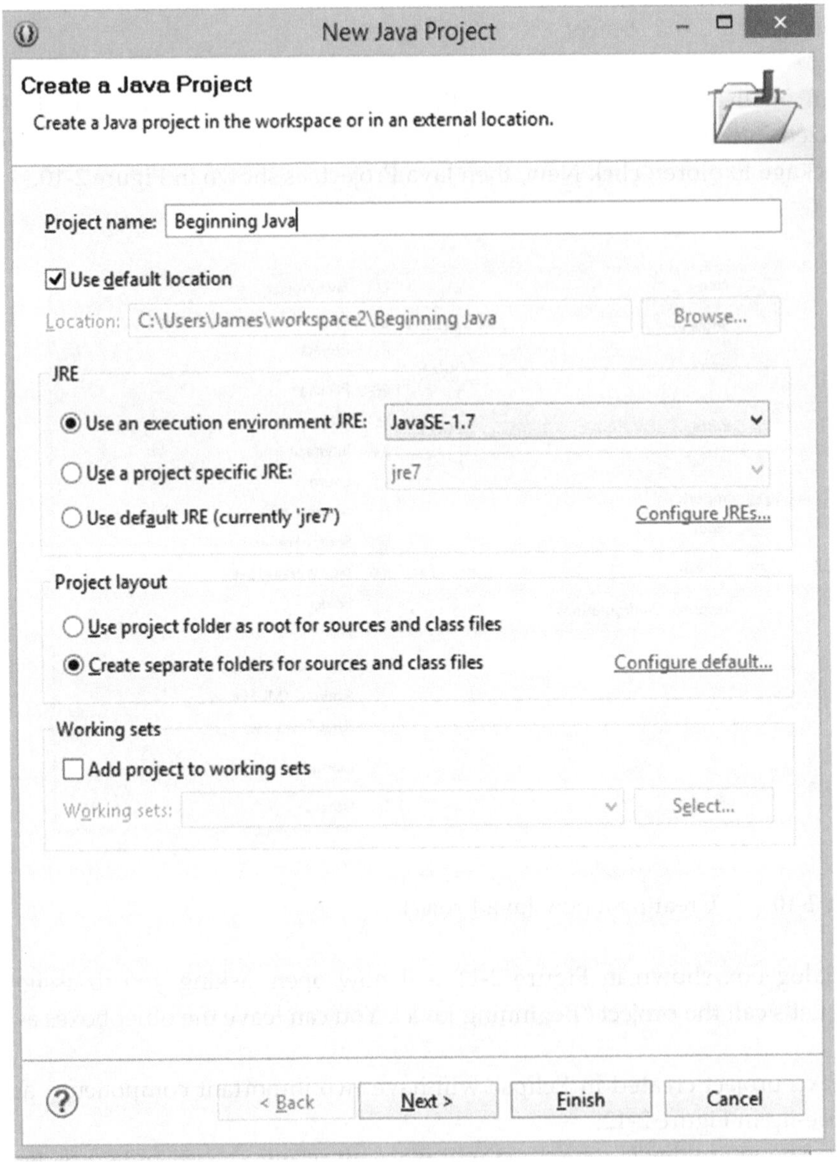

Figure 2-11   New Java Project Dialog

Figure 2-12   Java Project Structure

Creating a Java Class

Java requires us to write our code inside Java *classes*. You can create and modify classes inside a text editor (such as Notepad and TextEdit), or you can use an integrated development environment like Eclipse, as we will be doing.

To write our first program, we must create our first Java class. This is done by right clicking (Control + click for Mac) on the **src** folder, and selecting **New > Class**.

The *New Java Class* dialog will open. We will just provide the class name of **FirstProgram**, leave all the other settings as they are, and click **Finish**, ignoring the warning regarding default packages.

Figure 2-13   The New Java Class Dialog

Our **FirstProgram** class will open automatically in the Editor window. If it does not, double click on the **FirstProgram.java** file in the Package Explorer to the left.

Figure 2-14   Our First Class

Eclipse will generate some basic code for us – as shown in listing 2.1. Note that I have added some additional comments to this code (in green) in order to explain what each line is doing – these will not appear in your code unless you manually add them!

Listing 2.1   FirstProgram.java

```
1      public class FirstProgram {   // Denotes beginning of the class
2                     // methods go here!
3      } // Denotes the end of the class
```

Pay careful attention to the opening and closing curly braces: { and }. The former denotes where the class **FirstProgram** begins, and the latter denotes where the class ends. We will be writing our code in between these curly braces. Curly braces cause a lot of headache for beginning Java programmers, so I will help you with them by labeling them throughout the next several examples. You should pay attention to the curly braces, and get used to seeing the relationships between opening and curly braces.

Main Method

A Java program begins with the *main method*. The main method is called the starting point of a Java program. When you build and execute a program, whatever instructions you provide in the main method will be the first lines of code executed. Add the following code snippet inside the **FirstProgram** class (in between the curly braces).

Listing 2.2   The Main Method

```
public static void main(String[] args) {
            // This is the starting point of your program.
    } // End of main
```

The words `public`, `static`, `String[]` and `args` cause a lot of confusion for first time Java programmers. We will come back to all of these words very soon. For now, focus on three things that we know: the name of the method, the method parameter (input) and the return type.

Referring to the code in Listing 2.2, the name of the method, as you might have guessed, is **main**. It receives one argument – a group of **String** objects – to which we assign the name `args` (This name comes from convention. If it makes you happy, you can name it `rabbits` instead!). The return type, as indicated by the keyword **void**, is *none*; we do not provide any result or output in the main method.

Your program in Eclipse should now look as shown in Figure 2-15.

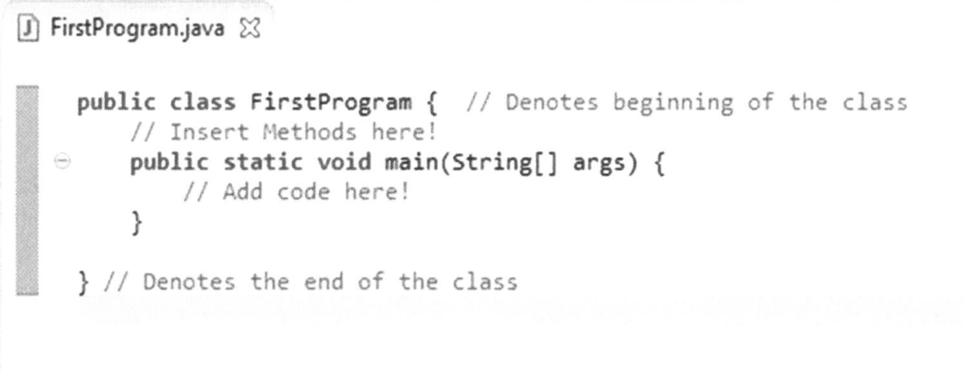

```
 FirstProgram.java ☒

    public class FirstProgram {  // Denotes beginning of the class
        // Insert Methods here!
        public static void main(String[] args) {
            // Add code here!
        }

    } // Denotes the end of the class
```

Figure 2-15   Adding the Main Method

If you are having trouble at this point, I would suggest that you visit the book's companion site at **jamescho7.com**. There's a video guide that will help you get this up and running smoothly!

Saying Hello

A traditional thing to do when learning a new programming language is to print the words "Hello, world" to the console. This is significant for two reasons. Firstly, if you are able to do this successfully, you know that your machine has been setup properly for development (that our IDE and Java installation is running smoothly behind the scenes).

Secondly, this means that you have executed your first line of code in a new environment, and you are ready to take things to the next level!

In Chapter 1, you learned that you can print things by using a `print()` function. Unfortunately, Java does not have such a simple print function due to its object-oriented design (which we will explore soon). Instead, we have to use: `System.out.println()`, where the last two letters are lowercase LN, short for the word line.

Add the following line of code to your main method (in between the curly braces), remembering that `println()` is spelled with an LN not IN.

```
System.out.println("Hello, world! I am now a Java programmer");
```

Your completed class should now look like that shown in listing 2.3.

Listing 2.3   FirstProgram.java – Hello World!

```
1 public class FirstProgram {  // Denotes beginning of the class
2
3       public static void main(String[] args) {  // Beginning of Main
4               System.out.println("Hello, world! I am now a Java programmer");
5       } // End of Main
6
7 } // Denotes the end of the class
```

Notice that we use indentations to represent a level of hierarchy. The **FirstProgram** class contains a `main` method, which is indented once. In turn, the main method contains our `println` statement, which is indented twice. Such formatting allows us to quickly determine how lines of code form structures and where each such section begins and ends.

Executing Java Programs

To execute a program, we simply right click (Control + click on Mac) on our project's **src** folder (or our **FirstProgram** class), click on **Run As > Java Application**, as shown in Figure 2-16.

When you run the program the Console should pop up (as shown in Figure 2-17) and display the message "Hello, world! I am now a Java Programmer". If, for any reason, the console doesn't appear then you can make it appear by clicking on the **Window** menu on the toolbar (top of the Eclipse window) and then selecting **Show View > Console**.

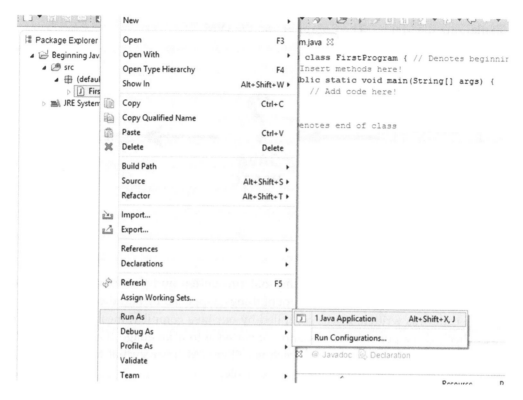

Figure 2-16   Running a Java Application

Figure 2-17   The Console displaying the output from FirstProgram.java

Success! If you were able to get this printed, congratulations! You have written your first Java program successfully.

If you are having trouble getting this message to show, please visit this book's companion website at **jamescho7.com**. There is a video guide that will walk you through the steps and make sure you are able to do this without any issues.

Explaining the Magic – The Compiler and the JVM

Figure 2-18   Java Magic?

What happened between our clicking that run button and the appearance of "Hello, world…?" Believe it or not, a whole lot of things happened behind the scenes. When our source code was written, it was compiled by our Java compiler, meaning that the code was checked for potential errors and converted into a language that only a machine could understand. This machine, which is called JVM (Java Virtual Machine) executed our code, printing the desired text to the console.

The JVM, as its name suggests, is a *virtual machine*. It runs on top of the operating system and is capable of executing Java instructions. The advantage of using such a virtual machine is that you can write cross-platform Java code on one operating system (such as Windows or Mac) that runs on another.

Building a Simple Calculator Program

Now that we've gotten our feet wet, let's bring back some of the concepts that we've discussed in Chapter 1 and build a simple calculator program. Let me give you some on-your-own practice with setting up a new Java program. Remember the major steps:

1. Create a new Java Project (call it **SecondProject**).
2. Create a new Class inside the **src** folder (call it **SimpleCalculator**).
3. Create a *main method*.

If at any time you get stuck, you should refer to the previous sections. Once you have followed the steps above, you should have something that looks like listing 2.4.

Listing 2.4 The SimpleCalcualtor class

```
public class SimpleCalculator {

        public static void main(String[] args) {

        }
}
```

The idea behind our calculator app will be simple. We will create two `float` variables, representing our two operands. We will create a third variable to represent the operation that we wish to perform.

We will represent our operation using an integer, with the following rules:
1: addition
2: subtraction
3: multiplication
4: division

Our source code will examine and use the values of our three variables to produce the arithmetic result that is requested. Add the following code to your **SimpleCalculator** class. The new code is shown on lines 04 to 31.

Listing 2.5 The SimpleCalcualtor class with Logic

```
01 public class SimpleCalculator {
02
03   public static void main(String[] args) {
04       float operand1 = 5;
05       float operand2 = 10;
06       int operation = 1;
07
08       if (operation == 1) {
09
10               // Addition
11               System.out.println(operand1 + " + " + operand2 + " =");
12               System.out.println(operand1 + operand2);
13
14       } else if (operation == 2) {
15
16               // Subtraction
17               System.out.println(operand1 + " - " + operand2 + " =");
18               System.out.println(operand1 - operand2);
19
20       } else if (operation == 3) {
21
22               // Multiplication
23               System.out.println(operand1 + " * " + operand2 + " =");
24               System.out.println(operand1 * operand2);
25
```

```
26        } else {
27
28                // Division
29                System.out.println(operand1 + " / " + operand2 + " =");
30                System.out.println(operand1 / operand2);
31        }
32
33    }
34 }
```

Run the program! You should get the following output:

```
5.0 + 10.0 =
15.0
```

Take a moment to look over the code. Let's make sure we can step through our code line by line and describe what is happening.

We begin by declaring two new `float` variables called `operand1` and `operand2`, initializing them with the values `5` and `10`. We declare a third variable called `operation`, and assign a value of `1`.

After that, we have a series of if-statements, which test the value of our `operation` variable to determine the correct operation to perform. When an if-statement is satisfied, two `System.out.println()` statements execute, printing the result that we see. Notice here that we are concatenating (combining) strings with `float` values by using the addition operator.

Now what do we have to modify if we want to calculate the value of 25 * 17? We simply change the value `operand1` to 25, `operand2` to 17 and `operation` to 3, as shown in listing 2.6.

Listing 2.6   The Modified SimpleCalcualtor class

```
public class SimpleCalculator {

        public static void main(String[] args) {
                float operand1 = 5;
                float operand2 = 10;
                int operation = 1;
                float operand1 = 25;
                float operand2 = 17;
                int operation = 3;

                if (operation == 1) {

                        // Addition
                        System.out.println(operand1 + " + " + operand2 + " =");
                        System.out.println(operand1 + operand2);
```

```
        } else if (operation == 2) {

                // Subtraction
                System.out.println(operand1 + " - " + operand2 + " =");
                System.out.println(operand1 - operand2);

        } else if (operation == 3) {

                // Multiplication
                System.out.println(operand1 + " * " + operand2 + " =");
                System.out.println(operand1 * operand2);

        } else {

                // Division
                System.out.println(operand1 + " / " + operand2 + " =");
                System.out.println(operand1 / operand2);
        }

    }
}
```

Running the program again, we should see:

```
25.0 * 17.0 =
425.0
```

Our **SimpleCalculator** isn't very useful right now. It requires us to change our code every time we want to perform a simple calculation. The better solution would be to ask the user of the program to provide us with the desired values for operand1, operand2 and operation. It turns out that Java gives us a way to do that, but that requires us to understand how to work with objects first, so we will hold off on that discussion for now.

Building a Simple Counting Program

For the next example, we will make use of the *for loop* that we have discussed in Chapter 1 to print all the even numbers between the numbers 5 and 12. This is a simple toy example, but mastering the tricky for loop syntax is important.

Create a new Java project called **CountingProject** and create a new class called **EvenFinder** and add the main method as given in listing 2.7.

Listing 2.7   The EvenFinder class

```
01 public class EvenFinder {
02
03      public static void main(String[] args) {
04              int startingNum = 5;
05              int endingNum = 12;
06
07              for (int i = startingNum; i < endingNum + 1; i++) {
08
09                      // Execute following code if i < endingNum + 1
10
11                      if (i % 2 == 0) {
12                              System.out.println(i + " is an even number.");
13                      } else {
14                              System.out.println(i + " is an odd number.");
15                      }
16
17                      // Repeat for loop
18              }
19      }
20 }
```

Running the program, you should see the following output:

```
5 is an odd number.
6 is an even number.
7 is an odd number.
8 is an even number.
9 is an odd number.
10 is an even number.
11 is an odd number.
12 is an even number.
```

Recall that a for loop has three components. We first *initialize* a counter variable i. We then provide a *terminating condition*, which says, "run this loop until this condition is no longer satisfied." Lastly, we provide a rule for *incrementing* the counter variable.

In the previous example, the counter begins with the value of 5 and increases as long as its value is less than endingNum + 1. When the value of i becomes equal to endingNum + 1, the loop terminates (its body is not executed), and the program ends.

Try walking yourself through this code, line by line, mentally incrementing i each time that the loop "runs." Make sure that you understand when and why the for loop terminates. If this is difficult, it may be helpful to review Chapter 1's section on loops.

Basics of Objects

We've applied the concepts discussed in Chapter 1 to write and run some very simple Java programs. Next, we turn our attention to objects, which will allow us to write more complex and powerful programs.

What are *objects*? It helps to think of Java objects in the same way you envision objects in the real world. Objects in our world have properties that we call *state* and *behavior*.

Let's take your phone for example. Your phone has *state* – it may have a black color, and it may be powered on. These attributes that can help you describe your phone make up its state. Your phone also has *behavior*. It may be able to play music or respond to your touch. Often (but not always), these behaviors are dependent on the phone's state. For example, if your phone is powered off (which is a property of its state), your phone will no longer be able to perform either of these behaviors.

Java objects are not so different. They also have both state and behavior. In fact, you've already been studying states and behaviors throughout this book. *Variables* are often used to describe an object's state. *Functions*, which we will refer to as *methods*, describe an object's behavior.

Figure 2-19 shows an example of how we might design a Java **Phone** object using variables and methods.

Phone object:
State (descriptive properties of the **Phone** object):

`boolean poweredOn;`
 	
 `boolean playingMusic;`
 	
 `String phoneManufacturer = "Samsung";`
 	
 `double androidVersionNumber = 4.4;`

Behavior (actions performed by the **Phone** object):

`togglePower();`
 	
 `playMusic();`
 	
 `upgrade(double newVersion);`

Figure 2-19　　An Outline of a Phone Object

Classes

How does an object outline such as the one in shown Figure 2-19 translate into Java code? We make use of *classes*. We've created many classes already, but we've yet to discuss what a class *is*.

A class provides a template for creating a Java object. A common analogy describes a class as a *blueprint*. Here is what a Phone *class* might look like:

Listing 2.8   An example Phone class

```
01  public class Phone {
02
03      // These variables describe the Phone object's state
04      boolean poweredOn;
05      boolean playingMusic;
06      String phoneManufacturer;
07      double androidVersionNumber;
08
09      // These methods are the Phone object's behaviors
10      void togglePower() {
11              if (poweredOn) {
12                      System.out.println("Powering off!");
13                      poweredOn = false;
14                      playingMusic = false;
15              } else {
16                      System.out.println("Powering on!");
17                      poweredOn = true;
18              }
19      } // ends togglePower method
20
21      void playMusic() {
22              if (poweredOn) {
23                      System.out.println("Playing music!");
24                      playingMusic = true;
25              }
26      } // ends playMusic method
27
28      void upgrade(double newVersion) {
29              if (newVersion > androidVersionNumber) {
30                      androidVersionNumber = newVersion;
31              } else {
32                      System.out.println("Upgrade failed!");
33              }
34      } // ends upgrade method
35
36  } // ends class
```

This **Phone** class shown in listing 2.8 is a blueprint for creating individual **Phone** objects. It tells us what properties (state and behavior) an object requires in order to be a **Phone** object. We will explore what this means using code, and discuss the implications of the class-object relationship in a later section.

KEY POINT

Quick note on naming conventions

You may have noticed that we follow some conventions when naming our classes, variables and methods. These are agreed upon rules that you should learn and follow. Let's go over them in detail.

Class names, variable names and method names should always be one word (multiple words are combined into one). When naming classes, we use what's referred to as UpperCamelCase, where we capitalize the first letter of every word. In this book, names of classes are written in bold, fixed-width font. The following are proper class names (notice that they are all nouns):

Game   **DragonKnight**   **SimpleCalculator**   **MathHelper**

When naming variables and methods, we use camelCase. We lowercase the *first* word of the name and capitalize the first letter of every *subsequent* word. In this book, names of variables and methods are written in regular, fixed-width font. The following are proper variable and method names (notice that variables names are nouns and that method names are verbs):

versionNumber   drawCharacter()   addNum()   failingStudent

Working with Objects

We will now practice working with Java objects. Create a new Java project called **BasicObjects**. Then, create a new class called **World** and give it a simple "Hello, world!" main method, as shown in listing 2.9.

Listing 2.9   World.java

```
public class World {

    public static void main(String[] args) {
        System.out.println("Hello, world!");
    }
}
```

The **World** class will represent a small virtual world that we can populate with objects. It will also be the entry point in our program (the class that we run to begin the program), and hence requires the main method.

Inside the same **src** folder, create a second class called **Phone**, as shown in Figure 2-20.

Figure 2-20   The Class Structure for `BasicObjects`

Copy the **Phone** class from listing 2.8 into the **Phone.java** file in Eclipse. The **Phone** class should *NOT* have a main method. The purpose of **Phone** is to simply hold information regarding a virtual device; it is a representation of an *imaginary* phone, nothing more. The **Phone** and **World** classes together make up one program, and in this book our programs will typically have just one main method – meaning that there will only be one way to start them.

Can you predict what would happen if we were to run our two class program? Will the code from the **World** class run? Will the code from the **Phone** class be run? There's only one way to find out. Start the program by right-clicking (Control + click on Mac) on the **src** folder and running the project as a Java application. You should see the following output:

```
Hello, world!
```

Our project had two classes, but Eclipse was able to locate the class containing the main method (**World.java**), and run it. Despite having a lot of code in the **Phone** class, none of it had any impact on our output, because we had never asked our *main* method to perform any behavior using the **Phone** class. Let's change that.

Creating New Object Variables

We are going to create a new **Phone** object variable using the **Phone** class as our blueprint. To do this, we use the following syntax:

```
Phone myPhone = new Phone();
```

Creating an object variable follows the same pattern that we've previously used to create primitive variables. We begin by declaring the type (**Phone**), then assign a name (myPhone), and lastly assign the value.

The syntactic difference arises in this final step. To create a new **Phone** object, we must use Java's built-in keyword **new** and declare the blueprint that we are using to create our **Phone** object, which is the **Phone** class. Let's add the above line of code into our main method as shown in listing 2.10 on line 5.

Listing 2.10   World.java - updated

```
1       public class World {
2
3               public static void main(String[] args) {
4                       System.out.println("Hello, world!");
5                       Phone myPhone = new Phone();
6               }
7       }
```

We will talk about the effect of the new keyword and what exactly happens when we declare new Phone() later on in the book.

Assigning and Accessing an Object's State

Now we have access to a **Phone** object! myPhone represents a single **Phone** *object* created using the **Phone** *class*. It is an independent entity from any other **Phone** objects that may be created using our blueprint (the **Phone** class) in the future. We use the word *instance* to describe this phenomenon.

To elaborate, let's think about what happens when we mass produce smartphones inside a factory. We use the same blueprint to create thousands of devices, yet they are all independent. They each have their own properties and behaviors, meaning that turning off one device won't affect other phones made using the same blueprint. In much the same way, each object created from a single class is an independent *instance* of that class, and receives its own copy of the various variables that describe the object's state. These variables are called *instance variables*.

We can now start to modify our myPhone's state and invoke its behavior. Let's first assign some initial values for our single **Phone** object's state, as shown in listing 2.11 (lines 06 through 09):

Listing 2.11   World.java - updated

```
01  public class World {
02
03      public static void main(String[] args) {
04              System.out.println("Hello, world!");
05              Phone myPhone = new Phone();
06              myPhone.poweredOn = true;
07              myPhone.playingMusic = false;
08              myPhone.phoneManufacturer = "Samsung";
09              myPhone.androidVersionNumber = 4.4;
10      }
11  }
```

Take note of how we access instance variables that belong to our **Phone** object. To retrieve a specific variable from an object, we use the *dot operator*. The dot operator is used to indicate ownership. For example, myPhone.poweredOn refers to the poweredOn variable that belongs to the myPhone object.

Now that we've assigned some initial values to our **Phone** object's variables, myPhone is a bundle of descriptive data. If someone has access to our myPhone object, he or she will know exactly what myPhone's current state is by printing their values, as shown in listing 2.12 (lines 11 through 15):

Listing 2.12   World.java - updated

```
01  public class World {
02
03      public static void main(String[] args) {
04              System.out.println("Hello, world!");
05              Phone myPhone = new Phone();
06              myPhone.poweredOn = true;
07              myPhone.playingMusic = false;
08              myPhone.phoneManufacturer = "Samsung";
09              myPhone.androidVersionNumber = 4.4;
10
11              System.out.println("myPhone's state:");
12              System.out.println("Powered on: " + myPhone.poweredOn);
13              System.out.println("Playing music: " + myPhone.playingMusic);
14              System.out.println("Manufacturer: " + myPhone.phoneManufacturer);
15              System.out.println("Version: " + myPhone.androidVersionNumber);
16      }
17  }
```

Run the program again. You should see the following output:

```
Hello, world!
myPhone's state:
Powered on: true
```

```
Playing music: false
Manufacturer: Samsung
Version: 4.4
```

As you see, we were able to group together meaningful data into one bundle – a **Phone** object called myPhone. myPhone is now a complex collection of information. We will explore how this can be useful in the coming sections.

Invoking an Object's Behavior

In the previous section, we discussed how to assign and access the state (variables) of objects that we create. We will next discuss *methods*, and learn how to invoke the object's behavior.

Invoking methods also requires us to use the dot operator. We use the dot operator to reference specific methods that belong to a particular object. Add the two lines of code at the bottom of the main method shown in listing 2.12:

```
myPhone.togglePower();
myPhone.upgrade(4.5);
```

If we refer back to our **Phone** class, we will see that the togglePower method checks the current value of the boolean poweredOn, and inverts it (true becomes false, false becomes true). Since myPhone was initially powered on when we created the object, we expect that myPhone will now be powered off. We also can predict that myPhone's androidVersionNumber has changed to 4.5, up from 4.4.

To test this, we will print our myPhone object's state once more, adding some print statements to the bottom of the main method as shown in listing 2.13.

Listing 2.13   Printing myPhone's State

```
01  public class World {
02
03      public static void main(String[] args) {
04              System.out.println("Hello, world!");
05              Phone myPhone = new Phone();
06              myPhone.poweredOn = true;
07              myPhone.playingMusic = false;
08              myPhone.phoneManufacturer = "Samsung";
09              myPhone.androidVersionNumber = 4.4;
10
11              System.out.println("myPhone's state:");
12              System.out.println("Powered on: " + myPhone.poweredOn);
13              System.out.println("Playing music: " + myPhone.playingMusic);
14              System.out.println("Manufacturer: " + myPhone.phoneManufacturer);
15              System.out.println("Version: " + myPhone.androidVersionNumber);
16
```

```
17              myPhone.togglePower();
18              myPhone.upgrade(4.5);
19
20              // include "\n" to skip a line when printing.
21              System.out.println("\nmyPhone's NEW state:");
22              System.out.println("Powered on: " + myPhone.poweredOn);
23              System.out.println("Playing music: " + myPhone.playingMusic);
24              System.out.println("Manufacturer: " + myPhone.phoneManufacturer);
25              System.out.println("Version: " + myPhone.androidVersionNumber);
26      }
27  }
```

The corresponding output is:

```
Hello, world!
myPhone's state:
Powered on: true
Playing music: false
Manufacturer: Samsung
Version: 4.4
Powering off!

myPhone's NEW state:
Powered on: false
Playing music: false
Manufacturer: Samsung
Version: 4.5
```

As predicted, our phone has powered off, and its version number is now 4.5. We were able to invoke our myPhone's behavior to perform specific behavior to modify myPhone's state.

Hiding Our Variables

Notice that, thus far, we were able to modify our **Phone** object's state in two different ways. We were able to access its variables *directly* using the dot operator and assign explicit values, and we were also able to use the behavior provided by the **Phone** object to *indirectly* modify our **Phone** object's state.

If we are able to *directly* reach into our myPhone object and pull out and modify its information, we say that the object's variables are exposed. From this point on, we will refrain from exposing our variables, as this can be problematic for many reasons.

For instance, what if someone tried to assign an *illegal* (or illogical) value to a variable? The following code would be accepted by our Java program, but it may cause problems later on if we were to extend this program, and these values actually mattered for some other functionality.

```
myPhone.androidVersionNumber = -10;    // Version should be positive
myPhone.poweredOn = false;             // This is fine
myPhone.playingMusic = true;           // Shouldn't play music while phone is off
```

Another reason that exposing variables can be problematic is that we may be dealing with sensitive information. If we were running the video-sharing website discussed in the first page of this chapter, we would not want people to be able to access our **User** object's `password` variable – it should always be hidden. Security is an issue here.

The third reason we want to hide our variables is for maintenance and scale. When we later have more complex programs and games with lots of different types of objects interacting with each other, we want to reduce dependencies (functionality that relies very heavily on specific interactions) as much as possible. We need to keep in mind that programs and games can change. You may choose to remove classes and create new ones, but you don't want to have to rewire an entire application to handle a minor change.

For example, let's say you have an **Enemy** class that interacts very well with a **Player** class and a **GameLevel** class. Later on, you decide that you want to remove the **Enemy** and replace it with a **SuperZombieOrangutan** class. If there are too many dependencies between the **Enemy** and the **Player** and **GameLevel** classes, you may end up rewriting both of those classes to handle your new enemy type – you'd be creating three new classes rather than one. This can become a malicious pattern. If this were a time-consuming undertaking, you might decide that the change isn't worth the effort, which would mean your game would have one fewer zombie orangutan. That's never a good thing.

In short, you want to be able to add the features you want to your games without worrying about what a nightmare it would be to modify your existing code. This means that we want to keep our classes as independent as possible, and hiding our variables is a step in the right direction. We will explore this concept further in a later chapter.

Improving Our Program

Let's keep the above principles in mind and try to improve our program. We begin by adding the built-in Java keyword `private` as a modifier to all of our **Phone** object's variables, as shown in listing 2.14, lines 04 to 07.

Listing 2.14   Hiding the variables in the Phone Class

```
01  public class Phone {
02
03      // These variables describe the Phone object's state
04      private boolean poweredOn;
05      private boolean playingMusic;
```

```
06        private String phoneManufacturer;
07        private double androidVersionNumber;
08
09        // These methods are the Phone object's behaviors
10        void togglePower() {
11                if (poweredOn) {
12                        System.out.println("Powering off!");
13                        poweredOn = false;
14                        playingMusic = false;
15                } else {
16                        System.out.println("Powering on!");
17                        poweredOn = true;
18                }
19        } // ends togglePower method
20
21        void playMusic() {
22                if (poweredOn) {
23                        System.out.println("Playing music!");
24                }
25        } // ends playMusic method
26
27        void upgrade(double newVersion) {
28                if (newVersion > androidVersionNumber) {
29                        androidVersionNumber = newVersion;
30                } else {
31                        System.out.println("Upgrade failed!");
32                }
33        } // ends upgrade method
34
35  } // ends class
```

Making our variables private means that other classes will no longer be able to access them directly, meaning that the variables are no longer exposed. Because of this, you will see errors appear in your **World** class, as shown in Figure 2-21 (you cannot directly refer to a private variable from a different class).

Your program currently has what we call compile-time errors (errors that occur during compilation of your code – review Figure 2-18 and the subsequent discussion). A program with compile-time errors will never run. The JVM won't even accept it. Let's remove all of the lines that are causing errors as shown in listing 2.15 (remove all the lines that have a line through them).

```
public class World {

    public static void main(String[] args) {
        System.out.println("Hello, world!");
        Phone myPhone = new Phone();
        myPhone.poweredOn = true;
        myPhone.playingMusic = false;
        myPhone.phoneManufacturer = "Samsung";
        myPhone.androidVersionNumber = 4.4;

        System.out.println("myPhone's state:");
        System.out.println("Powered on: " + myPhone.poweredOn);
        System.out.println("Playing music: " + myPhone.playingMusic);
        System.out.println("Manufacturer: " + myPhone.phoneManufacturer);
        System.out.println("Version: " + myPhone.androidVersionNumber);

        myPhone.togglePower();
        myPhone.upgrade(4.5);

        // include "\n" to skip a line when printing.
            System.out.println("\nmyPhone's NEW state:");
        System.out.println("Powered on: " + myPhone.poweredOn);
        System.out.println("Playing music: " + myPhone.playingMusic);
        System.out.println("Manufacturer: " + myPhone.phoneManufacturer);
        System.out.println("Version: " + myPhone.androidVersionNumber);
    }
}
```

Figure 2-21   A Catastrophic Error?

Listing 2.15   World.java – Removing the Errors

```
01  public class World {
02
03      public static void main(String[] args) {
04          System.out.println("Hello, world!");
05          Phone myPhone = new Phone();
06          myPhone.poweredOn = true;
07          myPhone.playingMusic = false;
08          myPhone.phoneManufacturer = "Samsung";
09          myPhone.androidVersionNumber = 4.4;
10
11          System.out.println("myPhone's state:");
12          System.out.println("Powered on: " + myPhone.poweredOn);
13          System.out.println("Playing music: " + myPhone.playingMusic);
14          System.out.println("Manufacturer: " + myPhone.phoneManufacturer);
15          System.out.println("Version: " + myPhone.androidVersionNumber);
16
17          myPhone.togglePower();
18          myPhone.upgrade(4.5);
19
20          // include "\n" to skip a line when printing.
21          System.out.println("\nmyPhone's NEW state:");
22          System.out.println("Powered on: " + myPhone.poweredOn);
23          System.out.println("Playing music: " + myPhone.playingMusic);
```

```
24                   System.out.println("Manufacturer: " + myPhone.phoneManufacturer);
25                   System.out.println("Version: " + myPhone.androidVersionNumber);
26       }
27   }
```

In performing this clean-up, we have just removed two features from our program. We are no longer able to assign starting values for our **Phone** objects' variables, and we are no longer able to access these variables to print them. We can bring these features back in a more efficient way by providing methods inside the **Phone** class that performs these tasks for us.

Let's add two new methods to our **Phone** class `initialize()` and `describe()`, as shown in listing 2.16, and provide starting values for our `playingMusic` and `androidVersionNumber` variables (lines 05 and 07 of listing 2.16):

Listing 2.16   Phone.java – Updated (New Lines are Highlighted)

```
01   public class Phone {
02
03       // These variables describe the Phone object's state
04       private boolean poweredOn;
05       private boolean playingMusic = false;
06       private String phoneManufacturer;
07       private double androidVersionNumber = 4.4;
08
09       // These methods are the Phone object's behaviors
10       void initialize(boolean poweredOn, String phoneManufacturer) {
11               this.poweredOn = poweredOn;
12               this.phoneManufacturer = phoneManufacturer;
13       }
14
15       void togglePower() {
16               if (poweredOn) {
17                       System.out.println("Powering off!");
18                       poweredOn = false;
19                       playingMusic = false;
20               } else {
21                       System.out.println("Powering on!");
22                       poweredOn = true;
23               }
24       }
25
26       void playMusic() {
27               if (poweredOn) {
28                       System.out.println("Playing music!");
29               }
30       }
31
32       void upgrade(double newVersion) {
33               if (newVersion > androidVersionNumber) {
34                       androidVersionNumber = newVersion;
35               } else {
36                       System.out.println("Upgrade failed!");
```

```
37            }
38        }
39
40        void describe() {
41                System.out.println("\nPhone's state:");
42                System.out.println("Powered on: " + poweredOn);
43                System.out.println("Playing music: " + playingMusic);
44                System.out.println("Manufacturer: " + phoneManufacturer);
45                System.out.println("Version: " + androidVersionNumber);
46        }
47
48    } // ends class
```

Let's discuss the describe method (lines 40 to 46 in listing 2.16): You will notice that it performs the same printing behavior that we were previously performing inside the **World** class. This time, we do not have to use the dot operator, because the variables are being accessed from within the same class.

In some cases, however, you do need to use the dot operator. Have a close look at the initialize() method (lines 10 to 13 in listing 2.16):

```
void initialize(boolean poweredOn, String phoneManufacturer) {
        this.poweredOn = poweredOn;
        this.phoneManufacturer = phoneManufacturer;
}
```

The initialize() method simply accepts two inputs: a boolean called poweredOn and a String called phoneManufacturer. The only function of this method is to initialize the two variables that we have not provided default values for: poweredOn and phoneManufacturer (recall that we have provided starting values for the other two variables).

Notice that we *do* use the dot operator here. Using the this keyword lets our program know that we are referring to *this instance* of the object – the current **Phone** object that we are calling the initialize() method on. This is how we can distinguish between the poweredOn variable that belongs to the *object* and the poweredOn variable that belongs to the *method* (received from the arguments).

Now that we've created two methods that will allow us to access our **Phone** objects' private variables, let's change our **World** class so that it calls these methods as highlighted on lines 06, 07 and 10 of listing 2.17.

```
public class Phone {

    private boolean poweredOn;
    private String phoneManufacturer;
    ...

    void initialize(boolean poweredOn, String phoneManufacturer) {
        this.poweredOn = poweredOn;
        this.phoneManufacturer = phoneManufacturer;
    }

    ...
}
```

Figure 2-22   Same Names Different Owners

Listing 2.17   World.java – Calling the New Methods

```
01  public class World {
02
03      public static void main(String[] args) {
04              System.out.println("Hello, world!");
05              Phone myPhone = new Phone();
06              myPhone.initialize(false, "Samsung");
07              myPhone.describe();
08              myPhone.togglePower();
09              myPhone.upgrade(4.5);
10              myPhone.describe();
11      }
12  }
```

The corresponding output is:

```
Hello, world!

Phone's state:
Powered on: false
Playing music: false
Manufacturer: Samsung
Version: 4.4
Powering on!

Phone's state:
Powered on: true
Playing music: false
Manufacturer: Samsung
Version: 4.5
```

Distinguishing Between Classes and Objects

It is important for us to understand the difference between a class and an object, so let's review. Objects are just collections of data – they comprise a set of bits that describe a relationship of variables and methods. Classes are the blueprints used for creating these objects.

To illustrate this, let's pretend that you are playing with Legos (you can never be too old for Legos). You pull out an instructions manual and start building a spaceship. The instruction manual includes all the information that you need in order to create your spaceship: the number of wings you need to build, the number of cannons to add and so on. Every Lego model that you build using this manual is a spaceship, but the *manual* itself is NOT a spaceship – it's a blueprint.

A similar relationship exists between classes and objects. While classes describe what an object's state and behavior are (what properties you need in order to have an object of that type), classes are NOT objects themselves.

Objects Are Independent

Let's review the concept of instances and object independence. Using one class, you may create as many objects as you would like. For example, you can create a **Spaceship** class and use it to *instantiate* (create instances of) fifty **Spaceship** objects. Each of these **Spaceship** objects are called instances of the **Spaceship** class. Instances are "tangible" representations of the more "generic" class, much like Lego sets are tangible representations of their respective instructions manuals.

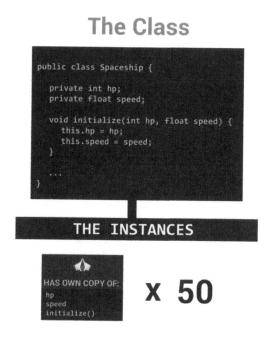

Figure 2-23   Spaceships: Class vs. Instances

Just like objects in real life, different instances of the same class are independent from one another. Extending the fifty **Spaceships** example, you can modify one *instance* of the **Spaceship** *class* (a single **Spaceship** object), and the other forty-nine will NOT be affected.

Working with Objects from the Java API

Now let's take a break from cooking up our own classes and enjoy some ready-made ones that ship with Java. The advantage of using an existing programming language rather than making your own is that you gain access to existing code that you can implement into your own projects. Luckily for us, Java classes ship with extensive documentation regarding the variables they contain, how they should be initialized and what behavior they perform, so that we can incorporate these into our programs and focus on the important problems that are unique to our projects.

You can access the full Java documentation for Java SE 7 at the following link: **http://docs.oracle.com/javase/7/docs/api/**

Practice with Strings

Let's practice using the Java documentation using a class that we are familiar with: **String**. Create a new Java project called **FunWithStrings**, and create a new class called **StringTester** with a main method, as shown in listing 2.18.

Listing 2.18   StringTester.java - Empty

```
01  public class StringTester {
02
03      public static void main(String[] args) {
04
05      }
06
07  }
```

The **String** class (which is hidden from us deep inside the Java Library) allows you to create **String** objects in our own code. Let's initialize a **String** object using the **new** keyword used to initialize objects. Add the following to the main method:

```
String s = new String("this is a string");
```

Strings are so commonly used that Java provides a special way of initializing them. Add this next line also:

```
String s2 = "this is also a string";
```

Listing 2.19 shows the updated class:

Listing 2.19   StringTester.java - Updated

```
01  public class StringTester {
02
03      public static void main(String[] args) {
04              String s = new String("this is a string");
05              String s2 = "this is also a string";
06
07      }
08
09  }
```

Like other Java objects, **Strings** have state and behavior. We will only focus on the behavior of **Strings** in this book – the state is not useful to us.

Let's now get some practice with the Javadocs. Search for the **String** class and scroll down to the *Method Summary*. You will find a list of methods available to a **String** object.

Method Summary

Methods

Modifier and Type	Method and Description
char	charAt(int index) Returns the char value at the specified index.
int	codePointAt(int index) Returns the character (Unicode code point) at the specified index.
int	codePointBefore(int index) Returns the character (Unicode code point) before the specified index.
int	codePointCount(int beginIndex, int endIndex) Returns the number of Unicode code points in the specified text range of this String.
int	compareTo(String anotherString) Compares two strings lexicographically.
int	compareToIgnoreCase(String str) Compares two strings lexicographically, ignoring case differences.
String	concat(String str) Concatenates the specified string to the end of this string.
boolean	contains(CharSequence s) Returns true if and only if this string contains the specified sequence of char values.

Figure 2-24   Partial Method Summary of the **String** Class

Individual entries in this table tell you the return type of each method, along with the method name, required parameters (input) and method summary.

String has a method that retrieves a single character (of type char) from a specified position (referred to as an *index*). This method is called charAt(), and accepts an integer value representing the index of the desired character.

Index values in Java are zero-based, meaning that the first character has an index of 0. Let's see what this means in our code. We will call the charAt() method and ask for the 3rd character in the String s (index 2), as shown on line 07 in listing 2.20:

Listing 2.20   Printing Characters from a String

```
01  public class StringTester {
02
03      public static void main(String[] args) {
04              String s = new String("this is a string");
05              String s2 = "this is also a string";
06
07              char ch = s.charAt(2);
08              System.out.println("The third character is " + ch);
09      }
10
11  }
```

The corresponding output is:

```
The third character is i
```

Let's practice using the Java documentation with one more example. Look through the *Method Summary*. Can you find a method that returns the length of the given **String**? Browsing through the Method Summary, you may find this:

Return Type	Method and Description
int	length()
	Returns the length of the String

Figure 2-25   The Summary of the length() Method

This table tells us all the information that we need in order to use the length method. We know that it returns an integer representing the length of the **String** invoking the method. The method takes no parameters. Let's try finding the length of both s and s2, and determine which one is longer! Change your **StringTester** class so that it is the same as listing 2.21; the new code is on lines 13 to 19.

Listing 2.21   StringTester.java (Updated)

```
01  public class StringTester {
02
03      public static void main(String[] args) {
04              String s = new String("this is a string");
05              String s2 = "this is also a string";
06
07              char ch = s.charAt(2);
08              System.out.println("The third character is " + ch);
09
10              int sLen = s.length();
11              int s2Len = s2.length();
12
13              if (sLen > s2Len) {
14                      System.out.println("s is longer than s2.");
15              } else if (sLen == s2Len) {
16                      System.out.println("They have the same length.");
17              } else {
18                      System.out.println("s2 is longer than s");
19              }
20
21      }
22
23  }
```

Running the code we get the following result:

```
The third character is i
s2 is longer than s
```

I encourage you to experiment with some of the other methods that are listed in the Javadocs. Being able to work with Javadocs is an important skill to have. Like all other things worth doing, you only get better by practicing. Remember to keep the following in mind:

1. The return type: (this determines what kind of variable you need to store the result in).
2. The method name: (you must spell it exactly as it is shown. Method names are case-sensitive).
3. The inputs: (you must always provide the required parameters in order for a method to work. This involves providing the correct number of values of the correct type).
4. Some of the methods ask for an input of type **CharSequence**. When you encounter such methods, you may provide a **String**. This is because of an

interesting property called **polymorphism** (i.e. the ability of an object to take many forms) that we will be discussing in detail in the next chapter.

More practice with Objects – Simulating a dice

In our next project, we will simulate the roll of a six-sided dice. Dice make appearances in many modern board games because they add an element of unpredictability. In this section, I will show you how you can simulate randomness inside a Java program.

Figure 2-26   A Standard Dice

We begin by creating a new Java project called "DiceProject." Inside, create a new class called **DiceMaker** and give it a main method, as usual.

To generate a random number, we must use a built-in class from the Java Library called **Random**. We create a new Random object using the familiar object-creation syntax as shown on line 4 of listing 2.22.

Listing 2.22   DiceMaker.java

```
1  public class DiceMaker {
2
3      public static void main(String[] args) {
4              Random r = new Random();
5      }
6
7  }
```

You should notice that Eclipse informs you that there is an error on the line which creates the Random object, as shown in Figure 2.27.

Once you mouse over the word Random, the following error message will appear.

```
Random cannot be resolved to a type
```

This is simply telling you that the compiler cannot create an object of type **Random**, because it does not know where **Random** is located!

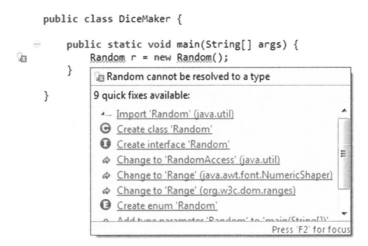

Figure 2-27   Random Cannot be Resolved to a Type

To fix this issue, we must let the compiler know where it can find **Random** by providing the full address. The desired **Random** class can be found at the address `java.util.Random` (this is in the form `UnitedKingdom.London.221BBakerSt`). Let's import this class as shown in line 1 of listing 2.23:

Listing 2.23   Importing `java.util.Random`

```
1 import java.util.Random;
2
3 public class DiceMaker {
4
5        public static void main(String[] args) {
6                Random r = new Random();
7        }
8
9 }
```

Now that we have informed the computer where the **Random** class is located, we are able to call its methods. The method we are interested in is the `nextInt()` method, which accepts an integer and returns a value between 0 (inclusive) and the accepted integer (exclusive).

For example: `r.nextInt(6)` would randomly generate one of these numbers:

`0, 1, 2, 3, 4, 5`

If we wanted to generate numbers 1 through 6 instead, we could simply add one to the result, as shown in lines 7 and 8 of listing 2.24:

Listing 2.24   Simulating a Dice Roll

```
01  import java.util.Random;
02
03  public class DiceMaker {
04
05      public static void main(String[] args) {
06              Random r = new Random();
07              int randNum = r.nextInt(6) + 1;
08              System.out.println("You have rolled a " + randNum);
09      }
10
11  }
```

When you run the program, you will see ONE of the following results:

```
You have rolled a 1
You have rolled a 2
You have rolled a 3
You have rolled a 4
You have rolled a 5
You have rolled a 6
```

What are some applications of the **Random** class? You may choose to implement a random number generator in determining what items drop once your heroes slay monsters. You may also use a random number generator to generate your map in a game resembling Minecraft. The possibilities are truly endless.

How random is java.util.Random?

The **Random** class we've used simulates randomness, but it does not achieve true randomness. Although it seems to generate numbers that are random, it is actually following a formula that generates a theoretically predictable outcome. We call this phenomenon **pseudo-random**. This is unlikely to have any effect on games that we write, but it makes for an interesting discussion. You can safely expect that in the long run, the random number generator will generate a uniform distribution of all the possible numbers. If you would like to learn more about true randomness, visit **Random.org** on the web!

More on importing

In the above example, we had to import from `java.util.Random`. This is the full name of the **Random** class that we are importing from the Java Library.

The Java Library is organized into packages, which contain various classes that you can use in your own code. Whenever you want to use a class from the Java Library, you must ask for it by telling your program where it can find its parent package (the full name).

Not all objects require imports. **String**, for example, belongs to the `java.lang` package, which is actually imported *automatically* due to its common usage. Arrays, which we discuss in the next section, can also be created without imports.

Grouping objects and primitives

Java allows us to group objects and primitives together. There are two categories of objects used for this purpose that you will encounter very often: arrays and lists.

Arrays

To denote an array (or group) of a certain type, we make use of the square brackets. For example, if you wanted an array of integers, you would declare it like so:

```
int[] numbers = new int[5];
```

The number 5 in the above example indicates how large the array called `numbers` should be. As it is written, `numbers` will have room for five integer values. To picture what an array looks like, we can draw a table:

numbers[0]	numbers[1]	numbers[2]	numbers[3]	numbers[4]
0	0	0	0	0

Figure 2-28   An Array of Integers (Default Values)

Initially, our array will have default values (0 when we create an array of integers). Java allows us to a assign number directly to each index (or position). Array indices are zero-based, just like characters in a String. Here's the syntax:

```
numbers[0] = 5;
numbers[1] = 10;
numbers[2] = 15;
numbers[3] = 20;
numbers[4] = 25;
```

The numbers array will now look like this:

numbers[0]	numbers[1]	numbers[2]	numbers[3]	numbers[4]
5	10	15	20	25

Figure 2-29   An Array of Integers (Assigned Values)

We can retrieve values from the array with the exact same syntax. For example:

```
int sum = numbers[0] + numbers[1] + numbers[2] + numbers[3] + numbers[4];
System.out.println(sum)          // will print 75
```

Arrays have a disadvantage. One you have created an array, you may not change its size. Why is this problematic? Imagine you are creating a shooting game, where each time the player clicks the left mouse button, a **Bullet** object is added into an array (representing all the bullets that have been fired). We do not know how many **Bullets** we will need ahead of time. Some players may use 42 bullets. Others may use their knives and grenades and complete the level without firing a single shot. In this situation, it is often better to use an **ArrayList** instead, which will dynamically resize as you put in more objects.

ArrayLists
ArrayLists are much more commonly used than arrays, and you should know how to use them (and how to use them well). To use an **ArrayList**, you must first import it:

```
import java.util.ArrayList
```

ArrayLists are created like any other objects:

```
ArrayList playerNames = new ArrayList();
```

We use the add() method to insert objects inside an **ArrayList** object:

```
playerNames.add("Mario");
playerNames.add("Luigi");
...
playerNames.add("Yoshi");
```

As you can tell, this is an **ArrayList** of **String** objects. You can retrieve an object (in this case a **String**) from an ArrayList using its zero-based index by calling the get() method (square brackets from arrays [ ] do not work with ArrayLists):

```
playerNames.get(2);          // will retrieve "Luigi" (kind-of)
```

Theoretically, we could place all kinds of objects inside a single **ArrayList**, regardless of type; however, this is not very useful, because once you have done so, you may not know what specific type of object is at, say, index 152. If you don't know what kind of object it is, you do not know what methods it has. Have a look at the following example:

```
someArrayList.get(152);    // What kind of object is this?
```

We pulled out the 153rd object (remember that indices are zero-based) from someArrayList. The problem is, we know nothing about this object. It might be a delicious **Sushi** object or even a dangerous **Bomb**. Imagine the consequences if we were to say:

```
Monster hungryOne = new Monster();
Object unknown = someArrayList.get(152);    // The Object is actually a Bomb
hungryOne.eat(unknown);                      // hungryOne thinks it's Sushi
// Boom!
```

In fact, modern Java allows us to limit **ArrayLists** to hold objects of exactly one type by adding the following notation: **<Type>**

```
ArrayList<String> playerNames = new ArrayList<String>();
playerNames.add("Mario");          // Works!
Bomb b = new Bomb();
playerNames.add(b);                // Gives type-mismatch error
```

Now we know that any object we retrieve from playerNames is guaranteed to be a **String**, and we can call **String** methods on it:

```
// Any object from playerNames will always be a String
String nameZero = playerNames.get(0);
System.out.println(nameZero.length());
```

Using ArrayLists with Primitives

You cannot directly insert primitives into an **ArrayList**. In fact, the following is NOT allowed:

```
ArrayList<int> numbers = new ArrayList<int>(); // not allowed
```

To get around this limitation, you can simply use one of the built-in wrapper classes – object versions of each of your primitives. These include **Integer** for int, **Character** for char, and so on. To do this, you first create the **ArrayList** and declare the wrapper class as the type:

```
ArrayList<Integer> numbers = new ArrayList<Integer>();
```

This initially has a size of zero:

```
System.out.println(numbers.size());      // Prints zero
```

Next, you simply call the add() method and pass in the int values that you want inside the **ArrayList**. These will *automatically* be wrapped inside an **Integer** object.

```
numbers.add(2);
numbers.add(3);
numbers.add(1);
```

At this point, your **ArrayList** looks like this (notice that it has grown dynamically):

index 0	index 1	index 2
2	3	1

Figure 2-30   numbers: an **ArrayList** of Integers

You can retrieve the primitives by calling the get() method, passing in the index of the desired value. For example, to get the number 3 back, we ask the ArrayList to give us the value at index 1. This value will automatically be converted to an int (from the wrapper **Integer** object), so you can store it inside an int variable.

```
int myNum = numbers.get(1);
System.out.println(myNum);        // Prints 3
```

Using ArrayLists with Loops
It's difficult to appreciate how powerful **ArrayLists** can be until you see them in action, so let's try an example.

We will be writing a simple program containing two classes. The first class will be our entry point, where we will store our main method and create our **ArrayList**. The second class will be a custom class representing a person.

We begin by creating a new Java project called **Groups**. Inside, create a new class called **ListTester** and give it a main method, as shown in listing 2.25.

Listing 2.25   ListTester.java

```
01  public class ListTester {
02
03      public static void main(String[] args) {
04
05      }
06
07  }
```

Now, create a second class in the same project and name it **Person**. Add the following variables and methods (listing 2.26):

Listing 2.26   Person.java

```
01  public class Person {
02
03      private String name;
04      private int age;
05
06      public void initialize(String name, int age) {
07              this.name = name;
08              this.age = age;
09      }
10
11      public void describe() {
12              System.out.println("My name is " + name);
13              System.out.println("I am " + age + " years old");
14      }
15
16  }
```

Our **Person** class describes a blueprint for a new **Person** object. Specifically, it says that a **Person** object's state will be described by two instance variables: name and age. We do not give default values for name and age, and we must call the initialize() method to provide these values. Once our **Person** object has a name and age, we can call the describe() method to print the information in human-friendly, readable format. Let's go back to our **ListTester** and make sure that we can do this.

Listing 2.27   ListTester.java (Updated)

```
1  public class ListTester {
2
3      public static void main(String[] args) {
4              Person p = new Person();
5              p.initialize("Marty", 40);
6              p.describe();
7      }
8
9  }
```

Let's walk through listing 2.27, line by line: We begin by creating a new instance of the **Person** class named p. At this point, p has two instance variables: name and age. These variables have not been initialized yet.

Next, we call the initialize() method, which accepts two values: a **String** and an integer. The initialize() method will take the value of each of these and assign them to the instance variables.

Now that our two instance variables have been initialized, we can ask our **Person** object to describe itself by calling the describe() method. The result follows:

```
My name is Marty
I am 40 years old
```

Now let's create multiple **Person** objects and group them together inside an **ArrayList**. Change the **ListTester** class so that it is exactly like listing 2.28.

Listing 2.28   Creating the ArrayList and Adding the First Loop

```
01  import java.util.ArrayList;
02  import java.util.Random;
03
04  public class ListTester {
05
06      public static void main(String[] args) {
07
08              ArrayList<Person> people = new ArrayList<Person>();
09              Random r = new Random();
10
11              for (int i = 0; i < 5; i++) {
12                      Person p = new Person();
13                      p.initialize("Person  #" + i, r.nextInt(50));
14                      people.add(p);
15              }
16      }
17
18  }
```

In the listing 2.28, we create a new **ArrayList** called people, and a new **Random** object called r. We then begin a for loop which will run five times. On each iteration (repetition) of the loop, we create a new **Person** object called p. We initialize the instance variables for that person with an appropriate name (Person #i, where i is between 0 and 4) and a randomly generated age. Lastly, we add the newly created **Person** object to our **ArrayList** (line 14). The loop repeats, creating an entirely new **Person**, initializing it and adding it again.

Pay careful attention to the following line:

```
Person p = new Person();
```

Any variables that you create inside a loop are only valid within that same iteration – meaning that its existence is limited to the current iteration of the loop. Because of this, we can reuse the variable name p on each repetition of our loop.

Each time that the above line is called, we are creating a new **Person** with variable name p. We then store the value held by the temporary variable p inside our more permanent **ArrayList** called people, so that we have a reference to each of these newly created **Person** objects later on in the code without assigning a unique variable name to each one of them.

To see how this works, we can try iterating through the loop again and calling the describe() method, as demonstrated in listing 2.29 (lines 17 through 20).

Listing 2.29   Adding the Second Loop

```
01  import java.util.ArrayList;
02  import java.util.Random;
03
04  public class ListTester {
05
06      public static void main(String[] args) {
07
08              ArrayList<Person> people = new ArrayList<Person>();
09              Random r = new Random();
10
11              for (int i = 0; i < 5; i++) {
12                      Person p = new Person();
13                      p.initialize("Person  #" + i, r.nextInt(50));
14                      people.add(p);
15              }
16
17              for (int i = 0; i < people.size(); i++) {
18                      Person p = people.get(i);
19                      p.describe();
20              }
21
22      }
23
24  }
```

The resulting output is (age may vary due to random generation):

```
My name is Person  #0
I am 29 years old
My name is Person  #1
I am 1 years old
My name is Person  #2
I am 4 years old
My name is Person  #3
I am 21 years old
My name is Person  #4
I am 47 years old
```

You may be wondering why we run this second loop from lines 17 through 20 `people.size()` times, rather than 5 times. The two values are identical and either solution would produce the same outcome; however, the above example is a more flexible loop, because we do not need to hardcode the number of times that the loop runs. Depending on the size of the **ArrayList** `people`, our second for loop will run an appropriate number of times. This means that we can change the number of times that the upper loop runs (the loop that adds to the **ArrayList**) from 5 to 8, and the bottom loop will not need to be changed, because `people.size()` will also increase to 8:

Listing 2.30   Iterating 8 Times

```
01      import java.util.ArrayList;
02      import java.util.Random;
03
04      public class ListTester {
05
06              public static void main(String[] args) {
07
08                      ArrayList<Person> people = new ArrayList<Person>();
09                      Random r = new Random();
10
11                      //for (int i = 0; i < 5; i++) {
12                      for (int i = 0; i < 8; i++) {
13                              Person p = new Person();
14                              p.initialize("Person  #" + i, r.nextInt(50));
15                              people.add(p);
16                      }
17                      // people.size() is now 8!
18                      for (int i = 0; i < people.size(); i++) {
19                              Person p = people.get(i);
20                              p.describe();
21                      }
22
23              }
24
25      }
```

The resulting output is (age may vary due to random generation):

```
My name is Person  #0
I am 27 years old
My name is Person  #1
I am 27 years old
My name is Person  #2
I am 20 years old
My name is Person  #3
I am 28 years old
My name is Person  #4
I am 5 years old
My name is Person  #5
```

```
I am 49 years old
My name is Person  #6
I am 2 years old
My name is Person  #7
I am 26 years old
```

The above example demonstrated how we can quickly create multiple objects using a loop and group them together in an **ArrayList**. We've also learned that we can iterate through a for loop to quickly retrieve all members of an **ArrayList** and invoke their methods.

Summary of Chapter 2

In the previous examples, our programs consisted of one or two small classes. As we progress through this book, we will be writing programs that have even more classes. In fact, some of our games will easily have over ten classes that each fulfill some role in the game architecture. Study the previous example very carefully, and if you have any lingering questions, visit the companion site for the book at **jamescho7.com**. Post any questions you have regarding the book, and I will try to address them.

We've covered a lot of material in this chapter, and all of these concepts will be reappearing throughout this book. It's difficult to remember the syntax of this new language, but the key is *practice*. Take a moment now to study the source code for the examples in this chapter (available on **jamescho7.com**), run the programs, experiment creatively and most importantly, try to understand the topics that we have discussed. You will get much more out of the later chapters if you understand the *core concepts* from this one. If you ever get stuck, please do post in our forums! We will actively monitor them and answer any questions you may have.

If you are ready to move on, join me in Chapter 3, where we will discuss some of Java's more advanced topics, including constructors, inheritance, interfaces, graphics and threads – all of the stuff you need to know in order to start writing Java games!

Chapter 3: Designing Better Objects

We've studied the fundamentals of object-oriented programming and learned the basic Java syntax for creating and using objects. In this chapter, we will explore some important object design concepts that will allow us to create meaningful classes and to organize them in intuitive ways.

This chapter will be dense, covering a lot of tough material in a very few pages. In fact, you might find yourself not remembering the details of the syntax behind these various concepts after a single reading, and that's completely okay. What is important is that you read through the explanations and *understand* the corresponding code listings. Later on, you will be able to return to these pages for reference and review as needed.

Constructors

We will ease into the more complex topics by reviewing an important idea from Chapter 2 and making some small changes. Begin by creating a project called **Constructors**, and create a **World** class as shown in Listing 3.1:

Listing 3.1   World.java

```
1  public class World {
2
3        public static void main(String[] args) {
4
5
6        }
7
8  }
```

We will also create a class called **Coder** as shown in Listing 3.2:

Listing 3.2   Coder.java

```
1  public class Coder {
2        private String name;
3        private int age;
4
5        public void initialize(String name, int age) {
6                this.name = name;
7                this.age = age;
8        }
```

```
9
10      public void writeCode() {
11              System.out.println(name + " is coding!");
12      }
13
14      public void describe() {
15              System.out.println("I am a coder");
16              System.out.println("My name is " + name);
17              System.out.println("I am " + age + " years old");
18      }
19
20 }
```

Your project should now have the setup as shown in Figure 3-1.

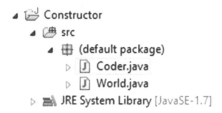

Figure 3-1   The Constructor Project

Let's make sure that we understand our **Coder** class before moving on. **Coder.java** is a blueprint for creating **Coder** objects. In this blueprint, we have declared that a **Coder** object should have two variables describing its *state*: a **String** representing the name and an integer representing the age.

Like other objects, our Coder object will have behavior. The `initialize()` method allows us to initialize our **Coder** object's instance variables with values that we provide. The `writeCode()` method will print text indicating that our **Coder** object is coding. The `describe()` method will simply list the values of all the instance variables in human-friendly form.

Variables Receive Default Values

Return to the **World** class and create an instance of a **Coder** object, and tell it to describe itself. Your code should look like that shown in Listing 3.3:

Listing 3.3   World.java (updated)

```
1  public class World {
2
3      public static void main(String[] args) {
4              Coder c = new Coder();
5              c.describe();
6      }
```

```
7
8  }
```

When we first declare our new **Coder** object, its instance variables have not been initialized (meaning that they retain the default values for each variable type). Running the **World** class, we get the following output:

```
I am a coder
My name is null
I am 0 years old
```

As shown above, the default value for an int is zero. An empty object reference variable (a variable that points to an object) defaults to a value of null, which means "nothing." This simply means that your object reference variable does not contain any values.

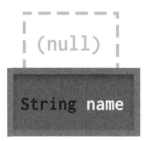

Figure 3-2   Empty Object Reference Variable

Avoiding Java Exceptions

Before we move on, I want to point out a very common error that causes a lot of Java programs to terminate unexpectedly: the NullPointerException. This runtime error (errors that occur during a program's execution) occurs when you attempt to call a method belonging to a null object variable. Have a look at the following example:

```
String a;        // Equivalent to String a = null;
a.length();
```

If you were to run this code inside your main method, you would get the following error (accompanied by the line number where everything went wrong):

```
Exception in thread "main" java.lang.NullPointerException
```

Whenever you come across this error message, the solution is to find and initialize all object variables with a value of null that are still in use.

Initializing Our Coder Object Using A Method

To avoid any potential NullPointerExceptions, we will now initialize the instance variables of our new **Coder** using its initialize() method (as shown on Line 7 of Listing 3.4).

Listing 3.4   Initializing the Coder and Its Instance Variables

```
1 public class World {
2
3       public static void main(String[] args) {
4               Coder c = new Coder(); // Initializes the variable c
5               c.describe();
6               System.out.println(""); // insert empty line for readability
7               c.initialize("Bill", 59);  // Initializes c's instance variables
8               c.describe();
9       }
10
11 }
```

When we run listing 3.4, we get the following output:

```
I am a coder
My name is null
I am 0 years old

I am a coder
My name is Bill
I am 59 years old
```

Initializing Our Coder Object Using A Custom Constructor

In the previous sections, we've learned to use the following syntax for object creation:

```
Coder c = new Coder();
```

The part shown in blue in the above line of code is how we invoke what we call the *default constructor*, which simply creates a new instance of a **Coder** object for us to use inside the variable c.

Java also allows the use of custom constructors, which, like methods, can accept values to be used by the object. To see this in action, let's focus on these two lines of code:

```
Coder c = new Coder(); // Uses the default constructor
```

```
...
c.initialize("Bill", 59);
```

Custom constructors allow us to reduce this code to the following:

```
Coder c = new Coder("Bill", 59);
```

To do this, we must first declare the desired custom constructor in the **Coder** class as shown below:

```
public Coder(String name, int age) {
        this.name = name;
        this.age = age;
}
```

A constructor appears similar to a method, but it has some big differences. Firstly, a constructor has no return type (not even void). Secondly, a constructor's name must be identical to that of its surrounding class.

Despite these differences, notice that our constructor accepts arguments and assigns them to the **Coder** object's instance variables just as the initialize() method did.

We can now add this constructor into the body of our **Coder** class and remove the initialize() method as shown below:

```
public class Coder {

        private String name;
        private int age;

        public Coder(String name, int age) {
                this.name = name;
                this.age = age;
        }

        public void initialize(String name, int age) {
                this.name = name;
                this.age = age;
        }

        public void writeCode() {
                System.out.println(name + " is coding!");
        }

        public void describe() {
                System.out.println("I am a coder");
                System.out.println("My name is " + name);
                System.out.println("I am " + age + " years old");
        }

}
```

You can think of constructors as a requirement – a rule for creating that object. It is a way of saying, "If you want to make my object, you must pass me the inputs I'm asking for!"

In creating your own constructor, you have just specified that a Coder object can only be created if values for its name and age are provided. Because of this, we can no longer create a Coder object using the familiar syntax:

```
Coder c = new Coder(); // no longer works!
```

Let's make changes to our **World** class to reflect this change, as shown in listing 3.5.

Listing 3.5   Calling the Custom Constructor

```
public class World {
        public static void main(String[] args) {
                Coder c = new Coder();
                c.describe();
                System.out.println(""); // insert empty line for readability
                c.initialize("Bill", 59);

                Coder c = new Coder("Bill", 59);
                c.describe();
        }

}
```

Running the code, we get:

```
I am a coder
My name is Bill
I am 59 years old
```

KEY POINTS

Object Constructors

- Constructors provide a means of initializing instance variables in your objects during their creation.
- The constructor is used with the **new** keyword.
- Java provides a default constructor if you choose not to create one.
- All constructors must be named after the class.
- You can have as many constructors as you want, but they each must have a unique set of parameters.

Getters and Setters

A constructor allows you to initialize an object's instance variables as the object is being created, but it does little to help you retrieve or modify these values afterwards. Moreover, because we are using the private modifier to hide our variables, we have no way of doing these two tasks directly. In fact, the following will result in an error:

```
...
// somewhere inside the World class...
Coder c3 = new Coder("Mark", 30);
String c3Name = c3.name; // cannot reference private variable from another class
c3.age = 25; // cannot modify private variable from another class
...
```

How can we get around these limitations? We could mark our Coder class' instance variables public, but we do not want to do that for the reasons discussed in Chapter 2. Instead, we can create *accessor* methods inside the Coder class. There are two types that we will be discussing:

1. A *getter method* returns a COPY of the value of a requested hidden variable (but leaves the hidden variable alone). By doing this, we can keep the instance variable safe from unauthorized changes while providing access to the variable's value

2. A *setter method* allows other classes to modify the values of a hidden variable, provided that they follow the rules you prescribe in the setter method.

Let's see these accessor methods in action. Add the following getter and setter methods to the **Coder** class: getAge(), setAge(), getName() and setName() (as shown on lines 26 to 48 in listing 3.6).

Listing 3.6   Adding Getter and Setter Methods to Coder.java

```
01  public class Coder {
02
03      private String name;
04      private int age;
05
06      public Coder(String name, int age) {
07              this.name = name;
08              this.age = age;
09      }
10
11      public void writeCode() {
12              System.out.println(name + " is coding!");
13      }
14
15      public void describe() {
16              System.out.println("I am a coder");
17              System.out.println("My name is " + name);
```

```
18                  System.out.println("I am " + age + " years old");
19          }
20
21      public String getName() {
22              return name;
23      }
24
25      public int getAge() {
26              return age;
27      }
28
29      public void setName(String newName) {
30              if (newName != null) {
31                      name = newName;
32              } else {
33                      System.out.println("Invalid name provided!");
34              }
35      }
36
37      public void setAge(int newAge) {
38              if (newAge > 0) {
39                      age = newAge;
40              } else {
41                      System.out.println("Invalid age provided");
42              }
43      }
44  }
```

Our two getter methods return the values of name and age variables to the caller of this method. This means that any class that has access (or reference) to a **Coder** object can call its getter methods and peek at the values of Coder's the instance variables. Values is the key word here. We are not giving access to the original copies of the instance variables, but to the *values* stored in them.

Our two setter methods allow other classes to modify the **Coder** objects' instance variables, but we can protect these instance variables from illegal or invalid changes by providing a set of rules. In listing 3.6, our setters reject non-positive age values and null name values.

Let's test our getters and setters in our **World** class by calling them in lines 08 and 09 as shown in listing 3.7:

Listing 3.7   Calling the Getter and Setters from World.java

```
01  public class World {
02      public static void main(String[] args) {
03
04              Coder c = new Coder("Bill", 59);
05              c.describe();
06              System.out.println(""); // empty line for readability
07
08              String cName = c.getName();
```

```
09                     int cAge = c.getAge();
10
11                     System.out.println(cName + ", " + cAge);
12                     System.out.println(""); // empty line for readability
13                     c.setName("Steve");
14                     c.setAge(-5); // This will be rejected by our setter method
15
16                     c.describe();
17        }
18
19  }
```

The printed result is:

```
I am a coder
My name is Bill
I am 59 years old

Bill, 59

I am a coder
My name is Steve
Invalid age provided!
```

In the previous example, we were able to create a means of keeping our Coder objects' instance variables private while allowing outside access to retrieve (get) and modify (set) these hidden variables via our public accessor methods. This allows us to keep the element of security obtained through the use of private variables and also allows us to access and modify values that we need. Notice that our setter method can reject invalid arguments, as we were able to prevent the **World** class from changing our **Coder** object's age to **-5**.

Interface

We will next discuss a way to group objects together into various categories using what we call an *interface*. An interface is an *abstract* category that describes the essential components of objects that belong to this category. To best understand this, we will study an example.

An interface resembles a class, but it has some notable differences. Here's what a **Human** interface may look like (do not worry about following along in Eclipse):

Listing 3.8   The Human Interface

```
public interface Human {
```

```
        public void eat();

        public void walk();

        public void urinate(int duration);
}
```

As shown in listing 3.8, an interface contains various *abstract* methods that have no method body. These disembodied abstract methods tell you what a **Human** category of objects MUST be able to do, but they do not specify how these actions must be done.

To explore what an interface really is, let's step away from the code. In your mind, create an idea of what it means to be a human being (you don't have to get too philosophical!). Next, have a look at the following list and tell me if each person satisfies your idea of humanity: your neighbor, your best friend and yourself.

You've probably answered yes to all of these people. This is because when I asked you to form an idea of humanity, you did not perceive of one *individual* human being. Instead, you formed some kind of rule – an idea of how a human being interacts with his or her world – and used this to determine the humanity of various people.

An interface is much the same. The **Human** interface from listing 3.8 is not used to create an individual **Human** object. Instead, it defines a pattern of interaction, stating how a **Human** object should be able to behave in your program. It provides a set of essential requirements that you must meet in order to create more concrete versions of type **Human** such as the **King** class, which is shown in listing 3.9.

Listing 3.9   The King Class

```
public class King implements Human {

 public void eat() {
        System.out.println("The King eats.");
 }

 public void walk() {
        System.out.println("The King walks.");
 }

 public void urinate(int duration) {
        System.out.println("The King urinates for " + duration + " minutes.");
 }

 public void rule() {
        System.out.println("The King reigns.");
 }

}
```

Study the relationship between the **King** class and the **Human** interface, and you will notice three things. Firstly, the class declares that it **implements Human**, which is how we as programmers specify that we want our **King** class to belong to the **Human** category. Secondly, the **King** class declares all three of the methods in the **Human** interface given in listing 3.8, and it class provides a concrete method body for each of these previously abstract methods. Thirdly, the **King** class has an additional method called rule() that distinguishes it from the generic **Human**.

An interface is a binding contract. If an object chooses to implement an interface, it is agreeing to implement each of the abstract methods from the interface. What does this all mean? It means that a **King** object, no matter how much he wishes to stay away from the privy, must implement all of the **Human** interface's abstract methods including urinate(), because a king is, after all, only human. If he foregoes this requirement, the angry JVM will shoot red error messages at him.

Polymorphism

You might be wondering why we had to create both an interface and a class to define a single **King** class. You might be telling yourself that, at this point, the **Human** interface doesn't really do much, and you'd be absolutely right.

Using an interface allows us to create a category of objects, but it's difficult to appreciate what this means for our program until we study polymorphism.

Have a look at the following method.

```
public void feed(Human h) {
        System.out.println("Feeding Human!");
        h.eat();
}
```

The method can accept a single argument of type **Human**. In fact, it can accept *any* object instance of a class that implements the **Human** interface. This is useful because, in a single program, we could create multiple classes that all extend the **Human** interface, such as **Villain**, **Professor** and **SushiChef**.

This means that the following examples will *all* work:

```
// Elsewhere in same program
King kong = new King();
Villain baddie = new Villain();
Professor x = new Professor();
SushiChef chef = new SushiChef();

// Any Human can be fed:
```

```
feed(kong); // A King is Human
feed(baddie); // A Villain is Human
feed(x); // A Professor is Human
feed(chef); // A SushiChef is Human
```

This is just a trivial example of what *polymorphism* can do, which is just a fancy way of describing a *common method* of interacting with *multiple* types of objects. We will explore interfaces and polymorphism in more practical situations in the coming chapters.

Inheritance

When designing categories of objects, you might find that another pattern called *inheritance* gives you more control. Inheritance describes a phenomenon in which a one class inherits the variables and methods from another. In such a case, the inheritor is referred to as the *subclass* (or child class), and the ancestor is referred to as the *superclass* (or parent class).

The advantage of inheritance over using an interface is the ability for you to reuse code. Recall that each class implementing an interface MUST provide a full implementation for every one of the abstract methods declared in the interface. Using the example from the previous section, this means that the **King**, **Villain**, **Professor** and **SushiChef** classes must ALL have their own eat(), walk() and urinate() methods. Inheritance is powerful in such situations, because it allows similar classes to *share* methods and variables. We will illustrate this using an example from a hypothetical role-playing game.

When creating an RPG, you might have a class called **Hero** representing the player character, as shown in listing 3.10.

Listing 3.10   The Hero Class

```
01 public class Hero {
02     protected int health = 10; // We will discuss 'protected' later in this section
03     protected int power = 5;
04     protected int armor = 3;
05
06     public void drinkPotion(Potion p) {
07        health += p.volume(); // Equivalent to health = health + p.volume();
08     }
09
10     public void takeDamage(int damage) {
11        int realDamage = damage - armor;
12        if (realDamage > 0) {
13            health -= realDamage; // Equivalent to health = health – realDamage.
14        }
15     }
16
17     // ....more methods
```

```
18
19 }
```

After creating the **Hero**, You later decide that your RPG would distinguish itself from the competition by implementing a unique class system in which players would choose between the never-before-seen Warrior, Mage and Rogue classes.

Next, as any respectable object-oriented programmer would, you create a separate Java class for each of these character classes, because your Warrior, Mage and Rogue should each have impossibly powerful *unique* abilities. You also decide that, since all of your character classes are first and foremost extensions of a generic **Hero** class, they should each have all of the variables and method from the **Hero** class in listing 3.10. This is where inheritance comes in.

Have a look at listings 3.11 through 3.13.

Listing 3.11   The Warrior Class

```java
public class Warrior extends Hero {

        //      ....other variables and methods
        public void shieldBash() {
            ....
        }
}
```

Listing 3.12   The Mage Class

```java
public class Mage extends Hero {

        //      ....other variables and methods
        public void useMagic() {
            ....
        }
}
```

Listing 3.13   The Rogue Class

```java
public class Rogue extends Hero {

        //      ....other variables and methods
        public void pickPocket() {
            ....
        }
}
```

Notice that we use the **extends** keyword to indicate inheritance. This is fitting because all three of these classes are extensions of the superclass **Hero**. In inheritance, each of the subclasses receive their own copies of ALL non-private variables and methods from the superclass (the **protected** variables from listing 3.10 are similar to **private** variables in that foreign classes cannot access them; however, unlike **private** variables, they ARE accessible by subclasses during inheritance).

The benefits of inheritance are most apparent when we apply polymorphism, which allows us to use any of the **Hero**'s subclasses in methods such as this one:

```
// Will attack any Hero regardless of Class
public void attackHero(Hero h, int monsterDamage) {
        h.takeDamage(monsterDamage);
}
```

Graphics

Text-based programs are easy to build, but text-based games are so out of style. In this section, we will discuss how to create a *graphical user interface* (GUI) by using classes from the Java Class Library – specifically from the **javax.swing** package. You will find that while adding a simple user interface is straight-forward; GUI is a massive topic. I will only be providing a quick introduction - the bare essentials you need in order to create a window and display a Java-based game. If you would like to learn more about Swing and creating professional applications, visit the following tutorial:

```
http://docs.oracle.com/javase/tutorial/uiswing/TOC.html
```

Introduction to JFrame

When developing a graphical application in Java, we begin by creating a window called a **JFrame** object (imported from **javax.swing.JFrame**). Inside this window is a content pane (think window pane), to which we can add various UI elements such as buttons, sliders and text areas.

The content pane's default layout is called **BorderLayout**. This allows you to place UI elements into one of five regions as shown in Figure 3-3.

Each of the five regions shown in the content pane in Figure 3-3 can hold just *one* UI element, meaning that the **BorderLayout** only supports five elements; however, this is not an issue for us, as we really only need one element called a **JPanel**.

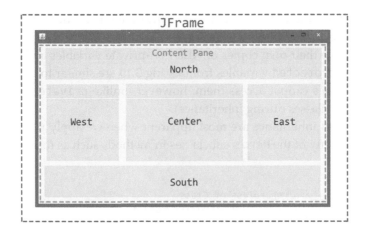

Figure 3-3   A JFrame on Windows 8 and its Content Pane

A **JPanel** object is a simple, empty container that can be added to one of the regions of a **BorderLayout**. We can draw everything that our players should see onto a single **JPanel** object, much as we might draw on a canvas. As an example, consider the screenshot shown in Figure 3-4. This screenshot is taken from a development version of the TUMBL game – which was one of the first games that I developed. Everything that you see from the player's score and pause button to the character and power-up has been drawn onto a single **JPanel**.

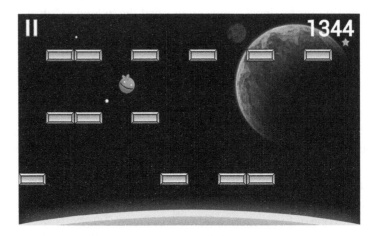

Figure 3-4   Screenshot from an Early Build of TUMBL

Explaining the Coordinate System
When we deal with graphics on a computer, we will use a pixel-based X, Y coordinate system. In addition, we will also treat the top-left pixel as our origin (0, 0). This means

that on a screen with a resolution of 1920 pixels by 1080 pixels, the bottom-right pixel will have the coordinates (1919, 1079).

Creating a JFrame

Now that we have discussed everything that we need in order to build a graphical application. It's time to get our hands dirty.

Create a new Java Project called **FirstGraphics** and create a class called **FirstFrame**, complete with a main method. We will then create a **JFrame** object by adding the following lines of code to the main method (make sure to import javax.swing.JFrame):

```
JFrame frame = new JFrame("My First Window");
frame.setDefaultCloseOperation(JFrame.EXIT_ON_CLOSE);
frame.setSize(480, 270);
frame.setVisible(true);
```

At this point your **FirstFrame** class should look like that shown in listing 3.14.

Listing 3.14   FirstFrame Class

```
01 import javax.swing.JFrame;
02
03 public class FirstFrame {
04
05     public static void main(String[] args) {
06             JFrame frame = new JFrame("My First Window");
07             frame.setDefaultCloseOperation(JFrame.EXIT_ON_CLOSE);
08             frame.setSize(480, 270);
09             frame.setVisible(true);
10     }
11
12 }
```

Run the **FirstFrame** class and you should see something similar to Figure 3-5.

Notice that a window has appeared with the title "My First Window." It is clear that the content pane (grey area in Figure 3-5) is currently empty.

In the non-graphical examples from previous sections, our programs terminated as soon as their last lines of code was executed by the JVM. Graphical applications do not behave this way. A **JFrame** will persist even after the last line of code, as indicated by the presence of the window. Let's terminate the program by clicking the exit button.

Let's make sure that we understand what is going on in these four lines of code that define the **JFrame** (lines 06 to 09 in listing 3.14). In line 06, we create a new **JFrame** object called frame by using a custom constructor. This allows us to set the title of our window.

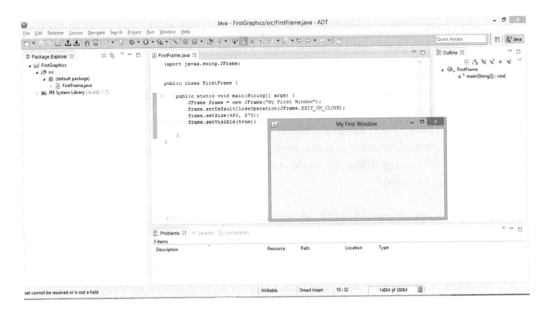

Figure 3-5   My First Window

Next on line 07, we specify what should happen when our window is closed. We want the entire program to terminate when the user closes the window, so we pass in a public `int` called `EXIT_ON_CLOSE` from the `JFrame` class to the `setDefaultCloseOperation()` method (remember that the dot operator is used to access public methods and variables from another class).

Line 08 simply tells the window to resize itself so that it is 480 pixels wide and 270 pixels tall. Once this is finished, we call the `setVisible()` method on line 09 to make the frame appear on our screen.

Adding a JPanel

Now that we have a `JFrame`, it's time to add to its content pane. To do this, we will create a new class called `MyPanel`. This class will be a *customized* version of `JPanel` created by using inheritance, so we must extend `JPanel`, importing `java.swing.JPanel`.

Copy the code shown in listing 3.15 into your `MyPanel` class. We will discuss it once we have run the program! Don't forget to add the proper imports as shown in lines 01, 02 and 04.

Listing 3.15   MyPanel Class

```
01 import java.awt.Color;
02 import java.awt.Graphics;
03
04 import javax.swing.JPanel;
```

```
05
06 public class MyPanel extends JPanel {
07
08      @Override
09      public void paintComponent(Graphics g){
10              g.setColor(Color.BLUE);
11              g.fillRect(0, 0, 100, 100);
12
13              g.setColor(Color.GREEN);
14              g.drawRect(50, 50, 100, 100);
15
16              g.setColor(Color.RED);
17              g.drawString("Hello, World of GUI", 200, 200);
18
19              g.setColor(Color.BLACK);
20              g.fillOval(250, 40, 100, 30);
21      }
22
23 }
```

Now we must go back to our **FirstFrame** class, construct an instance of **MyPanel**, and add it to one of the regions of our content pane. This is accomplished by adding the following lines of code to the bottom of our main method:

```
MyPanel panel = new MyPanel(); // Creates new MyPanel object.
frame.add(BorderLayout.CENTER, panel); // Adds panel to CENTER region.
```

The updated **FirstFrame** class should look exactly like listing 3.16 (notice the import statement on line 01):

Listing 3.16   Updated FirstFrame Class

```
01 import java.awt.BorderLayout;
02
03 import javax.swing.JFrame;
04
05 public class FirstFrame {
06
07      public static void main(String[] args) {
08              JFrame frame = new JFrame("My First Window");
09              frame.setDefaultCloseOperation(JFrame.EXIT_ON_CLOSE);
10              frame.setSize(480, 270);
11              frame.setVisible(true);
12
13              MyPanel panel = new MyPanel();   // Creates new MyPanel Object
14              frame.add(BorderLayout.CENTER, panel);   // adds panel to CENTER region
15      }
16
17 }
```

Run **FirstFrame** and you will see a screen similar to that shown in Figure 3-6.

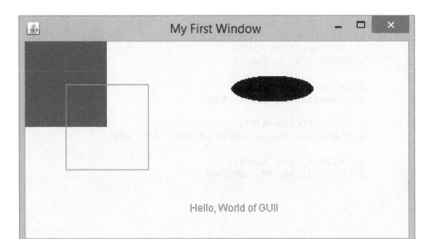

Figure 3-6   Output from the Updated FirstFrame Class

Explaining the Terms

Before we discuss what happened, we first need to clarify some terminology. Recall that we can add various graphical elements to the regions of our **JFrame**'s content pane. These graphical elements are also called *widgets*, and they belong to a category of generic objects called **JComponent**. This means that **JPanel**, along with other graphical elements used in Swing-based graphical applications, is a type of *component*.

Understanding the MyPanel

I will now explain what happened when we ran our program, beginning by explaining the **MyPanel** class. Refer to listing 3.15, and you will remember that **MyPanel** extends **JPanel** (line 06 of listing 3.15). This says that **MyPanel** is a subclass of **JPanel**; in other words, it is a more *specific version* of a *generic* **JPanel** class. It follows that **MyPanel** inherits all of the public methods that belong to **JPanel** (since **MyPanel** IS-A specific type of **JPanel** by inheritance).

One of the inherited methods is called paintComponent(). It is a method that describes how a component should be rendered (or drawn). We want to take control of this method so that we can tell our program how a **MyPanel** object should appear. To do so, we declare the paintComponent() method in our **MyPanel** class and add an @Override modifier (line 08), which is our way of letting the compiler know that we are replacing an existing paintComponent() method with our own.

Inside this paintComponent() method, we call eight methods using the provided **Graphics** object g (lines 10 to 20 in listing 3.15).

The **Graphics** object can draw one thing at a time, and it works like a paintbrush. You first select a color using the setColor() method and tell the **Graphics** object what to draw using one of several draw and fill methods.

The setColor() method accepts a **Color** object, which we can retrieve from the **Color** class (this class holds many **Color** objects as public variables that you can reference using the dot operator). Note that there are two variables for each color, one named in all uppercase and the other in all lowercase. These always return the same color to you.

As a general rule, a method that begins with the word draw will only draw the *outline* of the desired shape. Methods that begin with the word fill, on the other hand, will fill that entire shape. As an example, g.drawRect(50, 50, 100, 100); will draw a square outline that has its top left corner is anchored at (50, 50) and also has a side length of 100.

Refer to the Method Summary for the Graphics class for more information on the methods called in our paintComponent() method and what the parameters mean at the following link:

```
http://docs.oracle.com/javase/7/docs/api/java/awt/Graphics.html
```

Back to FirstFrame

Now that I have explained what is going on in **MyFrame**, let's discuss the two lines that we have added in listing 3.16 to our **FirstFrame** class.

```
MyPanel panel = new MyPanel(); // Creates new MyPanel object.
frame.add(BorderLayout.CENTER, panel); // Adds panel to CENTER region.
```

The first line of code simply creates a new **MyPanel** object using the familiar syntax. The second line then adds it to the center region from those shown in Figure 3-3. Note that empty regions take up no space.

Once our **MyPanel** object has been added to the **JFrame**, its paintComponent method is AUTOMATICALLY called. This means that we do not have to explicitly ask our panel to paint itself. This is why we are able to see the various graphics shown in Figure 3-6.

Make sure that you walk yourself through the code again and understand how we were able to produce the amazing artwork that even Picasso would have been proud of.

A Milestone

With that example, we wrap up Chapter 3 and Unit 1. If you've stuck with me this far, you have learned about the fundamentals of programming, mastered basic Java and studied advanced object-oriented design concepts. Java Game Development lies ahead, and it promises great challenges and even greater excitements.

Before we move on, I'd like to remind you that Java is an immense programing language. While I've tried to introduce you to all of the concepts that you will likely come across as you develop Java and Android games, I have by no means done the language justice. If you are interested in learning more about Java and exploring all of these concepts in much greater detail, you owe it to yourself to find a good book dedicated solely to Java alone. My favorite such book is *Head First Java* by Kathy Sierra and Bert Bates.

Secondly, I'd like to offer another reminder that you are not in this journey alone. If you are struggling with any concepts, want to learn more or just want to talk, please feel free to visit the book's companion site at **jamescho7.com**. I'd be happy to discuss any questions or concerns you may have.

Now take a deep breath. It's time to dive into the world of Java Game Development.

UNIT 2

JAVA GAME DEVELOPMENT

CHAPTER 4: LAYING THE FOUNDATIONS

We've spent much time discussing Java syntax and object-oriented design, but we've yet to see how these concepts translate into dynamic games. In this chapter, we will be putting our knowledge to use by building a game development framework. This will serve as the foundation for our first game, which we will be building in Chapter 5.

Coding a game seems daunting; you may spend months learning about Java and still have no idea where to even begin, because there seems to be this unbridgeable gap between calling basic functions and building an interactive game application. This chapter will teach you exactly how to bridge this gap. Once you realize that a Java game is made up of classes just like any other Java program, you will realize that it is not a difficult endeavor.

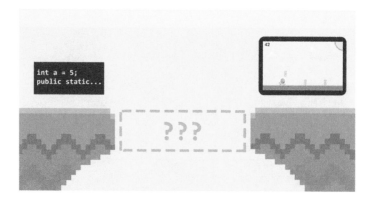

Figure 4-1   The Unbridgeable Gap

Java Game Development – An Overview

It helps to think of a Java game in terms of its three components:
- *Game development framework*: a collection of game-independent classes that will help you perform tasks that every game needs to perform, such as implementing a game screen and handling player input.

- *Game-specific classes*: Java classes representing characters, power-ups, levels and much more.
- *Resources*: images and sound files that are used throughout the game.

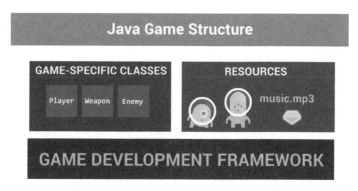

Figure 4-2   The Three Components of a Java Game

Learning to Build Games

Before we get started, I think it is important for you to understand my goals in writing Unit 2 (Chapters 4, 5 and 6), so that you know exactly what to expect.

Firstly, I aim to teach you how to build a Java game from scratch. I will walk you through the thought process behind creating a game development framework and writing game-specific classes, while sharing some tips on preparing resources.

Secondly, I hope to solidify your understanding of object-oriented design and programming. Specifically, I want you to walk away from Unit 2 with a clear understanding of how modular classes come together to form one coherent application. This will prepare you for building Android applications and games in Unit 3.

There's one additional skill that I hope you will develop from this unit. You may find that in many cases, to make the best game possible, it's easiest to work with an existing game development framework rather than building your own. This is because there are many open-source game development frameworks out there that you can incorporate into your project to build more impressive games in less time. Therefore, my hope is that you will learn how to go about working with an existing game development framework to build the games you want.

Building a Game Development Framework

The Purpose of a Game Development Framework

There are many tasks that EVERY game must be able to perform. For example, every game should be able to load images and draw them to a screen. In addition, every game needs to allow some kind of user interaction.

The role of a game development framework is to provide *reusable* classes that perform such tasks, so that you, as a game programmer, can focus on writing the game-specific code that will make or break your game.

As such, we will begin by creating a simple game development framework that will serve as the starting point for each Java game that we build in this book. This game development framework, with a few modifications, will even serve as a starting point for the Android games that we will build in Unit 3.

What Makes a Good Game Development Framework?

There is no correct way to create a game development framework. Some frameworks, such as the one we are building in this chapter, are written with fewer than ten classes. Others, such as the ever-growing, community-powered libGDX, provide hundreds of classes. As a solo developer, you will likely develop a small game development framework and add to it over time (as we will do in Chapters 5 and 6), as you find yourself needing the same features over and over again.

Despite there being no *correct* way to make a game development framework, a good game development framework should be *flexible*. You should be able to build turn-based puzzle games and real-time action games in different perspectives without making heavy modifications to the framework or sacrificing performance.

Essential Terminology

Before we can build our game, there are some terms that you must be familiar with.

- One thing that distinguishes a game from a regular Java program is the use of a game loop. A *game loop* is a block of code that runs continuously throughout the lifetime of a game, performing two important tasks on every iteration. It first updates the game logic, moving characters, handling collisions, and much more. Secondly, it takes those updates and renders (draws) images to the screen.
- FPS (frames-per-second) refers to the rate at which images on your screen are replaced to create an illusion of motion. This is directly related to the game loop, as the frequency of the render calls <u>is</u> our game's FPS.

Designing Our Framework

The framework we are going to build in this chapter will be very simple. We will be creating seven classes that belong to three categories. Read the basic overview for these classes, which is provided in Figure 4-3. If some of the explanations are unclear, return to them as we build our framework, and they should make more sense.

- Main classes
    - **GameMain**: The starting point for our game. The **GameMain** class will contain our main method, which will set our game into motion.
    - **Game**: The central class for our game. The **Game** class will host our game loop, and will have methods to start and exit out of our game.
    - **Resources**: A convenience class that will allow you to quickly load images and sound files. It will hold these resources in one location and allow you to use them across your game.

- State classes
    - **State**: Our game will be built one *state* at a time. Each state represents one screen in our game. The **State** class will serve as a blueprint for other states (through inheritance).
    - **LoadState**: It takes time to load resources. We will handle that in the **LoadState**, which will be the initial state of our game.
    - **MenuState**: A "welcome" screen that will display information regarding the game. It will be used to allow navigation to future states, such as the **GameState**, where gameplay happens.

- Utility class
    - **InputHandler**: Listens for user mouse and keyboard events and dispatches the game's state classes to handle these events.

Figure 4-3   Outline of the Game Framewok

Downloading the Source Code

The full source code (with comments) is available for you to download at `jamescho7.com`. If you are having trouble with your code at any point in this section, I recommend downloading the full code and comparing your classes.

Starting the Framework

Enough talk — it's time to start coding! Open up Eclipse and create a new Java Project called **SimpleJavaGDF**.

Next, we will create groups of classes called *packages* by right-clicking (Ctrl + click on Mac) on our **src** folder and choosing New -> Package as shown in Figure 4-4.

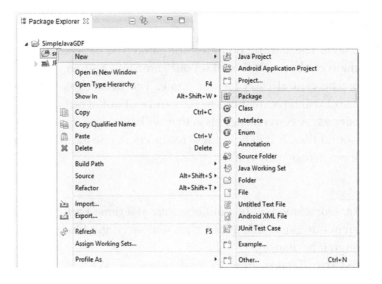

Figure 4-4   Creating a New Package

In the **New Java Package** dialog's **Name** field, enter the following:

```
com.jamescho.game.main
```

Your dialog should look like that shown in Figure 4-5.

Figure 4-5   Adding a Package Name

Click Finish, and your new package should appear under **src** in your Package Explorer. Repeat these steps to create four more packages with the following names:

1. com.jamescho.game.model

2. com.jamescho.game.state

3. com.jamescho.framework.util

4. resources

One you are done, your project should now look like Figure 4-6.

Figure 4-6   Our Five Pacakges

A Discussion of Packages

A Java package is a folder containing related files. For example, com.jamescho. framework.util refers to a folder inside our project's main src folder at .../com/jamescho/framework/util.

The classes we have discussed in Figure 4-3 will be added to these packages as follows:
- The com.jamescho.framework.util package will contain our Utility class.
- The com.jamescho.game.main package will contain our Main classes.
- The com.jamescho.game.state package will contain our State classes.

Two of our packages are *specific* to each game.
- The com.jamescho.game.model package will contain classes that will represent various objects in our game. We will keep this package empty until the next section, in which we will build a game using our framework.
- The resources package will contain images and sound files that we will use in our game.

Creating Our Classes

Now that our packages are setup, we will begin creating our classes.

KEY POINT

If at any point you get lost while following my explanations, read on. I will include a full code listing showing the most recent state of each class that we modify.

Our plan is to create a **GameMain** class, instantiate a **JFrame** object and populate its *content pane* with an instance of **Game** (which will inherit **JPanel**). Refer to Figure 4-7 if you need a refresher on these terms. If you need more review, I recommend re-reading Chapter 3's sections on *Inheritance* and *Graphics* before moving on.

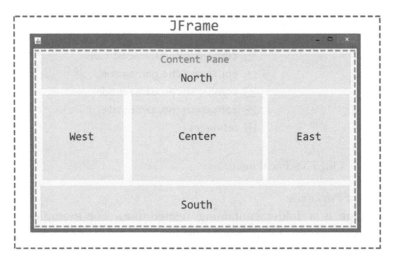

Figure 4-7   A JFrame and its Content Pane

Now, create two classes in com.jamescho.game.main, as shown in Figure 4-8. The first will be called **GameMain**, and the second will be called **Game**.

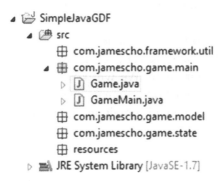

Figure 4-8   Adding GameMain and Game to the com.jamescho.game.main package.

Creating a JFrame in GameMain

We will now open up our **GameMain** class, add a main method, create some variables and initialize a new **JFrame** object representing our game's window as shown in listing 4.01.

Listing 4.01   GameMain.java (incomplete)

```
01 package com.jamescho.game.main;
02
03 import javax.swing.JFrame;
04
05 public class GameMain {
06      private static final String GAME_TITLE = "Java Game Development Framework
                             (Chapter 4)";
07      public static final int GAME_WIDTH = 800;
08      public static final int GAME_HEIGHT = 450;
09      public static Game sGame;
10
11      public static void main(String[] args) {
12              JFrame frame = new JFrame(GAME_TITLE);
13              frame.setDefaultCloseOperation(JFrame.EXIT_ON_CLOSE);
14              frame.setResizable(false); // Prevents manual resizing of window
15              frame.setVisible(true);
16      }
17
18 }
```

Before we discuss the code, let's run the program to make sure it works. You should get a window that looks like this (with minor differences based on OS):

Figure 4-9   An Empty JFrame Window (on Windows 8)

Our **JFrame** currently looks tiny, but once we start adding to its *content pane*, it should resize properly. Let's close out of our **JFrame** for now and discuss the code.

Looking at listing 4.01 again, you will find that all of the methods called in the main method are self-explanatory. (Refer to listing 3.16 if you have forgotten what some of these methods do). Let's spend some time talking about the variables.

The static *Keyword*

Notice that in listing 4.01 that all of **GameMain**'s variables are marked **static**. The word **static** denotes that these variables are NOT *instance* variables but *class* variables. This means that these variables do NOT belong to any particular instance; they belong to the class, and thus can be accessed without instantiating **GameMain**. To learn more about the **static** keyword, refer to Appendix A.

The final *Keyword*

Some variables shouldn't change throughout the course of our game. The following variables from listing 4.01 are all constants:

```
private static final String GAME_TITLE = "Java Game Development Framework (Chapter 4)";
public static final int GAME_WIDTH = 800;
public static final int GAME_HEIGHT = 450;
```

To make this clear, we first add the keyword **final** which prevents us from changing the values of these variables. We also use all uppercase letters in naming constant variables (the word *variable* still applies to *constants*, because *variable* just means something that stands in the place of another. In this case, for instance, GAME_WIDTH is a variable that stands in the place of an unchanging constant value of 800).

KEY POINT

Static Does <u>NOT</u> Mean Constant: To create constants, we use the **final** keyword.

Creating a Constructor for Game.java

Now, open up the **Game** class and extend **JPanel** (importing javax.swing.JPanel) as shown in listing 4.02.

Listing 4.02   The Game Class (incomplete)

```
1 package com.jamescho.game.main;
2
3 import javax.swing.JPanel;
4
5 @SuppressWarnings("serial")
```

```
6
7 public class Game extends JPanel {
8
9 }
```

By extending **JPanel**, **Game** *becomes* a type of **JPanel**. Our **Game** class can now be added to the *content pane* of the **JFrame** in **GameMain.**

Note:
The line: @SuppressWarnings("serial") tells Eclipse not to give us warnings regarding what is called a *serial version ID*, which is used when saving an object through a process called serialization. Serialization is beyond the scope of this book, so we will just ignore the warning. Don't worry, it will NOT affect our games!

Next, we will create several instance variables and provide a constructor we will use to initialize them. Add the following code to your **Game** class so that it looks like listing 4.03 (practice checking for new import statements to prevent errors whenever we use a new type of class):

Listing 4.03   The Game Class (updated)

```
01 package com.jamescho.game.main;
02
03 import java.awt.Color;
04 import java.awt.Dimension;
05 import java.awt.Image;
06
07 import javax.swing.JPanel;
08
09 @SuppressWarnings("serial")
10
11 public class Game extends JPanel{
12     private int gameWidth;
13     private int gameHeight;
14     private Image gameImage;
15
16     private Thread gameThread;
17     private volatile boolean running;
18
19     public Game(int gameWidth, int gameHeight) {
20         this.gameWidth = gameWidth;
21         this.gameHeight = gameHeight;
22         setPreferredSize(new Dimension(gameWidth, gameHeight));
23         setBackground(Color.BLACK);
24         setFocusable(true);
25         requestFocus();
26     }
27
28 }
```

Look at the five instance variables (lines 12 to 17 in listing 4.03) and you might see some unfamiliar terms. We have never encountered the **Image** and **Thread** types before, nor have we seen the keyword volatile. We will be discussing these shortly. Let's skip over them for the time being and move on to the constructor.

Recall that when an object is first created, its constructor is called. **Game**'s constructor asks for two values: integers called gameWidth and gameHeight. These values will be the width and height in pixels of our Java game window's content. In the first two lines of the constructor, we use these values to initialize two instance variables of the same name (we will need these values later).

Next, we call four methods that belong to **JPanel** (available to us by inheritance) as shown on lines 22 to 25 of listing 4.03.

The first of these methods requests that our **Game** object be resized to the dimensions given by gameWidth x gameHeight. We call the setPreferredSize() method by passing in a new **Dimension** object as required by the method (line 22). This **Dimension** object simply holds our width and height values in one place.

Secondly, we set the background color of our **Game** to black, by using the BLACK constant from the **Color** class (line 23).

Lines 24 and 25 allow us to start receiving user input (in the form of keyboard and mouse events). We first flag our **Game** as being *focusable*, and then ask for *focus*. This just means that keyboard events and buttons will now be available to our **Game** object.

Adding the Game to the JFrame

Now it's time to add an instance of **Game** to our **JFrame**. Return to **GameMain**, initialize sGame with a new instance of **Game**, then add it to our frame by adding the following lines of code shown in bold to the main method (the full class listing is shown in listing 4.04):

```
public static void main(String[] args) {
            ...
            sGame = new Game(GAME_WIDTH, GAME_HEIGHT);
            frame.add(sGame);
            frame.pack();

            frame.setVisible(true);
    }
```

Run the code, and you will see that our **JFrame** now has a proper size, as shown in Figure 4-10.

Let's discuss the changes we made. frame.add(sGame) is another way of saying **frame.add(BorderLayout.CENTER, sGame)**, which we have discussed in Chapter 3.

`frame.pack()` tells our **JFrame** object to resize to accommodate the preferred size of its contents (which is set using the method `setPreferredSize()` in each component).

Figure 4-10   **JFrame** with an Instance of **Game** Attached

Exit out of the program by closing the window. We are now nearly done with the **GameMain** class. The full class is reproduced in listing 4.04:

Listing 4.04   The GameMain Class (updated)

```
01 package com.jamescho.game.main;
02
03 import java.awt.BorderLayout;
04
05 import javax.swing.JFrame;
06
07 public class GameMain {
08     private static final String GAME_TITLE = "Java Game Development Framework
               (Chapter 4)";
09     public static final int GAME_WIDTH = 800;
10     public static final int GAME_HEIGHT = 450;
11     public static Game sGame;
12
13     public static void main(String[] args) {
14             JFrame frame = new JFrame(GAME_TITLE);
15             frame.setDefaultCloseOperation(JFrame.EXIT_ON_CLOSE);
16             frame.setResizable(false);
17             sGame = new Game(GAME_WIDTH, GAME_HEIGHT);
18             frame.add(sGame);
19             frame.pack();
20             frame.setVisible(true);
21     }
```

```
22
23 }
```

Adding Image Files to Our Project

We will now take a break from our code and add a few image files to our project. Go to **jamescho7.com/book/chapter7/** on your web browser, and download the following image files to any folder outside your project (alternatively, create two images of your own with the provided names and sizes):

`iconimage.png` `(20px x 20px) - to be used as icon image for JFrame`

`welcome.png` `(800px x 450px) - to be used as welcome screen for framework`

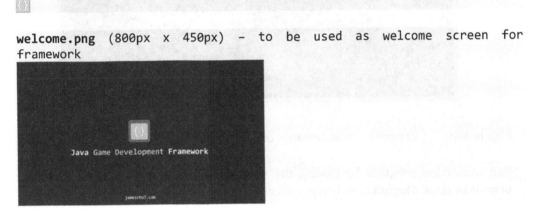

We will be adding these image files to our `resources` package. To do so, simply open the folder containing the two files and drag the files into the resources package in the Package Explorer. You will see a **File Operation** dialog. Make sure that you select **Copy files**, as shown in Figure 4-11, and press **OK**. This ensures that our project has access to these images even if they are removed from the original location.

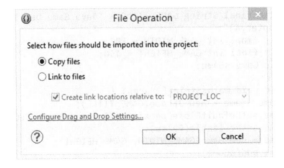

Figure 4-11   Copying Files into Our Project

Your project should now contain our two image files, as shown in Figure 4-12.

Figure 4-12   Resources Package with Images Added

Creating the Resources class

Now that we have some resources, we need a class that will manage them. We will create a **Resources** class that will allow us to quickly load image and sound files from the resources package and store them as public variables that can be accessed by other classes in our game. Create this class inside the com.jamescho.game.main package, as shown in Figure 4-13.

Figure 4-13   Creating the **Resources** Class

Our **Resources** class will have three methods. The first method, load(), will be a public method that will load all the resources in the game. To accomplish this, it will make use of two private helper methods: loadSound() and loadImage().

Add the three methods as given in listing 4.05, paying attention to the import statements to prevent errors.

Listing 4.05   The **Resources** Class

```
01 package com.jamescho.game.main;
02
03 import java.applet.Applet;
04 import java.applet.AudioClip;
05 import java.awt.image.BufferedImage;
06 import java.net.URL;
07
08 import javax.imageio.ImageIO;
09
10 public class Resources {
11      public static void load() {
12              // To-do
13      }
14
15      private static AudioClip loadSound(String filename) {
16              URL fileURL = Resources.class.getResource("/resources/" + filename);
17              return Applet.newAudioClip(fileURL);
18      }
19
20      private static BufferedImage loadImage(String filename) {
21              BufferedImage img = null;
22              img = ImageIO.read(Resources.class
                        .getResourceAsStream("/resources/" + filename));
23              return img;
24      }
25
26 }
```

Note that line 22 is wrapped in listing 4.05. Make sure that you treat any lines such as this one as one line.

You will see an error in loadImage() as shown in Figure 4-14. Ignore this for now. We will be fixing this shortly.

```
private static BufferedImage loadImage(String filename) {
    BufferedImage img = null;
    img = ImageIO.read(Resources.class.getResourceAsStream("/resources/" + filename));
    return img;
}
```

Figure 4-14   An Error in loadImage()

The `loadSound()` and `loadImage()` methods both receive a **String** parameter representing the name of the file you want to load from the `resources` package. These make use of two built-in methods for loading sound and image files that we will not discuss in-depth here.

These two methods will search the `resources` package for the requested file, and return it as either an **AudioClip** or **BufferedImage**, which are examples of Java object representations of image and sound files.

Try/Catch Block

Now let's go about fixing that error in Figure 4-14. Put your mouse over the error message, and you will see an explanation of the error.

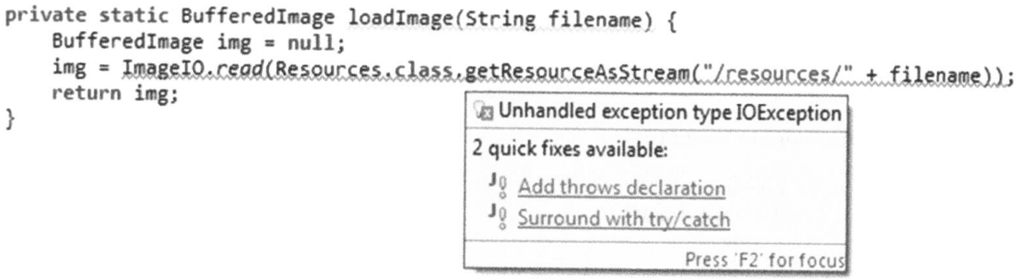

```
private static BufferedImage loadImage(String filename) {
    BufferedImage img = null;
    img = ImageIO.read(Resources.class.getResourceAsStream("/resources/" + filename));
    return img;
}
```

> Unhandled exception type IOException
>
> 2 quick fixes available:
>
> Add throws declaration
> Surround with try/catch
>
> Press 'F2' for focus

Figure 4-15 Error is due to an Unhandled Exception

Our compiler is telling us that the `ImageIO.read(...)` may throw an Exception (an error) and that we must provide a way of handling the error. To do so, we will choose the **Surround with try/catch** option. Your method should update as shown below, adding the lines shown in blue (you may see an IOException rather than an Exception, but that is perfectly okay! Either choice is fine here):

```
private static BufferedImage loadImage(String filename) {
    BufferedImage img = null;
    try {
        img = ImageIO.read(Resources.class
                        .getResourceAsStream("/resources/" + filename));
    } catch (Exception e) {
        // TODO Auto-generated catch block
        e.printStackTrace();
    }
    return img;
}
```

Whenever we call a method that is likely to fail (such as `ImageIO.read()`), we must surround it with a try/catch block, placing the risky method inside the try block and handling the error inside the catch block. We will keep the `e.printStackTrace()`, which will tell us what error occurred and where in our code it occurred.

A common exception in this case occurs when our game is unable to find a requested file, so let's add an appropriate error message to our catch block, replacing the //TODO line with the following line, so that it is easy for us to identify the problematic file:

```
System.out.println("Error while reading: " + filename);
```

Our **Resource** class should now look like listing 4.06.

Listing 4.06   The **Resources** Class (Updated with Try/Catch Block)

```
01 package com.jamescho.game.main;
02
03 import java.applet.Applet;
04 import java.applet.AudioClip;
05 import java.awt.image.BufferedImage;
06 import java.net.URL;
07
08
09 import javax.imageio.ImageIO;
10
11 public class Resources {
12        public static void load() {
13                // To-do
14        }
15
16      private static AudioClip loadSound(String filename) {
17                URL fileURL = Resources.class.getResource("/resources/" + filename);
18                return Applet.newAudioClip(fileURL);
19        }
20
21      private static BufferedImage loadImage(String filename) {
22                BufferedImage img = null;
23                try {
24                        img = ImageIO.read(Resources.class
                                .getResourceAsStream("/resources/" + filename));
25                } catch (Exception e) {
26                        System.out.println("Error while reading: " + filename);
27                        e.printStackTrace();
28                }
29                return img;
30        }
31 }
```

Loading Image Files from the resources Package

We will now go about loading the two image files **welcome.png** and **iconimage.png** into our project. This just requires two simple steps.

We first create appropriate `public static` variable for each file. Since we are working with image files, we will create two **BufferedImage** variables as shown in bold in the following example. Note that we are using the comma to declare multiple variables of the same type in one line.

```
....
public class Resources {

        public static BufferedImage welcome, iconimage;

        public static void load() {
                // To-do
        }
....
```

Secondly, we must initialize these two variables inside the load() method by calling the appropriate helper method with the desired file name as shown in bold in the example below:

```
....
public class Resources {

        public static BufferedImage welcome, iconimage;

        public static void load() {
                welcome = loadImage("welcome.png");
                iconimage = loadImage("iconimage.png");
        }
....
```

Take care to ensure that each String argument matches the name of the desired file *exactly*. Your completed class should look like listing 4.07:

Listing 4.07   The **Resources** Class (Complete)

```
01 package com.jamescho.game.main;
02
03 import java.applet.Applet;
04 import java.applet.AudioClip;
05 import java.awt.image.BufferedImage;
06 import java.net.URL;
07
08
09 import javax.imageio.ImageIO;
10
11 public class Resources {
12
13      public static BufferedImage welcome, iconimage;
14
15      public static void load() {
16              welcome = loadImage("welcome.png");
17              iconimage = loadImage("iconimage.png");
18      }
19
20      private static AudioClip loadSound(String filename) {
21              URL fileURL = Resources.class.getResource("/resources/" + filename);
22              return Applet.newAudioClip(fileURL);
```

```
23        }
24
25        private static BufferedImage loadImage(String filename) {
26                BufferedImage img = null;
27                try {
28                        img = ImageIO.read(Resources.class
                                    .getResourceAsStream("/resources/" + filename));
29                } catch (Exception e) {
30                        System.out.println("Error while reading: " + filename);
31                        e.printStackTrace();
32                }
33                return img;
34        }
35
36 }
```

We will be testing this class at a later time.

Checkpoint #1

Let's see what we have currently completed thus far within our framework. It's important for us to do this so that we don't get lost in our own code. In Figure 4-16, classes marked red have yet to be created. Classes marked orange are in-progress. Classes marked green are finished.

Note: If you are having problems with any of the classes at this point, you can download the source code at **jamescho7.com/book/chapter4/checkpoint1**.

Main Classes (com.jamescho.game.main)
GameMain: Created a **JFrame** and added an instance of **Game**.
Game: Inherited **JPanel** and created a constructor to resize and request focus.
Resources: Added load(), loadImage() and loadSound() methods and loaded two image files.

State Classes (com.jamescho.game.state)
State
LoadState
MenuState

Utility Classs (com.jamescho.game.util)
InputHandler

Figure 4-16   List of Classes and Notes

We have made a lot of progress with the main classes. In the next several pages, we will begin and complete the *state classes*.

Defining 'State'

Throughout a game session, the player passes through multiple screens. He or she may start in the main menu screen, go to the settings screen, return to the menu screen and then enter the gameplay screen.

To incorporate this feature into our framework, we will create a Java class for each screen in the game. We will be naming these classes *states*. (Following this idea, the menu screen will be represented by the **MenuState** class, the gameplay screen will be represented by the **PlayState** class, and so on).

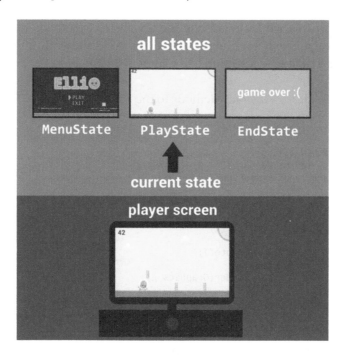

Figure 4-17   Representing States

Creating State Class

Inside the package com.jamescho.game.state, create a class called **State**. This class will serve as a generic template (i.e. a super-class) when we create other state classes (sub-classes). As such, **State** will NOT represent an actual screen in our game.

To indicate this vicarious role, we will mark this class as an *abstract class* by adding the abstract keyword in the class declaration as shown in listing 4.08.

Listing 4.08   Adding the **abstract** Keyword

```
package com.jamescho.game.state;

public abstract class State {

}
```

More on Abstract Classes

An abstract class is very similar to an interface. It contains abstract methods (methods with no method bodies) that *must* be implemented by any class inheriting from the abstract class. This means that the abstract **State** class (superclass) can declare abstract methods to provide a common structure for all state objects (subclasses) that we will create.

Let's see how this works by adding the six abstract methods that we will need to implement in each of our state objects. Add the code shown in lines 9 through 19 of listing 4.09 into **State** (pay attention to the import statements).

Listing 4.09   Adding Abstract Methods to the **State** Class

```
01 package com.jamescho.game.state;
02
03 import java.awt.Graphics;
04 import java.awt.event.KeyEvent;
05 import java.awt.event.MouseEvent;
06
07 public abstract class State {
08
09     public abstract void init();
10
11     public abstract void update();
12
13     public abstract void render(Graphics g);
14
15     public abstract void onClick(MouseEvent e);
16
17     public abstract void onKeyPress(KeyEvent e);
18
19     public abstract void onKeyRelease(KeyEvent e);
20
21 }
```

Each of these six methods will be called at very specific moments during gameplay.
- The init() method will be called when a we transition into to a new game state. It is a great place to initialize any game objects that will be used throughout the game state.

- The update() method of the current state will be called by the game loop on every frame. We use it to update every game object inside the game state.
- The render() method of the current state will be called by the game loop on every frame. We use it to render game images to the screen.
- The onClick() method of the current state will be called when the player makes a mouse click. It receives information regarding this mouse event as a parameter.
- The onKeyPress() method of the current state will be called when the player presses a keyboard button. It receives information regarding the key event, such as the identity of the key that was pressed. We use this method to make changes to our game (such as moving the character).
- The onKeyRelease() method of the current state will be called when the player releases a keyboard button. It receives information regarding the key event, such as the identity of the key was released. We use this method to make changes to our game (such as stopping a moving character).

Why We Use an Abstract Class

An abstract class, unlike an interface, allows us to declare concrete methods alongside its abstract methods to implement behavior that will be *shared* by its subclasses. In other words, an abstract class allows you to combine features of inheritance and interface!

In our framework, **State** has to be an abstract class rather than a simple interface, because we will later implement some concrete methods to perform shared behavior such as transitioning to another screen. This will make more sense later in this chapter.

Creating the LoadState Class

Let's put our **State** to use by using it as a template to create the **LoadState** class. This class will represent the loading screen of our game, where we will ask our **Resources** class to load all of our game resources.

Create the **LoadState** class inside the package com.jamescho.game.state, and extend **State** as shown in Figure 4-18.

```
package com.jamescho.game.state;

public class LoadState extends State{

}
```

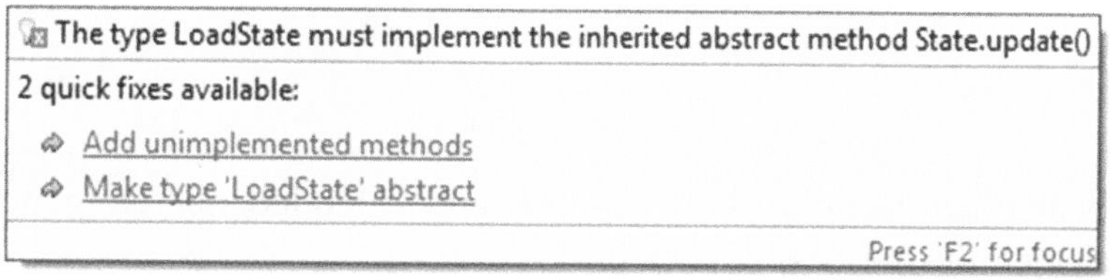

> The type LoadState must implement the inherited abstract method State.update()
>
> 2 quick fixes available:
> - Add unimplemented methods
> - Make type 'LoadState' abstract
>
> Press 'F2' for focus

Figure 4-18   Extending **State**

Just as when implementing an interface, you must implement ALL abstract methods of an inherited abstract class. Select the add "**unimplemented methods**" quick-fix, and your code should then look like that shown in listing 4.10.

Listing 4.10   The **LoadState** Class After Adding Unimplemented Methdos

```
01 package com.jamescho.game.state;
02
03 import java.awt.Graphics;
04 import java.awt.event.KeyEvent;
05 import java.awt.event.MouseEvent;
06
07 public class LoadState extends State {
08
09        @Override
10        public void init() {
11                // TODO Auto-generated method stub
12        }
13
14        @Override
15        public void update() {
16                // TODO Auto-generated method stub
17        }
18
19        @Override
20        public void render(Graphics g) {
21                // TODO Auto-generated method stub
22        }
23
24        @Override
25        public void onClick(MouseEvent e) {
26                // TODO Auto-generated method stub
27        }
28
29        @Override
30        public void onKeyPress(KeyEvent e) {
31                // TODO Auto-generated method stub
32        }
33
34        @Override
35        public void onKeyRelease(KeyEvent e) {
36                // TODO Auto-generated method stub
37        }
38
39 }
```

Now that we have created our class and extended our template, we need to start implementing the class's behavior.

In the `init()` method of the **LoadState**, we will ask our **Resources** class to load all of our game's resources. Add the following lines of code to the `init()` method, importing `com.jamescho.game.main.Resources`:

```
Resources.load();
System.out.println("Loaded Successfully");
```

You can leave the other methods empty. We will not be performing any updates or rendering any images inside the **LoadState**, and we will ignore any user interaction that happens via the keyboard or the mouse. Your **LoadState** should now look like that shown in listing 4.11.

Listing 4.11   LoadState.java

```
01 package com.jamescho.game.state;
02
03 import java.awt.Graphics;
04 import java.awt.event.KeyEvent;
05 import java.awt.event.MouseEvent;
06
07 import com.jamescho.game.main.Resources;
08
09 public class LoadState extends State{
10
11      @Override
12      public void init() {
13              Resources.load();
14              System.out.println("Loaded Successfully");
15      }
16
17      @Override
18      public void update() {
19              // TODO Auto-generated method stub
20      }
21
22      @Override
23      public void render(Graphics g) {
24              // TODO Auto-generated method stub
25      }
26
27      @Override
28      public void onClick(MouseEvent e) {
29              // TODO Auto-generated method stub
30      }
31
32      @Override
33      public void onKeyPress(KeyEvent e) {
34              // TODO Auto-generated method stub
35      }
36
37      @Override
38      public void onKeyRelease(KeyEvent e) {
39              // TODO Auto-generated method stub
40      }
41
42 }
```

This is all we need to do for now! Next, we will go to our **Game** class and set the **LoadState** as the initial state of our game.

Setting the Current State

Open the **Game** class, and declare the following instance variable (importing `com.jamescho.game.state.State`):

```
private volatile State currentState;
```

Our game will show one game state at a time. The variable `currentState` will be our framework's way of tracking this current game state. We will now add a method that accepts any **State** object (such as **loadState**), calls its `init()` method and sets it as the `currentState`. Add `setCurrentState()` as given in listing 4.12.

Listing 4.12   Adding the `setCurrentState()` method.

```
public void setCurrentState(State newState){
            System.gc();
            newState.init();
            currentState = newState;
}
```

Note: `System.gc()` is called to clean up any unused objects that are taking up valuable space in memory. The gc stands for "garbage collector". We will discuss the significance of this in more detail later on in this book.

Now we can create as many **State** objects as we want, and simply pass it into our **Game** object's `setCurrentState()` method to transition into it.

When our game begins, we want the initial game state to be the **LoadState**. Let's set this inside a new `addNotify()` method as shown on lines 38 to 42 in listing 4.13 (import accordingly):

Listing 4.13   Setting the Initial Game State

```
01 package com.jamescho.game.main;
02
03 import java.awt.Color;
04 import java.awt.Dimension;
05 import java.awt.Image;
06
07 import javax.swing.JPanel;
08
09 import com.jamescho.game.state.LoadState;
10 import com.jamescho.game.state.State;
11
12 @SuppressWarnings("serial")
13
```

```
14 public class Game extends JPanel {
15      private int gameWidth;
16      private int gameHeight;
17      private Image gameImage;
18
19      private Thread gameThread;
20      private volatile boolean running;
21      private volatile State currentState;
22
23      public Game(int gameWidth, int gameHeight) {
24              this.gameWidth = gameWidth;
25              this.gameHeight = gameHeight;
26              setPreferredSize(new Dimension(gameWidth, gameHeight));
27              setBackground(Color.BLACK);
28              setFocusable(true);
29              requestFocus();
30      }
31
32      public void setCurrentState(State newState) {
33              System.gc();
34              newState.init();
35              currentState = newState;
36      }
37
38      @Override
39      public void addNotify() {
40              super.addNotify();
41              setCurrentState(new LoadState());
42      }
43
44 }
```

Notice that I have added the @Override annotation above the addNotify() method. This is because addNotify() is an existing method that has been inherited by the **Game** class. The method addNotify() is called automatically when our **Game** object has been successfully added to the **JFrame** inside **GameMain**. It is a safe place to start setting up graphics, game state and user input.

Note that **super** (from line 40 of 4.13) refers to the superclass. super.addNotify(), then, calls **JPanel**'s addNotify() method. You will often see the superclass's methods being called inside an overriding subclass method. This means that when Game.addNotify() is called, JPanel.addNotify() will also be called.

We usually do this when a superclass's original method performs important tasks behind-the-scenes that would otherwise not be called if we were to replace the method with an overriding subclass method.

Now run your program! When our **Game** instance is added to our **JFrame**, our **LoadState** object is initialized as the currentState. At this point, **LoadState**'s init() method is called, meaning our resources will be loaded, as indicated by the friendly message that displays on the console, as shown in Figure 4-19.

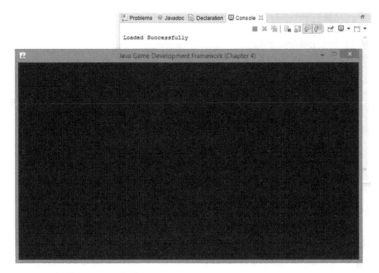

Figure 4-19   Loaded Successfully

Transitioning to MenuState

Our program claims that our resources have loaded, but we don't know this for sure until we have displayed some images. Let's ask our **LoadState** to transition to a new state called **MenuState** upon loading the resources, where we will display an image to the screen.

We first need to give our **LoadState** a way of transitioning to another state. We could implement a new method inside **LoadState** that accomplishes the state change by calling the **Game** object's setCurrentState() method. The problem with this approach is that *every* state class needs to be able to transition into another state class, so we must search for a more efficient solution.

Open the **State** class once more, and define the following concrete method that will be available via inheritance to any subclass of this abstract superclass (lines 23 to 25 of listing 4.14, checking for new import statements as always--hint: line 07):

Listing 4.14   Adding the setCurrentState() method to **State.java**

```
01      package com.jamescho.game.state;
02
03      import java.awt.Graphics;
04      import java.awt.event.KeyEvent;
05      import java.awt.event.MouseEvent;
06
07      import com.jamescho.game.main.GameMain;
08
09      public abstract class State {
10
11              public abstract void init();
12
13              public abstract void update();
```

```
14
15              public abstract void render(Graphics g);
16
17              public abstract void onClick(MouseEvent e);
18
19              public abstract void onKeyPress(KeyEvent e);
20
21              public abstract void onKeyRelease(KeyEvent e);
22
23              public void setCurrentState(State newState) {
24                      GameMain.sGame.setCurrentState(newState);
25              }
26
27      }
```

The setCurrentState() method accepts a target **State** object and passes it into the
setCurrentState() method of our **Game** object (which is stored as the variable sGame
inside our **GameMain** class). We can call this method from any state class, such as
LoadState, whenever we desire to transition to a new state.

Let's test this first by creating our **MenuState** class inside
com.jamescho.game.state. Once you have created the new class and extended State
(see Figure 4-18 if you don't remember how to do this), implement the init() and
render() methods as shown in listing 4.15. Make sure you pay attention to the import
statements. Care should be taken to import the correct **Resources** class.

Listing 4.15   The full **MenuState** Class

```
01 package com.jamescho.game.state;
02
03 import java.awt.Graphics;
04 import java.awt.event.KeyEvent;
05 import java.awt.event.MouseEvent;
06
07 import com.jamescho.game.main.Resources;
08
09 public class MenuState extends State {
10
11      @Override
12      public void init() {
13              System.out.println("Entered MenuState");
14      }
15
16      @Override
17      public void update() {
18              // Do Nothing
19      }
20
21      @Override
22      public void render(Graphics g) {
23              // Draws Resources.welcome to the screen at x = 0, y = 0
24              g.drawImage(Resources.welcome, 0, 0, null);
25      }
```

```
26
27      @Override
28      public void onClick(MouseEvent e) {
29              // To do
30      }
31
32      @Override
33      public void onKeyPress(KeyEvent e) {
34              // Intentionally ignored
35      }
36
37      @Override
38      public void onKeyRelease(KeyEvent e) {
39              // Intentionally ignored
40      }
41
42 }
```

We will discuss the g.drawImage(...) method in detail at a later time. For now, return to the **LoadState** class. We will add one statement inside the update() method to transition into the new **MenuState**, as shown below:

```
....

public class LoadState extends State {

....

        @Override
        public void update() {
                setCurrentState(new MenuState());      // This is the new line!
        }
....
```

This will allow us to transition from the **LoadState** to the **MenuState** when the LoadState.update() method is called.

Now, you may be wondering why our program still doesn't display the welcome image even though in the render() method of our **MenuState**, we are calling a function to draw an image.

The reason for this is that we never called the render() method in our **Game** class (nor the update(), onClick(), onKeyPress() and onKeyReleased() for that matter). To call the render() method, we need to add the heart of the game into the **Game** class: the game loop. We will be doing this after the following checkpoint.

Checkpoint #2

Let's take a second look at our progress. Figure 4-20 follows the same rules given for Figure 4-16.

Main Classes (`com.jamescho.game.main`)
`GameMain`: Unchanged.
`Game`: Added a `currentState` variable, implemented `addNotify()` and
`setCurrentState()` methods.
`Resources`: Unchanged.

State Classes (`com.jamescho.game.state`)
`State`: Added six abstract methods required by all other state objects. Defined a
concrete `setCurrentState()` method used to transition between states.
`LoadState`: Implemented **State**, added calls to load resources and transition to
MenuState.
`MenuState`: Implemented **State**, added a call to draw a welcome image to the screen.

Utility Classs (`com.jamescho.game.util`)
`InputHandler`

Figure 4-20   List of Classes and Changes Since Checkpoint #1

Remember: If you are having problems with any of the classes at this point, you can
download the source code at `jamescho7.com/book/chapter4/checkpoint2`.

We are nearly there! Let's return once again to **Game**, where we will implement the game
loop and hook up a new **InputHandler** object. We will then add a cool icon to our
JFrame in **GameMain**, and we will be ready to build our very first graphical game.

The Need to Multi-Task

You've probably heard of multi-core processors. Chances are you have one inside your
own computer. Having multiple cores allows you to execute various tasks
simultaneously.

As our game needs to perform all kinds of behavior simultaneously (we don't want
player input to be ignored while the game is rendering), our game will need to multi-
task as well. But we don't have to worry about whether our player runs an Intel i7
Processor Extreme Edition or a good old Pentium 4. Java allows us to accomplish multitasking even without multiple cores when we use *threads*.

Threads
Think of a thread as a process that executes instructions from a list. If we were to
chronologically list every method that is called when we run our framework, we would
have the list of the instructions that are being called by our default thread (called the
main thread). This list is called the call stack.

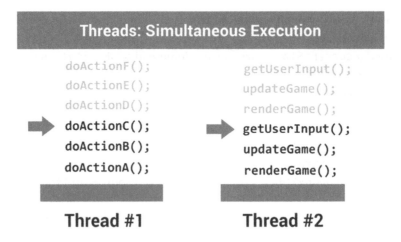

Figure 4-21   Threads / Game

Until now, we have been providing a single call stack for the JVM to execute; however, creating multiple stacks is easy. For starters, we can create a second thread and provide it with a list of instructions to perform. When our program executes, our two threads will execute their call stacks "simultaneously" (this is a simplification, but we will assume this). In the context of our framework, this would mean that one thread (the game thread) can handle the execution of our game loop, while the main thread can handle the rest! We will now be implementing this second thread into our game.

Adding the Game Thread

Creating a new call stack requires three steps. Firstly, you create the new thread. Secondly, you give it some instructions to perform. Thirdly, you tell our program to start executing these instructions. We will be performing all three of these steps to create our game thread.

Open the **Game** class. Back in listing 4.03, we added three instance variables that we have ignored until this point: gameImage, gameThread and running.

We will be making use of the **Thread** and boolean variables to implement a game loop. Add the initGame() method shown in bold below to **Game** (ignore the errors for now). Then, call this new method inside addNotify() (also shown in bold).

```
....

@Override
public void addNotify() {
        super.addNotify();
        setCurrentState(new LoadState());
        initGame();
}
```

126

```
private void initGame() {
      running = true;
      gameThread = new Thread(this, "Game Thread");
      gameThread.start();
}
```

....

initGame() initializes our running as true (we will be discussing volatile shortly). Then, we initialize our gameThread variable using a constructor that accepts two arguments. The first argument is a task for the new **Thread** to complete. The second argument is the name of the new **Thread**. At the moment, we have an error in our code, as shown in Figure 4-22.

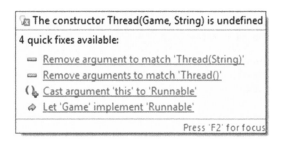

Figure 4-22   Error in the **Thread** Constructor

Mousing over the red lines, we see the error shown in Figure 4-23, along with a list of suggested quick-fixes.

> 🔲 The constructor Thread(Game, String) is undefined
>
> **4 quick fixes available:**
>
> ⇒ Remove argument to match 'Thread(String)'
>
> ⇒ Remove arguments to match 'Thread()'
>
> (↓ Cast argument 'this' to 'Runnable'
>
> ↻ Let 'Game' implement 'Runnable'
>
> Press 'F2' for focus

Figure 4-23   Give Me a Runnable!

The quick-fixes seem to suggest that the first argument of this constructor should be a variable of type **Runnable**, not **Game** (remember that the keyword this refers to the instance of **Game** that is calling the **Thread** constructor). Indeed, the Java Documentation describes the following constructor for **Thread**:

```
Thread (Runnable target, String name)
```

To solve this issue, we need to understand what a **Runnable** object is. Recall that a thread needs a list of instructions to execute. This list can be provided in the form of a **Runnable** object.

Now where do we get this **Runnable** object? It turns out that **Runnable** is a built-in Java interface. This means that we can implement **Runnable** in our **Game** class, and this will allow us to pass in the instance of our **Game** (using the keyword this) to the constructor for the Game Thread as shown in Figure 4-22. Let's do this by adding the implements... declaration shown in Figure 4-24 to our **Game** class:

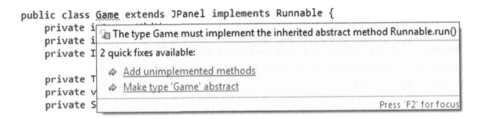

Figure 4-24   Game implements the Runnable Interface

As we are implementing an interface, we must implement all of its abstract methods. Select **Add unimplemented methods**.

This will automatically add the run() method as shown in listing 4.16, which shows what your **Game** class should look like at this point.

Listing 4.16   Implementing the run() method

```
01 package com.jamescho.game.main;
02
03 import java.awt.Color;
04 import java.awt.Dimension;
05 import java.awt.Image;
06
07 import javax.swing.JPanel;
08
09 import com.jamescho.game.state.LoadState;
10 import com.jamescho.game.state.State;
11
12 @SuppressWarnings("serial")
13
14 public class Game extends JPanel implements Runnable {
15       private int gameWidth;
16       private int gameHeight;
17       private Image gameImage;
18
19       private Thread gameThread;
20       private volatile boolean running;
21       private volatile State currentState;
22
23       public Game(int gameWidth, int gameHeight) {
24             this.gameWidth = gameWidth;
25             this.gameHeight = gameHeight;
26             setPreferredSize(new Dimension(gameWidth, gameHeight));
27             setBackground(Color.BLACK);
```

```
28                    setFocusable(true);
29                    requestFocus();
30            }
31
32        public void setCurrentState(State newState) {
33                    System.gc();
34                    newState.init();
35                    currentState = newState;
36            }
37
38        @Override
39        public void addNotify() {
40                    super.addNotify();
41                    setCurrentState(new LoadState());
42                    initGame();
43            }
44
45        private void initGame() {
46                    running = true;
47                    gameThread = new Thread(this, "Game Thread");
48                    gameThread.start();
49            }
50
51        @Override
52        public void run() {
53                    // TODO Auto-generated method stub
54            }
55
56 }
```

Implementing **Runnable** and its abstract run() method makes **Game** eligible to be used as a **Runnable** object. Thus, our error in the initGame() method is gone, as shown in Figure 4-25.

```
private void initGame() {
    running = true;
    gameThread = new Thread(this, "Game Thread");
    gameThread.start();
}
```

Figure 4-25   Game as Runnable

Based on this, you can probably guess that **Game**'s run() method has something to do with our gameThread, and you would be exactly right.

The gameThread needs a task to complete, and the run() method is that task. When we call gameThread.start() as shown in Figure 4-25, we are asking our gameThread to perform our run() method. Since gameThread is a separate thread that exists independently from our default main thread, we are letting our program multi-task.

Now when our **Game**'s addNotify() method is called, the initGame() will be called, starting the run() method in the gameThread. You can test this by adding a print statement to the run() method and running the program. You should be able to see your message once **LoadState** becomes the current state.

Note: You have probably been wondering what the keyword 'volatile' means and how it effects a variable. This is a quite advanced topic (Google: Java Concurrency). To understand this, you must first know that when two threads are sharing a variable (modifying or accessing the same variable), they may create their own copy of the shared variable before using it. To put simply, this means that changing the value of a shared variable in one thread may not change the copy of that variable in another, leading to inconsistent values.

What implications does this have? For one, the value of our boolean running can be true on one thread and false on another. Will our game continue or stop? We want to avoid ambiguous questions like this by marking the variable as volatile.

We also want currentState to be volatile, as there should only be one current state. Our game should not be stuck in limbo between one state and another.

Implementing the Game Loop

Now that we have added our game thread, it is time to add the game loop to it. We will be focusing on just the run() method for now.

Inside the run() method, add a while loop as shown below in bold, along with an exit command (also shown). As you can see, when the game loop ends, our game should also terminate.

....

```
    @Override
    public void run() {
            while (running) {

            }

            // End game immediately when running becomes false.
            System.exit(0);
    }
```

....

Our game loop terminates when running becomes false, meaning that, to terminate our game, we would need to change the value of running to false, but more on that later.

Inside the body of the game loop, we will perform two tasks: update and render. Updating will be simple. We just need to ask our currentState to call its update()

method. Rendering, however, will be more drawn out, and will take three steps to complete.

To render our game, we will rely on a technique called *double buffering*. Rather than drawing our images directly to the screen one at a time, we will prepare an off-screen empty image and draw all of our images onto that, before we finally draw the completed scene onto the screen once per frame. So, the three steps we must complete are as follows:

1. Prepare an off-screen empty image.
2. Render the `currentState`'s scene (all the game objects in the `currentState`) to this game image.
3. Draw the completed off-screen image onto the screen.

Double buffering allows us to reduce unwanted graphical tearing and flickering. We won't get into the details of that here. Suffice it to say that double buffering, although it will take more time to code, improves the gameplay experience.

It's time to add our code. Add the four lines in bold inside the game loop, and define a new method called `prepareGameImage()` as shown below (importing **Graphics**):

....

```
@Override
public void run() {
        while (running) {
                currentState.update();
                prepareGameImage();
                currentState.render(gameImage.getGraphics());
                repaint();
        }

        // End game immediately when running becomes false.
        System.exit(0);
}


private void prepareGameImage() {
        if (gameImage == null) {
                gameImage = createImage(gameWidth, gameHeight);
        }
        Graphics g = gameImage.getGraphics();
        g.clearRect(0, 0, gameWidth, gameHeight);
}
```
....

In the four lines of code that we have added inside the game loop, we update the `currentState` and then call three methods to handle the steps required for rendering. In `prepareGameImage()` we prepare an off-screen image by creating and initializing the `gameImage` variable with a width of `gameWidth` and a height of `gameHeight`. Next, on every frame, we clear this image using a rectangle of equal size to clear all images that have been drawn to the screen in the previous frame. This ensures that images from the previous frame do not bleed into the current frame. Every frame starts anew.

Frames per Second and the Timing Mechanism

Games rely on rapidly-switching static images (or frames) to provide an illusion of animation. As such, game performance is often measured in FPS or frames per second. Typically, the higher the FPS, the smoother the graphics and gameplay.

FPS, in our framework, is equivalent to our game loop's iterations (repetition) per second. This is because in each iteration, we update and render our game once, refreshing the screen one time.

So, the following equation is a great way to think about our game.

```
update + render = one iteration of game loop = one frame
```

Our framework will aim for about 60 FPS. This should be more than enough to ensure smooth gameplay. Therefore, we want our game loop to iterate about 60 times a second, which would mean that each iteration should take about 0.017 seconds (17 milliseconds) to execute. There are sophisticated ways of handling this that we will discuss later, but we will keep it extremely simple for now.

We build upon the assumption that, for most games we build on this framework, updating and rendering will complete in a very small amount of time (2-3 milliseconds). Of course, this will vary from system to system and from game to game, which is the reason that we will discuss a better timing mechanism in the future. For now, after each update and render, we are going to ask our game thread to *sleep* for 14 milliseconds. When added to the 2-3 milliseconds of updating and rendering, each iteration will thus take about 17 milliseconds total.

Note: Since our game loop is unending (it runs until we tell it to terminate by setting running to false), our game thread will hog much of our computer's CPU time. Asking our game thread to sleep will allow our CPU to spend time performing other tasks, such as taking user input.

To implement our sleep-driven timing mechanism, we simply have to add the following lines of code (shown in blue text) to our run() method.

```
...
@Override
public void run() {
        while (running) {
                currentState.update();
                prepareGameImage();
                currentState.render(gameImage.getGraphics());
                repaint();
                try {
```

```
                    Thread.sleep(14);
            } catch (InterruptedException e) {
                    e.printStackTrace();
            }
    }
    System.exit(0);
}
...
```

Note that we just call a simple static method called `Thread.sleep()` to ask our Game Thread to sleep for 14 milliseconds. We must surround this in a try-catch as it may throw an exception (specifically of type `InterruptedException`, a form of Exception. See Figure 4-15 and the following discussion on try/catch block if it is unfamiliar).

Our game loop is finished, and it should run approximately every 17 milliseconds. As you can tell, this timing mechanism is very limited and we will be modifying it soon in the coming chapters.

Exiting the Game

Our **Game** class is nearly finished. We will just be adding a few more methods. The first is trivial. It is a simple method that will be called when we want our game to exit. It will set the value of our `boolean running` to false, making our game loop terminate.

Add the following method to **Game** class:

```
public void exit() {
        running = false;
}
```

Fixing Paint

Recall that we must perform three steps to render our game. We have successfully created an empty off-screen image called `gameImage` and filled it with our images, but now we have to draw this image to our screen.

To accomplish this, we have called `repaint()` inside our game loop, but this is simply a request for the program to call the `paintComponent()` method of our **Game** object, which is a **JPanel** (see *Understanding the MyPanel* from Chapter 3).

At the moment, **Game** does not have a custom `paintComponent()` method, in which we must actually perform the drawing of our `gameImage` to the screen. Let's override it as shown below:

```
@Override
protected void paintComponent(Graphics g) {
        super.paintComponent(g);
        if (gameImage == null) {
                return;
        }
        g.drawImage(gameImage, 0, 0, null);
}
```

In our `paintComponent()` method, we first check if our `gameImage` is `null`, because we do not want to draw it if it does not exist. If it is, we call `return`, which, inside a `void` method, simply ends the method. The next time `prepareGameImage()` and `repaint()` are called, this `gameImage` should not be null.

The parameter for `paintComponent()` is a reference to a **Graphics** object called g, which you can think of as a canvas on our device's screen. We will take g and draw our off-screen `gameImage` onto it at the coordinates x = 0, y = 0 (top-left corner of game window).

Note: The third argument for `g.drawImage(…)` is an **ImageObserver** object which allows you to determine if an image has been fully loaded. We will not be using this in our framework, so we can safely pass in `null`.

The updated **Game** class is given in listing 4.17.

Listing 4.17   The Game class (Updated)

```
01 package com.jamescho.game.main;
02
03 import java.awt.Color;
04 import java.awt.Dimension;
05 import java.awt.Graphics;
06 import java.awt.Image;
07
08 import javax.swing.JPanel;
09
10 import com.jamescho.game.state.LoadState;
11 import com.jamescho.game.state.State;
12
13 @SuppressWarnings("serial")
14
15 public class Game extends JPanel implements Runnable {
16      private int gameWidth;
17      private int gameHeight;
18      private Image gameImage;
19
20      private Thread gameThread;
21      private volatile boolean running;
22      private volatile State currentState;
23
24      public Game(int gameWidth, int gameHeight) {
25              this.gameWidth = gameWidth;
26              this.gameHeight = gameHeight;
27              setPreferredSize(new Dimension(gameWidth, gameHeight));
28              setBackground(Color.BLACK);
29              setFocusable(true);
30              requestFocus();
31      }
32
33      public void setCurrentState(State newState) {
34              System.gc();
```

```
35              newState.init();
36              currentState = newState;
37          }
38
39      @Override
40      public void addNotify() {
41              super.addNotify();
42              setCurrentState(new LoadState());
43              initGame();
44          }
45
46      private void initGame() {
47              running = true;
48              gameThread = new Thread(this, "Game Thread");
49              gameThread.start();
50          }
51
52      @Override
53      public void run() {
54              while (running) {
55                      currentState.update();
56                      prepareGameImage();
57                      currentState.render(gameImage.getGraphics());
58                      repaint();
59
60                      try {
61                              Thread.sleep(14);
62                      } catch (InterruptedException e) {
63                              e.printStackTrace();
64                      }
65              }
66              System.exit(0);
67          }
68
69      private void prepareGameImage() {
70              if (gameImage == null) {
71              gameImage = createImage(gameWidth, gameHeight);
72              }
73              Graphics g = gameImage.getGraphics();
74              g.clearRect(0, 0, gameWidth, gameHeight);
75          }
76
77      public void exit() {
78              running = false;
79          }
80
81      @Override
82      protected void paintComponent(Graphics g) {
83              super.paintComponent(g);
84              if (gameImage == null) {
85                      return;
86              }
87              g.drawImage(gameImage, 0, 0, null);
88          }
89  }
```

Figure 4-26   Our First Image!

Run your code and you should see the image as shown in Figure 4-26.

We have finally gotten some graphics to display. There is one last thing we must do to complete our framework, and that is to add the ability to respond to user input.

Handling Player Input

Recall that each of our state classes implements methods to handle keyboard and mouse input; however, adding code to our states' `onClick()`, `onKeyPress()` and `onRelease()` methods will not have any effect at the moment. As with the `init()`, `update()` and `render()` methods, these methods are not called automatically. We must ask that the `currentState`'s input methods be called when the player interacts with our game, and that is where the **InputHandler** class comes in.

Inside `com.jamescho.framework.util`, create a new class called **InputHandler**, which we will designate to be notified when the player interacts with the game. For this to happen, we must implement two built-in Java interfaces **KeyListener** and **MouseListener** in this class, and attach an instance of the class to **Game**.

Update our class declaration as shown in listing 4.18 to begin the first step, paying attention to the `implements` and `import` statements:

Listing 4.18   Implementing `KeyListener` and `MouseListener`

```
package com.jamescho.framework.util;

import java.awt.event.KeyListener;
```

```
import java.awt.event.MouseListener;

public class InputHandler implements KeyListener, MouseListener {

}
```

Put your mouse over the error in the class declaration (shown in Figure 4-27) and select *Add unimplemented methods*).

```
package com.jamescho.framework.util;

import java.awt.event.KeyListener;
import java.awt.event.MouseListener;

public class InputHandler implements KeyListener, MouseListener {

}
```
```
  The type InputHandler must implement the inherited abstract method
  MouseListener.mouseClicked(MouseEvent)

2 quick fixes available:
  ♦ Add unimplemented methods
  ♦ Make type 'InputHandler' abstract

                                              Press 'F2' for focus
```

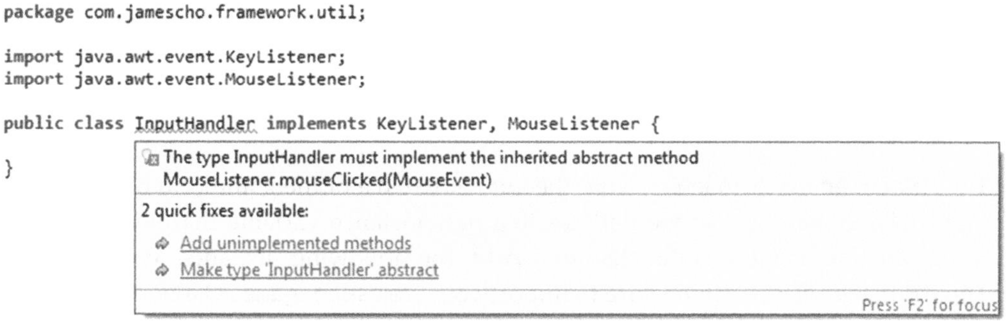

Figure 4-27   Implementing Abstract Methods

This will automatically add the mouseClicked(), mouseEntered(), mouseExited(), mousePressed(), mouseReleased(), keyPressed(), keyReleased() and keyTyped() methods to your class. We only care about three of them: mouseClicked(), keyPressed() and keyReleased(), as these are enough to implement any kind of user interaction that we want in our games.

As their names indicate, the methods mouseClicked(), keyPressed() and keyReleased() are called when the player clicks a mouse button, presses a key, or releases a key, respectively. When these methods are called, the role of our **InputHandler** is to ask the currentScreen of the game to call its own onClick(), onKeyPress() and onKeyRelease() methods. This relationship is elaborated in Figure 4-28.

Note: You can find more information on when the interfaces' methods are called by reading the Java Documentation for the **KeyListener** and **MouseListener** interfaces:
KeyListener:
http://docs.oracle.com/javase/7/docs/api/java/awt/event/KeyListener.html
MouseListener:
http://docs.oracle.com/javase/7/docs/api/java/awt/event/MouseListener.html

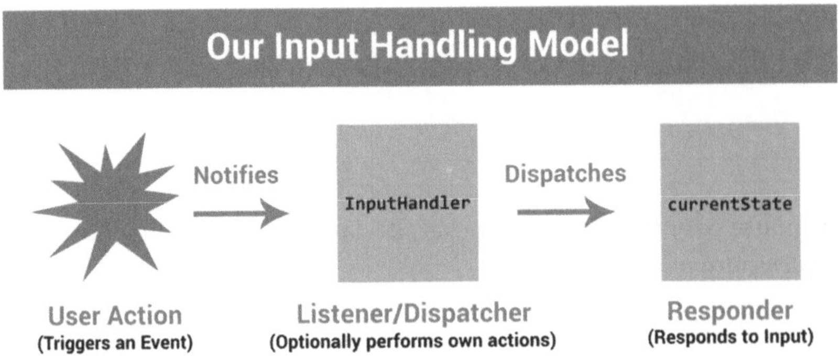

Our Input Handling Model

Notifies → InputHandler → Dispatches → currentState

User Action
(Triggers an Event)

Listener/Dispatcher
(Optionally performs own actions)

Responder
(Responds to Input)

Figure 4-28   Input Handling Model

InputHandler needs to know what the currentState of the game is in order to call its input-related methods, so we will create a new instance variable that will be updated whenever the game's state changes. Add the following instance variable to the **InputHandler** class, making sure to import com.jamescho.game.state.State.

```
private State currentState;
```

Create a corresponding setter method as shown below:

```
public void setCurrentState(State currentState) {
        this.currentState = currentState;
}
```

Let's now add some code to the mouseClicked(), keyPressed() and keyReleased() methods. Specifically, we will be asking the currentState of our game to call their versions of the three methods of the same name, as shown on lines 20, 45 and 50 of listing 4.19, which reflects the final version of **InputHandler**.

Listing 4.19   The **InputHandler** Class

```
01 package com.jamescho.framework.util;
02
03 import java.awt.event.KeyEvent;
04 import java.awt.event.KeyListener;
05 import java.awt.event.MouseEvent;
06 import java.awt.event.MouseListener;
07
08 import com.jamescho.game.state.State;
09
10 public class InputHandler implements KeyListener, MouseListener {
11
12     private State currentState;
13
```

```
14      public void setCurrentState(State currentState) {
15              this.currentState = currentState;
16      }
17
18      @Override
19      public void mouseClicked(MouseEvent e) {
20              currentState.onClick(e);
21      }
22
23      @Override
24      public void mouseEntered(MouseEvent e) {
25              // Do Nothing
26      }
27
28      @Override
29      public void mouseExited(MouseEvent e) {
30              // Do Nothing
31      }
32
33      @Override
34      public void mousePressed(MouseEvent e) {
35              // Do Nothing
36      }
37
38      @Override
39      public void mouseReleased(MouseEvent e) {
40              // Do Nothing
41      }
42
43      @Override
44      public void keyPressed(KeyEvent e) {
45              currentState.onKeyPress(e);
46      }
47
48      @Override
49      public void keyReleased(KeyEvent e) {
50              currentState.onKeyRelease(e);
51      }
52
53      @Override
54      public void keyTyped(KeyEvent arg0) {
55              // Do Nothing
56      }
57
58 }
```

Our work on the **InputHandler** class is finished. Next, we will attach an instance of **InputHandler** to our game.

Attaching the InputHandler

Being a **JPanel** subclass, **Game** inherits two methods that will allow us to listen to user input. These are addKeyListener(KeyListener l) and addMouseListener(Mouse Listener l). These two methods accept any instance of a class that implements the

KeyListener and **MouseListener** interfaces, respectively. We already have a class that does both (**InputHandler**), so this will be easy!

When addKeyListener() and addMouseListener() are called in **Game**, we will pass in an instance of **InputHandler** as the argument. This object will then be set as the key and mouse listener for our **JPanel**, and will hence be notified (in the form of its methods being called) when the player interacts with our game.

Open the **Game** class and add the following instance variable (remember to import com.jamescho.framework.util.InputHandler):

```
private InputHandler inputHandler;
```

Initialize it in a new method called initInput(), which should be defined as follows:

```
private void initInput() {
        inputHandler = new InputHandler();
        addKeyListener(inputHandler);
        addMouseListener(inputHandler);
}
```

Next, we will simply call this method in our addNotify() method as shown in bold below. This will initialize our inputHandler and set it as the key and mouse listener for our **Game**:

```
@Override
public void addNotify() {
        super.addNotify();
        initInput();  // This is the new line!
        setCurrentState(new LoadState());
        initGame();
}
```

Finally, we will add a line of code to set the currentState variable for our inputHandler inside the setCurrentState() method as shown in bold:

```
public void setCurrentState(State newState){
        System.gc();
        currentState = newState;
        newState.init();
        inputHandler.setCurrentState(currentState);     // This is the new line!
}
```

That finishes our input handling and our **Game** class, which should now look as shown in listing 4.20:

Listing 4.20   The Completed **Game** Class

```
001 package com.jamescho.game.main;
002
003 import java.awt.Color;
004 import java.awt.Dimension;
005 import java.awt.Graphics;
006 import java.awt.Image;
007
008 import javax.swing.JPanel;
009
010 import com.jamescho.framework.util.InputHandler;
011 import com.jamescho.game.state.LoadState;
012 import com.jamescho.game.state.State;
013
014 @SuppressWarnings("serial")
015
016 public class Game extends JPanel implements Runnable {
017     private int gameWidth;
018     private int gameHeight;
019     private Image gameImage;
020
021     private Thread gameThread;
022     private volatile boolean running;
023     private volatile State currentState;
024
025     private InputHandler inputHandler;
026
027     public Game(int gameWidth, int gameHeight){
028             this.gameWidth = gameWidth;
029             this.gameHeight = gameHeight;
030             setPreferredSize(new Dimension(gameWidth, gameHeight));
031             setBackground(Color.BLACK);
032             setFocusable(true);
033             requestFocus();
034     }
035
036     public void setCurrentState(State newState){
037             System.gc();
038             newState.init();
039             currentState = newState;
040             inputHandler.setCurrentState(currentState);
041     }
042
043     @Override
044     public void addNotify() {
045             super.addNotify();
046             initInput();
047             setCurrentState(new LoadState());
048             initGame();
049     }
050
051     private void initInput() {
052             inputHandler = new InputHandler();
053             addKeyListener(inputHandler);
054             addMouseListener(inputHandler);
055     }
056
```

```
057        private void initGame() {
058                running = true;
059                gameThread = new Thread(this, "Game Thread");
060                gameThread.start();
061        }
062
063        @Override
064        public void run() {
065                while (running) {
066                        currentState.update();
067                        prepareGameImage();
068                        currentState.render(gameImage.getGraphics());
069                        repaint();
070
071                        try {
072                                Thread.sleep(14);
073                        } catch (InterruptedException e) {
074                                e.printStackTrace();
075                        }
076
077                }
078                // End game immediatly when running becomes fales
079                System.exit(0);
080        }
081
082        private void prepareGameImage() {
083                if (gameImage == null) {
084                        gameImage = createImage(gameWidth, gameHeight);
085                }
086                Graphics g = gameImage.getGraphics();
087                g.fillRect(0, 0, gameWidth, gameHeight);
088        }
089
090        public void exit() {
091                running = false;
092        }
093
094        @Override
095        protected void paintComponent(Graphics g) {
096                super.paintComponent(g);
097                if (gameImage == null) {
098                        return;
099                }
100                g.drawImage(gameImage, 0, 0, null);
101        }
102
103 }
```

Now, try adding some print statements to the **MenuState** class's onClick(), onKeyPress() and onKeyRelease() methods, and you should be able to see them appear when you run the program and interact with the welcome screen using your keyboard and mouse as shown in Figure 4-29!

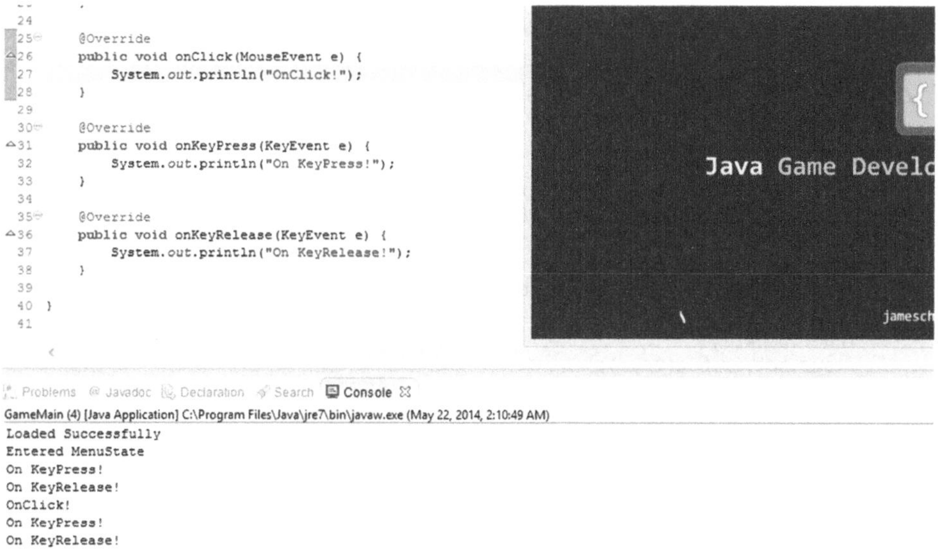

```
 24
 25    @Override
 26    public void onClick(MouseEvent e) {
 27        System.out.println("OnClick!");
 28    }
 29
 30    @Override
 31    public void onKeyPress(KeyEvent e) {
 32        System.out.println("On KeyPress!");
 33    }
 34
 35    @Override
 36    public void onKeyRelease(KeyEvent e) {
 37        System.out.println("On KeyRelease!");
 38    }
 39
 40  }
 41
```

```
Problems   Javadoc   Declaration   Search   Console
GameMain (4) [Java Application] C:\Program Files\Java\jre7\bin\javaw.exe (May 22, 2014, 2:10:49 AM)
Loaded Successfully
Entered MenuState
On KeyPress!
On KeyRelease!
OnClick!
On KeyPress!
On KeyRelease!
```

Figure 4-29   Interacting with the Game

Checkpoint #3

We are one small change away from finishing our framework. Figure 4-30 follows the same rules given for Figure 4-16.

Main Classes (com.jamescho.game.main)
GameMain: Unchanged.
Game: Implemented game loop and input.
Resources: Unchanged.

State Classes (com.jamescho.game.state)
State: Unchanged
LoadState: Unchanged
MenuState: Unchanged

Utility Classs (com.jamescho.game.util)
InputHandler: Implemented KeyListener and MouseListener, provided a method for setting currentState.

Figure 4-30   List of Classes and Changes Since Checkpoint #2

Note: If you are having problems with any of the classes at this point, you can download the source code at jamescho7.com/book/chapter4/checkpoint3.

The last change we need to make is to make use of the **iconimage.png** file that has been sitting inside the **resources** package by setting it equal to the framework's launch icon! To do so, open **GameMain** and add a single line of code as shown in bold below:

```
. . . .
public static void main(String[] args) {
        JFrame frame = new JFrame(GAME_TITLE);
        frame.setDefaultCloseOperation(JFrame.EXIT_ON_CLOSE);
        frame.setResizable(false); // Prevents manual resizing of window
        sGame = new Game(GAME_WIDTH, GAME_HEIGHT);
        frame.add(sGame);
        frame.pack();
        frame.setVisible(true);
        frame.setIconImage(Resources.iconimage); // This is the new line!
}
. . . .
```

Next, run the framework, and you should see your icon (Figure 4-31 shows the effect on Windows 8).

Figure 4-31   Setting the Icon Image

Note: The completed framework for Chapter 4 can be downloaded at jamescho7.com/book/chapter4/complete.

And, we're done! We will be making some improvements to the framework in the coming chapters, but for now, it's time to build a game. Skim through the note on license information that follows, and join me in the next section.

A Note on Licenses and Code Reuse

This framework is provided to you to use as you wish without restriction. You may modify the framework, redistribute the code and even build commercial games without permission from me or the publisher. You only have to include the following license by creating a text file called LICENSE.txt in every distribution (available for download at **jamescho7.com/book/license**).

```
The MIT License (MIT)

Copyright (c) 2014 James S. Cho

Permission is hereby granted, free of charge, to any person obtaining a copy of this
software and associated documentation files (the "Software"), to deal in the Software
without restriction, including without limitation the rights to use, copy, modify, merge,
publish, distribute, sublicense, and/or sell copies of the Software, and to permit
persons to whom the Software is furnished to do so, subject to the following conditions:

The above copyright notice and this permission notice shall be included in all copies or
substantial portions of the Software.

THE SOFTWARE IS PROVIDED "AS IS", WITHOUT WARRANTY OF ANY KIND, EXPRESS OR IMPLIED,
INCLUDING BUT NOT LIMITED TO THE WARRANTIES OF MERCHANTABILITY, FITNESS FOR A PARTICULAR
PURPOSE AND NONINFRINGEMENT. IN NO EVENT SHALL THE AUTHORS OR COPYRIGHT HOLDERS BE LIABLE
FOR ANY CLAIM, DAMAGES OR OTHER LIABILITY, WHETHER IN AN ACTION OF CONTRACT, TORT OR
OTHERWISE, ARISING FROM, OUT OF OR IN CONNECTION WITH THE SOFTWARE OR THE USE OR OTHER
DEALINGS IN THE SOFTWARE.
```

It All Starts Here

This long chapter has walked you through the design and development of a simple game development framework that will serve as the foundation for the games that we will be building in the next several chapters. This was the first serious application that we have built in this book, and we were able to see many Java concepts in practical situations.

Now that we have our initial game development framework, it's time to build a game. Join me in Chapter 5, where we will take this framework for a spin. It's going to be a fun ride.

Chapter 5: Keeping It Simple

A common pitfall in getting started with game development is being too specific about what you want to build. Aspiring developers want to make a great game with an immersive story that they think everyone will enjoy. They have an idea of what their character will look like, what he will do, whom he will fight, where and when the game will take place, and so on. They learn a programming language and rush head-on into the challenge of game development, only to find themselves realizing their ambitions were too great too soon.

This chapter is all about starting small. I won't be teaching you how to build the games of your dreams, but I will be teaching you how to work with an existing game development framework to build a simple game. I will guide you through the design and implementation of each game object in order to help you become a better programmer. By the end of this chapter, you may realize that there is still a long way to go before you release a groundbreaking title, but you will have a much greater understanding of the development process, and you will have made your first game from scratch.

Game Development: A High-Level Overview

Our game will be a clone of Pong called *LoneBall*, and it will challenge players to keep a ball bouncing left and right for as long as possible by pressing the up and down arrow keys to control both paddles, as the ball speeds up or slows down randomly. The player earns 1 point for each successful save and loses 3 points for each miss! The twist is that the paddles will always move in opposite directions, meaning that the paddle on the right will travel in the opposite direction of the arrow key you press. A screenshot of the final product is shown in Figure 5-1.

Why So Simple?
Despite our game's simplicity, it will capture many important aspects of game development. You will learn how to write classes in order to represent game objects, how to detect and handle collision, how to update objects in response to player input, how to render them on the screen and more. These skills will likely be used in every game you build, and it is important that you learn them without the distractions of fancy graphics and peripheral features.

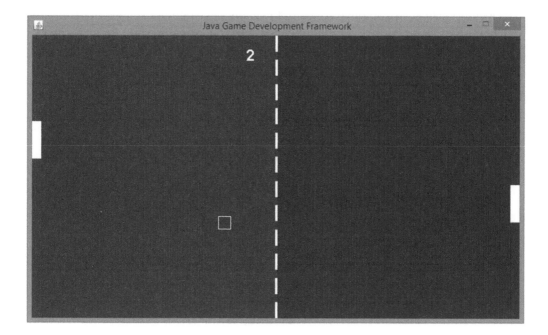

Figure 5-1   Screenshot of LoneBall

The Classes

We will represent our paddles by creating a **Paddle** class and instantiating it two times. We will also create an instance of a **Ball** class to represent our square "ball," which will encapsulate all of the logic needed to move and bounce the ball around the screen. Each of these objects will exist and interact on a game state that we will name **PlayState**, whose job is to update and render the objects while handling player keyboard input.

One of the advantages of object-oriented programming is its extensibility. We can easily add new classes and features without affecting our entire application. As we build our game, we might find that our framework is missing a useful feature or two that might come in handy in our game development process (such as easy random number generation), and we will add these features as necessary.

Now that you've read the overview, it's time to start building.

Preparing the LoneBall Project

Copying the Framework

In all of our game development projects, we will always start by making a copy of our game development framework. This allows us to start building our game immediately, without worrying about rewriting the game-independent code that we wrote in Chapter 4.

Open up Eclipse. If you have access to the game development framework from the end of Chapter 4, make a copy of it by right-clicking on it (Ctrl + Click on Mac), pressing **Copy**, and pasting it back into the Package Explorer with the new name of *LoneBall*. Once you have done so, and you have all the classes shown in Figure 5-2 inside your project, and you will be good to go.

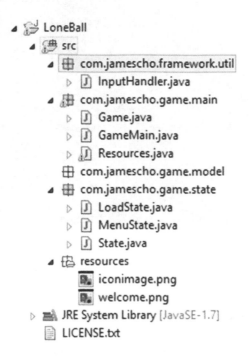

Figure 5-2   The LoneBall Project

Note: If you do not have access to the framework on your computer, the appropriate version can be downloaded in `.zip` format at: `jamescho7.com/book/chapter4/complete`.
To import the downloaded framework into your workspace, extract the `.zip` file to a convenient folder. Next, right click (Ctrl + click on Mac) on the Package Explorer, click *Import*, select *Existing Projects into Workspace* under *General* as your import source, Browse to the folder containing the extracted files, *Select All* projects and press *Finish*. Your Package Explorer should now show the game development framework's project. If you have trouble with any of these steps, please post on the forums at `jamescho7.com` for help!

Now that our game development framework is ready, our next step is to open **GameMain** and change the name of the **JFrame** window to **LoneBall (Chapter 5)**. This is accomplished by modifying the value of the **GAME_TITLE** constant as shown in listing 5.01.

Listing 5.01   The **GameMain** Class

```
package com.jamescho.game.main;

import javax.swing.JFrame;

public class GameMain {
    public static final String GAME_TITLE = "Java Game Development Framework (Chapter 4)";
    public static final String GAME_TITLE = "LoneBall (Chapter 5)";
    public static final int GAME_WIDTH = 800;
    public static final int GAME_HEIGHT = 450;
    public static Game sGame;

        public static void main(String[] args) {
                JFrame frame = new JFrame(GAME_TITLE);
                frame.setDefaultCloseOperation(JFrame.EXIT_ON_CLOSE);
                frame.setResizable(false);
                sGame = new Game(GAME_WIDTH, GAME_HEIGHT);
                frame.add(sGame);
                frame.pack();
                frame.setVisible(true);
                frame.setIconImage(Resources.iconimage);
        }

}
```

Let's make sure that our framework has been successfully copied and that its name has been changed. Run the project as a Java application. You should see the window shown in Figure 5-3 (note the title of the window):

Figure 5-3   LoneBall **JFrame**

149

Adding and Loading Resources

We are ready to start adding some content. The first thing we will do is add all of the resources that we will need throughout the development process. Having all of the assets ready prior to writing code will make it easy for us to quickly develop our game without jumping back and forth between our graphics/sound editing programs and the Eclipse IDE.

I have created *LoneBall*'s assets and uploaded them onto the book's companion site. You will now be able downloading these into your project and loading the new resources into the **Resources** class.

The following resources (images and sound files) are available for you to download at **jamescho7.com/book/chapter5**. You may also use your own by creating images and sound files of the appropriate dimensions and type.

`bounce.wav` (Duration: <1 sec) - to be played when the ball bounces off of a paddle

`hit.wav` (Duration: <1 sec) - to be played when the ball bounces off of a wall

`iconimage.png` (32px x 32px) - to be used as the icon image for JFrame

`welcome.png` (800px x 450px) - to be used as the new welcome screen for LoneBall.

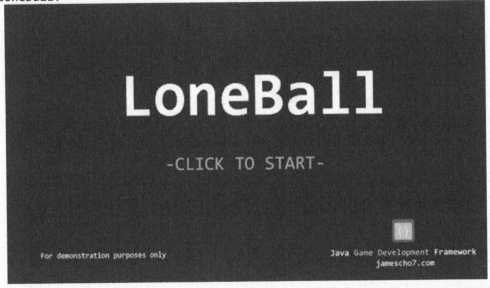

line.png (4px x 450px) – to be used as the divider between the two background colors

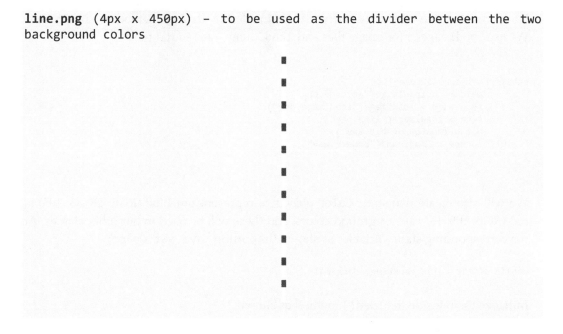

Download the five files and add them into your project's `resources` package, overwriting any existing files. Your `resources` package should now be identical to that shown in Figure 5-4.

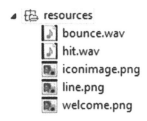

Figure 5-4   Adding the Resource Files

Note: If you want to work with your own assets, I recommend using GIMP or Photoshop to prepare your game's images. The sound files used here have been created using a free online tool at **www.bfxr.net** (you have full rights to anything you produce using **bfxr**, so there are no licensing issues to worry about).

Next, we will load the new resource files into our **Resources** class. This is done in two steps. Firstly, declare the following `static` variables (`welcome` and `iconimage` may already be declared for you):

```
public static BufferedImage welcome, iconimage, line;
public static AudioClip hit, bounce;
```

Next, initialize the newly created variables inside the load() method as shown below. We use loadImage() for image files and loadSound() for sound files:

```
....
public static void load() {
        welcome = loadImage("welcome.png");
        iconimage = loadImage("iconimage.png");
        line = loadImage("line.png");
        hit = loadSound("hit.wav");
        bounce = loadSound("bounce.wav");
}
....
```

We will also create two static **Color** objects to represent our blue (RGB: 25, 83, 105) and red (RGB: 105, 13, 13) background colors, and these will be used in our other classes. Add the corresponding static variables as shown (importing java.awt.Color):

```
public static Color darkBlue, darkRed;
```

Initialize them inside the load() method as shown:

```
....
public static void load() {
        welcome = loadImage("welcome.png");
        iconimage = loadImage("iconimage.png");
        line = loadImage("line.png");
        hit = loadSound("hit.wav");
        bounce = loadSound("bounce.wav");
        darkBlue = new Color(25, 83, 105); // Constructor accepts RGB
        darkRed = new Color(105, 13, 13); // Constructor accepts RGB
}
....
```

The completed **Resources** class is shown in listing 5.02 (check your import statements):

Listing 5.02   The Completed **Resources** Class

```
01 package com.jamescho.game.main;
02
03 import java.applet.Applet;
04 import java.applet.AudioClip;
05 import java.awt.Color;
06 import java.awt.image.BufferedImage;
07 import java.net.URL;
08
09 import javax.imageio.ImageIO;
10
11 public class Resources {
12        public static BufferedImage welcome, iconimage, line;
13        public static AudioClip hit, bounce;
14
15        public static Color darkBlue, darkRed;
16
```

```
17      public static void load() {
18              welcome = loadImage("welcome.png");
19              iconimage = loadImage("iconimage.png");
20              line = loadImage("line.png");
21              hit = loadSound("hit.wav");
22              bounce = loadSound("bounce.wav");
23              darkBlue = new Color(25, 83, 105);
24              darkRed = new Color(105, 13, 13);
25      }
26
27      public static AudioClip loadSound(String filename){
28              URL fileURL = Resources.class.getResource("/resources/" + filename);
29              return Applet.newAudioClip(fileURL);
30      }
31
32      public static BufferedImage loadImage(String filename){
33          BufferedImage img = null;
34           try {
35              img = ImageIO.read(Resources.class.getResource("/resources/" + filename));
36          } catch (Exception e) {
37              System.out.println("Error while reading: " + filename);
38              e.printStackTrace();
39          }
40          return img;
41      }
42 }
```

Now that our resources have been loaded, let's run the game once more to see the changes (note the new welcome screen and icon image):

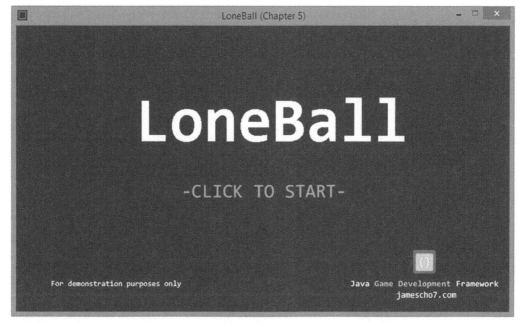

Figure 5-5   LoneBall Welcome Screen

Implementing the Gameplay Screen

Adding the PlayState

Our resources are all ready, and it's time to add the **PlayState** class, which will act as the gameplay screen for *LoneBall*. Create this class inside `com.jamescho.game.state`, and extend **State** (we must do this for every new screen of our game). Eclipse will immediately get angry (show an error message) and ask you to *Add unimplemented methods*. Perform this quick-fix, and your class should match that shown in listing 5.03:

Listing 5.03   The **PlayState** Class (Initial)

```
package com.jamescho.game.state;

import java.awt.Graphics;
import java.awt.event.KeyEvent;
import java.awt.event.MouseEvent;

public class PlayState extends State{

        @Override
        public void init() {
                // TODO Auto-generated method stub
        }

        @Override
        public void update() {
                // TODO Auto-generated method stub
        }

        @Override
        public void render(Graphics g) {
                // TODO Auto-generated method stub
        }

        @Override
        public void onClick(MouseEvent e) {
                // TODO Auto-generated method stub
        }

        @Override
        public void onKeyPress(KeyEvent e) {
                // TODO Auto-generated method stub
        }

        @Override
        public void onKeyRelease(KeyEvent e) {
                // TODO Auto-generated method stub
        }

}
```

The first thing we will do in our new state is add code to render the background (see Figure 5-1 for a reference). Recall that rendering is similar to painting with a brush. You must select a color before you draw any shapes, and whatever you draw first will appear *below* anything else you paint over it later. This means that the background must be drawn before anything else, as we want it to be below the ball and the paddles.

To draw the background for *LoneBall*, we will first fill the screen with our dark blue color, and then draw a red rectangle that covers the right half of the screen (order is important). Lastly, we will draw `line.png` in the center of the screen to accomplish the dotted line effect (see Figure 5-1) with ease.

Note: To draw our dotted line, we could also render multiple white rectangles instead of rendering a `.png` file. This alternative approach may save a bit of memory for us, as we have one fewer image to worry about, but it would take more code. Such trade-offs are common in game programming, and you must seek a balance between optimization (a faster program) and work efficiency (a faster programmer). The general rule of thumb is to optimize only when necessary by identifying bottlenecks in your program and improving them.

Add the code shown in bold to the **PlayState**'s render() method, importing `com.jamescho.game.main.GameMain` and `com.jamescho.game.main.Resources`:

```
....
import java.awt.event.MouseEvent;
import com.jamescho.game.main.GameMain;
import com.jamescho.game.main.Resources;
....
@Override
public void render(Graphics g) {
        // Draw Background
        g.setColor(Resources.darkBlue);
        g.fillRect(0, 0, GameMain.GAME_WIDTH, GameMain.GAME_HEIGHT);
        g.setColor(Resources.darkRed);
        g.fillRect(GameMain.GAME_WIDTH / 2, 0, GameMain.GAME_WIDTH / 2,
                        GameMain.GAME_HEIGHT);
        // Draw Separator Line
        g.drawImage(Resources.line, (GameMain.GAME_WIDTH / 2) - 2, 0, null);
}
....
```

This code is self-explanatory, so I will let you review the additions by yourself. Keep in mind that when drawing graphics, the origin of the screen (0, 0) is at the top-left corner of the screen.

If you get stuck, remember that the four arguments used for drawing rectangles are x, y, width and height, where (x, y) are the coordinates of the top-left corner of the image or rectangle to be drawn. In the case of drawing images, the first argument is the image to be drawn, and the next two arguments are the x and y values. The final argument will always be null in this book. (As a final hint, the width of Resources.Line is 4px, and this has something to do with subtracting 2 from the x coordinate).

Note: We have access to the game's width and height through the GameMain.GAME_WIDTH and GameMain.GAME_HEIGHT variables.

Transitioning into PlayState

Now that we have a **PlayState** that renders the background, let's make sure that it works by opening the **MenuState** and asking it to transition to the **PlayState** when the mouse is clicked. This requires just one line of code to be added to the onClick() method, as shown in line 28 of listing 5.04.

Listing 5.04   From **MenuState** to **PlayState**

```
01 package com.jamescho.game.state;
02
03 import java.awt.Graphics;
04 import java.awt.event.KeyEvent;
05 import java.awt.event.MouseEvent;
06
07 import com.jamescho.game.main.Resources;
08
09 public class MenuState extends State{
10
11     @Override
12     public void init() {
13             System.out.println("Entered MenuState");
14     }
15
16     @Override
17     public void update() {
18
19     }
20
21     @Override
22     public void render(Graphics g) {
23             g.drawImage(Resources.welcome, 0, 0, null);
24     }
25
26     @Override
27     public void onClick(MouseEvent e) {
28             setCurrentState(new PlayState());
29     }
30
31     @Override
32     public void onKeyPress(KeyEvent e) {
33
34     }
35
36     @Override
37     public void onKeyRelease(KeyEvent e) {
38
39     }
40
41 }
```

Run the program. Once you see the menu screen, click a button on your mouse. The game should then transition to the gameplay screen, which renders the beautiful blue and red background as shown in Figure 5-6, complete with a dotted line effect.

Figure 5-6   MenuState to PlayState

Designing the Paddles

A game, even one as simple as *LoneBall*, must have something for the player to control (a video game minus player interaction is a video)! We will next implement the controllable paddles into the game.

The blueprint (class) for these paddles will be called **Paddle**. Having such a class allows us to easily create a **Paddle** object, which will store all of the information and behavior needed to represent a paddle in our game.

KEY POINT

Advantages of Object-Oriented Programming in Game Development
Creating game objects demonstrates the benefits of object-oriented programing. Each object, created using a class, represents an actual entity on the screen, and this makes it very easy for a programmer to wrap his or her mind around the project. Behind each character, wall or background element in any game we build, there will be an object and thus a class responsible for its representation.

Before we create the **Paddle** class, let's outline its variables and methods.

The Variables in Paddle
When creating variables for a new game object, you should ask yourself the following question: what information do I need to store inside each of my game objects?

In the case of each paddle, we will need to know where it is and how big it is. We also need to know how fast it is moving and which direction it is moving. These requirements can help us determine what variables we will need to create for our **Paddle** class, as listed below.

Coordinates and Dimensions: We will create four variables to allow us to locate each paddle and draw it in our coordinate plane. These are x, y, width and height. The purpose of these four values are shown in Figure 5-7.

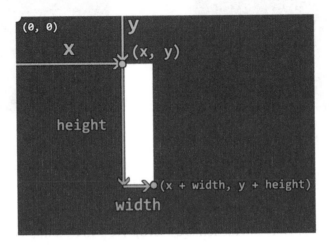

Figure 5-7   Overview of a Paddle

Bounding Box: **Rectangle** is a built in Java class that represents a simple quadrilateral. This class has a built-in method that allows us to easily check if two **Rectangle** objects are overlapping. Have a look at the example below:

```
Rectangle r = new Rectangle(0, 0, 10, 10);
Rectangle r2 = new Rectangle(5, 5, 10, 10);
System.out.println(r.intersects(r2));
```

To figure out what the result would be, let's draw it out. Take a look at Figure 5-8, where the origin is at the top-left. The two rectangles overlap, and so r.intersects(r2) returns true.

We will make use of this simple intersection check to determine whether a collision occurred between our ball and the paddles. This can be done by creating an instance of **Rectangle** as a *bounding box* for each of these objects and checking for overlaps on every frame.

Velocity: Our paddles will move up and down, so we will create a variable called velY to store information regarding each paddle's current movement speed and direction. This variable represents the number of pixels that a paddle should traverse in one frame. Therefore, adding velY to a paddle's y-coordinate in one frame allows us to calculate the y-coordinate of the next frame. This means that a positive `velY` value indicates that a paddle is moving downwards (remember that y increases downwards in our coordinate plane) and that a negative `velY` value indicates that a paddle is moving upwards.

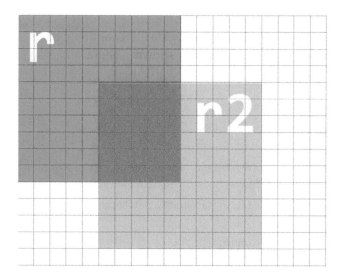

Figure 5-8   Do They Overlap?

Note: If the above discussion is confusing to you or you just want to review the simple laws of physics that will govern our game, please see **Appendix B**.

The Methods

As with creating variables, asking yourself a question can help you determine what methods you need to create for your game object: what should my game object be able to do?

Each paddle needs to be able to increase velocity, decrease velocity, update its position, and update its bounding box. We will be creating methods to perform these behaviors as outlined below.

Acceleration/Deceleration Methods: To change the velocity of each paddle, we will implement `accelUp()`, `accelDown()` and `stop()`. These methods will update the y-velocity of our paddle appropriately (making it negative, positive and zero, respectively).

Update Methods: The `update()` method will determine a new position for each paddle given its current position and velocity . We will also create a method called `updateRect()`, which will simply move our bounding box to keep it aligned with our paddle objects.

Creating the Paddle Class

We have outlined the Paddle class in the previous section, now let's write some code.

Adding the Variables

Inside the package `com.jamescho.game.model`, create the **Paddle** class. Then, create the instance variables and constructor shown below, making sure to import `java.awt.Rectangle`:

```
package com.jamescho.game.model;

import java.awt.Rectangle;

public class Paddle {
        private int x, y, width, height, velY;
        private Rectangle rect;

        public Paddle(int x, int y, int width, int height) {
                this.x = x;
                this.y = y;
                this.width = width;
                this.height = height;
                rect = new Rectangle(x, y, width, height);
                velY = 0;
        }

}
```

Our constructor will accept the `x`, `y`, `width` and `height` values to initialize our **Paddle**'s coordinates and dimensions, and also create a new bounding box with the same coordinates and dimensions. We will lastly set the initial y-velocity as zero.

Adding the Methods

Add the `update()`, `updateRect()`, `accelUp()`, `accelDown()` and `stop()` methods into **Paddle** as shown in listing 5.05 (lines 18 through 37).

Listing 5.05   The **Paddle** Class with Five Methods

```
01 package com.jamescho.game.model;
02
03 import java.awt.Rectangle;
04
05 public class Paddle {
06        private int x, y, width, height, velY;
07        private Rectangle rect;
08
09        public Paddle(int x, int y, int width, int height) {
10                this.x = x;
11                this.y = y;
12                this.width = width;
13                this.height = height;
14                rect = new Rectangle(x, y, width, height);
```

```
15                  velY = 0;
16          }
17
18          public void update() {
19                  y += velY;
20                  updateRect();
21          }
22
23          private void updateRect() {
24                  rect.setBounds(x, y, width, height);
25          }
26
27          public void accelUp() {
28                  velY = -5;
29          }
30
31          public void accelDown() {
32                  velY = 5;
33          }
34
35          public void stop() {
36                  velY = 0;
37          }
38
39 }
```

Note: Always keep methods `public` if they will be called by other classes. Otherwise, keep them `private`. In the example above, `updateRect()` is a method that will only be called inside the `update()` method in the same class, so it remains `private`.

The code in the five methods is pretty simple. Our `update()` method simply adds `velY` to the y once per frame. This has the effect of moving the paddle to a y-position of y + `velY` (if you need elaboration on this, see Appendix B). The `update()` method also calls the `updateRect()` method, which takes the updated coordinates of the paddle and moves the bounding box to the same position.

The three acceleration/deceleration methods, `accelUp()`, `accelDown()` and `stop()`, simply change `velY` to an appropriate value: -5, 5 and zero, respectively.

Notice here that the movement speed will be 5 or -5 pixels per frame, depending on direction (or zero if the paddle is not moving). What if we wanted to change the movement speed to be 4 or -4? Then we would have to make changes to two places in code (inside the `accelUp()` and `accelDown()` methods). This is easy in *LoneBall*; however, in more complex game classes, a simple change such as this one might require you to modify 10 lines of code (or more). If you were making such a game class, you might decide that a change is simply not worth it. This is bad. Your code should help you *realize* your vision of the game, not *restrict* it! Let's explore how we can reduce dependencies, so that we can avoid this trap in the future.

Reducing Dependencies with Constants

Create a new constant in **Paddle** by declaring the `final static` variable shown in bold below:

```
. . . .

public class Paddle {
        private int x, y, width, height, velY;
        private Rectangle rect;
        private final static int MOVE_SPEED_Y = 4;    // This is the new line
. . . .
```

Next, change the implementation of the `accelUp()` and `accelDown()` methods to make use of this constant rather than hardcoded integer values (shown in lines 29 and 34 of listing 5.06):

Listing 5.06   Making Use of Constants

```
01 package com.jamescho.game.model;
02
03 import java.awt.Rectangle;
04
05 public class Paddle {
06        private int x, y, width, height, velY;
07        private Rectangle rect;
08        private final static int MOVE_SPEED_Y = 4;
09
10        public Paddle(int x, int y, int width, int height) {
11                this.x = x;
12                this.y = y;
13                this.width = width;
14                this.height = height;
15                rect = new Rectangle(x, y, width, height);
16                velY = 0;
17        }
18        public void update() {
19                y += velY;
20                updateRect();
21        }
22
23        private void updateRect() {
24                rect.setBounds(x, y, width, height);
25        }
26
27        public void accelUp() {
28                velY = -5;
29                velY = -MOVE_SPEED_Y;
30        }
31
32        public void accelDown() {
33                velY = 5;
34                velY = MOVE_SPEED_Y;
35        }
36
```

```
37      public void stop() {
38            velY = 0;
39      }
40
41 }
```

Now, if I want to modify our paddles' movement speeds, all I would have to do is change the value of the constant MOVE_SPEED_Y to the desired value, because the methods accelUp() and accelDown() will automatically receive the changed value! By adding MOVE_SPEED_Y to the class, we have reduced the number of lines of code dependent on the value of our movement speed.

This change may seem insignificant now, but making an effort to reduce dependencies whenever possible makes it much more pleasant to maintain your code. With this change, determining what values you must modify in order to make your paddles go faster is easy, because a quick glance reveals that there is a constant called MOVE_SPEED_Y.

Benefits such as these mean that if you were to take a vacation and return to your code weeks later, you wouldn't have to reason through your own code to figure out how to make simple changes. Naturally, in a team-based environment, this means that others can look through your code and readily add, modify or remove features without needing to know inconvenient details such as which methods must always change together.

Adding the Getters

Our **Paddle** class's instance variables are all private. This means that other classes cannot, for instance, modify our paddles' x and y positions illegally (x should *not* change, and y should *only* change inside the **Paddle**'s update() method). This protects our variables, but this also means that **PlayState** cannot access the x and y values to render the **Paddle** objects in the correct position with the correct dimensions.

We will finish up our **Paddle** class by creating five getter methods so that other classes can peek at our **Paddle** objects' instance variables, but not modify them. The five getters are shown in bold below:

```
package com.jamescho.game.model;

import java.awt.Rectangle;

public class Paddle {
        ....

        public void stop() {
                velY = 0;
        }

        public int getX() {
                return x;
        }

        public int getY() {
```

```
            return y;
    }

    public int getWidth() {
            return width;
    }

    public int getHeight() {
            return height;
    }

    public Rectangle getRect() {
            return rect;
    }

}
```

Our **Paddle** class is now complete! We can now instantiate the class to make **Paddle** objects as necessary.

Implementing the Paddle Objects inside PlayState

Our game, as shown in Figure 5-1, needs two paddle objects. Open the **PlayState** class and declare the following variables (importing `com.game.model.Paddle`):

```
private Paddle paddleLeft, paddleRight;
private static final int PADDLE_WIDTH = 15;
private static final int PADDLE_HEIGHT = 60;
```

Inside the `init()` method, initialize our two new **Paddle** variables as shown in bold below:

```
@Override
public void init() {
        paddleLeft = new Paddle(0, 195, PADDLE_WIDTH, PADDLE_HEIGHT);
        paddleRight = new Paddle(785, 195, PADDLE_WIDTH, PADDLE_HEIGHT);
}
```

The two paddles should be created at the coordinates (x = 0, y = 195) and (x = 785, y = 195). The provided x positions place `paddleLeft` on the left side of the screen, and place `paddleRight` on the right side of the screen.

The given y values indicate where the top-left corner of each paddle should be located in order to keep them vertically centered. These values are simply calculated by taking 225 (the vertical center) and subtracting 30 (half of a paddle's height).

Note: At the moment, our two paddles will only be centered if the game's resolution remains 800 x 450 (this is set in **GameMain**). We *could* eliminate this dependency on screen resolution by deriving the x and y coordinates using **GameMain**'s GAME_WIDTH and

GAME_HEIGHT constants, but we will keep things simple by leaving the hardcoded values for now.

Rendering the Paddles

To make sure that we have initialized our two paddles at the correct coordinates, let's draw them on our screen. Add the lines of code shown in bold to your render() method in **PlayState** (import java.awt.Color accordingly):

```
@Override
public void render(Graphics g) {
        // Draw Background
        g.setColor(Resources.darkBlue);
        g.fillRect(0, 0, GameMain.GAME_WIDTH, GameMain.GAME_HEIGHT);
        g.setColor(Resources.darkRed);
        g.fillRect(GameMain.GAME_WIDTH / 2, 0, GameMain.GAME_WIDTH / 2,
                    GameMain.GAME_HEIGHT);
        // Draw Separator Line
        g.drawImage(Resources.line, 398, 0, null);

        // Draw Paddles
        g.setColor(Color.white);
        g.fillRect(paddleLeft.getX(), paddleLeft.getY(), paddleLeft.getWidth(),
                    paddleLeft.getHeight());
        g.fillRect(paddleRight.getX(), paddleRight.getY(), paddleRight.getWidth(),
                    paddleRight.getHeight());

}
```

These three lines simply draw two white rectangles at the coordinates stored by each of the paddles. These draw calls are at the bottom of the render method, so that the paddles are drawn *after* (thus on top of) the background.

Try running the game. You should see two vertically-centered paddles hugging the left and right sides of the window as shown in Figure 5-9.

Handling Player Input

We want our paddles to move when the player presses the up and down arrow keys. We can implement this with ease using the onKeyPress() and onKeyRelease() methods, thanks to our framework.

Our two input-related methods are called automatically (and accordingly) when the game detects a key press or release. Notice these methods have the same parameter: (KeyEvent e). This passed in **KeyEvent** object stores information regarding the key that has triggered the method, and you can retrieve this information by calling its getKeyCode() method.

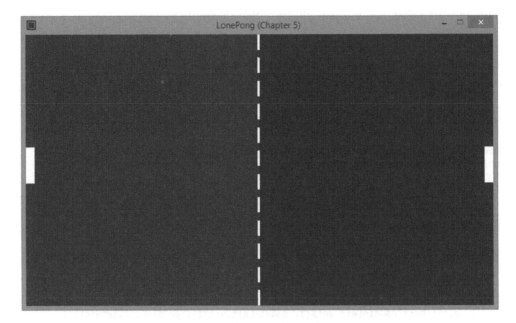

Figure 5-9   Rendering the Padels

This means that, in order to determine which key was pressed or released, you compare the value of `e.getKeyCode()` with various constants representing each keyboard button (these are defined within the **KeyEvent** class with the prefix VK_...).

As with other explanations, this will make much more sense when you see it in action. Update your onKeyPress() and onKeyRelease() methods in **PlayState** by adding the lines in bold below:

```
....
@Override
public void onKeyPress(KeyEvent e) {
        if (e.getKeyCode() == KeyEvent.VK_UP) {
                paddleLeft.accelUp();
                paddleRight.accelDown();
        } else if (e.getKeyCode() == KeyEvent.VK_DOWN) {
                paddleLeft.accelDown();
                paddleRight.accelUp();
        }
}

@Override
public void onKeyRelease(KeyEvent e) {
        if (e.getKeyCode() == KeyEvent.VK_UP ||
                        e.getKeyCode() == KeyEvent.VK_DOWN) {
                paddleLeft.stop();
                paddleRight.stop();
        }
}
....
```

Our onKeyPress() method only cares about two keys: VK_UP (the up arrow key) and VK_DOWN (the down arrow key). If either of these keys is pressed, it calls the accelUp() and accelDown() methods of the two paddles as appropriate. Note that we send paddleLeft in the direction of the arrow key pressed and paddleRight in the opposite direction.

The onKeyRelease() method only cares about the same keys. In this opposite case, whether the key released is VK_UP or VK_DOWN, it reacts by stopping both paddles.

Try running your code and pressing the up and down arrow keys. Nothing will happen! This is because although we are changing the velY property of each paddle, we are not allowing the paddles to update. Let's change that.

Updating the Paddles by Delegation

Ask each paddle to update itself inside **PlayState**'s update() method, as shown below:

```
@Override
public void update() {
        paddleLeft.update();
        paddleRight.update();
}
```

Notice that our update() method delegates two other objects to update(). It does *very little work* on its own. This pattern is called *delegation*, and you will find that it is very useful in maintaining a hierarchy of objects. In this example, **PlayState** represents an entire gameplay screen and contains various objects, including paddleLeft and paddleRight. You update **PlayState**, and everything *inside* **PlayState** updates as well. Every object inside the **PlayState** behaves together. This is a powerful pattern. With that change, your **PlayState** should currently look like listing 5.07:

Listing 5.07   PlayState (Updated)

```
01 package com.jamescho.game.state;
02
03 import java.awt.Color;
04 import java.awt.Graphics;
05 import java.awt.event.KeyEvent;
06 import java.awt.event.MouseEvent;
07
08 import com.jamescho.game.main.GameMain;
09 import com.jamescho.game.main.Resources;
10 import com.jamescho.game.model.Paddle;
11
12 public class PlayState extends State{
13
14      private Paddle paddleLeft, paddleRight;
15      private static final int PADDLE_WIDTH = 15;
16      private static final int PADDLE_HEIGHT = 60;
17
18      @Override
19      public void init() {
```

```
20              paddleLeft = new Paddle(0, 195, PADDLE_WIDTH, PADDLE_HEIGHT);
21              paddleRight = new Paddle(785, 195, PADDLE_WIDTH, PADDLE_HEIGHT);
22      }
23
24      @Override
25      public void update() {
26              paddleLeft.update();
27              paddleRight.update();
28      }
29
30      @Override
31      public void render(Graphics g) {
32              // Draw Background
33              g.setColor(Resources.darkBlue);
34              g.fillRect(0, 0, GameMain.GAME_WIDTH, GameMain.GAME_HEIGHT);
35              g.setColor(Resources.darkRed);
36              g.fillRect(GameMain.GAME_WIDTH / 2, 0, GameMain.GAME_WIDTH / 2,
37                              GameMain.GAME_HEIGHT);
38              // Draw Separator Line
39              g.drawImage(Resources.line, (GameMain.GAME_WIDTH / 2) - 2, 0, null);
40              // Draw Paddles
41              g.setColor(Color.white);
42              g.fillRect(paddleLeft.getX(), paddleLeft.getY(), paddleLeft.getWidth(),
43                              paddleLeft.getHeight());
44              g.fillRect(paddleRight.getX(), paddleRight.getY(), paddleRight.getWidth(),
45                                  paddleRight.getHeight());
46
47      }
48
49      @Override
50      public void onClick(MouseEvent e) {
51              // TODO Auto-generated method stub
52      }
53
54      @Override
55      public void onKeyPress(KeyEvent e) {
56              if (e.getKeyCode() == KeyEvent.VK_UP) {
57                      paddleLeft.accelUp();
58                      paddleRight.accelDown();
59              } else if (e.getKeyCode() == KeyEvent.VK_DOWN) {
60                      paddleLeft.accelDown();
61                      paddleRight.accelUp();
62              }
63
64      }
65
66      @Override
67      public void onKeyRelease(KeyEvent e) {
68              if (e.getKeyCode() == KeyEvent.VK_UP ||
69                              e.getKeyCode() == KeyEvent.VK_DOWN) {
70                      paddleLeft.stop();
71                      paddleRight.stop();
72              }
73
74      }
75
76 }
```

Try running the code once more. If you press the up and down arrows, your paddles should begin to move in opposite directions! There is one bug, however. Once you reach the top or bottom of the screen, the paddles will go straight through the window as shown in Figure 5-10.

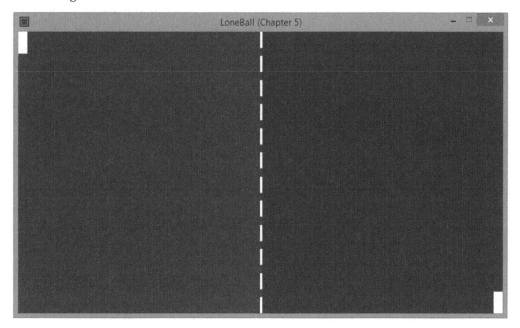

Figure 5-10   Our First Bug!

Fixing the Bug

This is actually not, strictly speaking, a *bug*. We never told the paddles that they should never leave the screen. To do so, we need to make a small change to our `update()` method inside the **Paddle** class, as shown in bold below (import **GameMain** as needed):

```
public void update() {
        y += velY;

        if (y < 0) {
                y = 0;
        } else if (y + height > GameMain.GAME_HEIGHT) {
                y = GameMain.GAME_HEIGHT - height;
        }

        updateRect();
}
```

What does this change do? After updating our paddle's y-position, we now check if our paddle has left the screen. This can happen either when y is less than zero (meaning that the top of the paddle has left the top of the screen) or when y + height is greater than the game height (meaning that the bottom of the paddle has left the bottom of the screen).

Once we have detected that our paddle has moved outside of our window, we simply correct its y-position in the same frame (before update() ends).

We correct collision in the same frame for an important reason. The render() method will never be called before the update() method is finished. This means that by resolving collisions at the end of each iteration of update(), we ensure that the player will never see a paddle leave the screen (even if its y-position temporarily leaves the window)!

Run the game once more, and your paddles will remain on the screen no matter how hard you push down on your arrow keys.

Note: The above technique is applied in resolving collision between two game objects as well.

At this point, we have implemented our two paddles, and now we must implement a scoring system and the ball.

Implementing a Score System

We will implement the score system by creating an integer to represent the score and then using the g.drawString() method from Chapter 3 to draw the score to the screen. Declare the following instance variables for **PlayState** (import java.awt.Font as needed):

```
private int playerScore = 0;
private Font scoreFont;
```

The variable scoreFont is an instance of **Font**—a built-in Java class that allows you to customize the appearance of Strings that you draw. Initialize it inside the init() method as shown in bold below:

```
@Override
public void init() {
        paddleLeft = new Paddle(0, 195, PADDLE_WIDTH, PADDLE_HEIGHT);
        paddleRight = new Paddle(785, 195, PADDLE_WIDTH, PADDLE_HEIGHT);
        scoreFont = new Font("SansSerif", Font.BOLD, 25);
}
```

This creates a new bold, sans-serif **Font** object with a size of 25.

Working with fonts is similar to working with **Colors**. In the render() method, we will first set scoreFont as the current font for our **Graphics** object and then draw text to the screen. Add the following lines at the END of the render() method:

```
// Draw UI
g.setFont(scoreFont); // Sets scoreFont as current font
g.drawString(playerScore, 350, 40); // Draws String using current font
```

The second line will produce the following error:

```
The method drawString(String, int, int) in the type Graphics is not applicable for the
arguments (int, int, int)
```

This is saying that the drawString() method expects arguments of types **String**, int and int, but you have provided int, int and int instead. This error is expected, because the method name is drawString() not drawInt(). The solution is to convert our playerScore into a **String** before we ask it to be drawn. One way to do so is to call the following method:

```
String playerScoreStr = String.valueOf(playerScore);
```

The above static method of the **String** class accepts an integer and returns a **String** copy of it. I personally don't like it. The fancier way of doing the same thing involves a simple concatenation:

```
String playerScoreStr = "" + playerScore;
```

This approach appends an integer to the end of an empty string and thus produces the **String** version of the integer. This is quicker and easier to remember. Add this fix into your method as shown in bold below:

```
@Override
public void render(Graphics g) {
        // Draw Background
        g.setColor(Resources.darkBlue);
        g.fillRect(0, 0, GameMain.GAME_WIDTH, GameMain.GAME_HEIGHT);
        g.setColor(Resources.darkRed);
        g.fillRect(GameMain.GAME_WIDTH / 2, 0, GameMain.GAME_WIDTH / 2,
                        GameMain.GAME_HEIGHT);
        // Draw Separator Line
        g.drawImage(Resources.line, 398, 0, null);

        // Draw Paddles
        g.setColor(Color.white);
        g.fillRect(paddleLeft.getX(), paddleLeft.getY(), paddleLeft.getWidth(),
                        paddleLeft.getHeight());
        g.fillRect(paddleRight.getX(), paddleRight.getY(),
                        paddleRight.getWidth(), paddleRight.getHeight());

        // Draw UI
        g.setFont(scoreFont);
        g.drawString(playerScore, 350, 40);
        g.drawString("" + playerScore, 350, 40);
}
```

Run the program once more, and you should see the score rendered as shown in Figure 5-1. As we have not started incrementing it yet, it will remain zero.

Implementing the RandomNumberGenerator Class

Before we create the **Ball** class, we are going to add a new class which will allow us to quickly generate random numbers. Review pages 62 through 64, you will remember that we had to perform the following steps to generate a random number:

- Create a new **Random** object.
- Import java.util.Random.
- Call the nextInt(int n) method, which generates a random number between 0 (inclusive) and n (exclusive).

The problem with this approach is that we must create a new **Random** object before generating a random number, and creating a new **Random** object costs memory. Making ten or even a hundred **Random** objects is perfectly fine, but recall that every line of code that we write is being executed inside the game loop (at ~60 times per second). That means that if we were to create a **Random** object inside our **Paddle**'s update() method, we would get 60 new **Random** objects every *second*. Sure, there are ways of getting around this problem by creating the **Random** object inside methods that are only called when necessary (init(), for example), but that does not solve the problem of needing to create a new **Random** object for every object that wants access to a random number once in a while.

It would be extremely convenient if our framework provided a way of generating a random number without requiring a new **Random** object every time. It would also be awesome if we could generate a number between two arbitrary numbers, not just 0 and n. Wait. You are a programmer, so you can add this feature! Inside com.jamescho.framework.util, create a class named **RandomNumberGenerator**, and implement it as shown in listing 5.08:

Listing 5.08   The **RandomNumberGenerator** Class

```
01 package com.jamescho.framework.util;
02
03 import java.util.Random;
04
05 public class RandomNumberGenerator {
06
07     private static Random rand = new Random();
08
09     public static int getRandIntBetween(int lowerBound, int upperBound) {
10         return rand.nextInt(upperBound - lowerBound) + lowerBound;
11     }
12
13     public static int getRandInt(int upperBound) {
14         return rand.nextInt(upperBound);
15     }
16 }
```

The class has a *single*, static **Random** object called `rand` that will be shared across the entire application. `rand` is used in the class's two methods to generate a random number (see Appendix A if you need help with `static`). I will let you work out the logic, reviewing pages 62 through 64 if necessary.

Note that both of these methods are `public` and `static`, meaning that they can be accessed by other classes within the framework without instantiating a new **Random** object or a new **RandomNumberGenerator** object! In other words, you can generate a random number with ease as shown below:

```
.... // Elsewhere in the framework
import com.jamescho.framework.util.RandomNumberGenerator;
....
System.out.println(RandomNumberGenerator.getRandIntBetween(-10, 11));
....
```

The line of code shown in bold in the example above will generate a random integer between -10 (inclusive) and 11 (exclusive), and it doesn't even require you to create a new **Random** object. We will make use of **RandomNumberGenerator** throughout the **Ball** class and in our future games.

Designing the Ball

We can push up paddles all day long, but where's the fun in that? Let's add some bounce to our game by adding a ball. As with our paddles, we begin by outlining the class that we will be creating. (Note the similarities to the Paddle class)!

The Variables in the Ball Class
Coordinates and Dimensions: We will create `x`, `y`, `width` and `height` variables analogous to those in the **Paddle** class.

Bounding Box: Our ball will also have a bounding box created using the **Rectangle** class. This allows us to check for collision with the two paddles.

Velocity: The ball also has a `velY` variable like the paddles; but it will also be moving horizontally. This requires that we add a second velocity variable called `velX`.

The Methods in the Ball Class
Update Methods: As with the **Paddle** class, the **Ball** class will have the `update()` and `updateRect()` methods used to calculate a new position for the ball and its bounding box. The `update()` method will make use of a helper method called `correctYCollisions()` which will check for and resolve collisions with the top and bottom of the screen (recall that this same functionality was added directly into the `update()` method in the **Paddle** class).

<u>Miscellaneous Methods:</u> The **Ball** class will feature three `public` methods that will notify our **PlayState** when certain events occur and allow the state to react accordingly. For instance, we will have a method called `isDead()` which will return `true` if the ball has hit the left or right side of the game's screen.

Once this occurs, our ball is considered dead. The player will lose 3 points, and the ball will reset. To make this happen, we will implement a `reset()` method, which will return the ball to the center of the screen. We will also add an `onCollideWith()` method that is triggered when our ball collides with a paddle.

Creating the Ball Class

We know what variables and methods we need to create, so let's start creating the class inside Eclipse. Much of this will be similar to the procedure for creating the **Paddle** class, so we will move more quickly.

Adding the Variables

Create a new **Ball** class inside the package `com.jamescho.game.model`. Declare the following variables:

```
private int x, y, width, height, velX, velY;
private Rectangle rect;
```

Initialize them by adding the following constructor:

```
public Ball(int x, int y, int width, int height) {
        this.x = x;
        this.y = y;
        this.width = width;
        this.height = height;
        velX = 5;
        velY = RandomNumberGenerator.getRandIntBetween(-4, 5);
        rect = new Rectangle(x, y, width, height);
}
```

Take note that we are putting our **RandomNumberGenerator** class to use by calling its `getRandIntBetween()` method to generate a random `velY`. Since the class is in a different package, we must import `com.jamescho.framework.util.RandomNumberGenerator`. Make sure to import **Rectangle** as well.

Adding the Update Methods

Next, add the `update()` method and its two helpers (import `GameMain` and `Resources` accordingly):

```
public void update() {
        x += velX;
```

174

```
        y += velY;
        correctYCollisions();
        updateRect();
}

private void correctYCollisions() {
        if (y < 0) {
                y = 0;
        } else if (y + height > GameMain.GAME_HEIGHT) {
                y = GameMain.GAME_HEIGHT - height;
        } else {
                return;
        }

        velY = -velY;
        Resources.bounce.play();
}

private void updateRect() {
        rect.setBounds(x, y, width, height);
}
```

You've seen most of what happens in these three methods in the **Paddle** class, but some things are worth discussing:

- As expected, our `update()` method will update both the x and y values using the two velocity variables.
- The logic for `correctYCollisions()` follows an interesting pattern. We first check if the ball has gone past the top or bottom of the screen and correct it. If it turns out that the ball has not left the window, we simply call `return` to end the method there. This means that the following two lines are only called if the ball HAS gone outside of the window (this indicates a collision with the top or bottom wall, so we deflect the ball and play a bounce sound).

```
velY = -velY;
Resources.bounce.play();
```

Adding the Misc. Methods

Declare three more methods inside the **Ball** class, as shown below.

```
public void onCollideWith(Paddle p) {
        if (x < GameMain.GAME_WIDTH / 2) {
                x = p.getX() + p.getWidth();
        } else {
                x = p.getX() - width;
        }
        velX = -velX;
        velY += RandomNumberGenerator.getRandIntBetween(-2, 3);
}

public boolean isDead() {
        return (x < 0 || x + width > GameMain.GAME_WIDTH);
}
```

```
public void reset() {
        x = 300;
        y = 200;
        velX = 5;
        velY = RandomNumberGenerator.getRandIntBetween(-4, 5);
}
```

The onCollideWith() method is called when the game determines that the ball has collided with one of the two paddles. Just as with the onKeyPress() method from **PlayState**, the onCollideWith() method receives a reference to the paddle object that has triggered it.

Inside onCollideWith(), we can check whether the ball is currently on the left side of the screen or the right side of the screen to determine whether it hit the paddle on the left or the paddle on the right. We then use this information to resolve the collision by moving the ball outside of the paddle's bounding box (which is either the right side of the left paddle and left side of the right paddle). Once collision has been resolved, we send the ball on its way, deflecting it horizontally and randomly modifying velY.

The isDead() method checks two conditions: whether the ball has hit the left side of the screen or the right side of the screen. If either of these events occurred, the method returns true to the caller. We will be calling this method inside **PlayState** to determine when our ball is out of play and react accordingly.

The reset() method will be called by the **PlayState** in response to the death of the ball. It simply moves the ball to its initial position and gives it a random velocity.

Adding the Getter Methods
We will be creating the same getter methods that **Paddle** has for our **Ball** class as shown:

```
public int getX() {
        return x;
}

public int getY() {
        return y;
}

public int getWidth() {
        return width;
}

public int getHeight() {
        return height;
}

public Rectangle getRect() {
        return rect;
}
```

Our **Ball** class is now finished. If you have errors, compare it to listing 5.09, which shows the full class.

Listing 5.09   The **Ball** Class (Completed)

```
01      package com.jamescho.game.model;
02
03      import java.awt.Rectangle;
04
05      import com.jamescho.framework.util.RandomNumberGenerator;
06      import com.jamescho.game.main.GameMain;
07      import com.jamescho.game.main.Resources;
08
09      public class Ball {
10              private int x, y, width, height, velX, velY;
11              private Rectangle rect;
12
13              public Ball(int x, int y, int width, int height) {
14                      this.x = x;
15                      this.y = y;
16                      this.width = width;
17                      this.height = height;
18                      velX = 5;
19                      velY = RandomNumberGenerator.getRandIntBetween(-4, 5);
20                      rect = new Rectangle(x, y, width, height);
21              }
22
23              public void update() {
24                      x += velX;
25                      y += velY;
26                      correctYCollisions();
27                      updateRect();
28              }
29
30              private void correctYCollisions() {
31                      if (y < 0) {
32                              y = 0;
33                      } else if (y + height > GameMain.GAME_HEIGHT) {
34                              y = GameMain.GAME_HEIGHT - height;
35                      } else {
36                              return;
37                      }
38
39                      velY = -velY;
40                      Resources.bounce.play();
41              }
42
43              private void updateRect() {
44                      rect.setBounds(x, y, width, height);
45              }
46
47              public void onCollideWith(Paddle p) {
48                      if (x < GameMain.GAME_WIDTH / 2) {
49                              x = p.getX() + p.getWidth();
50                      } else {
51                              x = p.getX() - width;
52                      }
53                      velX = -velX;
54                      velY += RandomNumberGenerator.getRandIntBetween(-2, 3);
55              }
56
57              public boolean isDead() {
```

177

```
58                      return (x < 0 || x + width > GameMain.GAME_WIDTH);
59            }
60
61        public void reset() {
62                x = 300;
63                y = 200;
64                velX = 5;
65                velY = RandomNumberGenerator.getRandIntBetween(-4, 5);
66        }
67
68        public int getX() {
69                return x;
70        }
71
72        public int getY() {
73                return y;
74        }
75
76        public int getWidth() {
77                return width;
78        }
79
80        public int getHeight() {
81                return height;
82        }
83
84        public Rectangle getRect() {
85                return rect;
86        }
87    }
```

Implementing the Ball Object inside PlayState

Adding the ball will require the same basic steps as adding the paddles. We will declare and initialize it, ask it to update, and then render it.

Declaring and Initializing the Ball

Begin by declaring the new ball as an instance variable, along with a constant representing its diameter (don't forget the import statement com.jamescho.game. model.Ball). The changes to **PlayState** class are shown below in bold:

```
....
import com.jamescho.game.model.Ball;
import com.jamescho.game.model.Paddle;

public class PlayState extends State {
        private Paddle paddleLeft, paddleRight;
        private static final int PADDLE_WIDTH = 15;
        private static final int PADDLE_HEIGHT = 60;

        private Ball ball;
        private static final int BALL_DIAMETER = 20;
....
```

Next, initialize the ball variable inside the `init()` method:

```
@Override
public void init() {
        paddleLeft = new Paddle(0, 195, PADDLE_WIDTH, PADDLE_HEIGHT);
        paddleRight = new Paddle(785, 195, PADDLE_WIDTH, PADDLE_HEIGHT);
        scoreFont = new Font("SansSerif", Font.BOLD, 25);
        ball = new Ball(300, 200, BALL_DIAMETER, BALL_DIAMETER);
}
```

This places the ball at an arbitrary initial position of (300, 200) with a `width` and `height` equal to the value of the BALL_DIAMETER constant (remember that our ball really is a square).

Updating the Ball

Next, we will be delegating once more by asking the ball to update inside the **PlayState**'s `update()` method.

```
@Override
public void update() {
        paddleLeft.update();
        paddleRight.update();
        ball.update();
}
```

Rendering the Ball

Finally, draw the ball inside the `render()` method by adding the line of code shown below in bold:

```
@Override
public void render(Graphics g) {
        // Draw Background
        g.setColor(Resources.darkBlue);
        g.fillRect(0, 0, GameMain.GAME_WIDTH, GameMain.GAME_HEIGHT);
        g.setColor(Resources.darkRed);
        g.fillRect(GameMain.GAME_WIDTH / 2, 0, GameMain.GAME_WIDTH / 2,
                        GameMain.GAME_HEIGHT);
        // Draw Separator Line
        g.drawImage(Resources.line, 398, 0, null);

        // Draw Paddles
        g.setColor(Color.white);
        g.fillRect(paddleLeft.getX(), paddleLeft.getY(), paddleLeft.getWidth(),
                        paddleLeft.getHeight());
        g.fillRect(paddleRight.getX(), paddleRight.getY(),
                        paddleRight.getWidth(), paddleRight.getHeight());

        // Draw Ball
        g.drawRect(ball.getX(), ball.getY(), ball.getWidth(), ball.getHeight());

        // Draw UI
        g.setFont(scoreFont);
        g.drawString("" + playerScore, 350, 40);
}
```

Note that we draw the ball on top of the paddles, but this is arbitrary, as the ball and paddles should never visibly overlap.

With those changes, your `PlayState` should match that shown in listing 5.10.

Listing 5.10   The PlayState Class (Updated)

```
01 package com.jamescho.game.state;
02
03 import java.awt.Color;
04 import java.awt.Font;
05 import java.awt.Graphics;
06 import java.awt.event.KeyEvent;
07 import java.awt.event.MouseEvent;
08
09 import com.jamescho.game.main.GameMain;
10 import com.jamescho.game.main.Resources;
11 import com.jamescho.game.model.Ball;
12 import com.jamescho.game.model.Paddle;
13
14 public class PlayState extends State{
15
16     private Paddle paddleLeft, paddleRight;
17     private static final int PADDLE_WIDTH = 15;
18     private static final int PADDLE_HEIGHT = 60;
19
20     private Ball ball;
21     private static final int BALL_DIAMETER = 20;
22
23     private int playerScore = 0;
24     private Font scoreFont;
25
26     @Override
27     public void init() {
28             paddleLeft = new Paddle(0, 195, PADDLE_WIDTH, PADDLE_HEIGHT);
29             paddleRight = new Paddle(785, 195, PADDLE_WIDTH, PADDLE_HEIGHT);
30             scoreFont = new Font("SansSerif", Font.BOLD, 25);
31             ball = new Ball(300, 200, BALL_DIAMETER, BALL_DIAMETER);
32     }
33
34     @Override
35     public void update() {
36             paddleLeft.update();
37             paddleRight.update();
38             ball.update();
39     }
40
41     @Override
42     public void render(Graphics g) {
43             // Draw Background
44             g.setColor(Resources.darkBlue);
45             g.fillRect(0, 0, GameMain.GAME_WIDTH, GameMain.GAME_HEIGHT);
46             g.setColor(Resources.darkRed);
47             g.fillRect(GameMain.GAME_WIDTH / 2, 0, GameMain.GAME_WIDTH / 2,
48                                     GameMain.GAME_HEIGHT);
49
50             // Draw Separator Line
51             g.drawImage(Resources.line, (GameMain.GAME_WIDTH / 2) - 2, 0, null);
```

```
52
53                  // Draw Paddles
54                  g.setColor(Color.white);
55                  g.fillRect(paddleLeft.getX(), paddleLeft.getY(), paddleLeft.getWidth(),
56                              paddleLeft.getHeight());
57                  g.fillRect(paddleRight.getX(), paddleRight.getY(), paddleRight.getWidth(),
58                              paddleRight.getHeight());
59
60                  // Draw Ball
61                  g.drawRect(ball.getX(), ball.getY(), ball.getWidth(), ball.getHeight());
62
63                  // Draw UI
64                  g.setFont(scoreFont); // Sets scoreFont as current font
65                  g.drawString("" + playerScore, 350, 40);
66
67          }
68
69          @Override
70          public void onClick(MouseEvent e) {
71                  // TODO Auto-generated method stub
72          }
73
74          @Override
75          public void onKeyPress(KeyEvent e) {
76                  if (e.getKeyCode() == KeyEvent.VK_UP) {
77                          paddleLeft.accelUp();
78                          paddleRight.accelDown();
79                  } else if (e.getKeyCode() == KeyEvent.VK_DOWN) {
80                          paddleLeft.accelDown();
81                          paddleRight.accelUp();
82                  }
83
84          }
85
86          @Override
87          public void onKeyRelease(KeyEvent e) {
88                  if (e.getKeyCode() == KeyEvent.VK_UP ||
89                                  e.getKeyCode() == KeyEvent.VK_DOWN) {
90                          paddleLeft.stop();
91                          paddleRight.stop();
92                  }
93
94          }
95
96 }
```

Unfortunately, our game still isn't finished. Run the code, and you will see that the ball never collides with the paddles and that it disappears into the void (through the side of the window). Let's fix this.

Handling Collision: Ball vs. Paddles and Ball vs. the Void

To complete our game, we must do three things:
- Check if the ball collides with the left *paddle* and react accordingly.

- Check if the ball collides with the right *paddle* and react accordingly.
- Check if the ball collides with the left or right *sides of the screen* and react accordingly.

The third case can be checked by calling `ball.isDead()`. To handle the first two cases, declare this new method inside **PlayState**:

```
private boolean ballCollides(Paddle p) {
        return ball.getRect().intersects(p.getRect());
}
```

This helper method checks whether the ball and a given paddle collide by determining whether the bounding boxes of the ball and the paddle intersect.

Next, let's handle the three cases of collision by make the changes shown in bold to the `update()` method in **PlayState**. Note that we call `ballCollides()` two times and `ball.isDead()` once:

```
@Override
public void update() {
        paddleLeft.update();
        paddleRight.update();
        ball.update();

        if (ballCollides(paddleLeft)) {
                playerScore++;
                ball.onCollideWith(paddleLeft);
                Resources.hit.play();
        } else if (ballCollides(paddleRight)) {
                playerScore++;
                ball.onCollideWith(paddleRight);
                Resources.hit.play();
        } else if (ball.isDead()) {
                playerScore -= 3;
                ball.reset();
        }
}
```

Let's discuss the changes we made to the `update()` method.

If the ball hits either paddle, we now call `ball.onCollideWith()`, which will handle the deflection of the ball. We also increment the score by 1 using the post-increment ++ operator (remember that `playerScore++` is equivalent to `playerScore = playerScore + 1`), and play `hit.wav`.

If the ball hits the left or right sides of the screen, we now subtract 3 from the score and reset the ball at its initial position, so that the gameplay continues over and over (and over and over...) again.

Running the Final Product

That completes the **PlayState** class, and *LoneBall* has been implemented in its entirety. Run the game and make sure everything is working! If you are having trouble with your code, the full source code can be found at: **jamescho7.com/book/chapter5/complete**.

Exporting the Game

Before I let you enjoy your game, I will teach you how to perform one more task with Eclipse. You want people to be able to enjoy your game without having access to the source code or having an IDE. The easiest way to do that is to export your project as a *.jar file, which can be executed by most machines with Java 7 or 8 installed.

Exporting the project as a runnable .jar file is easy. Simply right click on the project in the Package Explorer and select **Export**. The Export window will pop up, at which time you will select *Runnable JAR file* under the Java category as shown in Figure 5-11.

Figure 5-11   Exporting as a Runnable JAR

Click **Next >**, and you will see the screen shown in Figure 5-12:

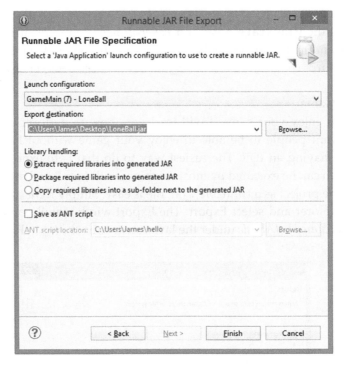

Figure 5-12   Choosing a Destination for the JAR file

Make sure that the Launch configuration is set to run the **GameMain** class inside the *LoneBall* project, choose an export destination (<u>copy the destination into your clipboard</u>), and press **Finish**. This should create a runnable .jar file in that directory.

 Note: The number (7) shown in the Launch configuration box in Figure 5-12 may be different on your machine. That number indicates that this **GameMain** class of project **LoneBall** was the seventh of its name of those that have been recently run on my computer. Yours may be as low as (2) or just say `GameMain - LoneBall`.

Executing the Game

Exit out of Eclipse. We won't be needing it to execute our game anymore. To execute the newly-created `.jar` file, open a command-line interpreter (Command Prompt on Windows, Terminal on Mac) and type the following command:

```
java -version
```

This should show you a screen similar to that in Figure 5-13, telling you what version of Java is installed on your computer (mine says 1.7.0_55, meaning Java 7 update 55).

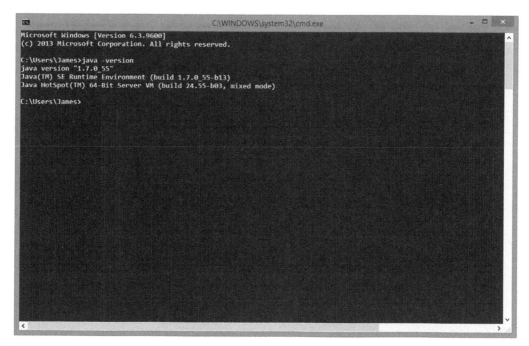

Figure 5-13   Java Version Command

Note: If you get an error saying **java: Command not found**, your terminal is unable to find your installation of Java. To fix this, follow the instructions at the link below:
`http://docs.oracle.com/javase/tutorial/essential/environment/paths.html`

The next step is easy, provided that you have copied your JAR file's export destination in the previous section. If you haven't, that's perfectly okay. It's still easy.

Type the `java -jar` command into your command-line, followed by your export destination (you can paste by right-clicking and selecting **Paste** on Windows):

```
java -jar INSERT_YOUR_EXPORT_DESTINATION_HERE
(e.g. java -jar C:\Users\James\Desktop\LoneBall.jar)
```

If you do not have the export destination copied, simply locate your JAR file in Explorer or Finder and drag it into your terminal after typing the same command (don't forget the whitespace after `-jar`). This should automatically print its full path.

Once you execute the command, you should see *LoneBall*'s window pop open as shown in Figure 5-14! It will run just like it used to on Eclipse, but it now executes from a packaged, sharable `.jar` file.

Before Moving Forward

Before you move on to Chapter 6, here are a couple of things you should do.

Firstly, play your new game to your heart's content, and review the code that you have written in the past two chapters. Make sure that you understand how each class was written and why each class was written, and then draw a diagram of how classes interact with each other.

Next, study some of the example game projects posted on the book's companion site at **jamescho7.com/book/samples/**. Play the games and dissect its classes and methods. Reading code is a great way to improve, especially if you take the time to analyze and understand.

Finally, *try your hand at making your own simple game*. You can start by making simple modifications to *LoneBall*, and then build a game on your own. If you need help, post on the forums at the book's companion site. If you've created a game and want feedback, upload your .JAR file (and optionally your source code) and share it with us! The important thing is that you start coding without the help of this book. Reading code can only take you so far. Remember: practice makes perfect, and there is much material to practice and experiment with in this chapter.

The Next Level

In Chapter 6, the final chapter of Unit 2, we will be adding fancier (and more complicated) features to our framework such as animation. Using this upgraded framework, we will build an infinite-runner complete with an animated character and scrolling obstacles. This one final challenge stands between you and Android game development. Take a well-deserved break, thinking about all that you've learned so far. When you are ready for the next level, join me in Chapter 6.

CHAPTER 6: THE NEXT LEVEL

You may have thought that *LonePong* was fun, but it sure is no *Flappy Bird*. In this chapter, we will be making a frustratingly challenging infinite runner type game in which you take control of an alien named Ellio, who is trying to adjust to gravity on our little blue planet with the help of his toy blocks (which can float above the ground). The game will look as shown in Figure 6-1.

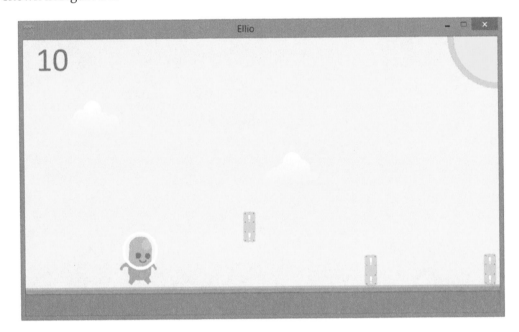

Figure 6-1   Ellio: An Infinite Runner

In the game *Ellio*, the character will run infinitely without player control. As blocks scroll from the right side of the screen, the player will need to react accordingly by sliding and jumping to avoid them. Each time the player is hit by a set of blocks, Ellio will be pushed slightly left. Once Ellio has been pushed completely off the screen, the game will end.

The Framework Needs an Update

Before we get started with developing *Ellio*, we need to update our framework. As with *LonePong*, we will be using the game development framework from Chapter 4 as a starting point; however, the current version of the framework has some limitations that require our attention.

Framerate-Dependent vs. Framerate-Independent Movement

The core problem with our framework is in our game loop, which is reproduced below:

```
@Override
public void run() {
        while (running) {
                currentState.update();
                prepareGameImage();
                currentState.render(gameImage.getGraphics());
                repaint();

                try {
                        Thread.sleep(14);
                } catch (InterruptedException e) {
                        e.printStackTrace();
                }
        }

        System.exit(0);
}
```

We've previously assumed that each iteration of our game loop will take about 17 milliseconds (3 milliseconds of update/render and 14 milliseconds of sleep). While this assumption served us well in *LoneBall*, this is not a valid assumption to make. The update and render steps can take much longer or much fewer than 3 milliseconds. This means that the game loop will not be iterating at a consistent rate. This can lead to problems in games where timing is important, especially when a game fails to take framerate into account when calculating its physics (movement, collision, etc.). To understand why, consider the following scenario:

Let's say that we were to create a side-scrolling game where the **Player** object moves 3 pixels to the right in every iteration of its update() method (which is called once per frame). Assuming that the game runs smoothly at 60 FPS, this translates to 180 pixels per second. What happens if our game were to slow down as the game progresses because we introduce more enemy types and special effects? Our FPS might drop; the game loop will slow down and thus update() will be called less frequently. Assuming a new FPS of 50, the movement speed will have decreased to 150 pixels per second.

If a game behaves as discussed above, we say that the game has *framerate-dependent movement*, because movement speed directly correlates with the framerate. This means that as framerate changes, the game will appear to run slower or faster. In most cases, this does not result in a fun gaming experience.

In games such as *Flappy Bird* or *Megaman*, precise timing of jumps and movement is crucial to staying alive. As such, these games require what is called *framerate-independent movement*, in which movement speed does NOT change with framerate. Instead, these games calculate the amount of time spent per frame and scales the velocity of their objects with this value, so that movement speed is affected by change in *time*, not change in framerate.

To visualize *framerate-independent movement*, imagine that you've built the same side-scrolling game described previously, except that the **Player** object's movement speed inside update() is no longer 3 but the product of **180** and delta, where delta is the number of seconds elapsed since the previous iteration of update(). This has the effect of creating a constant speed independent of framerate. If framerate were to decrease, delta will increase, as will velocity. In this scenario, the **Player** will always move at 180 pixels per second.

Ellio will require players to be precise with their movement. As such, we will be improving our framework by adding framerate-independent movement.

Animation

A second limitation of our framework is its inability to create and display animations. We were able to get away with having static images as our ball and paddles in *LoneBall*, but in our infinite runner, even an alien like Ellio will need to appear as if he's actually running. We will be creating a set of classes in order to implement this new feature.

Planning the Changes: A High-Level Overview

- The game loop: We will be modifying our game loop to add time-measuring functionality for the following reasons:
  - Measuring the duration of the update and render steps allows us to calculate how much our game should sleep in order to maintain a constant framerate.
  - Having a measurement of time allows our state classes to implement framerate-independent movement, so that—in the event the FPS *does* drop—we can keep the game speed constant.
  - An animation needs to know how much time has elapsed in the current frame to determine when to transition to the next frame.
- The state classes: We must modify the update() method of the state classes so that they can receive information regarding the amount of time elapsed since the previous frame and thus implement *framerate-independent movement*.
- Animation: Our game will incorporate animations. We will be creating a **Frame** class and an **Animation** class to make this happen.

Methods to Know Before Getting Started

Math.max()

The Math.max() is a method that belongs to the **Math** class (note that it is static). It determines and returns the greater value of two numbers that you pass in as arguments. For example, if you were to call:

```
System.out.println(Math.max(-1, 5));
```

...the resulting value will be 5.

Why is this method static? This is because the behavior of `Math.max()` should NOT change across *instances* of **Math**—all **Math** objects should perform the `max()` method the exact same way (in fact all methods inside **Math** are static, and you cannot instantiate the class). See Appendix A for more information on static methods.

System.nanoTime()

In order to accomplish animation and framerate-independent movement, we need a way of measuring the amount of time that passes between each iteration of the game loop.

This functionality can be implemented using Java's built-in method called `System.nanoTime()`. Before we discuss what this method does, let's first learn how it may be used:

```
long before = System.nanoTime();
for (int i = 0; i < 100; i++) {
    System.out.println(i);
}
long after = System.nanoTime();
System.out.println("The loop took " + (after - before) + " nanoseconds to run!");
```

In the above example, the `System.nanoTime()` method helps us measures the amount of time that it takes for a for loop to print one hundred numbers. This works because the `System.nanoTime()` method returns the number of nanoseconds (one billionth of a second) that has passed since some arbitrary fixed point in time. Since this point in time is fixed, any subsequent call of `System.nanoTime()` is guaranteed to return a value greater than the previous call by the number of nanoseconds that have elapsed between the two calls. As such, subtracting `long after` by `long before` gives us an accurate measure of time.

Note: One caveat regarding `System.nanoTime()` is the fact that the fixed point in time used as the reference point is arbitrary and can *vary*. As such, it cannot be used to measure *current* time. If you are interested in determining the current time in your program, look into the method `System.currentTimeMillis()`.

Updating the Game Loop

Now that we have planned the changes and studied the methods that we will be using, let's begin coding.

Note: If you get lost while making changes to the Game class, see listing 6.01 on page 199. You can also visit the book's companion site at `jamescho7.com/book/chapter6/`

Fixing the Timing Mechanism

As mentioned, the current version of the game loop iterates at varying intervals. Some iterations take 15 milliseconds while others take 17 or 19. We are going to make this interval consistent, fixing it at 17 milliseconds. To understand the specific changes that we will be making, let's first break down our game loop into a series of stages for simplicity:

Our Game Loop (Simplified):
- Update
- Render
- Sleep
- (Repeat)

As the goal is to have the game loop iterate every 17 milliseconds, the steps update, render and sleep should collectively take 17 milliseconds in total.

We *cannot* modify the number of milliseconds that the update and render calls take to complete (this value will vary depending on the number of objects in our game and the whims of our OS); however, we *can* modify the duration of sleep. For example, if our update and render steps were to take 15 milliseconds to complete, we can sleep for 2 milliseconds (for a total of 17). On the other hand, if our update and render steps were to take 3 milliseconds to complete, we can sleep for 14 milliseconds (also for a total of 17).

We now know that to fix our timing mechanism, we must know how long the update and render methods take to execute. Open the **Game** class of your game development framework project (optionally make a new copy of it called **SimpleJavaGDF2**), and make the changes shown in bold below:

```
@Override
public void run() {
    // These variables should sum up to 17 on every iteration
    long updateDurationMillis = 0; // Measures both update AND render
    long sleepDurationMillis = 0; // Measures sleep

    while (running) {
        long beforeUpdateRender = System.nanoTime();

        currentState.update();
        prepareGameImage();
        currentState.render(gameImage.getGraphics());
        repaint();

        updateDurationMillis = (System.nanoTime() - beforeUpdateRender) / 1000000L;
        sleepDurationMillis = Math.max(2, 17 - updateDurationMillis);

        try {
                Thread.sleep(14);
                Thread.sleep(sleepDurationMillis);
        } catch (InterruptedException e) {
                e.printStackTrace();
        }
```

```
    }
    System.exit(0);
}
```

Wrapping your mind around timing lines of code executing inside loops can be a little confusing because a loop jumps from place to place, but bear with me! It will make sense in time.

Let's discuss the changes. We start by creating two variables of type `long` (`updateDurationMillis`, used for measuring duration of update AND render, and `sleepDurationMillis`, for measuring sleep duration). Note that these two variables are both declared OUTSIDE of the loop, for reasons we will discuss later.

Before calling the series of update and render methods, we check the time and store it inside the variable `beforeUpdateRender`. Once the update and render methods finish executing, we calculate the duration of the two steps by checking the time once more (`System.nanoTime()`) and subtracting the original time (`beforeUpdateRender`). This result in nanoseconds is divided by a million to convert it into the same result milliseconds (a nanosecond is a millionth of a millisecond).

Finally, we calculate the amount of sleeping time as `17 - updateDurationMillis` and ask our thread to sleep by this amount. This value can be negative if `updateDurationMillis` is greater than 17, and so we use the `Math.max()` method to enforce a minimum of 2 seconds as the sleep time. If this is confusing, consider the following block of code:

```
for (int updateTime = 0; updateTime < 20; updateTime++) {
    long sleepTime = Math.max(2, 17 - updateTime);
    System.out.println(sleepTime);
}
```

This simulates what would happen to `sleepTime` if `updateTime` were to range from 0 to 20 (a value greater than 17). Write down the values that `sleepTime` would take on each iteration of the loop, and the purpose of calling the `Math.max()` method in this situation will become clear.

Calculating Delta

Now that we have a timing mechanism in place, we can calculate the duration of each iteration of the game loop. This value, which we will refer to as *delta*, is simply the sum of `updateDurationMillis` and `sleepDurationMillis`. *Delta* will be passed into our `currentState`'s update method for the purposes of animation and framerate-independent movement.

Add the line of code in bold shown below to your game loop:
```
@Override
public void run() {
    long updateDurationMillis = 0;
```

```
    long sleepDurationMillis = 0;

    while (running) {
        long beforeUpdateRender = System.nanoTime();
        long deltaMillis = updateDurationMillis + sleepDurationMillis;  // New line!

        currentState.update();
        prepareGameImage();
        currentState.render(gameImage.getGraphics());
        repaint();

        updateDurationMillis = (System.nanoTime() - beforeUpdateRender) / 1000000L;
        sleepDurationMillis = Math.max(2, 17 - updateDurationMillis);

        try {
            Thread.sleep(sleepDurationMillis);
        } catch (InterruptedException e) {
            e.printStackTrace();
        }
    }

    System.exit(0);
}
```

The value of the newly-created deltaMillis *should* be 17 milliseconds in most cases, but if updateDurationMillis were to take an abnormally long time, this number can be higher.

Allowing Framerate-Independent Movement

We have our deltaMillis value, and now we must use it to allow frame-rate independent movement. But first, we are going to clean up our game loop a little bit. It is a bit messy.

We will "refactor" our code (restructure how the code is written without modifying its behavior) by creating a new method. Select the following four lines of code inside the loop using your mouse:

```
....
currentState.update();
prepareGameImage();
currentState.render(gameImage.getGraphics());
repaint();
....
```

We could manually create a new method, copy these four lines into the new method, and replace the original four lines with a call to that method, but there is an easier (and faster) way.

Right-click on the four selected lines (Ctrl + Click on Mac), and choose *Refactor > Extract Method*, as shown in Figure 6-2.

Figure 6-2　Refactoring by Extraction

Enter the name `updateAndRender` for the new method as shown in Figure 6-3. Keep the access as **private**. We will only be calling the method inside the game loop.

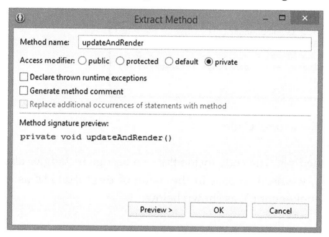

Figure 6-3　The New Method Name

Once you click **OK**, Eclipse will automatically refactor your code as shown in Figure 6-4!

```
@Override
public void run() {
    long updateDurationMillis = 0;
    long sleepDurationMillis = 0;

    while (running) {
        long beforeUpdateRender = System.nanoTime();
        long deltaMillis = updateDurationMillis + sleepDurationMillis;

        updateAndRender();

        updateDurationMillis = (System.nanoTime() - beforeUpdateRender) / 1000000L;
        sleepDurationMillis = Math.max(2, 17 - updateDurationMillis);

        try {
            Thread.sleep(sleepDurationMillis);
        } catch (InterruptedException e) {
            e.printStackTrace();
        }
    }

    System.exit(0);
}

private void updateAndRender() {
    currentState.update();
    prepareGameImage();
    currentState.render(gameImage.getGraphics());
    repaint();
}
```

Figure 6-4   Refactored Code

We are not finished yet. The code inside the two orange rectangles above must be slightly modified. Firstly, we need to pass in the value of deltaMillis as an argument for the method updateAndRender(), as shown below:

```
updateAndRender();
updateAndRender(deltaMillis);
```

Next, the updateAndRender() method needs to be changed to accept this new argument, and we must pass on the argument into the currentState.update() method! By doing so, each of our states' update() methods will have access to the time it has taken since the previous iteration of update(), for reasons we have discussed. I prefer to have this value be in seconds, so we will divide by 1000f (this allows us to denote movement later in pixels per second, rather than pixels per millisecond). The changes you must make are shown in bold below:

```
private void updateAndRender(long deltaMillis) {
    currentState.update(deltaMillis / 1000f);
    prepareGameImage();
    currentState.render(gameImage.getGraphics());
    repaint();
}
```

You will see an error inside the updated method, as shown in Figure 6-5:

```
private void updateAndRender(long deltaMillis) {
    currentState.update(deltaMillis / 1000f);
    prepareGameI  The method update() in the type State is not applicable for the arguments (float)
    currentState
    repaint();   3 quick fixes available:
}                  Remove argument to match 'update()'
                   Change method 'update()': Add parameter 'float'
private void pre    Create method 'update(float)' in type 'State'
    if (gameImag
        gameImag
    }
    Graphics g = gameImage.getGraphics();
    g.clearRect(0, 0, gameWidth, gameHeight);
}
```

Figure 6-5   An Error in `updateAndRender()`

This error is telling us that the `update()` method inside the **State** class does not accept a numerical argument. We will be fixing this soon.

Declaring Variables outside of a Loop

Now that we have the delta calculation in place, we can discuss the reason why we previously declared `updateDurationMillis` and `sleepDurationMillis` outside the game loop.

To understand this, you should know that variables declared inside a loop are only accessible within that current iteration only. Their values *cannot* be accessed in the next iteration. Since the concept of delta is the amount of time that has passed since the *previous* iteration of the game loop, we need access to the `updateDurationMillis` and `sleepDurationMillis` of the previous iteration to calculate delta. This is why we have declared the two `long` variables outside of the loop. Keeping this in mind, have a look at the game loop again. The timing variables will make much more sense.

Switching to Active Rendering

At the moment, we are taking three steps to perform our rendering. We first prepare a blank game image, fill it with content from the `currentState` and then draw the image to the screen using `repaint()` (which *requests* that the method `paintComponent()` be called).

Of the above steps, the third step is *passive*. Again, we *request* that `paintComponent()` be called, but the JVM does not *have to* listen to us—there is no guarantee that `paintComponent()` *will* be called.

This is problematic because the variable `deltaMillis` should represent the amount of time that has passed since the previous update and render, but we have no guarantee that the render method actually was called in the previous iteration. When we have animations, precisely-timed drawing is important, so we must fix this.

We will be employing something called *active rendering* which will improve our game's performance and make its rendering more predictable. When actively rendering, we do not just *request* for the game to render—we *tell* it to. This is actually easy. Rather than calling `repaint()`, which will *sometimes* call `paintComponent()`, we will create a new method that will *always* be called. This method will be nearly identical to `paintComponent()`, as shown below.

```
private void renderGameImage(Graphics g) {
        if (gameImage != null) {
                g.drawImage(gameImage, 0, 0, null);
        }
        g.dispose();
}
```

Add this new method into your **Game** class, and REMOVE the existing `paintComponent()` method.

Next, we simply replace the call to `repaint()` inside `updateAndRender()` as shown in bold below:

```
private void updateAndRender(long deltaMillis) {
        currentState.update(deltaMillis / 1000f);
        prepareGameImage();
        currentState.render(gameImage.getGraphics());
        repaint();
        renderGameImage(getGraphics());
}
```

The `getGraphics()` method returns the **Graphics** object of our **JPanel** (remember that the **Game** class inherits from **JPanel**), and having access to it allows us to draw on the **JPanel**. We give this to our `renderGameImage()` method by passing it in as an argument.

Whenever we finish working with a Graphics object that we've request ourselves, it is recommended that we manually dispose of this object as shown inside the `renderGameImage()` method from earlier.

Reviewing the Code

We have made all the adjustments that we need in the **Game** class, incorporating timing, delta calculation and active rendering. You should still have an error on the line:

```
currentState.update(deltaMillis / 1000f);
```

We will be fixing this error next. The full **Game** class is reproduced in listing 6.01 for reference:

Listing 6.01   The **Game** Class (Completed)

```
001 package com.jamescho.game.main;
002
003 import java.awt.Color;
004 import java.awt.Dimension;
005 import java.awt.Graphics;
006 import java.awt.Image;
007
008 import javax.swing.JPanel;
009
010 import com.jamescho.framework.util.InputHandler;
011 import com.jamescho.game.state.LoadState;
012 import com.jamescho.game.state.State;
013
014 @SuppressWarnings("serial")
015
016 public class Game extends JPanel implements Runnable{
017     private int gameWidth;
018     private int gameHeight;
019     private Image gameImage;
020
021     private Thread gameThread;
022     private volatile boolean running;
023     private volatile State currentState;
024
025     private InputHandler inputHandler;
026
027     public Game(int gameWidth, int gameHeight){
028             this.gameWidth = gameWidth;
029             this.gameHeight = gameHeight;
030             setPreferredSize(new Dimension(gameWidth, gameHeight));
031             setBackground(Color.BLACK);
032             setFocusable(true);
033             requestFocus();
034     }
035
036     public void setCurrentState(State newState) {
037             System.gc();
038             newState.init();
039             currentState = newState;
040             inputHandler.setCurrentState(currentState);
041     }
042
043     @Override
044     public void addNotify() {
045             super.addNotify();
046             initInput();
047             setCurrentState(new LoadState());
048             initGame();
049     }
050
051     private void initInput() {
052             inputHandler = new InputHandler();
053             addKeyListener(inputHandler);
054             addMouseListener(inputHandler);
055     }
056
057     private void initGame() {
```

```
058                 running = true;
059                 gameThread = new Thread(this, "Game Thread");
060                 gameThread.start();
061         }
062
063     @Override
064     public void run() {
065
066         long updateDurationMillis = 0; // Measures both update AND render
067         long sleepDurationMillis = 0; // Measures sleep
068
069             while (running){
070                     long beforeUpdateRender = System.nanoTime();
071                     long deltaMillis = updateDurationMillis + sleepDurationMillis;
072
073                     updateAndRender(deltaMillis);
074
075                     updateDurationMillis = (System.nanoTime() - beforeUpdateRender) /
                                1000000L;
076                     sleepDurationMillis = Math.max(2, 17 - updateDurationMillis);
077
078                     try {
079                             Thread.sleep(sleepDurationMillis);
080                     } catch (InterruptedException e) {
081                             e.printStackTrace();
082                     }
083             }
084             System.exit(0);
085     }
086
087     private void updateAndRender(long deltaMillis) {
088             currentState.update(deltaMillis / 1000f);
089             prepareGameImage();
090             currentState.render(gameImage.getGraphics());
091             renderGameImage(getGraphics());
092     }
093
094     private void prepareGameImage() {
095             if (gameImage == null) {
096                     gameImage = createImage(gameWidth, gameHeight);
097             }
098             Graphics g = gameImage.getGraphics();
099             g.fillRect(0, 0, gameWidth, gameHeight);
100     }
101
102     public void exit() {
103             running = false;
104     }
105
106     private void renderGameImage(Graphics g) {
107             if (gameImage != null) {
108                     g.drawImage(gameImage, 0, 0, null);
109             }
110             g.dispose();
111     }
112
113 }
```

Updating the State Classes

We must make some minor changes to the State classes in order to take advantage of the delta calculation from the game class. This will fix the error inside our updateAndRender() method and allow us to do perform animations later on! Open your **State** class, and make the change shown in Listing 6.02 to your update() method:

Listing 6.02   The **State** Class (Updated)

```
package com.jamescho.game.state;

import java.awt.Graphics;
import java.awt.event.KeyEvent;
import java.awt.event.MouseEvent;

import com.jamescho.game.main.GameMain;

public abstract class State {

        public abstract void init();

        public abstract void update();
        public abstract void update(float delta);

        public abstract void render(Graphics g);

        public abstract void onClick(MouseEvent e);

        public abstract void onKeyPress(KeyEvent e);

        public abstract void onKeyRelease(KeyEvent e);

        public void setCurrentState(State newState) {
                GameMain.sGame.setCurrentState(newState);
        }
}
```

Now update() will receive a float value called delta, representing the amount of time that has passed since the previous iteration of update. This value will typically be .017 (17 milliseconds in 60 FPS).

That rids us of the error in the **Game** class, as **State** now has an update() method that is capable of receiving a numerical value; however, since we have changed this method inside an abstract superclass (remember that **LoadState** and **MenuState** both inherit from **State**), we must make changes to our subclasses as well. Make the changes to **LoadState**'s and **MenuState**'s update() methods as shown in listings 6.03 and 6.04.

Listing 6.03   The **LoadState** Class (Updated)

```java
package com.jamescho.game.state;

import java.awt.Graphics;
import java.awt.event.KeyEvent;
import java.awt.event.MouseEvent;

import com.jamescho.game.main.Resources;

public class LoadState extends State {

    @Override
    public void init() {
        Resources.load();
        System.out.println("Loaded Successfully");
    }

    @Override
    public void update() {
    public void update(float delta){
        setCurrentState(new MenuState());
    }

    @Override
    public void render(Graphics g) {
        // TODO Auto-generated method stub
    }

    @Override
    public void onClick(MouseEvent e) {
        // TODO Auto-generated method stub
    }

    @Override
    public void onKeyPress(KeyEvent e) {
        // TODO Auto-generated method stub
    }

    @Override
    public void onKeyRelease(KeyEvent e) {
        // TODO Auto-generated method stub
    }

}
```

Listing 6.04   The **MenuState** Class (Updated)

```java
package com.jamescho.game.state;

import java.awt.Graphics;
import java.awt.event.KeyEvent;
import java.awt.event.MouseEvent;

import com.jamescho.game.main.Resources;
```

```java
public class MenuState extends State{

        @Override
        public void init() {
                System.out.println("Entered MenuState");

        }

        @Override
        public void update(float delta){

        }

        @Override
        public void render(Graphics g) {
                g.drawImage(Resources.welcome, 0, 0, null);
        }

        @Override
        public void onClick(MouseEvent e) {

        }

        @Override
        public void onKeyPress(KeyEvent e) {

        }

        @Override
        public void onKeyRelease(KeyEvent e) {

        }

}
```

With those changes, all the errors should be gone from our project.

Adding RandomNumberGenerator

Before moving on, our framework should have a copy of the **RandomNumberGenerator** class from Chapter 5. Check your com.jamescho.framework.util package to see if you have it. If not, the class can be found in listing 5.08. Add this to your com.jamescho.framework.util package prior to proceeding.

After that change, your current project structure should match that shown in Figure 6-6:

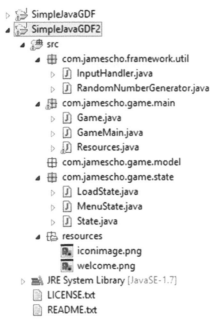

Figure 6-6   Project Structure, Checkpoint 1

Note: If you are having problems with any of the classes at this point, you can download the source code at `jamescho7.com/book/chapter6/checkpoint1`.

Adding Animation

Now that our State classes have access to the delta values, we can incorporate animation into our framework. Before we can start writing classes though, we first need to understand what an animation is.

As I'm sure you've heard many times, an animation is an illusion. It is a series of still images drawn in quick succession in order to trick our brains into seeing motion. Each of these images is called a frame, and each frame lasts for a certain amount of time. We will use this idea to create an **Animation** class and a **Frame** class.

Designing and Implementing the Frame Class

Our **Frame** object should be a simple class containing one image and its duration (the time it should be displayed for). As such, **Frame** should have an instance variable for each of these properties. We will keep these two variables private and provide public getters for access.

Create a new package called `com.jamescho.framework.animation`, which will soon contain our **Animation** and **Frame** classes. Create the **Frame** class inside the package, and implement it as shown in listing 6.05.

Listing 6.05   The **Frame** Class (Completed)

```java
package com.jamescho.framework.animation;

import java.awt.Image;

public class Frame {
        private Image image;
        private double duration;

        public Frame(Image image, double duration) {
                this.image = image;
                this.duration = duration;
        }

        public double getDuration() {
                return duration;
        }

        public Image getImage() {
                return image;
        }
}
```

The **Frame** class is a very simple. As there is nothing new to discuss here, we will move on to the harder part.

Designing the Animation Class

The **Animation** class is a collection of associated frames. For example, if we needed seven frames to animate a walk cycle, where each frame has a duration of .1 seconds, we might diagram it as shown in Figure 6-7.

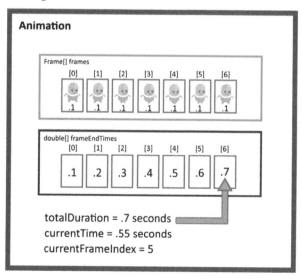

Figure 6-7   A Walk Animation

Study the diagram and its five variables for three minutes. You might be able to glean our animation strategy. If you want to check your predictions, read on!

For each animation, we will create an array that holds multiple frames (images and corresponding durations). Using each frame's duration value, we can determine when we should switch from one frame to another. For example, frame 0 should finish at a `currentTime` of .1 seconds, frame 1 should finish at .2, and so on. These end time values are stored in a second, *parallel array* called `frameEndTimes`. Make sure that you can see this relationship in Figure 5-7 before moving on.

Note: The term parallel array indicates that there is some relationship between elements in the two arrays, such as between the element at `frame[5]` and the element at `frameEndTimes[5]`. In this case, `frame[5]` should END at the time given in `frameEndTimes[5]`, at which point `frame[6]` will become current.

In our implementation, we will create an **Animation** object for each desired animation, such as the one for walking. Next, we will update this animation using the delta value from the game loop, so that the animation's `currentTime` variable increases every frame by the correct number of seconds. Using `currentTime` to determine `currentFrameIndex` (the index of the frame that should be being displayed), our **Animation** will be able to render itself using `g.drawImage(...)`.

Implementing the Animation Class

Now that we have discussed the logic for our **Animation** class, let's begin implementing it, starting with the variables. Create the **Animation** class in the `com.jamescho. framework.animation` package, and declare the following instance variables:

```
private Frame[] frames;
private double[] frameEndTimes;
private int currentFrameIndex = 0;

private double totalDuration = 0;
private double currentTime = 0;
```

We will be creating a constructor to receive an array of **Frame** objects, and we will use this array to create the parallel `frameEndTimes` array. `totalDuration` can also be determined by iterating through `frames`, while `currentTime` and `currentFrame` index will be incremented inside the `update()` method later.

Add the constructor as shown below:
```
public Animation(Frame... frames) {
        this.frames = frames;
        frameEndTimes = new double[frames.length];

        for (int i = 0; i < frames.length; i++) {
                Frame f = frames[i];
```

```
                    totalDuration += f.getDuration();
                    frameEndTimes[i] = totalDuration;
            }
    }
}
```

You will notice that this constructor has a single parameter of type `Frame...`; this is not a typo. The `...` is how you can specify a *variable* number of arguments in Java. This means that our constructor can accept *any* number of **Frame** objects, as shown below (this is just an example. Do NOT add the following to your own code). :

```
Frame f1 = new Frame(...); // Constructor call simplified
Frame f2 = new Frame(...);
Frame f3 = new Frame(...);
Frame f4 = new Frame(...);
Frame f5 = new Frame(...);

Animation anim = new Animation(f1, f2, f3);
Animation anim2 = new Animation(f4, f5);
```

Refer to the **Animation** constructor one more time. Notice that when the constructor receives this variable number of **Frame** objects, the frames are bundled together into a single array for ease of use. We will assign this array as the value of the `frames` variable.

Inside the constrcutor, we also create a new array of `doubles` called `frameEndTimes`. As this array should be parallel to the array `frames`, we give it an identical length. Then we use a for loop to determine the end time for *each* frame and the `totalDuration` of all the frames. If this logic is confusing, please refer to Figure 6-7, and walk yourself through the constructor using the diagram as a reference.

The variables are ready and initialized. Next, all we have to add are the four methods: `update()`, `wrapAnimation()`, `render()` and a second `render()`, as shown below (import accordingly to remove errors):

```
public synchronized void update(float increment) {
        currentTime += increment;

        if (currentTime > totalDuration) {
                wrapAnimation();
        }

        while (currentTime > frameEndTimes[currentFrameIndex]) {
                currentFrameIndex++;
        }
}

private synchronized void wrapAnimation() {
        currentFrameIndex = 0;
        currentTime %= totalDuration; // equal to cT = cT % tD
}

public synchronized void render(Graphics g, int x, int y) {
        g.drawImage(frames[currentFrameIndex].getImage(), x, y, null);
}
```

```
public synchronized void render(Graphics g, int x, int y, int width, int height) {
        g.drawImage(frames[currentFrameIndex].getImage(), x, y, width, height, null);
}
```

Note: The synchronized keyword is used to ensure that animations will update accurately in a multi-threaded environment. It is used to denote that a method should be executed in its entirety. This also is an advanced topic that we will not get into in this book.

We have two render methods with the same name but different parameters. In Java, this is called *overloading a method*. Typically, methods of the same name allow you to perform the same behavior in different ways. In our example, our render(Graphics g, int x, int y) method allows you to draw an animation's current frame image at x and y, but it does not let you specify how large the image should be. In contrast, render(Graphics g, int x, int y, int width, int height) *does* allow you to specify an image size.

The update() method is where the important action happens. This method has two responsibilities. Firstly, it keeps track of currentTime (how long the animation has been running for) and handles irregularities. Secondly it determines the currentFrameIndex by comparing the updated currentTime value to the frameEndTimes array.

To make these steps happen, the method receives a parameter—a float value called increment. This will be the delta value from the game loop. The currentTime is then incremented with this value. If the value of currentTime is greater than that of totalDuration, we know that the animation has completed. In this situation, our **Animation** class chooses to repeat the animation by calling the wrapAnimation() method.

The wrapAnimation() method, called when currentTime has exceeded the totalDuration, resets the currentFrameIndex at zero and calculate a new currentTime as currentTime % totalDuration. The modulus (%) operator has the effect of calculating overflow, or how many seconds PAST the end of the animation we were at before resetting the animation.

The **Animation** and **Frame** classes are now complete. The full Animation class is reproduced below in listing 6.06.

Listing 6.06   The **Animation** Class (Completed)

```
01 package com.jamescho.framework.animation;
02
03 import java.awt.Graphics;
04
05 public class Animation {
06         private Frame[] frames;
07         private double[] frameEndTimes;
08         private int currentFrameIndex = 0;
09
10         private double totalDuration = 0;
```

```
11          private double currentTime = 0;
12          public Animation(Frame... frames) {
13                  this.frames = frames;
14                  frameEndTimes = new double[frames.length];
15
16                  for (int i = 0; i < frames.length; i++) {
17                          Frame f = frames[i];
18                          totalDuration += f.getDuration();
19                          frameEndTimes[i] = totalDuration;
20                  }
21          }
22
23          public synchronized void update(float increment) {
24                  currentTime += increment;
25
26                  if (currentTime > totalDuration) {
27                          wrapAnimation();
28                  }
29
30                  while (currentTime > frameEndTimes[currentFrameIndex]) {
31                          currentFrameIndex++;
32                  }
33          }
34
35          private synchronized void wrapAnimation() {
36                  currentFrameIndex = 0;
37                  currentTime %= totalDuration; // equal to cT = cT % tD
38          }
39
40          public synchronized void render(Graphics g, int x, int y) {
41                  g.drawImage(frames[currentFrameIndex].getImage(), x, y, null);
42          }
43
44          public synchronized void render(Graphics g, int x, int y, int width,
                                            int height) {
45                  g.drawImage(frames[currentFrameIndex].getImage(), x, y, width,
                          height,null);
46          }
47
48 }
```

Our framework is now in a much better state than it was in Chapter 5. Let's start building *Ellio*.

Note: If you are having problems with any of the classes at this point, you can download the source code at **jamescho7.com/book/chapter6/checkpoint2**.

Ellio: Optimization Matters

Ellio is a simple two-button game, but the nature of this infinite runner necessitates a discussion of optimization.

The Issue of Memory Management

Until now, we've largely ignored memory usage; we've created objects at will, assuming that our machine will always have plenty of memory (RAM) to store these as variables for as long as we need. When we start developing for Android, this assumption may not always hold. Mobile devices tend to have smaller amounts of memory than do computers, and this memory tends to be shared across multiple applications simultaneously. This makes memory management an important issue that you should actively think about when developing games, and we will start this process with *Ellio*.

If you look again at Figure 6-1, you will notice that Ellio has to avoid a series of yellow blocks coming from the right. Let me ask you this question. What should we do with the yellow blocks that have gone past the left side of the screen? These blocks are no longer visible, so keeping them around means that they will take up memory for no reason. Continuing to waste processing power to update them and render them will mean that our game will slow down with time.

You may have answered the question by saying, "We should destroy the unused blocks." While that may sound like a great idea, that would mean we must create a new set of blocks to replace the destroyed ones. This is bad for a couple of reasons. To understand why, let's talk about some optimization techniques that will make our game run faster.

Optimizing Techniques
- <u>Minimize the CPU's workload:</u> As you increase the number of operations that your CPU must perform on every frame, you risk decreasing the game's framerate. This usually results in a poorer gameplay experience. Aim to minimize your CPU's workload, only performing calculations that are absolutely necessary. For example, only check for collision (which involves many operations and if-statements) when there is a CHANCE for collision in the first place. If an object is halfway across the screen from your character, there is no need to perform expensive calculations to check if the character's left foot, right foot, head, left hand, right hand (and so on) collide with the object.
- <u>Avoid object creation:</u> One of the most important things you can do is to avoid creating new objects inside a loop. In fact, you should only use the new keyword when absolutely necessary! Remember that our update and render methods are called inside the game loop, meaning that if you were to create a new object on every iteration of the update method, you would get 60 new objects every second. This would fill up your memory really fast. What happens if your machine runs out of memory, you ask? Garbage collection.

Meet the Garbage Collector
Have a look at the following loop:

```
for (int i = 0; i < 1000000; i++) {
```

```
        Random r = new Random();
        System.out.println(r.nextInt(5));
}
```

The above loop demonstrates wasteful object creation. In every iteration of the loop, we create a new **Random** object and assign it to the variable r. As the loop iterates, we lose access to the **Random** r object from the previous iteration. These lost r objects sit inside RAM taking up valuable space, and you have no way of getting them back. They are completely useless.

When the JVM realizes that you are beginning to run out of memory, it will call the *garbage collector* into action. Without being too anthropomorphic, you can think of the garbage collector as an autonomous "entity" that will determine which objects inside memory are still useable (it is autonomous because you have no control over this process). Objects that are no longer useable (such as the Random objects from the loop shown above) are discarded, creating new memory space for new objects.

Fear the Garbage Collector

The garbage collector is a great tool. It automatically does the hard work of managing memory for you; however, autonomous garbage collection can be a curse. Every time the garbage collector runs, your machine will devote its processing power to performing garbage collection tasks (identifying and removing unnecessary objects).

What happens if your player is about to make an important jump and garbage collection kicks in? The FPS drops, the gameplay stutters and slows, and your player dies without any fault of his own. Protect your player from the garbage collector by avoiding object creation!

Memory Management and Ellio

Let's go back to the question, "What should we do with yellow blocks that have gone past the left side of the screen?" The answer is to reuse them. Send them back over to the right side and let them try to hit Ellio again. In *Ellio*, this means that we can create five sets of blocks and use them infinitely, rather than create a new set of blocks every few frames.

Ellio: A High-Level Overview

We've discussed some issues you need to be aware of in order to make *Ellio* run as smoothly as possible. Let's apply these principles to create our game.

The Classes

<u>Main Classes:</u> Our game development framework allows us to create *Ellio* simply by creating new model classes and state classes. For the most part, we can stay outside of our framework! We only need to make a simple change to **GameMain** to configure the title of the game, and load our new resources inside the **Resources** class.

<u>State Classes:</u> We will be modifying **MenuState** to display selections as shown in Figure 6-8. The two state classes we will create anew are **PlayState** and **GameOverState**. The

PlayState will handle the gameplay. Once the player loses (everyone loses in an infinite runner eventually), we will transition to the **GameOverState** to display the score.

<u>Model Classes:</u> The three model classes we will create are **Cloud**, **Block** and **Player**. Each **Cloud** object will represent the **Cloud** images that scroll in the sky (see Figure 6-1), as each **Block** object will represent a stack of yellow blocks that can be avoided by jumping or ducking. The single **Player** instance will represent Ellio the alien.

Figure 6-8   Ellio: **MenuState** Screenshot

Preparing the Ellio Project

Copying the Framework

Open up Eclipse, and make a copy of the game development framework project (with all of the changes that we have made in this chapter). Give the copy the name *Ellio*. Your project should appear in your Package Explorer as shown in Figure 6-9:

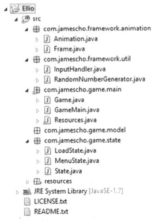

Figure 6-9   Ellio: Package Explorer

Note: If you do not have access to the framework on your computer, the appropriate version can be downloaded in .zip format at **jamescho7.com/book/chapter6/checkpoint2**. To import the downloaded framework into your workspace, follow the instructions provided on page 147-148.

The very first thing that we will do is change the name of our game. Open up **GameMain** and change the name of the **JFrame** window to Ellio (Chapter 6) by modifying the value of GAME_TITLE as shown in listing 6.07.

Listing 6.07   The **GameMain** Class

```
package com.jamescho.game.main;

import javax.swing.JFrame;

public class GameMain {
    public static final String GAME_TITLE = "Java Game Development Framework (Chapter 4)";
    public static final String GAME_TITLE = "Ellio (Chapter 6)";
    public static final int GAME_WIDTH = 800;
    public static final int GAME_HEIGHT = 450;
    public static Game sGame;

    public static void main(String[] args) {
                JFrame frame = new JFrame(GAME_TITLE);
                frame.setDefaultCloseOperation(JFrame.EXIT_ON_CLOSE);
                frame.setResizable(false);
                sGame = new Game(GAME_WIDTH, GAME_HEIGHT);
                frame.add(sGame);
                frame.pack();
                frame.setVisible(true);
                frame.setIconImage(Resources.iconimage);
    }

}
```

Run the program, and check that Ellio (Chapter 6) displays properly as the title of the **JFrame** window.

Adding and Loading Resources

For *Ellio's* artwork, we will be using some beautiful public domain images that can be used without restriction. With the exception of a few images that I have created or modified, these images have all been created by Kenney, an awesome programmer and artist who has made thousands of assets (images, sounds and fonts) available for free! Feel free to use these assets as you would like. Attribution is optional, but I'd like to ask you include Kenney's name in your project and share his amazing work with others.

Note: If you would like to see more of Kenney's free assets, visit his website at the following link: **http://www.kenney.nl/assets**. If you want to support Kenney's work, make a donation! You will get access/updates to all of his work. For more information, see **http://kenney.itch.io/kenney-donation**.

The following resources (images and sound files) are available for you to download at **jamescho7.com/book/chapter6**. You may also use your own by creating images and sound files of the appropriate dimensions and type.

iconimage.png (32px x 32px) – to be used as the icon image for JFrame.

welcome.png (800px x 450px) – to be used as the new welcome screen for Ellio.

selector.png (25px x 45px) – to be used as a selection arrow in MenuState.

cloud1.png (128px x 71px) – to be used in the background.

Cloud2.png (129px x 71px) – also to be used in the background.

runanim1.png (72px x 97px) – used as part of running animation for Ellio.

runanim2.png (72px x 97px) – used as part of running animation for Ellio.

runanim3.png (72px x 97px) – used as part of running animation for Ellio.

runanim4.png (72px x 97px) – used as part of running animation for Ellio.

runanim5.png (72px x 97px) – used as part of running animation for Ellio.

duck.jpg (72px x 97px) – used to show a ducking Ellio.

jump.png (72px x 97px) – used to show a jumping Ellio.

grass.png (800px x 45px) – used to draw the grass in PlayState.

block.png (20px x 50px) – used to draw obstacles in PlayState.

onjump.wav (Duration: <1 sec) – to be played when Ellio jumps. Created using bfxr.

hit.wav (Duration: <1 sec) – to be played when the player gets hit by the blocks. Created using bfxr.

Download (or create) the sixteen files and add them into your project's resources package, overwriting any existing files. Your resources package should be identical to that shown in Figure 6-10.

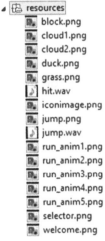

Figure 6-10   Adding the Resources Files to the Ellio Project

Next, we will load the new resource files into our **Resources** class. This is done in two steps. Firstly, declare the following static variables (welcome and iconimage may already be declared for you):

```
public static BufferedImage welcome, iconimage, block, cloud1, cloud2,
                duck, grass, jump, run1, run2, run3, run4, run5, selector;

public static AudioClip hit, onjump;
```

Next, initialize the newly created variables inside the load() method as shown below. We use loadImage() for image files and loadSound() for sound files.

```
....
public static void load() {
        welcome = loadImage("welcome.png");
        iconimage = loadImage("iconimage.png");
        block = loadImage("block.png");
        cloud1 = loadImage("cloud1.png");
        cloud2 = loadImage("cloud2.png");
        duck = loadImage("duck.png");
        grass = loadImage("grass.png");
```

```
        jump = loadImage("jump.png");
        run1 = loadImage("run_anim1.png");
        run2 = loadImage("run_anim2.png");
        run3 = loadImage("run_anim3.png");
        run4 = loadImage("run_anim4.png");
        run5 = loadImage("run_anim5.png");
        selector = loadImage("selector.png");
        hit = loadSound("hit.wav");
        onjump = loadSound("onjump.wav");
}
....
```

Note: Variable names do not always match the corresponding file names. Make sure you double check both to avoid errors!

We will also create a static **Color** object to represent our sky color (RGB: 25, 83, 105). Add the corresponding static variable as shown (importing `java.awt.Color`):

```
public static Color skyBlue;
```

Initialize `skyBlue` inside the `load()` method as shown in bold:

```
....
public static void load() {
        welcome = loadImage("welcome.png");
        iconimage = loadImage("iconimage.png");
        block = loadImage("block.png");
        cloud1 = loadImage("cloud1.png");
        cloud2 = loadImage("cloud2.png");
        duck = loadImage("duck.png");
        grass = loadImage("grass.png");
        jump = loadImage("jump.png");
        run1 = loadImage("run_anim1.png");
        run2 = loadImage("run_anim2.png");
        run3 = loadImage("run_anim3.png");
        run4 = loadImage("run_anim4.png");
        run5 = loadImage("run_anim5.png");
        selector = loadImage("selector.png");
        hit = loadSound("hit.wav");
        onjump = loadSound("onjump.wav");
        skyBlue = new Color(208, 244, 247);
}
....
```

The last thing we need to do is create our running animation. First, declare the static variable as shown (importing `com.jamescho.framework.animation`):
```
public static Animation runAnim;
```

We will initialize `runAnim` using the constructor for the **Animation** class, which accepts any number of **Frame** arguments. To achieve the deired running effect, we will add run1, run2, run3, run4, run5, run3 (repeated) and run2 (also repeated) in that order as **Frame** objects with duration of .1 seconds each.

To do as described, begin by importing our Frame class (make sure you import `com.jamescho.framework.animation.Frame`, not `java.awt.Frame`), and add the following to the bottom of the `load()` method:

```
Frame f1 = new Frame(run1, .1f);
Frame f2 = new Frame(run2, .1f);
Frame f3 = new Frame(run3, .1f);
Frame f4 = new Frame(run4, .1f);
Frame f5 = new Frame(run5, .1f);
runAnim = new Animation(f1, f2, f3, f4, f5, f3, f2);
```

The completed **Resources** class is provided in listing 6.08 (double-check your imports, making sure that the imported **Frame** class is from OUR framework, NOT from Java's AWT package):

Listing 6.08   The **Resources** Class (Completed)

```
01 package com.jamescho.game.main;
02
03 import java.applet.Applet;
04 import java.applet.AudioClip;
05 import java.awt.Color;
06 import java.awt.image.BufferedImage;
07 import java.net.URL;
08
09 import javax.imageio.ImageIO;
10
11 import com.jamescho.framework.animation.Animation;
12 import com.jamescho.framework.animation.Frame;
13
14 public class Resources {
15     public static BufferedImage welcome, iconimage, block, cloud1, cloud2,
16                         duck, grass, jump, run1, run2, run3, run4, run5, selector;
17     public static AudioClip hit, onjump;
18     public static Color skyBlue;
19     public static Animation runAnim;
20
21     public static void load() {
22             welcome = loadImage("welcome.png");
23             iconimage = loadImage("iconimage.png");
24             block = loadImage("block.png");
25             cloud1 = loadImage("cloud1.png");
26             cloud2 = loadImage("cloud2.png");
27             duck = loadImage("duck.png");
28             grass = loadImage("grass.png");
29             jump = loadImage("jump.png");
30             run1 = loadImage("run_anim1.png");
31             run2 = loadImage("run_anim2.png");
32             run3 = loadImage("run_anim3.png");
33             run4 = loadImage("run_anim4.png");
34             run5 = loadImage("run_anim5.png");
35             selector = loadImage("selector.png");
36             hit = loadSound("hit.wav");
```

```
37              onjump = loadSound("onjump.wav");
38              skyBlue = new Color(208, 244, 247);
39
40              Frame f1 = new Frame(run1, .1f);
41              Frame f2 = new Frame(run2, .1f);
42              Frame f3 = new Frame(run3, .1f);
43              Frame f4 = new Frame(run4, .1f);
44              Frame f5 = new Frame(run5, .1f);
45              runAnim = new Animation(f1, f2, f3, f4, f5, f3, f2);
46      }
47
48      public static AudioClip loadSound(String filename){
49              URL fileURL = Resources.class.getResource("/resources/" + filename);
50              return Applet.newAudioClip(fileURL);
51      }
52
53      public static BufferedImage loadImage(String filename){
54          BufferedImage img = null;
55          try {
56              img = ImageIO.read(Resources.class.getResource("/resources/" + filename));
57          } catch (Exception e) {
58              System.out.println("Error while reading: " + filename);
59              e.printStackTrace();
60          }
61          return img;
62      }
63 }
```

Now that our resources have been loaded, let's run the game once more to see the changes (note the new welcome screen and icon image):

Figure 6-11   Ellio Welcome Screen

We've finished setting up our framework! Now, it's time to start adding our game's three model classes. I will be repeating much of the design and implementation process from

Chapter 5. I will only be going into depth to explain important and novel concepts, with the assumption that you are familiar with the overall process for creating model classes.

Designing and Implementing the Player

We will get started right away by designing and implementing the most important class in *Ellio*: the **Player** class. Before we write any code, it's best if we understand exactly what we want the **Player** object to do. As you read these descriptions, try to predict which variables and methods we will be creating (some have been written for you).

Describing the Properties and Behavior

<u>Basics</u>: We want the player to have a position (x and y) and dimensions (width and height).

<u>Jumping</u>: When the spacebar is pressed, we want our **Player** object to jump. This requires that we have a velY variable that will be changed to a negative value (to go upwards) when a spacebar press is detected.

<u>Ducking</u>: When the down arrow key is pressed, we want our **Player** object to duck. In *Ellio*, ducking is limited to a certain duration to emphasis the precise timing of jumps and ducks.

<u>Collision</u>: Upon getting hit by a block, the player should get knocked back. Once the player is no longer visible, the game is considered to be over.

To check for collisions in Chapter 5, we created a single bounding rectangle for each object on the screen. This time, we will be making two different sized rectangles as shown in Figure 6-12.

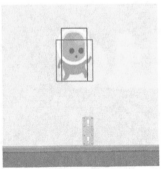

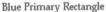
Blue Primary Rectangle   Red Duck Rectangle

Figure 6-12   Primary Rectangle and Duck Rectangle

The proposed use of the two rectangles is due to the fact that our character's dimensions change as he jumps and ducks. Rather than creating one rectangle and constantly changing its width and height, we will implement two rectangles. The blue primary rectangle shown in Figure 6-12 will be used to check for collision when the player is standing still (running) or jumping. The red rectangle will be used to check for collision when the player is ducking.

Update: Our **Player** object's update() method has many responsibilities. Two of these may be of interest.

- As mentioned before, we want Ellio to duck for a limited duration before standing up again. This behavior will be implemented inside the update() method.
- Since Ellio can jump, we need to have some sort of gravity to bring Ellio back to the ground. This will also be implemented inside the update() method.

Creating the Player Class and Its Variables

Inside the package com.jamescho.game.model, create the **Player** class. Declare the variables that we will be using, and initialize the variables inside the constructor as shown in listing 6.09 (remember to import any classes you use):

Listing 6.09   The **Player** Class (Variables and Constructor)

```
01      package com.jamescho.game.model;
02
03      import java.awt.Rectangle;
04
05      public class Player {
06              private float x, y;
07              private int width, height, velY;
08              private Rectangle rect, duckRect, ground;
09
10              private boolean isAlive;
11              private boolean isDucked;
12              private float duckDuration = .6f;
13
14              private static final int JUMP_VELOCITY = -600;
15              private static final int ACCEL_GRAVITY = 1800;
16
17              public Player(float x, float y, int width, int height) {
18                      this.x = x;
19                      this.y = y;
20                      this.width = width;
21                      this.height = height;
22
23                      ground = new Rectangle(0, 405, 800, 45);
24                      rect = new Rectangle();
25                      duckRect = new Rectangle();
26                      isAlive = true;
27                      isDucked = false;
28                      updateRects(); // This will give an error.
29              }
30
31              // More Methods
32
33      }
```

Note: Once you have created the class as shown, you will get an error regarding `updateRects()`. Ignore this for now. We will soon create this method to set the initial positions for `rect` and `duckRect`.

You've encountered most of **Player**'s variables before. The variables `x`, `y`, `width`, `height` and `velY` handle the player's position and movement. We declare `x` and `y` to be floats here, so that we can allow the player to have a decimal value as its velocity. This is important because we will soon be scaling our velocity value with the delta value to accomplish framerate-independent movement.

The **Rectangle** objects `rect` and `duckRect` represent the primary and duck rectangles from Figure 6-12. For later convenience, we create a third **Rectangle** called `ground`, which represents the bounding rectangle for the grass, which is located at (x= 0, y = 405) with a width and height of 800 and 45, respectively (see Figure 6-1). By creating this third **Rectangle**, we can easily determine if the player is standing on the ground. This tells us if the player should be able to jump (or duck).

As its name suggests, the `isAlive` boolean will keep track of whether the player is alive. Once this value becomes false, the **PlayState** will act by finishing the game and transitioning to the **GameOverState**.

The `isDucked` boolean works in conjunction with the `duckDuration` variable. When the player presses the down arrow key, `isDucked` will become true, and `duckDuration` (which is .6 seconds), will begin to decrement in every frame. Once .6 seconds have passed (when `duckDuration` is zero), we reset `duckDuration` to .6, and we tell the player to stand up by setting `isDucked` back to false.

To handle jumping, we employ a simple technique. When the player presses the spacebar, we send the player upwards by setting the `velY` to a negative value. To apply gravity, we accelerate `velY` (make its value more positive) on every frame. This results in the player moving up quickly, slowing down and falling back down again.

The two constants `JUMP_VELOCITY` and `ACCEL_GRAVITY` will be used to determine how high the player jumps and how fast the player falls down. The `ACCEL_GRAVITY` is the amount by which the `JUMP_VELOCITY` will be increased in every second. The values -600 and 1800 have been determined experimentally. Feel free to do your own experimenting with these values later until the game feels right for you!

Adding the Methods

The **Player** class needs methods for updating the **Player**'s position, updating the position of the rectangles, performing a jump, performing a duck, and handling collision. The methods shown below will implement these behaviors. Add them to the **Player** class:

```java
public void update(float delta) {

        if (duckDuration > 0 && isDucked) {
            duckDuration -= delta;
```

```
        } else {
                isDucked = false;
                duckDuration = .6f;
        }

        if (!isGrounded()) {
                velY += ACCEL_GRAVITY * delta;
        } else {
                y = 406 - height;
                velY = 0;
        }

        y += velY * delta;
        updateRects();
}

public void updateRects() {
        rect.setBounds(x + 10, y, width - 20, height); // Should have an error
        duckRect.setBounds(x, y + 20, width, height - 20); // Should have an error
}

public void jump() {
        if (isGrounded()) {
                Resources.onjump.play();
                isDucked = false;
                duckDuration = .6f;
                y -= 10;
                velY = JUMP_VELOCITY;
                updateRects();
        }
}

public void duck() {
        if (isGrounded()) {
                isDucked = true;
        }
}

public void pushBack(int dX) {
        Resources.hit.play();
        x -= dX;
        if (x < -width / 2) {
                isAlive = false;
        }
        rect.setBounds((int) x, (int) y, width, height);
}

public boolean isGrounded() {
        return rect.intersects(ground);
}
```

When the five methods have been added as shown above, you will have an error inside your updateRects() method as shown in Figure 6-13. Ignore this, and we will discuss it later.

```
public void updateRects() {
    rect.setBounds(x + 10, y, width - 20, height); // Should have an error
    duckR
}                 The method setBounds(int, int, int, int) in the type Rectangle is not applicable for the arguments (float, float,
                  int, int)

public vo                                                                                        Press 'F2' for focus
    if (isGrounded()) {
```

Figure 6-13   Error in updateRects()

Discussing the update() and isGrounded()methods:

You may notice that the update() method is different from those found in Chapters 5. This is because it has accepts parameter called delta, which it will be receiving from the **PlayState** class. In the first if-statement of the update() method, we check if the player is ducked and decrement duckDuration if necessary.

Next, we check if the player is in the middle of a jump by checking if the value of isGrounded() returns false (the isGrounded() method, as shown, returns true if the primary rectangle rect collides with the ground rectangle)! If the player is in the air—i.e. not grounded—we apply gravity.

With velocity updated, we update our player's y-position. Note that we must scale velY by delta in order to calculate the *true velocity* as determined by the amount of time that has passed since the previous iteration of update(). This is how we are able to implement *framerate-independent movement* for our character!

Discussing the updateRects() Method:

At the end of update()—more generally, whenever the player's position variables have been modified, we must call the updateRects() method to update the position of our bounding rectangles.

Refer to the error message shown in Figure 6-13. Right now, the compiler is getting angry because the setBounds() method inside the **Rectangle** class requests four integer values, but you have allegedly provided a combination of floats and integers.

Casting a Value

As we've learned in Chapter 1, adding an integer to a float results in a float. As such, x + 10 is not a valid integer input.

There are a couple of ways of converting a float into an integer, and the simplest way is shown in bold in the following example:

```
rect.setBounds((int) x + 10, (int) y, width - 20, height);
```

The addition of (int) in front of a float value or variable allows you to convert it into an integer. This process is called *casting* and has the effect of flooring (or rounding down) a float value to the nearest lesser integer value.

As a rule, casting is necessary when you have a chance of losing precision or information. In the case of converting a float—say 3.14—into the integer 3, you would lose two decimal points of precision. You must acknowledge this risk by explicitly adding (int). When converting from an integer to a float, however, casting is not necessary. Converting from the integer 3 to the float 3.00 does not result in a loss of precision, so you are safe from data loss. You do not have to add (float).

Now that you know how to cast a float into an integer, fix the errors inside your updateRects() method. If you get stuck, the solution is shown below, with the changes in bold:

```
public void updateRects() {
        rect.setBounds((int) x + 10, (int) y, width - 20, height);
        duckRect.setBounds((int) x, (int) y + 20, width, height - 20);
}
```

Note: Casting a variable does not change the variable's original value; it simply creates a new, modified copy. Consider the following:
```
float pi = 3.14f;
int rottenPi = (int) pi;
```
If you were to execute those two lines of code, the value of pi would remain 3.14f. The value of rottenPi would be 3 (casting always rounds down to the nearest lesser integer value).

Discussing the duck(), jump() and pushBack() Methods

Let's finish up our discussion of the methods by talking about the remaining methods.

The duck() method is very simple. It checks if Ellio is currently grounded. If he's not grounded, this means that he is in a state of jump, thus we do nothing. If he is grounded, we set the boolean isDucked to true. Throughout gameplay **PlayState** will access this value to determine which image to draw for our **Player** (ducked, running or jumping).

The method jump() will be called when the player presses the spacebar. To make Ellio jump, the method first checks if Ellio isGrounded() before sending him upwards. When jumping, we change isDucked to false and reset the duckDuration to indicate that the player is no longer ducking.

The pushBack() method, called when Ellio collides with a block, accepts a parameter called dX. This dX value is the amount of pixels by which the player should get knocked back on collision. After the knockback, if we determine that more than half of the player is off of the screen, we set isAlive to false, signaling to the **PlayState** that the game is over.

Adding the Getters

To finish the **Player** class, we just have to provide public getter methods so that our **PlayState** can access our **Player** object's variables for rendering and collision detection, among other tasks. Add the following getter methods to your **Player** class:

```
public boolean isDucked() {
        return isDucked;
```

```
        }

        public float getX() {
                return x;
        }

        public float getY() {
                return y;
        }

        public int getWidth() {
                return width;
        }

        public int getHeight() {
                return height;
        }

        public int getVelY() {
                return velY;
        }

        public Rectangle getRect() {
                return rect;
        }

        public Rectangle getDuckRect() {
                return duckRect;
        }

        public Rectangle getGround() {
                return ground;
        }

        public boolean isAlive() {
                return isAlive;
        }

        public float getDuckDuration() {
                return duckDuration;
        }
```

The completed **Player** class is provided in listing 6.10.

Listing 6.10   The **Player** Class (Completed)

```
001 package com.jamescho.game.model;
002
003 import java.awt.Rectangle;
004
005 public class Player {
006     private float x, y;
007     private int width, height, velY;
008     private Rectangle rect, duckRect, ground;
009
010     private boolean isAlive;
011     private boolean isDucked;
012     private float duckDuration = .6f;
```

```
013
014        private static final int JUMP_VELOCITY = -600;
015        private static final int ACCEL_GRAVITY = 1800;
016
017        public Player(float x, float y, int width, int height) {
018                this.x = x;
019                this.y = y;
020                this.width = width;
021                this.height = height;
022
023                ground = new Rectangle(0, 405, 800, 45);
024                rect = new Rectangle();
025                duckRect = new Rectangle();
026                isAlive = true;
027                isDucked = false;
028                updateRects();
029        }
030
031        public void update(float delta) {
032
033                if (duckDuration > 0 && isDucked) {
034                        duckDuration -= delta;
035                } else {
036                        isDucked = false;
037                        duckDuration = .6f;
038                }
039
040                if (!isGrounded()) {
041                        velY += ACCEL_GRAVITY * delta;
042                } else {
043                        y = 406 - height;
044                        velY = 0;
045                }
046
047                y += velY * delta;
048                updateRects();
049        }
050
051        public void updateRects() {
052                rect.setBounds((int)x + 10, (int)y, width - 20, height);
053                duckRect.setBounds((int)x, (int)y + 20, width, height - 20);
054        }
055
056        public void jump() {
057                if (isGrounded()) {
058                        Resources.onjump.play();
059                        isDucked = false;
060                        duckDuration = .6f;
061                        y -= 10;
062                        velY = JUMP_VELOCITY;
063                        updateRects();
064                }
065        }
066
067        public void duck() {
068                if (isGrounded()) {
069                        isDucked = true;
070                }
071        }
```

```
072
073         public void pushBack(int dX) {
074                 Resources.hit.play();
075                 x -= dX;
076                 if (x < -width / 2) {
077                         isAlive = false;
078                 }
079                 rect.setBounds((int) x, (int) y, width, height);
080         }
081
082         public boolean isGrounded() {
083                 return rect.intersects(ground);
084         }
085
086         public boolean isDucked() {
087                 return isDucked;
088         }
089
090         public float getX() {
091                 return x;
092         }
093
094         public float getY() {
095                 return y;
096         }
097
098         public int getWidth() {
099                 return width;
100         }
101
102         public int getHeight() {
103                 return height;
104         }
105
106         public int getVelY() {
107                 return velY;
108         }
109
110         public Rectangle getRect() {
111                 return rect;
112         }
113
114         public Rectangle getDuckRect() {
115                 return duckRect;
116         }
117
118         public Rectangle getGround() {
119                 return ground;
120         }
121
122         public boolean isAlive() {
123                 return isAlive;
124         }
125
126         public float getDuckDuration() {
127                 return duckDuration;
128         }
129 }
```

Designing and Implementing the Cloud

Refer to Figure 6-1, and you will notice two beautiful cloud images in the background. These are there to help create a sense of depth in our game (and for aesthetic purposes). When coupled with the unmoving sun (also shown in Figure 6-1), the slow-moving clouds will add a layer of immersion.

Note: This is a simple implementation of *parallax scrolling*, which creates an illusion of depth in a 2D game by scrolling objects closer to the camera at a faster speed than objects farther away.

These clouds will need to be represented at some position and will also be moving left (you should be thinking about the variables we will be creating). When the clouds have scrolled off of the screen, we will reset their positions to the right, so that they can scroll back onto the screen.

Following this description, the implementation of the **Cloud** class is very simple. Create the **Cloud** class inside com.jamescho.game.model, and implement it as shown in Listing 6.11 (paying attention to the import statement).

Listing 6.11   The **Cloud** Class (Completed)

```
package com.jamescho.game.model;

import com.jamescho.framework.util.RandomNumberGenerator;

public class Cloud {
        private float x, y;
        private static final int VEL_X = -15;

        public Cloud(float x, float y) {
                this.x = x;
                this.y = y;
        }

        public void update(float delta) {
                x += VEL_X * delta;

                if (x <= -200) {
                        // Reset to the right
                        x += 1000;
                        y = RandomNumberGenerator.getRandIntBetween(20, 100);
                }
        }

        public float getX() {
                return x;
        }

        public float getY() {
                return y;
        }
```

```
}
```

The **Cloud** class's update() method accepts a delta value, as did the update() method inside **Player**. This allows us to incorporate framerate-independent movement for our clouds. This may seem pointless (the game won't break if the cloud speed is dependent on framerate), but people do notice these details when playing games, and you should always provide care even for the small details.

Note that when the cloud is no longer visible, we reset it by sending it an arbitrary 1000 pixels to the right and giving a random y-position. Once reset, the cloud will continue to scroll left, appearing on the screen again as a "new" cloud and disappearing to the left to repeat this process. This is object-reuse at work.

Designing and Implementing the Block Class

The logic behind the **Block** class will be slightly more complicated than that behind the **Cloud** class, but not by much. **Block** will share many properties of **Cloud**, such as position. Each **Block** object will behave similarly to the **Cloud** objects, scrolling to the left and resetting to the right. Upon resetting, we will use our **RandomNumberGenerator** class to determine whether the **Block** should be an upper block (to be avoided by ducking) or a lower block (to be avoided by jumping).

One thing that a **Block** object can do that a **Cloud** object cannot do, however, is collide with the player. We will create a bounding rectangle (just like we did for our **Ball** in *LoneBall*), and use this to check for collision with the bounding rectangle of the **Player**. This logic will be handled inside the **PlayState**.

In our game, it is very important that all of the **Block** objects work together. As such, the velocity value used inside the update() method will be passed in from the **PlayState** to ensure that every **Block** object has the same speed.

Create the **Block** class inside com.jamescho.game.model as shown in listing 6.12.

Listing 6.12   The **Block** Class (Completed)

```
01 package com.jamescho.game.model;
02
03 import java.awt.Rectangle;
04
05 import com.jamescho.framework.util.RandomNumberGenerator;
06
07 public class Block {
08     private float x, y;
09     private int width, height;
10     private Rectangle rect;
11     private boolean visible;
12
13     private static final int UPPER_Y = 275;
```

```
14        private static final int LOWER_Y = 355;
15
16        public Block(float x, float y, int width, int height) {
17                this.x = x;
18                this.y = y;
19                this.width = width;
20                this.height = height;
21                rect = new Rectangle((int) x, (int) y, width, height);
22                visible = false;
23        }
24
25        // Note: Velocity value will be passed in from PlayState!
26        public void update(float delta, float velX) {
27                x += velX * delta;
28                if (x <= -50) {
29                        reset();
30                }
31                updateRect();
32        }
33
34        public void updateRect() {
35                rect.setBounds((int) x, (int) y, width, height);
36        }
37
38        public void reset() {
39                visible = true;
40                // 1 in 3 chance of becoming an Upper Block
41                if (RandomNumberGenerator.getRandInt(3) == 0) {
42                        y = UPPER_Y;
43                } else {
44                        y = LOWER_Y;
45                }
46
47                        x += 1000;
48        }
49
50        public void onCollide(Player p) {
51                visible = false;
52                p.pushBack(30);
53        }
54
55        public float getX() {
56                return x;
57        }
58
59        public float getY() {
60                return y;
61        }
62
63        public boolean isVisible() {
64                return visible;
65        }
66
67        public Rectangle getRect() {
68                return rect;
69        }
70
71 }
```

The **Block** class in listing 6.12 represents a standard game object with a position and dimensions. There are not many surprises here, but I will make a few comments regarding the details of the implementation.

Resetting: As we've done with **Cloud**, we incorporate delta inside our update() method and reset when our block leaves the screen, which we consider to be when x <= -50. This value ensures that, in the case the player is hanging on for dear life at edge of the left side of the screen like shown in Figure 6-14, the block does not reset too early after leaving the screen and make dodging easier for the player.

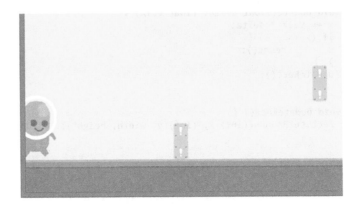

Figure 6-14   Don't Reset Too Early!

Each block is reset by moving a 1000 pixels to the right. This value is NOT arbitrary. In *Ellio*, we will create five **Block** objects that are evenly spaced out (each **Block** object will be 200 pixels away from another, as shown in Figure 6-15).

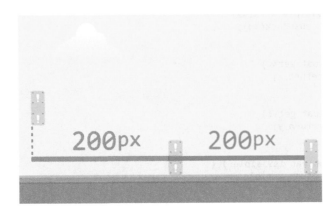

Figure 6-15   **Block** Objects are Evenly Spaced (200px)

Once a block is no longer visible, it will be recycled by being sent to the right, creating the illusion that there is an endless chain of blocks. This means that to maintain this even spacing, each block has to reset 1000 pixels to the right of its current position once it leaves the left side of the screen. (If block 1 is at -50, block 2 is at 150, block 3 is at 350, block 4 is at 550 and block 5 is at 750. This means that block 1 should reset at 950 (+1000) to set a 200 pixel gap with block 5).

<u>Colliding:</u> When the player collides with a block, the player should get knocked back 30 pixels. We do this by calling the pushBack() method of the **Player** object. Once this happens, the block that has sent the player away should probably not collide with the player again.

There are many ways of implementing this behavior. One way would be to take the traditional approach found in many old platformers: make the player blink and become immune to damage for a short period of time. The way *Ellio* will handle this is by making the block invisible (so that it cannot damage the player multiple times). For this purpose, we have created a boolean variable called visible, which will become false on collision and true on reset.

Our three model classes have been designed and fully implemented! All that is left is for us to implement the state classes.

Note: If you are having problems with any of the classes at this point, you can download the source code at jamescho7.com/book/chapter6/checkpoint3.

Designing and Implementing the Supporting State Classes

The GameOverState

We will design and implement the easiest state first. The **GameOverState** will be a simple score screen, as shown in Figure 6-16.

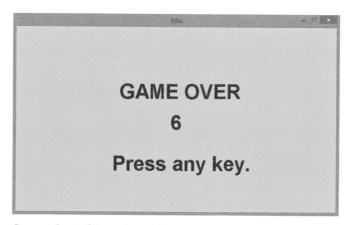

Figure 6-16   Screenshot of **GameOverState**

The **GameOverState** will be created inside the **PlayState** when the player loses the game. As such, we are able to create a custom constructor for it and pass in the player's score during the transition. This is how we can access a value created in one state from another state!

Create the **GameOverState** class inside the com.jamescho.game.state package. Extend **State** (**com.jamescho.game.state.State**), and add the unimplemented methods. Your **GameOverState** should now look like this:

```java
package com.jamescho.game.state;

import java.awt.Graphics;
import java.awt.event.KeyEvent;
import java.awt.event.MouseEvent;

public class GameOverState extends State {

    @Override
    public void init() {
        // TODO Auto-generated method stub
    }

    @Override
    public void update(float delta) {
        // TODO Auto-generated method stub
    }

    @Override
    public void render(Graphics g) {
        // TODO Auto-generated method stub
    }

    @Override
    public void onClick(MouseEvent e) {
        // TODO Auto-generated method stub
    }

    @Override
    public void onKeyPress(KeyEvent e) {
        // TODO Auto-generated method stub
    }

    @Override
    public void onKeyRelease(KeyEvent e) {
        // TODO Auto-generated method stub
    }

}
```

We will need to create two new variables: one for the score and one for the font. Declare them as shown, importing java.awt.Font:

```java
private String playerScore;
private Font font;
```

Initialize these in a custom constructor as shown below. Notice that the following constructor accepts a `playerScore` integer. As mentioned, This will be passed in from the **PlayState** as **GameOverState** is constructed.

```java
public GameOverState(int playerScore) {
        this.playerScore = playerScore + ""; // Convert int to String
        font = new Font("SansSerif", Font.BOLD, 50);
}
```

Next, we will use these two variables to display the score to the screen, along with some additional information. Add the code shown below to your `render()` method (importing `java.awt.Color` and `com.jamescho.game.main.GameMain`):

```java
@Override
public void render(Graphics g) {
        g.setColor(Color.ORANGE);
        g.fillRect(0, 0, GameMain.GAME_WIDTH, GameMain.GAME_HEIGHT);
        g.setColor(Color.DARK_GRAY);
        g.setFont(font);
        g.drawString("GAME OVER", 257, 175);
        g.drawString(playerScore, 385, 250);
        g.drawString("Press any key.", 240, 350);
}
```

Finally, we update the `onKeyPress()` method, so that any key press will take us to the **MenuState**:

```java
@Override
public void onKeyPress(KeyEvent e) {
        setCurrentState(new MenuState());
}
```

The completed **GameOverState** class is shown in listing 6.13.

Listing 6.13   The **GameOverState** Class (Completed)

```java
01 package com.jamescho.game.state;
02
03 import java.awt.Color;
04 import java.awt.Font;
05 import java.awt.Graphics;
06 import java.awt.event.KeyEvent;
07 import java.awt.event.MouseEvent;
08
09 import com.jamescho.game.main.GameMain;
10
11 public class GameOverState extends State {
12
13     private String playerScore;
14     private Font font;
15
16     public GameOverState(int playerScore) {
```

```
17              this.playerScore = playerScore + ""; // Convert int to String
18              font = new Font("SansSerif", Font.BOLD, 50);
19      }
20
21      @Override
22      public void init() {
23              // TODO Auto-generated method stub
24      }
25
26      @Override
27      public void update(float delta) {
28              // TODO Auto-generated method stub
29      }
30
31      @Override
32      public void render(Graphics g) {
33              g.setColor(Color.ORANGE);
34              g.fillRect(0, 0, GameMain.GAME_WIDTH, GameMain.GAME_HEIGHT);
35              g.setColor(Color.DARK_GRAY);
36              g.setFont(font);
37              g.drawString("GAME OVER", 257, 175);
38              g.drawString(playerScore, 385, 250);
39              g.drawString("Press any key.", 240, 350);
40      }
41
42      @Override
43      public void onClick(MouseEvent e) {
44              // TODO Auto-generated method stub
45      }
46
47      @Override
48      public void onKeyPress(KeyEvent e) {
49              setCurrentState(new MenuState());
50      }
51
52      @Override
53      public void onKeyRelease(KeyEvent e) {
54              // TODO Auto-generated method stub
55      }
56
57 }
```

The MenuState

As shown in Figure 6-8, we will be implementing a selection arrow in our menu screen to allow the player to either play the game or exit. This creates a fancy effect, but the code behind it is pretty simple.

To represent the currently selected option (PLAY or EXIT), we will create an integer called currentSelection and initialize it with a value of zero. When the player presses the up and down arrow keys, the value of currentSelection will move between 0 and 1 (0 for up, 1 for down).

The value of currentSelection will be used to determine where the selection arrow image will be drawn on every frame. If currentSelection has a value of zero, we will draw the arrow next to the PLAY button. If the currentSelection has a value of one, we will draw the arrow next to the EXIT button.

When the player presses the spacebar or the enter key, we will check the currentSelection to perform the selected action. For PLAY this will involve transitioning to the soon-to-be-created **PlayState**. For EXIT we will be calling our Game's exit() method to terminate the game loop and the **JFrame**.

Open your **MenuState** class inside com.jamescho.game.state, and modify it as shown in in listing 6.14 to fully implement the behavior described. Changes should be made to the import statements, the init(), render() and onKeyPress() methods.

Listing 6.14   The **MenuState** Class (Completed)

```
01 package com.jamescho.game.state;
02
03 import java.awt.Graphics;
04 import java.awt.event.KeyEvent;
05 import java.awt.event.MouseEvent;
06
07 import com.jamescho.game.main.GameMain;
08 import com.jamescho.game.main.Resources;
09
10 public class MenuState extends State{
11
12     private int currentSelection = 0;
13
14     @Override
15     public void init() {
16         // Do Nothing
17     }
18
19     @Override
20     public void update(float delta){
21         // Do Nothing
22     }
23
24     @Override
25     public void render(Graphics g) {
26         g.drawImage(Resources.welcome, 0, 0, null);
27         if (currentSelection == 0) {
28             g.drawImage(Resources.selector, 335, 241, null);
29         } else {
30             g.drawImage(Resources.selector, 335, 291, null);
31         }
32     }
33
34     @Override
35     public void onClick(MouseEvent e) {
36         // Do Nothing
37     }
38
39     @Override
40     public void onKeyPress(KeyEvent e) {
41         int key = e.getKeyCode();
42
```

```
43                    if (key == KeyEvent.VK_SPACE || key == KeyEvent.VK_ENTER) {
44                        if (currentSelection == 0) {
45                            setCurrentState(new PlayState());
46                        } else if (currentSelection == 1) {
47                            GameMain.sGame.exit();
48                        }
49                    } else if (key == KeyEvent.VK_UP) {
50                        currentSelection = 0;
51                    } else if (key == KeyEvent.VK_DOWN) {
52                        currentSelection = 1;
53                    }
54
55        }
56
57        @Override
58        public void onKeyRelease(KeyEvent e) {
59                // Do Nothing
60        }
61
62 }
```

Designing and Implementing the PlayState

We have an error inside onKeyPress() of the **MenuState** because the **PlayState** class has not been created yet. Create this class inside the com.jamescho.game.state package. Extend **State** (com.jamescho.game.state.State), and add the unimplemented methods. Your **PlayState** should look as shown below:

```
package com.jamescho.game.state;

import java.awt.Graphics;
import java.awt.event.KeyEvent;
import java.awt.event.MouseEvent;

public class PlayState extends State{

        @Override
        public void init() {
                // TODO Auto-generated method stub
        }

        @Override
        public void update(float delta) {
                // TODO Auto-generated method stub
        }

        @Override
        public void render(Graphics g) {
                // TODO Auto-generated method stub
        }

        @Override
        public void onClick(MouseEvent e) {
                // TODO Auto-generated method stub
```

```
        }

        @Override
        public void onKeyPress(KeyEvent e) {
                // TODO Auto-generated method stub
        }

        @Override
        public void onKeyRelease(KeyEvent e) {
                // TODO Auto-generated method stub
        }

}
```

The Variables of PlayState

Being the game's core state, the **PlayState** needs to have many variables. Declare them as shown below (I will not explicitly tell you what classes to import throughout this section! Practice doing this on your own):

```
private Player player;
private ArrayList<Block> blocks;
private Cloud cloud, cloud2;

private Font scoreFont;
private int playerScore = 0;

private static final int BLOCK_HEIGHT = 50;
private static final int BLOCK_WIDTH = 20;
private int blockSpeed = -200;

private static final int PLAYER_WIDTH = 66;
private static final int PLAYER_HEIGHT = 92;
```

The purpose of these variables are indicated by their nomenclature. Study it carefully. Note that we have an ArrayList of Blocks rather than five Block variables. If you need a refresher on ArrayLists, please see Chapter 2's discussion (page 66)!

Note: A game's difficulty should not be static. By making the blockSpeed faster (making it more negative), we will be making our game harder with time. Rather than having some kind of timer, however, we will simply increment the playerScore variable by 1 on every frame and use this value to determine the difficulty. Every 500 frames (that is, when playerScore is divisible by 500), we will make the blocks move faster.

Initializing the Variables

Initialize the newly-created variables by making the following changes to your init() method:

```
@Override
public void init() {
```

```
player = new Player(160, GameMain.GAME_HEIGHT - 45 - PLAYER_HEIGHT,
                         PLAYER_WIDTH, PLAYER_HEIGHT);
blocks = new ArrayList<Block>();
cloud = new Cloud(100, 100);
cloud2 = new Cloud(500, 50);
scoreFont = new Font("SansSerif", Font.BOLD, 25);

for (int i = 0; i < 5; i++) {
        Block b = new Block(i * 200, GameMain.GAME_HEIGHT - 95,
                         BLOCK_WIDTH, BLOCK_HEIGHT);
        blocks.add(b);
    }
}
```

The initialization of the variables is straightforward, so I will leave you to study the method on your own. Note that the (x, y) coordinates have been experimentally determined. If you get stuck with the for loop, try to figure out how many times the for loop would run, and determine what the (x, y) coordinates of each new **Block** object will be. You should see a pattern in the x values. (Hint see Figure 6-15).

Adding User Input

Recall that *Ellio* will feature a 2-button control scheme. This is easy to add! Change your onKeyPress() method, so that it looks like this:

```
@Override
public void onKeyPress(KeyEvent e) {
        if (e.getKeyCode() == KeyEvent.VK_SPACE) {
                player.jump();
        } else if (e.getKeyCode() == KeyEvent.VK_DOWN) {
                player.duck();
        }
}
```

Updating the PlayState

Now that we have initialized our variables, we must update them in every frame. Look at the code below, and make the changes shown to your update() method:

```
@Override
public void update(float delta) {
        if (!player.isAlive()) {
                setCurrentState(new GameOverState(playerScore / 100));
        }
        playerScore += 1;
        if (playerScore % 500 == 0 && blockSpeed > -280) {
                blockSpeed -= 10;
        }

        cloud.update(delta);
        cloud2.update(delta);
        Resources.runAnim.update(delta);
        player.update(delta);
        updateBlocks(delta); // Should give an error
}
```

Ignore the error regarding `updateBlocks()` for now. You will find that the `update()` method is very simple. We check if the player is dead, increment the score, make the `blockSpeed` faster (given some conditions are met) and update the game objects.

One thing you are seeing for the first time is the **Animation** (`Resources.runAnim`) being updated. By passing in delta into the animation's `update()` method, it begins to iterate through its frames. If we call this method on every frame, requesting `Resources.runAnim` to render will draw the correct frame later on.

We will create a separate `updateBlocks()` method, because it requires multiple steps. Add this method to your code:

```
private void updateBlocks(float delta) {
    for (Block b : blocks) {
        b.update(delta, blockSpeed);

        if (b.isVisible()) {
            if (player.isDucked() && b.getRect().intersects(player.getDuckRect())) {
                    b.onCollide(player);
            } else if (!player.isDucked() && b.getRect().intersects(player.getRect())) {
                    b.onCollide(player);
            }
        }
    }
}
```

Note: The syntax shown in the previous example is called a foreach loop:

```
for (Blocks b: blocks) {
    ....
}
```

It iterates through every element inside block one at a time. It is equivalent to the following:

```
for (int i = 0; i < blocks.size(); i++) {
    Block b = blocks.get(i);
    ....
}
```

Inside the `updateBlocks()` method, we use a foreach loop to iterate through every **Block** object inside the **ArrayList blocks**. Each **Block** is thus updated. Note that we pass in the same `blockSpeed` to every **Block** object for reasons discussed during its implementation.

After updating the blocks, we check if any of them collide with the player. Collision is only possible in one of two conditions, given that the block is visible (Start with this general case. There is no need to check for collision if the block is invisible. Doing this minimizes the CPU's workload as per our discussion on optimization!):

  o If the player is ducked and his **Rectangle** duckRect intersects the block
  o If the player is not ducked and his **Rectangle** rect intersects the block.

If collision is detected, we simply call `b.onCollide(player)`.

Rendering the PlayState

After updating every game object, we must render them to the screen at the appropriate location. Add the following code to `render()`:

```java
@Override
public void render(Graphics g) {
        g.setColor(Resources.skyBlue);
        g.fillRect(0, 0, GameMain.GAME_WIDTH, GameMain.GAME_HEIGHT);
        renderPlayer(g);
        renderBlocks(g);
        renderSun(g);
        renderClouds(g);
        g.drawImage(Resources.grass, 0, 405, null);
        renderScore(g);
}
```

Rather than calling all of the individual render and draw calls inside one method, we split things into smaller chunks. Add these new methods below your render method:

```java
private void renderScore(Graphics g) {
    g.setFont(scoreFont);
    g.setColor(Color.GRAY);
    g.drawString("" + playerScore / 100, 20, 30);
}

private void renderPlayer(Graphics g) {
    if (player.isGrounded()) {
        if (player.isDucked()) {
            g.drawImage(Resources.duck, (int) player.getX(),(int) player.getY(), null);
        } else {
            Resources.runAnim.render(g, (int) player.getX(),(int) player.getY(),
                    player.getWidth(),player.getHeight());
        }
    } else {
        g.drawImage(Resources.jump, (int) player.getX(),
                (int) player.getY(), player.getWidth(), player.getHeight(),null);
    }
}

private void renderBlocks(Graphics g) {
    for (Block b : blocks) {
        if (b.isVisible()) {
                g.drawImage(Resources.block, (int) b.getX(), (int) b.getY(),BLOCK_WIDTH,
                        BLOCK_HEIGHT, null);
        }
    }
}

private void renderSun(Graphics g) {
    g.setColor(Color.orange);
    g.fillOval(715, -85, 170, 170);
    g.setColor(Color.yellow);
    g.fillOval(725, -75, 150, 150);
}

private void renderClouds(Graphics g) {
```

```
    g.drawImage(Resources.cloud1, (int) cloud.getX(), (int) cloud.getY(),100, 60, null);
    g.drawImage(Resources.cloud2, (int) cloud2.getX(), (int) cloud2.getY(),100, 60, null);
}
```

The full source code for PlayState is shown in listing 6.15. Walk yourself through the primary render() method and the secondary methods called by render(). You have called a vast majority of the same draw calls before, so it will be easy to understand. If you get stuck, Figure 6-1 might help answer some questions. Remember that most of the (x, y) coordinates have been experimentally or mathematically determined.

Listing 6.15   The **PlayState** Class (Completed)

```
001 package com.jamescho.game.state;
002
003 import java.awt.Color;
004 import java.awt.Font;
005 import java.awt.Graphics;
006 import java.awt.event.KeyEvent;
007 import java.awt.event.MouseEvent;
008 import java.util.ArrayList;
009
010 import com.jamescho.game.main.GameMain;
011 import com.jamescho.game.main.Resources;
012 import com.jamescho.game.model.Block;
013 import com.jamescho.game.model.Cloud;
014 import com.jamescho.game.model.Player;
015
016 public class PlayState extends State {
017
018     private Player player;
019     private ArrayList<Block> blocks;
020     private Cloud cloud, cloud2;
021     private Font scoreFont;
022     private int playerScore = 0;
023     private static final int BLOCK_HEIGHT = 50;
024     private static final int BLOCK_WIDTH = 20;
025     private int blockSpeed = -200;
026     private static final int PLAYER_WIDTH = 66;
027     private static final int PLAYER_HEIGHT = 92;
028
029     @Override
030     public void init() {
031         player = new Player(160, GameMain.GAME_HEIGHT - 45 - PLAYER_HEIGHT,
                                PLAYER_WIDTH, PLAYER_HEIGHT);
032         blocks = new ArrayList<Block>();
033         cloud = new Cloud(100, 100);
034         cloud2 = new Cloud(500, 50);
035         scoreFont = new Font("SansSerif", Font.BOLD, 25);
036         for (int i = 0; i < 5; i++) {
037             Block b = new Block(i * 200, GameMain.GAME_HEIGHT - 95,
                        BLOCK_WIDTH, BLOCK_HEIGHT);
038             blocks.add(b);
039         }
040     }
041
042     @Override
```

```
043     public void update(float delta) {
044             if (!player.isAlive()) {
045                     setCurrentState(new GameOverState(playerScore / 100));
046             }
047             playerScore += 1;
048             if (playerScore % 500 == 0 && blockSpeed > -280) {
049                     blockSpeed -= 10;
050             }
051             cloud.update(delta);
052             cloud2.update(delta);
053             Resources.runAnim.update(delta);
054             player.update(delta);
055             updateBlocks(delta);
056     }
057
058     private void updateBlocks(float delta) {
059             for (Block b : blocks) {
060                     b.update(delta, blockSpeed);
061                     if (b.isVisible()) {
062                             if (player.isDucked() &&
                                        b.getRect().intersects(player.getDuckRect())) {
063                                     b.onCollide(player);
064                             } else if (!player.isDucked() &&
                                        b.getRect().intersects(player.getRect())) {
065                                     b.onCollide(player);
066                             }
067                     }
068             }
069     }
070
071     @Override
072     public void render(Graphics g) {
073             g.setColor(Resources.skyBlue);
074             g.fillRect(0, 0, GameMain.GAME_WIDTH, GameMain.GAME_HEIGHT);
075             renderPlayer(g);
076             renderBlocks(g);
077             renderSun(g);
078             renderClouds(g);
079             g.drawImage(Resources.grass, 0, 405, null);
080             renderScore(g);
081     }
082
083     private void renderScore(Graphics g) {
084             g.setFont(scoreFont);
085             g.setColor(Color.GRAY);
086             g.drawString("" + playerScore / 100, 20, 30);
087     }
088
089     private void renderPlayer(Graphics g) {
090             if (player.isGrounded()) {
091                     if (player.isDucked()) {
092                             g.drawImage(Resources.duck, (int) player.getX(), (int)
                                        player.getY(), null);
093                     } else {
094                             Resources.runAnim.render(g, (int) player.getX(), (int)
                                    player.getY(), player.getWidth(), player.getHeight());
095                     }
096             } else {
097                     g.drawImage(Resources.jump, (int) player.getX(), (int)
```

244

```
                         player.getY(), player.getWidth(), player.getHeight(), null);
098                  }
099          }
100
101      private void renderBlocks(Graphics g) {
102              for (Block b : blocks) {
103                      if (b.isVisible()) {
104                              g.drawImage(Resources.block, (int) b.getX(), (int)
                                        b.getY(), BLOCK_WIDTH, BLOCK_HEIGHT, null);
105                      }
106              }
107      }
108
109      private void renderSun(Graphics g) {
110              g.setColor(Color.orange);
111              g.fillOval(715, -85, 170, 170);
112              g.setColor(Color.yellow);
113              g.fillOval(725, -75, 150, 150);
114      }
115
116      private void renderClouds(Graphics g) {
117              g.drawImage(Resources.cloud1, (int) cloud.getX(), (int) cloud.getY(), 100,
                          60, null);
118              g.drawImage(Resources.cloud2, (int) cloud2.getX(), (int) cloud2.getY(),
                          100, 60, null);
119      }
120
121      @Override
122      public void onClick(MouseEvent e) {
123
124      }
125
126      @Override
127      public void onKeyPress(KeyEvent e) {
128              if (e.getKeyCode() == KeyEvent.VK_SPACE) {
129                      player.jump();
130              } else if (e.getKeyCode() == KeyEvent.VK_DOWN) {
131                      player.duck();
132              }
133      }
134
135      @Override
136      public void onKeyRelease(KeyEvent e) {
137
138      }
139
140 }
```

Running the Game

With the final state in place, our game is now finished. Try running your project! If you experience errors, try to identify the problem by reading the error messages. They should tell you what went wrong in what line in what class. If you need help resolving errors, please post in the forums on the book's companion site.

Note: If you are having problems with any of the classes at this point, you can download the source code at `jamescho7.com/book/chapter6/complete`.

Another Journey Begins

Congratulations! You've reached the end of Unit 2. At this point, you are probably feeling a lot more comfortable with Java and object-oriented programming. With two games and a game development framework under your belt, I hope that you are getting some of your questions answered and beginning to see where this path leads.

You are now ready to begin Android Development. Entering this new world, you may feel a bit like Ellio on his first trip to Earth; you will be introduced to a new set of topics, some confusing Android vocabulary and lots of code that makes no sense at first sight. However, after a little bit of practice with this book as your guide, you will easily navigate these obstacles and become a successful Android game developer. So grab the nearest Android device (if you have one), and turn the page! Let's have some fun with the green robot.

Unit 3

Android Game Development

CHAPTER 7: BEGINNING ANDROID DEVELOPMENT

In the previous two units, you've studied Java and its applications. Now, it's time to jump into the world of mobile application development. This chapter introduces you to Android—the most popular mobile operating system in the world (and perhaps the very reason you are reading this book). We will be taking a break from game development to build an Android application, study its structure and learn about its fundamental components. This will prepare us for Chapters 8 and 9, in which we will apply everything that we have discussed so far to build a game on the Android platform.

Android: Same Language in a New World

Android provides hundreds of classes in its API (Application Programming Interface), allowing developers to quickly build powerful, feature-rich and user-friendly applications using the Java programming language. This means that you will feel right at home in this new world, as there's no need to learn a new programming language or get acquainted to an unfamiliar IDE; however, you will find that Android development is, well, quite different from Java development.

The Challenges of Android Development

Being an Android developer means that you have a few additional things to worry about, and most of these concerns revolve around the issue of compatibility.

Building an Android application or game, you must consider the fact that Android runs on everything from cars and smartwatches to tablets and refrigerators (really)! To make matters more complicated, devices in each of these categories come in various shapes and sizes; under the hood, they cover the whole spectrum of tech specs.

Compatibility issues don't end there. Despite the fact that Google releases timely updates for its OS, Android's open source nature and customizability means that device manufacturers and mobile network providers have the ability to heavily modify the operating system before it ends up in the hands of consumers (often infused with clunky bloatware amounting to a watered-down Android experience). As a developer, these challenges mean that that you have to write code that will run well both on older versions of Android and the new.

In recent history, Google has been making an effort to combat fragmentation by making the latest versions of Android more friendly for older devices, so the future of

Android development seems brighter. Still, the fact that device manufacturers spend their resources on building the latest devices rather than on keeping their older devices updated means that, for the foreseeable future, you will need to take your target devices' version limitations into account when building an Android application.

Note: To learn more about Android's fragmentation and the distribution of devices by version number and screen size & density, please see Android's dashboards at the following URL: `https://developer.android.com/about/dashboards/index.html`

The Joys of Android Development

I hope I didn't scare you away from Android development because, as you will soon experience, its joys far outweigh the challenges (and it's extremely fun).

The Android platform is flexible and versatile, and its apps are delightfully interactive—just as you would expect from an operating system that names its major releases after confections like ice cream sandwich. Android developers get to build event-driven applications to provide or enrich some experience for their users, who will tap and drag away with smiles on their faces when using an application that does something beneficial.

In addition, Android development has a low barrier to entry. As of this writing, all it takes is a one-time $25 USD fee to register a developer account with Google Play to begin sharing your work with the world! This means that those who are serious about building and sharing useful apps will be able to do so without breaking the bank. There are few things that are better than seeing a stranger holding a smartphone playing a game that you made. With Android, that is a real possibility.

Hello, Android: Your First Android App

Now that you have been introduced to Android, let's build our first application.

Creating a New Android Application

In Chapter 2, we downloaded the ADT Bundle, which included both Eclipse and the Android SDK. Until now, we have completely ignored the Android-components of our bundle, but no longer. Right click (Ctrl + Click on Mac) your Package Explorer, select **New** > **Other**. This should open the dialog shown in Figure 7-1.

Under the **Android** group, select **Android Application Project** and click **Next**.

Note: As new releases of Android become available, the following steps may change. If you are unable to follow along due to major differences, please consult the book's companion site, which will have the latest information: `http://jamescho7.com /book/chapter7/`

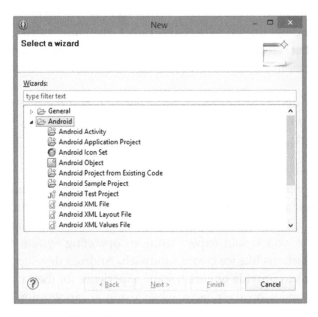

Figure 7-1   New Project Wizard

Before we fill in the values of the **New Android Application** dialog, let's talk about what they mean first.

- **Application Name** refers to the name that will be shown when you upload your project onto the Google Play Store.
- The **Project Name** will be shown in the Package Explorer for this application.
- **Package Name** should be a *unique* identifier (two applications with the same Package Name cannot be uploaded on the Play Store). The convention is to use reverse domain name notation. If you have a website at example.com, your package name should be com.example.firstapp. If you do not have a website, just use your name or an alias.
- **Minimum Required SDK** specifies the minimum version of Android that a user must have in order to install your application. This is used as a filter in the Play Store (i.e. an app with a Minimum Required SDK of 2.3 will not appear on devices that run 2.2 or below).
- **Target SDK** should specify the latest version of Android that your app is known to work with. This should be the most recent version.
- The **Compile With** option allows you to select the version of Android that you will use in Eclipse when writing your code. Each version of Android adds or removes methods and classes, so using the latest version is recommended.

Now that we know what each field is about, fill in the information as shown in Figure 7-2.

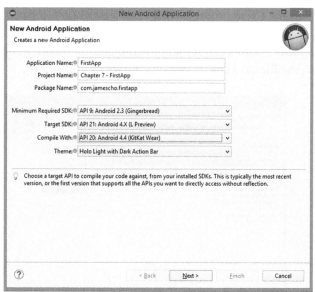

Figure 7-2   New Android Application

Note: Choose the latest version of the API for **Target SDK** and **Compile With**. At the time of writing, this is 4.4. You may have a more recent version.

Click **Next**. This should bring you to the project configuration screen (Figure 7-3)

Figure 7-3   Configuring the Android Project

Uncheck the option for **Create custom launcher icon** (I will not be showing you how to make an icon using this wizard, but if you are feeling adventurous, feel free to experiment). The other options can remain unchanged, as shown in Figure 7-3. Click **Next** again, and choose the **Blank Activity** option (shown in Figure 7-4).

Figure 7-4   Creating a Blank Activity

Hit **Next** one last time. You should see the dialog shown in Figure 7-5.

Figure 7-5   Naming the Activity and Layout

Make sure that you have the same values for the two boxes: **Activity Name** and **Layout Name** as those shown in Figure 7-5. We will talk about what each of these terms mean later!

Click **Finish**, and you should see the newly-created Android project inside your **Package Explorer** along with a project named **appcompat**. Your editor might also display a "Hello World!" application, as shown in Figure 7-6.

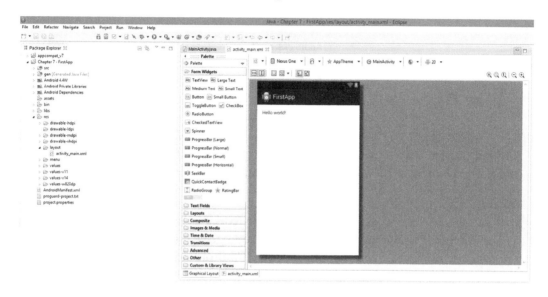

Figure 7-6   FirstApp has been Created

Exit out of any editor windows like **MainActivity.java** and **activity_main.xml**. As you can see, a "Hello world!" application has been created automatically for us, but that's no fun. We will be creating a "Hello, Android" app ourselves!

Before I teach you how you can print those ubiquitous words onto your Android device, spend some time looking through the project you have just created. It contains lots of directories and files. Study the icons for each of these directories and files, and try opening your **Android 4.4.2** hierarchy (version may vary) and the **android.jar** within. Look inside the **res/values** folder and see if you can make sense of its contents. Finally, compare this project to a regular Java project and ask yourself, what is the same? What is different?

Navigating Around an Android Application Project

Let's quickly talk about how an Android Application Project is structured. Figure 7-7 shows all of our new app's primary directories along with some supporting files.

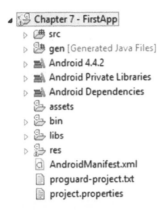

Figure 7-7   FirstApp's File Structure

The Android Developer Tools includes many files by default when you create a new Android project, but you will be working with just a handful of them. Some files can be completely ignored, as they are managed automatically for you.

The Important Stuff

In nearly every Android application, you will be working with the following components:

The **src** folder is where all of your source code goes, just like with our Java projects. You will spend most of your time developing Android apps in the **src** folder, creating classes to represent screens and data.

The **assets** folder is primarily used to store files that you want access to throughout your application. Later on, we will be storing our games' images and sounds inside this folder.

The **res** folder is the *resources* folder. You can store anything from images to pre-defined GUI layouts inside it to control how your application looks. The **res** folder allows you to include multiple versions of the same file. For example, you can provide text data in multiple languages, and Android will utilize the correct one depending on the user device's language settings!

The **AndroidManifest.xml** is an essential configuration file that allows the Android operating system to know key details about your application. Here, you can choose which image to display as your app's icon, which permissions to request during installation (such as the ability to send text messages or access the internet), and so on.

The Other Important Stuff

Many of the files and folders inside your application's project do not need to be touched. For the most part, they can be ignored. Even so, it is best if you have a basic understanding of the roles these files play (if only to know not to mess around with them).

First up is the **gen** folder, which contains automatically generated Java classes that all echo the same warning:

```
/* AUTO-GENERATED FILE.  DO NOT MODIFY.
....
*/
```

These Java files are generated automatically as you add resources into the **res** folder. If you look in the R.java file under com.jamescho.firstapp (without modifying it, of course), you will see that it has hundreds of constants. These come into use when you are coding and you want to access, for example, a file called image.png from the **res** folder. When the image.png file is added to **res**, R.java will automatically create a variable you can use to reference that new image!

In Unit 2, we made an extensive use of the Java API, importing various pre-written classes and calling their methods. To use Android's API in our application, we need to make Android's classes available to our app. Conveniently, this is done automatically for us in the form of the included library, which in Figure 7-7 is **Android 4.4.2** (you may have a different version of Android installed on your machine). Inside you will find the **android.jar** file (shown in Figure 7-8), which contains many packages full of Android-related Java classes with extensive documentation.

Figure 7-8   The Android Library

To learn more about the Android APIs, visit the following site:
http://developer.android.com/reference/packages.html

The **Android Dependencies** lists JAR files that our project needs in order for it to work. As shown in Figure 7-9, our project relies on the JAR file appcompat_v7.jar. This can be found inside the appcompat_v7 project, which is a supplementary project that includes some classes that allows you to write backwards-compatible code. Importing this JAR means that your app can take advantage of newly-added features on older versions of Android.

Figure 7-9   Android Dependencies

Note: Version numbers, such as `appcompat_v7`, may vary.

When you add JAR files to the **libs** folder, the **Android Private Libraries** will automatically update and allow you to use the JAR's contents throughout your application.

As shown in Figure 7-10, expanding each of these JAR files reveals packages of Java classes that you could import from. (The name `android.support` suggests that the packages inside our Private Libraries folder are used to provide support for older devices).

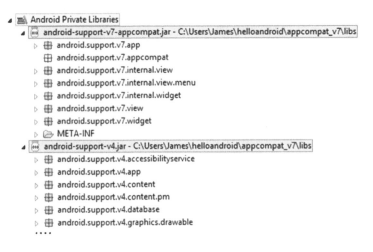

Figure 7-10   Android Private Libraries

Android makes use of a tool called ProGuard to optimize your code. It also obfuscates your code, making your code more difficult to reverse engineer. The **proguard-project.txt** file provides information on enabling and configuring ProGuard. To enable ProGuard, you must open the **project.properties** file and follow the provided instructions.

The **bin** folder's contents are generated by your compiler, and these files are used when building your app's **.apk** (Android application package file—the file that is installed on the Android device). Everything inside the **bin** folder is generated automatically.

Fundamental Android Concepts

You must be itching to write some code! We are almost there. Let's talk about a few important Android concepts, and we will be on our way.

Activities

Android applications are built one Activity at a time. An Activity is a screen—a single page inside your application. Each Activity has a Java class behind it, which allows you to write code to respond to events that occur throughout that activity's life.

XML

As you develop Android applications and games, you will come across various XML files. XML stands for **extensible markup language**, and it is used to store information. Although you do not need a degree in XML to write Android apps, it helps to know how to read and write in XML (it's very easy to learn). We won't discuss the XML syntax in much depth here, but there are a few things you should know that will help you get by.

An XML file comprises **elements**, denoted with the symbols < and >. For example, if I were writing an XML file detailing a smartphone item being sold at an electronics store, I would create the tags `<smartphone> </smartphone>` as shown.

```
<smartphone>
</smartphone>
```

The first tag denotes the beginning of the `smartphone` element, and the second tag denotes the end, *closing* the element. In between the two, I can nest smaller elements, as shown below:

```
<smartphone>

  <screen name = "super screen HD powered by A.W.E.S.O.M.E. technology"/>
  <processor
    name = "quad-core beast: even-more-extreme edition"
    speed = "3.5 ghz" />

</smartphone>
```

Notice that an XML element can have **attributes**. For instance, the `processor` element has the `name` and `speed` attributes. Also note that you can close elements using the following syntax, provided that the elements do not contain more elements:

```
<element ... />
```

Layouts

To create a GUI (graphical user interface) representation for an Activity, we create what is called a layout. These layout files are created using XML files that explicitly state what GUI elements should be present inside your Activity and how they should behave. Layout XML files look something like this:

```xml
<?xml version="1.0" encoding="utf-8"?>
<LinearLayout xmlns:android="http://schemas.android.com/apk/res/android"
    android:layout_width="match_parent"
    android:layout_height="match_parent"
    android:background="@android:color/black"
    android:orientation="vertical" >

    <TextView
        android:id="@+id/textView1"
        android:layout_width="wrap_content"
        android:layout_height="wrap_content"
        android:background="@android:color/white"
        android:text="This is TextView1 inside a LinearLayout" />

    <TextView
        android:id="@+id/textView2"
        android:layout_width="match_parent"
        android:layout_height="wrap_content"
        android:background="@android:color/darker_gray"
        android:text="This is TextView2 inside a LinearLayout" />

</LinearLayout>
```

In the example layout above, we have a **LinearLayout**, a type of layout that arranges its contents in vertical, linear order. Inside the **LinearLayout**, we have two **TextView elements**, GUI components that display text.

Using XML layout files such as this one, the Android operating system will create a layout as specified for each Activity, creating each element on the screen. Have a look at the location of the symbols < and > above, try to guess what each attribute is doing to modify the element, and try to envision the entire layout might look like on an Android screen. Pay special attention to the width of each element. The correct answer is shown in Figure 7-11.

Let's explain the solution. Every GUI element needs a width and a height (specified using the attributes android:layout_width and android:layout_height), and there are two permitted values: match_parent and wrap_content. The former, as the name suggests, makes the element's width equal to its container's width. The latter will make the element only as wide as it needs to be to wrap the content.

Note: The width and height describe how much space that element should take up inside the layout *without* changing the size of the content!

Our primary container, the **LinearLayout**, matches the width and height of its parent, which is the entire screen (minus some UI elements such as the title and notification bar). This is shown by all the areas colored black in Figure 7-11. The first **TextView**'s width and height are both `wrap_content`, meaning that it will only take up as much area as it needs to display its content, no more. This is made apparent by the white region in Figure 7-11. The second **TextView**'s width, on the other hand, is `match_parent`, so it will take up the entire width of its parent (the **LinearLayout**). This is demonstrated by the dark gray region also shown in Figure 7-11.

Note: In older versions of Android, `fill_parent` was used instead of `match_parent`. You may occasionally come across this value as you read other people's example code.

Figure 7-11   Example Layout Solution

Fragments

Fragments were introduced in Honeycomb (Android 3.0), and they allow more flexibility when building your application's GUI. Prior to Fragments, you could only have a single XML layout per Activity. With Fragments, you could have multiple, swappable layouts or even display multiple columns. Figure 7-12 shows some examples.

   Building Fragments is a slightly more advanced topic. As we will not need Fragments inside our games, we will not be discussing them here. If you'd like to learn more about Fragments, I recommend the book *Android Programming: The Big Nerd Ranch Guide* by Bill Phillips and Brian Hardy.

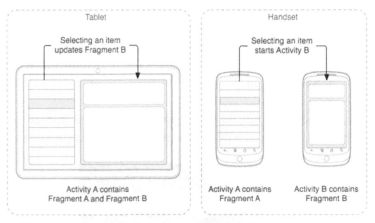

Figure 7-12   Fragment Examples[1]

AndroidManifest.xml

Recall that the `AndroidManifest.xml` file is a configuration file that reveals essential information about the application to the system. The Manifest for FirstApp is reproduced in listing 7.01 below:

Listing 7.01   FirstApp: AndroidManifest.xml

```xml
<?xml version="1.0" encoding="utf-8"?>
<manifest xmlns:android="http://schemas.android.com/apk/res/android"
    package="com.jamescho.firstapp"
    android:versionCode="1"
    android:versionName="1.0" >

    <uses-sdk
        android:minSdkVersion="9"
        android:targetSdkVersion="21" />

    <application
        android:allowBackup="true"
        android:icon="@drawable/ic_launcher"
        android:label="@string/app_name"
        android:theme="@style/AppTheme" >
        <activity
            android:name="com.jamescho.firstapp.MainActivity"
            android:label="@string/app_name" >
            <intent-filter>
                <action android:name="android.intent.action.MAIN" />
                <category android:name="android.intent.category.LAUNCHER" />
            </intent-filter>
        </activity>
    </application>
</manifest>
```

---

[1] Reproduced without modification from http://developer.android.com/guide/components/fragments.html and used according to terms described in the Creative Commons 2.5 Attribution License.

Let's discuss some of the tags inside the AndroidManifest. The largest element, the `Manifest` element, has the attribute xmlns:android… that specifies the XML namespace for the document. Think of this as an import statement that allows you to use Android-related terms throughout the XML document. The `Manifest` element allows you to set three important properties:

- The package attribute is used to specify the name of the primary package (inside **src**).
- The `android:versionCode` should be incremented by one (by you) whenever you make an update to your app and want to upload it to the Play Store (regardless of magnitude of update). The initial version should take `versionCode` 1, the second release should have `versionCode` 2 and so on. This value is used to by the system for update purposes.
- The `android:versionName` can follow any rule that you wish. This value is shown to the user but not used by the system for any other purpose.

The `Manifest` element contains a `uses-sdk` element, which allows you to change the minimum SDK version and the target SDK version (see Figure 7-2 and the preceding discussion for a refresher on these terms).

Figure 7-13   The **res** Folder

The core of the AndroidManifest is the application element, which allows you to configure your application's icon, theme, label (displayed name) and other properties. Notice in our example—reproduced below—that we use the @ symbol to specify some of the attributes' values:

```
android:icon="@drawable/ic_launcher"
android:label="@string/app_name"
android:theme="@style/AppTheme"
```

The @ indicates that each of these attributes are referencing a value from an existing file or folder inside the **res** folder. The file `ic_launcher` is an image file inside the `drawable` folder (ignore the multiple `drawable` folders for now), while `app_name` and `AppTheme` are two entries inside the XML files `string.xml` and `styles.xml`, respectively. The relevant files are shown in Figure 7-13.

The application element contains all the Activities that make up our application. Any time we create a new Activity to be used inside our application, we <u>must</u> declare it inside the application element. As we only have one Activity inside our application for now, we have one activity element:

```
....
    <activity
        android:name="com.jamescho.firstapp.MainActivity"
        android:label="@string/app_name" >
        <intent-filter>
            <action android:name="android.intent.action.MAIN" />
            <category android:name="android.intent.category.LAUNCHER" />
        </intent-filter>
    </activity>
....
```

The `android:name` attribute requires you to specify where the Activity can be found (in this case it can be found at the **MainActivity** class inside `com.jamescho.firstapp`). The `android:label` allows you to choose a name to be displayed in the Title Bar. You can keep this consistent throughout your app or vary it with each Activity.

The `intent-filter` element and its content elements `action` and `category` are used to denote which Activity should launch when the user taps the app's icon from the App Drawer. This is a required element even when you only have a single Activity, and is needed to specify the starting Activity in a multi-activity application.

Note: For details on various tags used inside the Manifest, please see the official Android API Guides at: `http://developer.android.com/guide/topics/manifest/manifest-intro.html`

Rewriting Hello, World

We've covered the essentials, so let's write some code. Recall that when creating FirstApp, we created a Blank Activity (see Figures 7-3 and 7-4). In the dialog shown in Figure 7-5, we gave this Activity and its layout the names `MainActivity` and `activity_main`, respectively.

We will be deleting both of these files and recreating the Activity and its layout manually.

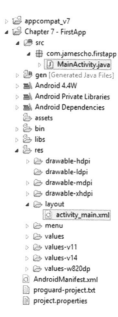

Figure 7-14   Files to Delete

Creating MainActivity

Go to the **src** folder, open the package for your app (`com.jamescho.firstapp`) and delete `MainActivity.java` by right clicking on it (Ctrl + click on Mac) and selecting Delete. Also open the folder **res/layout** and delete `activity_main.xml`.

Now that we have a blank slate, let's recreate our "Hello, World" application. Start by creating a new Java class called `MainActivity` (inside `com.jamescho.firstapp`). To make this class an Activity, we must extend the **Activity** class as shown below, importing `android.app.Activity`.

```
package com.jamescho.firstapp;

import android.app.Activity;

public class MainActivity extends Activity {

}
```

Note: Although we usually would need to add a new `activity` element to our Manifest whenever we create a new Activity, we do not have to do that for **MainActivity** because we never removed the existing reference to **MainActivity** from the Manifest—see listing 7.01.

By extending Activity and registering the class inside the Manifest, we allow **MainActivity** to interact with the Android system in interesting ways. For example, because of the `action` and `category` tags previously mentioned, **MainActivity** will be the first screen launched when the user starts our application. In addition, when **MainActivity** is created, the Android system will automatically call a method inside our Activity called onCreate(), which we can treat as the "main method" of our **MainActivity**.

Adding onCreate()

You might look at our **MainActivity** class and say, "There is no onCreate() in here!" On the contrary, there is! The onCreate() method is *inherited* from the **Activity** class (remember that **MainActivity** extends **Activity**). Even though we can't see it, **MainActivity** has one via its superclass (who has the action implementation of onCreate()). To add custom functionality to this method, we can override it inside the subclass as shown:

```java
package com.jamescho.firstapp;

import android.app.Activity;
import android.os.Bundle;

public class MainActivity extends Activity{
        @Override
        protected void onCreate(Bundle savedInstanceState) {
                super.onCreate(savedInstanceState);
                // Your own code here.
        }

}
```

As mentioned before, this method will be called automatically by the Android system when **MainActivity** is first created; we override the method so that we can provide some kind of initialization for our Activity. onCreate() receives a parameter of type **Bundle** (thus we import android.os.Bundle), which can be used to retain stored variable values when the Activity is recreated (for example when we rotate the screen). You do not have to understand what **Bundle** does.

Notice that we call super.onCreate(...) inside the method body, which goes to the superclass and calls its implementation of onCreate(). This *mandatory* call takes care of some system-related tasks behind-the-scenes.

Creating the Layout

Inside the onCreate() method, we have to call a method called setContentView(int layoutResId) to attach an XML layout to our Activity. In order for us to do so, we must first create a layout.

Right-click (Ctrl + click on Mac) on the **res/layout** folder, and select New > Other. Choose **Android XML Layout File** under the Android category, as shown in Figure 7-15, and press next.

Figure 7-15   Creating an Android XML Layout File

In the next dialog box, enter the file name `activity_main`, select `LinearLayout` as the root element (as shown in Figure 7-16) and hit finish.

Figure 7-16   Creating a Linear Layout

Once you have done this, you will be presented with the XML layout's editor window. Looking at the bottom left corner of this window, you will notice that you are currently in the Graphical Layout tab (see Figure 7-17). This mode shows you a graphical preview of the XML layout you are currently editing, which is accessible via the `activity_main.xml` tab (also shown in Figure 7-17).

Figure 7-17   Switching Between Graphical Layout and XML View.

Before we add anything to our blank layout, let's see its XML contents by selecting the `activity_main.xml` tab. You should see the standard editor display the following XML document:

Listing 7.02   `activity_main.xml` (with a vertical `LinearLayout` as the root element)

```
<?xml version="1.0" encoding="utf-8"?>
<LinearLayout xmlns:android="http://schemas.android.com/apk/res/android"
    android:layout_width="match_parent"
    android:layout_height="match_parent"
    android:orientation="vertical" >


</LinearLayout>
```

Notice that `activity_main.xml` contains a `LinearLayout` element, which we've previously selected as the root element for our new XML layout.

Adding Widgets

Return to the Graphical Layout. On the left side of the screen, you will find the Palette. Inside, you will find tens of widgets you can play around with on the screen! To add one into your layout (and thus your Activity), you simply drag and drop into your layout's preview.

The widget that we are interested in is called `TextView`. Select this, drag it over to the layout preview screen and snap it onto the top-left corner of the screen. Your preview should look like that shown in Figure 7-18.

Note: If you make a mistake following these steps, simply click on the problematic widget and hit the Delete/Backspace key before trying again.

Figure 7-18   LinearLayout + TextView

Dragging on the `TextView` automatically modified the XML layout. To see the changes, return to the `activity_main.xml` tab shown in Figure 7-17. Your XML listing should now look like that shown in listing 7.03:

Listing 7.03   `activity_main.xml` (with TextView added)

```
<?xml version="1.0" encoding="utf-8"?>
<LinearLayout xmlns:android="http://schemas.android.com/apk/res/android"
    android:layout_width="match_parent"
    android:layout_height="match_parent"
    android:orientation="vertical" >
    <TextView
        android:id="@+id/textView1"
        android:layout_width="wrap_content"
        android:layout_height="wrap_content"
        android:text="TextView" />

</LinearLayout>
```

Compare the XML contents of listings 7.02 and 7.03. You will see that a `TextView` element has been added *inside* of the existing `LinearLayout` root element. Now here's your challenge. Try to make our XML layout display "Hello, Android!" by modifying one line inside `activity_main.xml`. The solution is shown in Listing 7.04.

Listing 7.04   Hello Android!

```xml
<?xml version="1.0" encoding="utf-8"?>
<LinearLayout xmlns:android="http://schemas.android.com/apk/res/android"
    android:layout_width="match_parent"
    android:layout_height="match_parent"
    android:orientation="vertical" >
    <TextView
        android:id="@+id/textView1"
        android:layout_width="wrap_content"
        android:layout_height="wrap_content"
        android:text="Hello, Android!"
        android:text="TextView" />

</LinearLayout>
```

We have created the **MainActivity** class and a simple XML layout. Can you predict what would happen if we were to run our application now? It turns out that we would just get a blank screen representing our **MainActivity** class, as shown in Figure 7-19.

Figure 7-19   Why is is Blank?

We get this result because we never populated our **MainActivity** with the contents of `activity_main.xml`! As mentioned before, **MainActivity** is just an empty Java class until we call `setContentView(...)`.

The setContentView(...) Method
The `setContentView(...)` method allows us to add content to our view. It accepts a single argument—a reference to an XML layout. The trouble is, the XML layout is not a Java file. We can't instantiate it like we can a Java class and pass in a reference to `setContentView()`. Instead, we must retrieve the layout using its ID.

Recall that the **R.java** file inside the **gen** folder automatically creates a Java variable for resources added to the **res** folder. In our case, **R** has automatically created an ID called R.layout.activity_main. This can be used to retrieve our XML layout!

Note: When Eclipse is first starting up, it will take some time for it to completely load up your Android Application Project. There will be errors as Eclipse tries to build the application and find the required libraries. Some people get impatient and try to import android.R to make some of the errors go away, but this will cause compiler errors until the import statement is removed!
Always wait for everything to fully load, and NEVER add the statement import android.R into your class declaration!

Call setContentView()inside the onCreate() method as shown in Listing 7.05.

Listing 7.05   **MainActivity** + R.layout.activity_main

```
package com.jamescho.firstapp;

import android.app.Activity;
import android.os.Bundle;

public class MainActivity extends Activity{
        @Override
        protected void onCreate(Bundle savedInstanceState) {
                super.onCreate(savedInstanceState);
                setContentView(R.layout.activity_main);
        }

}
```

Our "Hello, Android!" application is now finished. Let's run it!

Running an Android Application

Using the Emulator

The ADT comes with a built-in emulator that is useful for testing apps while varying screen size, RAM and etc. To test our application on the emulator, right-click (Ctrl + click on Mac) on the FirstApp Android Project in the Package Explorer, and click **Run As > 1 Android Application**.

If you don't have any development devices setup on your computer, a dialog will appear saying, "No compatible targets were found. Do you wish to add a new Android Virtual Device?" Select **Yes**, and a new dialog will appear as shown in Figure 7-20.

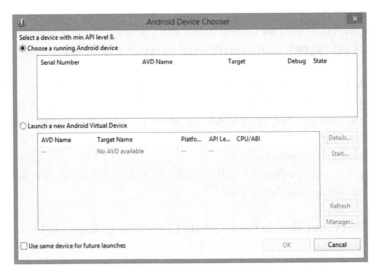

Figure 7-20   Android Device Chooser

Select the **Launch a new Android Virtual Device** radio button and click the **Manager...** button. Both of these options are highlighted in Figure 7-21.

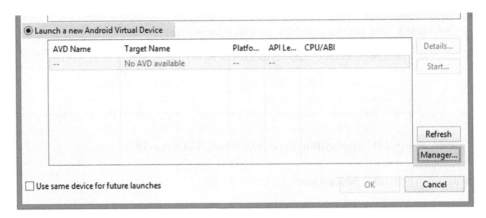

Figure 7-21   Launching a new Android Virtual Device

When the Android Virtual Device Manager dialog appears, switch over to the Device Definitions tab, select **Galaxy Nexus** and click **Create AVD...** as shown in Figure 7-22. This will allow us to create a virtual device that emulates Google's old flagship device.

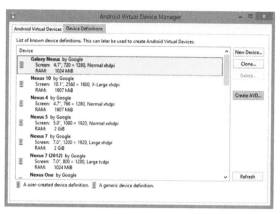

Figure 7-22   Launching a new Android Virtual Device

Once the Create new AVD dialog appears, the Skin option should be switched to HVGA (as shown in Figure 7-23). Keep the rest of the settings as they are, and select **OK**.

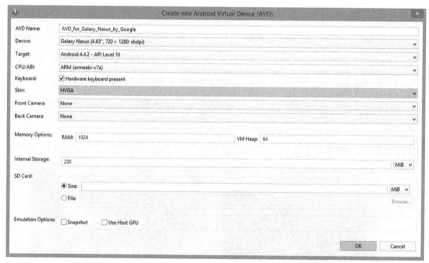

Figure 7-23   Creating a new AVD

<u>Note</u>: If you get an error message saying 'No system images installed...', please see 'Known Issues' at: http://jamescho7.com/book/chapter7

Our virtual Galaxy Nexus is now ready! Return to the Android Device Chooser (Figure 7-20) and hit **Refresh**. Your new AVD will now be available for you to launch your applications on, as shown in Figure 7-24. Select the device and hit **OK**.

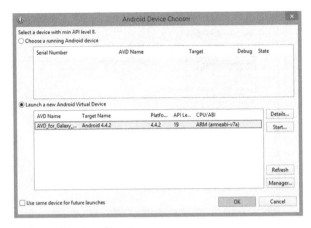

Figure 7-24   Launching the Application

You will begin to see a series of messages in the Console similar to those shown below:

```
[Chapter 7 - FirstApp] ------------------------------
[Chapter 7 - FirstApp] Android Launch!
[Chapter 7 - FirstApp] adb is running normally.
[Chapter 7 - FirstApp] Performing com.jamescho.firstapp.MainActivity activity launch
[Chapter 7 - FirstApp] Automatic Target Mode: launching new emulator with compatible AVD
'AVD_for_Galaxy_Nexus_by_Google'
[Chapter 7 - FirstApp] Launching a new emulator with Virtual Device 'AVD_for_Galaxy_Nexus_by_Google'
[Chapter 7 - FirstApp] New emulator found: emulator-5554
[Chapter 7 - FirstApp] Waiting for HOME ('android.process.acore') to be launched...
[Chapter 7 - FirstApp] HOME is up on device 'emulator-5554'
[Chapter 7 - FirstApp] Uploading Chapter 7 - FirstApp.apk onto device 'emulator-5554'
[Chapter 7 - FirstApp] Installing Chapter 7 - FirstApp.apk...
```

The emulator will also launch and display the boot animation shown in Figure 7-25:

Figure 7-25   The Dreaded Boot Animation

Now step away from your computer, make yourself some coffee and check back in ten minutes. This booting process can take quite a long time.

Note: If you do not have a physical Android device and would like to reduce the boot time, I recommend studying the emulator snapshot feature at the following link: `http://tools.android.com/recent/emulatorsnapshots`

Once booting is complete, you should be able to find FirstApp inside the App Drawer as shown in Figure 7-26.

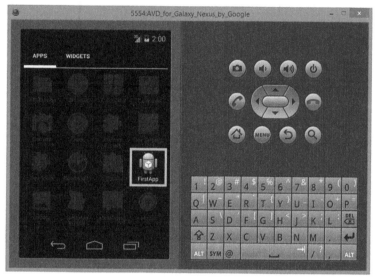

Figure 7-26   Opening FirstApp

Open up the FirstApp. If you see the screen shown in Figure 7-27, congratulations! You have just created your own "Hello, Android" application with minimal help from the Android Development Tools.

Note: If you are having problems with any of the classes or .xml files at this point, you can download the source code at **jamescho7.com/book/chapter7/checkpoint1**.

Debugging FirstApp

If you are having issues, follow the steps listed below in order to diagnose your issue.

- Check that you have the **MainActivity** class inside com.jamescho.firstapp, and compare it carefully to listing 7.05. There should be no errors in your code.
- Make sure that activity_main.xml is inside **res/layout** and that its contents match that of listing 7.04.
- Double check your AndroidManifest.xml, comparing it carefully to listing 7.01.

- If you have any lingering errors, look for any red error messages and search for a solution on your favorite search engine.
- Post your issue on the forums at the book's companion site.
- If all else fails, download the source code at the link provided above before moving on.

Figure 7-27   Hello, Android!

Using a Physical Device

If you have an Android device available then testing applications will be much easier. Follow the steps listed below in order to setup your device for testing.

1. Unplug your device from your computer.
2. Download the latest USB drivers for your device. In order to do this, consult the forums at `xda-developers.com` or refer to your hardware manufacturer's website.
3. Check the version of Android installed on your device. On most devices, this information can be accessed inside the Settings app under About phone, as shown in Figure 7-28.
4. Enable USB Debugging on your device, following the instructions provided for your device's Android version.
     i.   If you have Android 4.2 or newer, tap on Build number (highlighted in Figure 7-28) seven times. Developer options will now become enabled on your device.

Return to the main settings, select Developer options and enable USB debugging.

ii. If you have Android 4.0.x to 4.1.x, follow the same steps as above, skipping the Build number tapping step.

iii. On older versions of Android, open Settings, select Applications and check the Development settings to enable USB Debugging.

5. Plug in your device into your computer. If a dialog on your device asks you to Allow USB debugging, select "Always allow from this computer" and hit OK.

Figure 7-28 Checking your Android Version

Your device is ready! Return to Eclipse and run your project as an Android Application. The Android Device Chooser will appear, as shown in Figure 7-29. Select the connected device, and hit **OK**. Your app should begin to run on your device (if any security dialogs appear on your device, read them and grant permissions as necessary).

From now on, your device will be recognized by your computer. As you make changes to your application or create new ones, simply run the project as an Android Application to use your device for testing. The Android Device Chooser will appear and allow you to launch the app on your device.

Note: You can enable the "Use same device for future launches" option in the Android Device Chooser to speed up this process.

Figure 7-29   Android Device Chooser

The Activity Lifecycle

Activities are the building blocks of Android Applications. As the user interacts with Activities, transitioning from screen to screen, they will be created, hidden, paused or destroyed appropriately. This transition from one state to another can be understood by studying the Activity Lifecycle, which is shown in Figure 7-30.

You do not have to memorize the Activity Lifecycle. All you need to know is that an Activity passes through various stages and that you can choose to be notified when it enters a specific state. For example, if you want to be notified when your Activity is about to pause, you override the onPause() method. If you want to know when an Activity is resuming from a paused state, you override the onResume() method.

Note: Remember that the word override is used when we are inheriting a method from a superclass and changing its behavior.

Why the Activity Lifecycle Matters
The reason we want to be notified when our Activity enters certain states has to do with Android's multitasking capabilities. Android users switch from application to application all the time for various reasons. When these changes happen, it's best if your application is notified, so that it can decide when to get out of the way, when to save data, and when to shine.

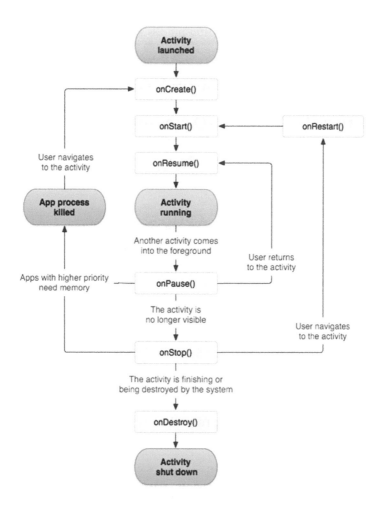

Figure 7-30   The Activity Lifecycle[2]

For instance, if someone is playing our game and receives a phone call, we probably want our game to pause. So, we would override the onPause() or onStop() method and put our game on hold. When the player returns to the game, onResume() or onRestart() is called by the Android system. Overriding these methods allows us to resume the game right away.

Before moving on, study the Activity Lifecycle, following the arrows starting at the oval labeled *Activity is launched*. Try to move your finger over the lines, drawing some possible sequences of states that an Activity may pass through during its typical use.

---

[2] Reproduced without modification from http://developer.android.com/guide/components/activities.html and used according to terms described in the Creative Commons 2.5 Attribution License

Whenever you reach an orange oval (*App process killed* or *Activity shut down*), you must start over from the top.

From this exercise, you will realize that some methods are not guaranteed to be called even when your Activity enters a certain state. For example, when your Activity's process is killed due to lack of memory, onDestroy() will not be called. Saving user progress, then, shouldn't occur inside onDestroy() to prevent loss of data occurring with a forced termination of our application. We need to keep these things in mind when designing our game.

Views

View objects are interactive, visual components used to build your app's user interface. You've seen some examples of View objects before. In activity_main.xml from FirstApp, we created a LinearLayout, a type of View. This was the parent of another View—the TextView.

When calling the method setContentView() inside an Activity, we pass in a reference to a View object—typically a layout. Inside this layout, we can add various Views such as Button and ImageView. Each of these Views has some unique characteristic that sets it apart from the others.

Event Handling

Views can respond to events in various ways. For example, a Button can react to a touch event and make something happen. A TextView can perform an action when its contents are changed by the user.

Drawing Views

A View needs to be visible (after all, it's called "View" not "Hide"). Every View we deal with will have a method called onDraw(), which will be called by the Android system to render that particular view.

Responding to Events and Starting a Second Activity

Now that you know all about Activities and Views, let's add a second Activity to our FirstApp. To do so, we will follow these steps:
1. Create a new Activity class and register it with the AndroidManifest.
2. Provide a Content View for the newly-created Activity.
3. Create a Button inside **MainActivity** that will take us to the new Activity.

Note: We are adding to the FirstApp project created in the previous sections. If you do not have a working version, you can download a copy at **jamescho7.com/book/ chapter7/checkpoint1** prior to continuing.

Creating the SecondActivity Class

Our very first task is to create a simple second Activity that displays a blue background and a rather clingy magenta square. A screenshot of Activity is shown in Figure 7-31:

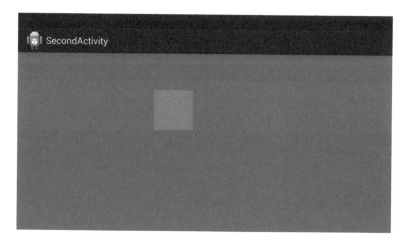

Figure 7-31   SecondActivity displays a square on a blue background

Begin by creating a class called **SecondActivity** inside the com.jamescho.firstapp package of FirstApp. Next, extend **Activity** (importing android.app.Activity) and override the onCreate() method (importing android.os.Bundle) as shown in listing 7.06.

Listing 7.06   **SecondActivity**

```
package com.jamescho.firstapp;

import android.app.Activity;
import android.os.Bundle;

public class SecondActivity extends Activity {

        @Override
        protected void onCreate(Bundle savedInstanceState) {
                super.onCreate(savedInstanceState);
        }
}
```

Whenever we create a new Activity in an Android application, we must register it with the AndroidManifest. Open up AndroidManifest.xml, and add the following element inside your application element:

<activity

```
        android:name="com.jamescho.firstapp.SecondActivity"
        android:label="SecondActivity"
        android:screenOrientation="Landscape" >
</activity>
```

Once this step is complete your Manifest should match that shown in listing 7.07 (note: your API numbers may vary):

Listing 7.07   Registering **SecondActivity** in the Manifest

```
<?xml version="1.0" encoding="utf-8"?>
<manifest xmlns:android="http://schemas.android.com/apk/res/android"
    package="com.jamescho.firstapp"
    android:versionCode="1"
    android:versionName="1.0" >

    <uses-sdk
        android:minSdkVersion="9"
        android:targetSdkVersion="21" />

    <application
        android:allowBackup="true"
        android:icon="@drawable/ic_launcher"
        android:label="@string/app_name"
        android:theme="@style/AppTheme" >
        <activity
            android:name="com.jamescho.firstapp.MainActivity"
            android:label="@string/app_name" >
            <intent-filter>
                <action android:name="android.intent.action.MAIN" />

                <category android:name="android.intent.category.LAUNCHER" />
            </intent-filter>
        </activity>
        <activity
                android:name="com.jamescho.firstapp.SecondActivity"
                android:label="SecondActivity"
                android:screenOrientation="Landscape" >
                </activity>

    </application>.

</manifest>
```

Note that we've requested the newly-added Activity to be displayed in landscape mode (as opposed to the default portrait mode on smartphone devices). We also provide a name for the Activity independent from the application name via the android:label attribute.

Creating a Content View
Now that **SecondActivity** has been created and registered, let's provide it with a Content View. To do so, we will be creating a custom **View** object that will fill up the entire screen and make a square follow your fingertip.

Inside the com.jamescho.firstapp package, create a class called **CustomView**, extending **View** (import android.view.View). Once you have done so, you will see the error shown in Figure 7-32:

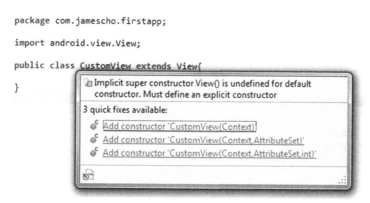

```
package com.jamescho.firstapp;

import android.view.View;

public class CustomView extends View{

}
```

Implicit super constructor View() is undefined for default constructor. Must define an explicit constructor

3 quick fixes available:
- Add constructor 'CustomView(Context)'
- Add constructor 'CustomView(Context,AttributeSet)'
- Add constructor 'CustomView(Context,AttributeSet,int)'

Figure 7-32   Constructor Required!

Our problem is that, for **CustomView** to be instantiated, we must instantiate its parent also—the **View** class (by inheritance, **CustomView** IS-A **View**). To complicate matters, the **View** class can only be instantiated using one of three allowed custom constructors, so we must provide an explicit constructor inside **CustomView** will construct the **View** superclass. The constructor that we will be calling has the signature View(Context).

Add the following constructor for **CustomView** into your class, importing android.content.Context.

```
public CustomView(Context context) {
        super(context); // Calls View(Context)
}
```

Note that this constructor calls super(context); this is the syntax used to call the constructor of a superclass. This means that—when **CustomView** is instantiated using the above constructor—it will automatically instantiates itself as a subclass of **View** by calling one of **View**'s constructors.

The single parameter of this constructor, a **Context** object, stores information regarding the application. When passed into the **View** class's constructor, the newly-created **View** instance will know important details about the application (such as its Target SDK Version).

Adding the Variables to CustomView

Our **CustomView** will draw a clingy square to follow the user's finger. In order for us to represent this square, we will create a **Rect** object (a built-in rectangle object that stores x, y, width and height values as `left`, `top`, `right` and `bottom`). To give this **Rect** object a color, we will create a **Paint** object, which is used to style elements drawn to the screen.

Add the following import statements to your class:

```
import android.graphics.Color;
import android.graphics.Paint;
import android.graphics.Rect;
```

Next, declare the following variables:

```
private Rect myRect;
private Paint myPaint;
private static final int SQUARE_SIDE_LENGTH = 200;
```

We now initialize the **Rect** and **Paint** objects inside the constructor as shown in bold below:

```
myRect = new Rect(30, 30, SQUARE_SIDE_LENGTH, SQUARE_SIDE_LENGTH);
myPaint = new Paint();
myPaint.setColor(Color.MAGENTA);
```

At this point, your **CustomView** should match that shown in listing 7.08.

Listing 7.08   The **Game** Class (Completed)

```
package com.jamescho.firstapp;

import android.content.Context;
import android.view.View;

import android.graphics.Color;
import android.graphics.Paint;
import android.graphics.Rect;

public class CustomView extends View{

        private Rect myRect;
        private Paint myPaint;
        private static final int SQUARE_SIDE_LENGTH = 200;

        public CustomView(Context context) {
                super(context);
                myRect = new Rect(30, 30, SQUARE_SIDE_LENGTH, SQUARE_SIDE_LENGTH);
                myPaint = new Paint();
                myPaint.setColor(Color.MAGENTA);
        }

}
```

Drawing the CustomView

To define how our **CustomView** should draw itself, we must override the onDraw(Canvas) method from **Activity**. Add the following method to your **CustomView** class (importing android.graphics.Canvas):

```
@Override
protected void onDraw(Canvas canvas) {
        canvas.drawRGB(39, 111, 184);
        canvas.drawRect(myRect, myPaint);
}
```

The overridden onDraw() method simply fills the Canvas (the area of our application that can be drawn on) with the color (R = 39, G = 111, B = 184)—a simple blue color. It then calls canvas.drawRect(...), which will reference myRect's coordinates and dimensions to draw it at the correct location on the Canvas (using the style specified in myPaint).

Handling Touch Events

To specify what should happen when a touch event is detected, we must override the onTouchEvent(MotionEvent) method. Add the following method to your **CustomView** class (importing android.view.MotionEvent):

```
@Override
public boolean onTouchEvent(MotionEvent event) {
        myRect.left = (int) event.getX() - (SQUARE_SIDE_LENGTH / 2);
        myRect.top = (int) event.getY() - (SQUARE_SIDE_LENGTH / 2);
        myRect.right = myRect.left + SQUARE_SIDE_LENGTH;
        myRect.bottom = myRect.top + SQUARE_SIDE_LENGTH;
        invalidate();
        return true; // Indicates that a touch event was handled.
}
```

The onTouchEvent() method receives a **MotionEvent** object, which reveals information about the touch event that has triggered this method. As such, we can determine the X and Y of the player's touch using the methods event.getX() and event.getY(). Using these two values, we update the position of our myRect so that it is centered at the player's touch location.

The purpose of the invalidate() call is to let the Android system know that there has been a change in our **CustomView**, and that its onDraw() method should be called again. This has the effect of refreshing the screen after myRect has been updated to a new position.

With the onDraw() and onTouchEvent() methods added, the **CustomView** is complete. The full class code is shown in listing 7.09.

Listing 7.09   **CustomView** (Completed)

```
package com.jamescho.firstapp;
```

```
import android.content.Context;
import android.view.MotionEvent;
import android.view.View;

import android.graphics.Canvas;
import android.graphics.Color;
import android.graphics.Paint;
import android.graphics.Rect;

public class CustomView extends View{

        private Rect myRect;
        private Paint myPaint;
        private static final int SQUARE_SIDE_LENGTH = 200;

        public CustomView(Context context) {
                super(context);
                myRect = new Rect(30, 30, SQUARE_SIDE_LENGTH, SQUARE_SIDE_LENGTH);
                myPaint = new Paint();
                myPaint.setColor(Color.MAGENTA);
        }

        @Override
        protected void onDraw(Canvas canvas) {
                canvas.drawRGB(39, 111, 184);
                canvas.drawRect(myRect, myPaint);
        }

        @Override
        public boolean onTouchEvent(MotionEvent event) {
                myRect.left = (int) event.getX() - (SQUARE_SIDE_LENGTH / 2);
                myRect.top = (int) event.getY() - (SQUARE_SIDE_LENGTH / 2);
                myRect.right = myRect.left + SQUARE_SIDE_LENGTH;
                myRect.bottom = myRect.top + SQUARE_SIDE_LENGTH;
                invalidate();
                return true;
        }

}
```

Setting the New CustomView

Now we must return to **SecondActivity** and set the **CustomView** as its Content View. To do so, we simply call setContentView(), passing in an instance of **CustomView** rather than a layout ID. The completed **SecondActivity** class is provided in listing 7.10.

Listing 7.10   **SecondActivity** (Completed)

```
package com.jamescho.firstapp;

import android.app.Activity;
import android.os.Bundle;

public class SecondActivity extends Activity {
```

```
        @Override
        protected void onCreate(Bundle savedInstanceState) {
                super.onCreate(savedInstanceState);
                setContentView(new CustomView(this));
        }
}
```

Note that we pass in `this` (the current instance of **SecondActivity**) as the argument for the `CustomView(Context)` constructor. This is allowed because an Activity is a subclass of **Context**, and thus stores information regarding the application needed by the newly-instantiated **CustomView**.

Creating a Button

As we have told our Manifest, our application has two Activities: **MainActivity** and **SecondActivity**. At the moment, we have asked **MainActivity** to be launched when the user starts the application (see the `action` and `category` elements inside the Manifest). Once **MainActivity** is running, however, it has no way of starting **SecondActivity** and letting it take over. To resolve this issue, we will create a new Button (which is a View) inside **MainActivity**.

Open `activity_main.xml` in the editor interface and add the following Button element below the existing **TextView** element:

```
<Button
        android:id="@+id/button1"
        android:layout_width="wrap_content"
        android:layout_height="wrap_content"
        android:text="Take me away!" />
```

Listing 7.11 shows the updated `activity_main.xml` file.

Listing 7.11   activity_main.xml (updated)

```
<?xml version="1.0" encoding="utf-8"?>
<LinearLayout xmlns:android="http://schemas.android.com/apk/res/android"
    android:layout_width="match_parent"
    android:layout_height="match_parent"
    android:orientation="vertical" >
    <TextView
        android:id="@+id/textView1"
        android:layout_width="wrap_content"
        android:layout_height="wrap_content"
        android:text="Hello, Android" />
    <Button
        android:id="@+id/button1"
        android:layout_width="wrap_content"
        android:layout_height="wrap_content"
        android:text="Take me away!" />
</LinearLayout>
```

Note that we have created a new `Button` with the id of `button1`. We can now preview the changes by switching to the Graphical Layout tab (shown in Figure 7-33).

Figure 7-33   Graphical Layout of activity_main.xml showing the Button

Our `Button` is now on the screen, but as of now, it does nothing! To provide some kind of action, we must reference the `Button` inside our **MainActivity** class, and attach what is called an **OnClickListener**.

Setting a Button's OnClickListener
An Activity has a method called `findViewById(int id)`, which will return a View object whose ID matches the `int` argument passed into the method. When creating our `Button`, we've assigned the ID of `button1`, so we can reference it inside our **MainActivity** as shown in bold below (don't forget the import statement):

```
package com.jamescho.firstapp;

import android.app.Activity;
import android.os.Bundle;
import android.widget.Button;

public class MainActivity extends Activity{
        @Override
        protected void onCreate(Bundle savedInstanceState) {
                super.onCreate(savedInstanceState);
                setContentView(R.layout.activity_main);
                Button button1 = (Button) findViewById(R.id.button1);
        }
}
```

Note that we must cast the returned **View** object as a **Button** in order to store it as a **Button** object rather than a generic **View** object.

Once we have access to the Button, we must provide it with an **OnClickListener**. Implement an **OnClickListener** by adding the changes shown below in bold to your **MainActivity** (keep an eye out for the new import statements):

```
package com.jamescho.firstapp;

import android.app.Activity;
import android.os.Bundle;
import android.view.View;
import android.view.View.OnClickListener;
import android.widget.Button;

public class MainActivity extends Activity implements OnClickListener{
        @Override
        protected void onCreate(Bundle savedInstanceState) {
                super.onCreate(savedInstanceState);
                setContentView(R.layout.activity_main);
                Button button1 = (Button) findViewById(R.id.button1);
                button1.setOnClickListener(this);
        }

        @Override
        public void onClick(View v) {

        }

}
```

As you can see, **OnClickListener** is an interface with one method: onClick(). When you register an instance of **OnClickListener** as the **OnClickListener** of a button, that instance's onClick() method will be called whenever the button is clicked.

Optional: The Anonymous Inner Class
Without changing your own code, have a look at the following example, which demonstrates an alternate solution for implementing an **OnClickListener**:

Listing 7.12   Alternative Syntax for OnClickListener (Example Only!)

```
package com.jamescho.firstapp;

import android.app.Activity;
import android.os.Bundle;
import android.view.View;
import android.view.View.OnClickListener;
import android.widget.Button;

public class ExampleActivity extends Activity {
        @Override
        protected void onCreate(Bundle savedInstanceState) {
                super.onCreate(savedInstanceState);
                setContentView(R.layout.activity_main);
```

```
        Button button1 = (Button) findViewById(R.id.button1);
        button1.setOnClickListener(new OnClickListener() {

                @Override
                public void onClick(View v) {

                }
        });
    }
}
```

You may come across the syntax shown in listing 7.12 as you develop Android apps. Figure 7-34 is provided to help you see the individual components of the bizarre multi-line statement inside onCreate().

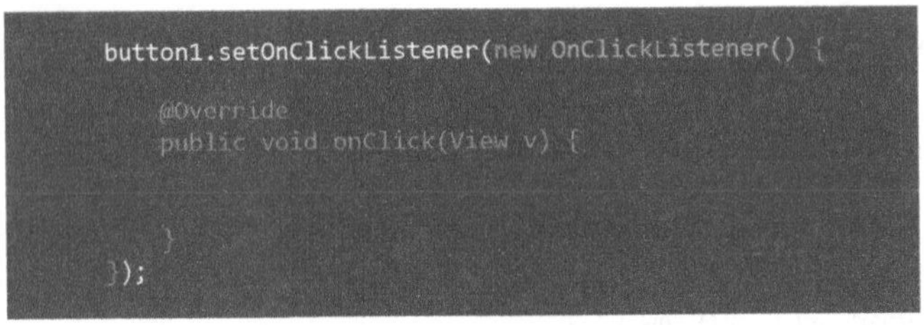

Figure 7-34   Anonymous Inner Class

Look at Figure 7-34 and focus just on just the white portion of the multi-line block. You will notice that you are just looking at a simple single statement: button1.setOnClickListener(...).

Everything in between the parentheses (colored pink, green and orange) form the single parameter required by the aforementioned statement. In other words, the parameter is a single **OnClickListener** object required by button1.setOnClickListener().

Listing 7.12 and Figure 7-34 demonstrate the syntax for creating an anonymous inner class: an in-line implementation of an interface. Rather than declaring a full class and implementing an interface, we can instantiate an interface directly as an anonymous inner class (the green and orange portions of Figure 7-34).

Starting a New Activity
The newly-created onClick() method will be called when our Button is pressed. We will use this to transition to a new screen. Implement onClick() as shown in listing 7.13, importing android.content.Intent.

Listing 7.13   **MainActivity** (Completed)

```
package com.jamescho.firstapp;
```

```
import android.app.Activity;
import android.content.Intent;
import android.os.Bundle;
import android.view.View;
import android.view.View.OnClickListener;
import android.widget.Button;

public class MainActivity extends Activity implements OnClickListener{
        @Override
        protected void onCreate(Bundle savedInstanceState) {
                super.onCreate(savedInstanceState);
                setContentView(R.layout.activity_main);
                Button button1 = (Button) findViewById(R.id.button1);
                button1.setOnClickListener(this);
        }

        @Override
        public void onClick(View v) {
                Intent intent = new Intent(MainActivity.this, SecondActivity.class);
                startActivity(intent);
        }
}
```

In Android, an **Intent** object is used to switch from one Activity to another. In our example, we instantiate a new **Intent** object, passing in the current instance of **MainActivity** (the source) and the desired target **SecondActivity** into the constructor. Once we pass in the Intent into startActivity(), **SecondActivity** will be instantiated and set as the current activity! Run your application, and it should behave as shown in Figure 7-35.

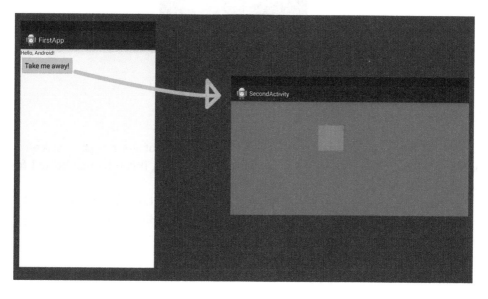

Figure 7-35   Calling startActivity()

Note: If you are having problems with any of the classes or .xml files at this point, you can download the source code at `jamescho7.com/book/chapter7/complete`.

LogCat: Basics of Debugging

As you develop Android applications and games, you will no doubt encounter the dialog box shown in Figure 7-36 many times. The error message shown in Figure 7-36 indicates that something wrong has happened to your application. To see detailed log messages regarding this fatal error, we use a tool called LogCat.

To make LogCat visible in Eclipse, click Window > Show View > Other. When the **Show View** dialog box opens, search for LogCat and select the non-deprecated version (as shown in Figure 7-37).

Figure 7-36   Unfortunately.......

You should notice LogCat is now docked to the bottom of your Eclipse screen near the console. Clicking on the LogCat tab opens up LogCat and it can be maximised for easier viewing, as shown in Figure 7-38.

The next time your application crashes, switch to the LogCat line and see if you can find an error message that describes the issue. In Figure 7-38, you can see that my app has crashed and LogCat is printing out a bunch of red error messages.

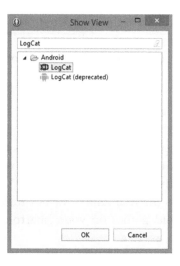

Figure 7-37   Showing LogCat

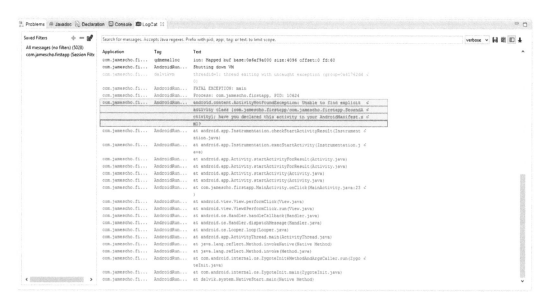

Figure 7-38   The LogCat Tab (Maximised)

Looking through some of the error messages in Figure 7-38, we can see the following:

```
android.content.ActivityNotFoundException: Unable to find explicit activity class
{com.jamescho.firstapp/com.jamescho.firstapp.SecondActivity}; have you declared this
activity in your AndroidManifest.xml?
```

The error message makes it apparent that I have not registered **SecondActivity** with the Manifest yet. After fixing this error, my application runs perfectly. Error messages such as this one can help you debug your code and fix broken code. We will talk about LogCat in more detail at a later time.

Onward to Android Game Development

We've taken an Android application apart, studied its building blocks and created our own application complete with user interaction. Next, we turn our attention to Android Game Development. As we did with Java, we will build an Android Game Development Framework that will serve as the foundation for our future games. Before long, you will be playing your own Android games on your smartphone and sharing your creations with the world!

CHAPTER 8: THE ANDROID GAME FRAMEWORK

This is where the fun begins. This chapter will combine the knowledge you've gained from building a Java game development framework and a simple Android application and walk you through the design and implementation of an Android game development framework.

Think back to the overarching architecture of our Java game development framework. You will recall that our framework was constructed one block at a time—we started with a **JFrame**, added a **JPanel**, implemented a game loop, attached an input handler and so on. You will find parallels to all of these components in our Android game development framework. In fact, with minor changes, most of the classes that we have written for our Java game development framework will translate directly into our new game development framework.

In reading this chapter, you will learn a lot more than just how to put together an Android game development framework. You will begin to appreciate the modularity, scalability and reusability of Java classes and truly understand why we use object-oriented programming.

Understanding the General Principles

As we create our Android game development framework, these are the principles that we will be following.

1. The goal of this chapter is to create an Android game development framework that provides all of the features implemented in the Java game development framework from Unit 2. We will be focusing on simplicity and ease of use.

2. The core architecture of our framework will not change from the Java game development framework, but specific implementations may change as many Java-based classes are not available to us in Android.

3. As we are developing for a mobile platform, we will emphasize performance by minimizing memory usage. We will only instantiate new objects when absolutely necessary, reusing existing objects whenever possible.

Building the Android Game Framework

Designing Our Framework

As previously mentioned, we will be maintaining the core architecture of the Java game development framework. The outline of the Android framework is provided in Figure 8-1. As you read through this, compare it with Figure 4-3 to see the parallels.

- Main classes

    - **GameMainActivity**: The starting point for our game, replaces **GameMain** class. Will serve as the Activity containing our **GameView**
    - **GameView**: The central class for our game, replaces the **Game** class. **GameView** will host our game loop, and will have methods to start and exit out of our game.
    - **Assets**: A convenience class that will allow you to quickly load images and sound files. Replaces the **Resource** class.

- State classes
    - **State**: Minor modifications from Unit 2.
    - **LoadState**: Minor modifications from Unit 2.
    - **MenuState**: Minor modifications from Unit 2.

- Utility classes
    - **InputHandler**: Listens for user touch events and dispatches the game's state classes to handle these events.
    - **RandomNumberGenerator**: Unchanged
    - **Painter**: A convenience class that will allow you to draw graphics much as you would in Java.

- Animation classes
    - **Animation**: Minor modifications from Unit 2.
    - **Frame**: Minor modifications from Unit 2.

Figure 8-1   Outline of the Android Framework

Explaining the Changes

Despite the fact that we will be using the Java programming language to build this framework, many Java classes are not available to us in Android. The packages `java.awt` and `javax.swing`, for example, which previously handled our graphics and input, are not included as part of the Android library. As such, we must rely on Android-specific code to implement these things. This requires us to modify all classes that were previously dependent on such packages.

Note: The full source code for the framework built-in this chapter can be found at the following link: **jamescho7.com/book/chapter8/complete**. If you get stuck, you might find it helpful to download the full source and see how a specific component fits into the overall framework. The architecture of this framework is very similar that that of Unit 2's framework, so you will find it easy to understand.

Creating the Project

We begin by creating an Android application named SimpleAndroidGDF. Inside Eclipse, right-click on your Package Explorer (Ctrl + Click on Mac) and select New > Android Application Project.

In the New Android Application dialog, enter the names shown in Figure 8-2. Set your Minimum Required SDK to API 9, and choose the latest version of the SDK available for Target SDK and Compile With options. As of this writing, the latest version of the SDK was API 21. Yours may be newer. Keep the Theme option as None and click Next.

Figure 8-2   New Android Application

Uncheck "Create custom launcher icon" and "Create activity" as shown in Figure 8-3. We will be providing our own icon and Activity. Keep the rest of the settings as they are (as shown in Figure 8-3). Your workspace location will differ depending on your setup.

Creating the GameMainActivity

Now that our project has been created, we must create our **GameMainActivity**—the starting point of our Android application. **GameMainActivity** will serve as the screen on which our game is drawn, hosting a custom SurfaceView as we've seen in Chapter 7.

Create a new package called com.jamescho.simpleandroidgdf (this matches the package name shown in Figure 8-2) and add a new class called **GameMainActivity** as shown in Figure 8-4.

Inside **GameMainActivity**, extend **Activity** and override an onCreate() method as shown in listing 8.01.

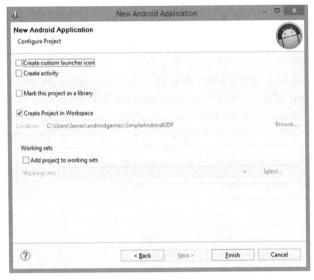

Figure 8-3   Continuing to Create the New Android Application

Figure 8-4   Creating **GameMainActivity**

Listing 8.01   GameMainActivity

```java
package com.jamescho.simpleandroidgdf;

import android.app.Activity;
import android.os.Bundle;

public class GameMainActivity extends Activity {
        @Override
        protected void onCreate(Bundle savedInstanceState) {
                super.onCreate(savedInstanceState);
        }

}
```

Registering the Activity

Now that our Activity has been created, we must declare it inside the AndroidManifest. Open `AndroidManifest.xml`, switch to the editor tab labeled `AndroidManifest.xml`, and declare your new Activity as shown highlighted below (note: your SDK versions may differ):

```xml
<manifest xmlns:android="http://schemas.android.com/apk/res/android"
    package="com.example.simpleandroidgdf"
    android:versionCode="1"
    android:versionName="1.0" >

    <uses-sdk
        android:minSdkVersion="9"
        android:targetSdkVersion="21" />

    <application
        android:allowBackup="true"
        android:icon="@drawable/ic_launcher"
        android:label="@string/app_name"
        android:theme="@style/AppTheme" >

        <activity
            android:screenOrientation="sensorLandscape"
            android:name="com.jamescho.simpleandroidgdf.GameMainActivity"
            android:label="@string/app_name"
            android:theme="@android:style/Theme.NoTitleBar.Fullscreen" >
            <intent-filter>
                <action android:name="android.intent.action.MAIN" />
                <category android:name="android.intent.category.LAUNCHER" />
            </intent-filter>
        </activity>

    </application>

</manifest>
```

In our Manifest, we set our new **GameMainActivity** as the launcher Activity, so that it becomes the starting point of our application. Note that we set `android:screenOrientation` as "`sensorLandscape`", which allows the player to hold the phone horizontally and use it in with either the left side or the right side facing up. Note also that we use the `android:theme` attribute to remove the title bar and set our application to full screen using the built in style `@android:style/Theme.NoTitleBar.Fullscreen`. This has the effect of removing the regions colored red in Figure 8-5, providing us with valuable screen estate we can use to display more of our game.

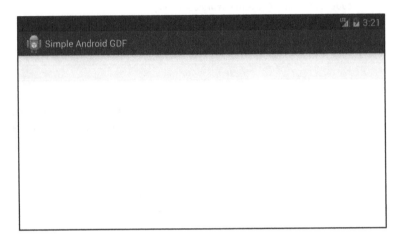

Figure 8-5   The Title Bar and Notification Bar

Running your Application

Now try running your application by right-clicking (Ctrl+click on Mac) on the SimpleAndroidGDF project and selecting Run As > 1 Android Application. You can run this either on an emulator or a physical device (refer to Chapter 7 if you need help with either option). Once your application is running, you should see a totally blank screen! Don't panic. This is the correct behavior, and you are looking at the emptiness of the **GameMainActivity**.

A Single Activity Game

As you know, Android applications typically use multiple Activities, transitioning from one screen to the next via the use of Intents. In our game development framework, however, we will only have a single Activity (**GameMainActivity**) and will rely on a dynamic SurfaceView which will display the currently selected state (**LoadState**, **PlayState** and so on). This is identical to the pattern we've used with our Java game development framework.

Working with a single Activity keeps our game's footprint small and provides us with the maximum control over our game's behavior in the Android ecosystem, which consists of multiple Activities running simultaneously. Using a SurfaceView grants us flexibility when drawing graphics, allowing us to draw pixel-perfect art just like we did with a **JPanel**.

Creating the GameView

We will now create a custom SurfaceView and attach it to our Activity. Create a new class called **GameView** inside com.jamescho.simpleandroid.gdf as shown in listing 8.02.

Listing 8.02   **GameView** (Incomplete)

```
package com.jamescho.simpleandroidgdf;

import android.content.Context;
import android.view.SurfaceView;

public class GameView extends SurfaceView {
        public GameView(Context context, int gameWidth, int gameHeight) {
                super(context);
        }

}
```

We will make use of the gameWidth and gameHeight values at a later time, so leave them alone for now.

Once the **GameView** has been created, you may (or may not) see the error shown in Figure 8-6:

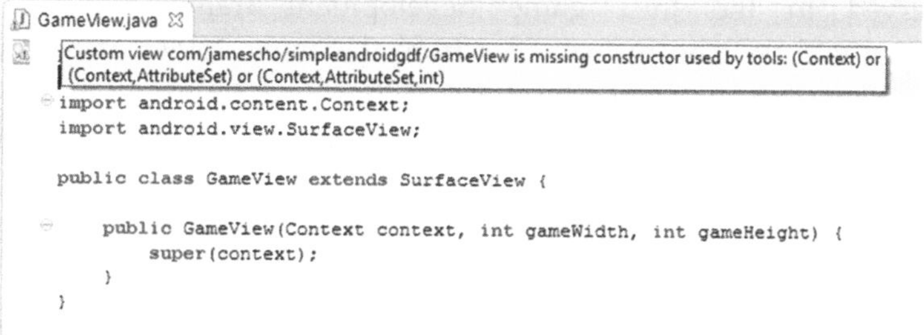

Figure 8-6   Missing Constructor

The warning in Figure 8-6 says that the Android developer tools uses one of the following constructors with every custom view: (Context) or (Context, AttributeSet) or (Context, AttributeSet, int). As our **GameView** only has a (Context, int, int) constructor, we will need to provide the following constructor (shown in bold) to make this warning disappear:

```
package com.jamescho.simpleandroidgdf;

import android.content.Context;
import android.view.SurfaceView;

public class GameView extends SurfaceView {
        public GameView(Context context, int gameWidth, int gameHeight) {
                super(context);
        }

        public GameView(Context context) {          // The new Constructor!
                super(context);
        }

}
```

This newly-added constructor is purely for our tools and will not affect our code.

Setting the GameView as the Content View

Now that we have a custom SurfaceView, we will set it as the content of our Activity. Start by navigating to the **GameMainActivity** and declaring the following class variables, importing android.content.res.AssetManager:

```
public static final int GAME_WIDTH = 800;
public static final int GAME_HEIGHT = 450;
public static GameView sGame;
public static AssetManager assets;
```

The variables GAME_WIDTH, GAME_HEIGHT, and sGame will serve the same purpose that they've served in the Java game development framework. The newly-added **AssetManager** will be used to load files from the assets folder of our Android project. This object will be accessed from other classes when loading images and sounds.

Inside the Activity's onCreate() method, we now initialize the variables sGame and assets then call setContentView(sGame) to set our new **GameView** as the content view of our Activity. This is shown in listing 8.03, which contains the full **GameMainActivity** class.

Listing 8.03   **GameMainActivity** Class

```
package com.jamescho.simpleandroidgdf;

import android.app.Activity;
import android.content.res.AssetManager;
import android.os.Bundle;

public class GameMainActivity extends Activity {

        public static final int GAME_WIDTH = 800;
        public static final int GAME_HEIGHT = 450;
        public static GameView sGame;
```

```
    public static AssetManager assets;

    @Override
    protected void onCreate(Bundle savedInstanceState) {
            super.onCreate(savedInstanceState);
            assets = getAssets();
            sGame = new GameView(this, GAME_WIDTH, GAME_HEIGHT);
            setContentView(sGame);
    }

}
```

Note: If you are having problems with any of the classes at this point, you can download the source code at **jamescho7.com/book/chapter8/checkpoint1**.

Discussing the GameView's Components

At the moment, our **GameView** is nothing more than a blank Canvas. Before we start building the **GameView**, let's first discuss what its role would be in our game development framework.

The **GameView**, like its Unit 2 counterpart **Game**, will contain our game loop. In this game loop, **GameView** will do the following: accept the player's input, update the current state and render the current state. To accomplish these tasks, **GameView** will require some helper classes.

Current State

As mentioned previously, **GameView** will manage a series of state classes. This remains virtually unchanged from the **Game** class's implementation.

Handling Input

As we are working with Android devices, our **GameView** will need to respond to touch events. To make this happen, we must provide it with an **OnTouchListener** (rather than a key or mouse listener). This will involve the following steps:
1. Create an **InputHandler** class.
2. Implement the **OnTouchListener** interface.
3. Set an instance of **InputHandler** as the **GameView**'s **OnTouchListener**

The **InputHandler** will then be notified whenever the player touches the **GameView**.

Handling Drawing

Recall that in Java, drawing is handled by the **Graphics** class. If you want to draw images onto an **Image** object, you must retrieve that **Image** object's **Graphics** object and call its drawing methods.

In Unit 2, to get images onto our screen in our Java game development framework, we created an empty, off-screen **Image** called gameImage. On every frame, we passed this gameImage's **Graphics** object to the current state, which asked the **Graphics** object to draw the appropriate images. Lastly, we took the prepared gameImage and drew it to the screen.

In Android, we follow the same pattern with minor differences. We use the **Bitmap** class instead of an **Image** class, and replace the **Graphics** class with the **Canvas** class.

To perform our drawing, we will create an empty, off-screen **Bitmap** called gameImage. On every frame, we will provide the gameImage's Canvas object to the current state, which will tell the received Canvas to draw the appropriate graphics. Once our gameImage is ready, we will draw it to the screen (or more accurately, to the Canvas object of our **GameView**, which is later drawn onto the screen).

Canvas and Memory Management

The **Canvas** class provides many drawing methods that are parallel to those in the **Graphics** class. For example, the **Canvas** class has a drawBitmap() method that draws an image (**Graphics** has a similar drawImage() method).

Despite the similarities to **Graphics**, Canvas has a limitation: many of its drawing calls require a Rectangle object as an argument, rather than integer position and dimension values. This means that if you wanted to draw a game object based on its x and y positions with its width and height, you would have to wrap those values inside a Rectangle object and pass it into the Canvas.

Given limitation, there are two routes we could take directly to implement graphics for our game:

1. We could create a new Rectangle object inside the render call of each game object using the game object's x, y, width and height values and pass it into the Canvas's drawing methods.
2. We could create a single Rectangle object for each game object and reuse it on every frame by updating its x, y, width and height values and passing it to the Canvas's drawing methods.

The first approach is great—if you enjoy playing games with lag. Excessive object allocation is your worst enemy. If we were to create a new Rectangle object on every render call (i.e. every frame) of each rendered game object, we would have 60 new Rectangle objects per second per game object (assuming 60 FPS). When working with an Android device with a limited amount of RAM, this would quickly fill up the heap (the location in memory where new objects are stored), causing the Garbage Collector to come in frequently and clean up any useless Rectangle objects to free memory. Every time this happens, your game will stutter. This results in a poor performance and a poor gameplay experience.

The second approach is better—we limit the number of Rectangles that are created. Assuming we have about 10-50 game objects, this means we would only need a couple dozen Rectangle objects, which likely will not merit garbage collection by themselves. In many games, this would work perfectly—especially if your game objects' bounding rectangles match the x, y, width and height values used to draw the its image, in which case you can use the bounding rectangles to check for collision *and* draw images. In games where the bounding box and the game objects' graphics are not perfectly aligned (such as Ellio), however, we would have to manually go into each class, create a new Rectangle and update it whenever the position or width of the game object changes. This reduces the programmer's efficiency, because you need to do more work.

The best approach is an indirect one: to create a middleman class between your state and the gameImage's Canvas object. This class, which we will call **Painter**, will make the Canvas behave more like a **Graphics** object by doing the work of creating and updating the Rectangles on behalf of the states and their game objects. This will make much more sense when you see it in action.

Screen Resolution vs. Game Resolution

It is important we distinguish the terms screen resolution and game resolution. Screen resolution describes the width and height in pixels of a physical device. Game resolution, on the other hand, describes the width and height of the game.

In the Java game development framework, our screen resolution and the game resolution were identical. We created a game image of size 800 x 450 and filled a window of equal size. When developing for Android, however, the two resolutions may not be the same, as different devices have different screen sizes and screen resolutions.

In Chapters 8 and 9, rather than matching our game resolution to the screen resolution, we will set a fixed game resolution of 800 x 450 (this was done in GameMainActivity). When performing rendering, we will create a game image of size 800 x 450 and scale it appropriately (up for higher screen resolutions and down for lower screen resolutions).

This method has both pros and cons. An advantage is that we can pretend that all Android devices have the same screen resolution of 800 x 450. We can build our game using this assumption and the game will behave identically on every device.

The obvious disadvantage is that not all Android devices actually have the screen resolution of 800 x 450. This means that, while the game will *behave* the same on every screen resolution, it may not *look* the same. The game will look pixel-perfect on 800 x 450 screens, lose detail on 1600 x 900 screens, and so on. If a device's screen has a completely different aspect ratio (the ratio of width and height—16:9 for our game) than our game, the game will stretch unevenly.

For most cases, I've found that the pros outweigh the cons. Games built with the aforementioned approach look good on many devices. In Appendix C, you will find a link to sample projects that show a more flexible solution.

Building the State, InputHandler and Painter Classes

Now that we have discussed the **GameView** in great detail, let's start building its individual components.

Painter

Create a new package called com.jamescho.framework.util and create a new **Painter** class as shown in listing 8.04.

Listing 8.04   **Painter** Class (Completed)

```
01 package com.jamescho.framework.util;
02
03 import android.graphics.Bitmap;
04 import android.graphics.Canvas;
05 import android.graphics.Paint;
06 import android.graphics.Rect;
07 import android.graphics.RectF;
08 import android.graphics.Typeface;
09
10 public class Painter {
11
12      private Canvas canvas;
13      private Paint paint;
14      private Rect srcRect;
15      private Rect dstRect;
16      private RectF dstRectF;
17
18      public Painter(Canvas canvas) {
19              this.canvas = canvas;
20              paint = new Paint();
21              srcRect = new Rect();
22              dstRect = new Rect();
23              dstRectF = new RectF();
24      }
25
26      public void setColor(int color) {
27              paint.setColor(color);
28      }
29
30      public void setFont(Typeface typeface, float textSize) {
31              paint.setTypeface(typeface);
32              paint.setTextSize(textSize);
33      }
34
35      public void drawString(String str, int x, int y) {
36              canvas.drawText(str, x, y, paint);
37      }
38
39      public void fillRect(int x, int y, int width, int height) {
40              dstRect.set(x, y, x + width, y + height);
41              paint.setStyle(Paint.Style.FILL);
42              canvas.drawRect(dstRect, paint);
43      }
44
45      public void drawImage(Bitmap bitmap, int x, int y) {
46              canvas.drawBitmap(bitmap, x, y, paint);
47      }
48
49      public void drawImage(Bitmap bitmap, int x, int y, int width, int height) {
50              srcRect.set(0, 0, bitmap.getWidth(), bitmap.getHeight());
51              dstRect.set(x, y, x + width, y + height);
```

```
52                    canvas.drawBitmap(bitmap, srcRect, dstRect, paint);
53        }
54
55        public void fillOval(int x, int y, int width, int height) {
56                paint.setStyle(Paint.Style.FILL);
57                dstRectF.set(x, y, x + width, y + height);
58                canvas.drawOval(dstRectF, paint);
59        }
60 }
```

The purpose of this class is to make the rendering process in our Android framework resemble that from our Java framework. Notice that our **Painter** class's methods are very similar to the ones we are familiar with from the Java **Graphics** class. This means that a **Painter** object can be used like a Java **Graphics** object, and it will do the work of translating your draw calls into Canvas draw calls.

The Canvas object inside our **Painter** class will belong to the gameImage. To render images onto our gameImage, we simply ask our **Painter** to draw. In the **GameView**, this gameImage will be drawn to the screen.

The Paint object is used for various styling options. We use it to set the **TypeFace** (font), font size, color of drawn polygons, and etc. For more information on the **Paint** class, please see the Android API Reference for the **Paint** class:

http://developer.android.com/reference/android/graphics/Paint.html

Notice that the **Rectangle** class from Java AWT (java.awt.Rectangle) has been replaced with the Android equivalent **Rect** (android.graphics.Rect) and **RectF** (android.graphics.RectF which is used to store float-based positions rather than integer-based positions).

Note: The constructors for android.graphics.Rect and android.graphics.RectF are different from that of java.awt.Rectangle.
The java.awt.Rectangle is created using the parameters:
(int x, int y, int width, int height).
The Android **Rect** objects are created using the parameters:
(int left, int top, int right, int bottom).
The Rect.set(...) and RectF.set(...) use the same conventions to change the position of an existing Rect object.

I will not go into individual Canvas drawing calls here, as they are mostly self-explanatory. For a complete discussion of all the methods used, please visit the Android API Reference for the Canvas class:

`http://developer.android.com/reference/android/graphics/Canvas.html`

State

Create a new package called `com.jamescho.game.state`, and create a new class called **State** as shown in Listing 8.05.

Listing 8.05   **State** (Completed)

```
package com.jamescho.game.state;

import android.view.MotionEvent;

import com.jamescho.framework.util.Painter;
import com.jamescho.simpleandroidgdf.GameMainActivity;

public abstract class State {

        public void setCurrentState(State newState) {
                GameMainActivity.sGame.setCurrentState(newState);
        }

        public abstract void init();

        public abstract void update(float delta);

        public abstract void render(Painter g);

        public abstract boolean onTouch(MotionEvent e, int scaledX, int scaledY);

}
```

After doing this you will have the error shown in Figure 8-7. Choose the option "Create method 'setCurrentState(State)' in type '**GameView**'." This will automatically create the method shown in Figure 8-8 inside **GameView**.

Import **State**, making sure you choose the correct one: (`com.jamescho.game.state`). At this point, our **GameView** class should look that shown in listing 8.06. Leave the class alone for now. We will come back to it later.

Figure 8-7   Method Undefined

Figure 8-8   setCurrentState()

Listing 8.06   GameView (Updated)

```
package com.jamescho.simpleandroidgdf;

import com.jamescho.game.state.State;

import android.content.Context;
import android.view.SurfaceView;

public class GameView extends SurfaceView {
    public GameView(Context context, int gameWidth, int gameHeight) {
        super(context);
    }

    public GameView(Context context) {
        super(context);
    }
```

```
    public void setCurrentState(State newState) {
        // TODO Auto-generated method stub

    }

}
```

Let's go back to **State** class from listing 8.05. All the errors should now be gone. Notice that the **State** class is virtually identical to its Unit 2 counterpart with the exception of the following changes.

- The **Graphics** parameter of render() has been updated to a **Painter**.
- All of the keyboard and mouse input methods have been removed and replaced with onTouch(). This method will be implemented inside each individual state class, and will be called by **InputHandler** when the player touches the screen.

The **MotionEvent** parameter of the onTouch() method provides information regarding the touch that has triggered the method to be called (such as whether the touch was a drag, a tap or a release). The parameters scaledX and scaledY will be described in detail with the **InputHandler** class.

InputHandler

Inside the package com.jamescho.framework.util, create the **InputHandler** class as shown in listing 8.07.

Listing 8.07   InputHandler

```
package com.jamescho.framework.util;

import android.view.MotionEvent;
import android.view.View;
import android.view.View.OnTouchListener;

import com.jamescho.game.state.State;
import com.jamescho.simpleandroidgdf.GameMainActivity;

public class InputHandler implements OnTouchListener {

    private State currentState;

    public void setCurrentState(State currentState) {
        this.currentState = currentState;
    }

    @Override
    public boolean onTouch(View v, MotionEvent event) {
        int scaledX = (int) ((event.getX() / v.getWidth()) *
                GameMainActivity.GAME_WIDTH);
        int scaledY = (int) ((event.getY() / v.getHeight()) *
                GameMainActivity.GAME_HEIGHT);
        return currentState.onTouch(event, scaledX, scaledY);
```

```
        }
}
```

The **InputHandler**'s role remains unchanged since Unit 2. Instead of implementing a **KeyListener** or a **MouseListener**, however, we implement the **OnTouchListener** by implementing the following method:

```
public boolean onTouch(View v, MotionEvent event)...
```

This allows us to set an instance of **InputHandler** as the **OnTouchListener** of our **GameView** (we will do this later). From that point on, our **InputHandler**'s onTouch() method will be called whenever the player touches the screen. We return `true` if we responded to the touch event, `false` otherwise.

When onTouch() is called, it receives two parameters from the Android system: the **View** that the player has interacted with and the **MotionEvent** that represents the touch that triggered onTouch().

The x and y coordinates retrieved using event.getX() and event.getY() tell you the coordinates of the touch with respect to the screen resolution. For our framework, we want these values scaled with respect to the the game resolution. This is accomplished inside onTouch() by dividing the event coordinates by the screen's dimensions (v.getWidth() and v.getHeight()) and multiplying by the game's dimensions (GameMainActivity.GAME_WIDTH and GameMainActivity.GAME_HEIGHT).

Note: If you are having problems with any of the classes at this point, you can download the source code at jamescho7.com/book/chapter8/checkpoint2.

Adding the Assets

The res Folder

Let's take a short break from coding and start adding some images that we will need in order to complete our game development framework. Open your **res** folder inside your Android project, as shown in Figure 8-9.

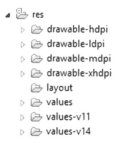

Figure 8-9   The res folder

You will notice that you have four folders named **drawable** each with a suffix. Ldpi, mdpi, hdpi, xhdpi stand for low, medium, high and extra high density, respectively. These folders allow you to create multiple versions of the same images to cater to various screen types. Depending on the device running your application, the Android system will determine the optimal resource to use. We will make use of this feature to provide an icon image that looks good on a range of screens.

Note: For more information on multiple screen sizes, please visit the following page: `http://developer.android.com/guide/practices/screens_support.html`

Downloading the Image Files

Go to **jamescho7.com/book/chapter8/** on your web browser, and download the following image files to any folder outside your project (alternatively, create images of your own with the provided names and sizes):

ic_launcher_36.png (36px x 36px) – to be used as the icon image for ldpi devices

ic_launcher_48.png (48px x 48px) – to be used as icon image for mdpi devices

ic_launcher_72.png (72px x 72px) – to be used as icon image for hdpi devices

ic_launcher_96.png (96px x 96px) – to be used as icon image for xhdpi devices

welcome.png (800px x 450px) – to be used as welcome screen for framework

Adding the Icon Images

Copy the four icon images into your **drawable** folders, as shown in Figure 8-10. You should put the 36 x 36 image inside the ldpi folder, 48 x 48 image inside the mdpi folder, and so on.

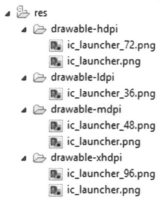

Figure 8-10   Adding the Icon Images

Next, remove the previously existing `ic_launcher.png` images, if present, as shown in Figure 8-11.

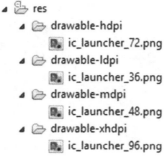

Figure 8-11   After Removing the Original `ic_launcher` images

Now rename all four files as `ic_launcher.png` as shown in Figure 8-12 (this is the name we specified for our icon inside our Manifest earlier on).

Figure 8-12   Renaming the Icon Images

And now our icons are ready! After running your application on your device (sending over the latest build), your application's icon will change as shown in Figure 8-13. Of course, the application will still not do anything.

Figure 8-13   Updated App Icon

Adding the Welcome Image

All game-related images and sound files used inside our game will go inside of the **assets** folder. Copy the downloaded (or created) `welcome.png` image into the **assets** folder as shown in Figure 8-14.

Figure 8-14   Place the welcome.png image in the assets folder.

Creating the Assets Class

Inside the package `com.jamescho.simpleandroidgdf`, create the **Assets** class as shown in listing 8.08. We will discuss it afterwards.

Listing 8.08   Assets (Completed)

```
01 package com.jamescho.simpleandroidgdf
02
03 import java.io.IOException;
04 import java.io.InputStream;
05
06 import android.graphics.Bitmap;
07 import android.graphics.Bitmap.Config;
08 import android.graphics.BitmapFactory;
09 import android.graphics.BitmapFactory.Options;
10 import android.media.AudioManager;
11 import android.media.SoundPool;
12
13 public class Assets {
14
15     private static SoundPool soundPool;
16     public static Bitmap welcome;
17
18     public static void load() {
19         welcome = loadBitmap("welcome.png", false);
20     }
21
22     private static Bitmap loadBitmap(String filename, boolean transparency) {
23         InputStream inputStream = null;
24         try {
25             inputStream = GameMainActivity.assets.open(filename);
26         } catch (IOException e) {
27             e.printStackTrace();
28         }
29         Options options = new Options();
30         if (transparency) {
31             options.inPreferredConfig = Config.ARGB_8888;
32         } else {
33             options.inPreferredConfig = Config.RGB_565;
34         }
35         Bitmap bitmap = BitmapFactory.decodeStream(inputStream, null,
36                 new Options());
37         return bitmap;
38     }
39
```

```
40      private static int loadSound(String filename) {
41              int soundID = 0;
42              if (soundPool == null) {
43                      soundPool = new SoundPool(25, AudioManager.STREAM_MUSIC, 0);
44              }
45              try {
46                  soundID = soundPool.load(GameMainActivity.assets.openFd(filename),1);
47              } catch (IOException e) {
48                      e.printStackTrace();
49              }
50              return soundID;
51      }
52
53      public static void playSound(int soundID) {
54              soundPool.play(soundID, 1, 1, 1, 0, 1);
55      }
56
57 }
```

Review the code in listing 8.08. You will find that much of it is self-explanatory. I will not discuss individual built-in method calls here, as many of these really need to be studied and memorized, not just described. For information on specific methods and arguments, please see the Android API Reference as needed at the following page:

`http://developer.android.com/reference/packages.html`

The **Assets** class in lising 8.08 replaces the **Resources** class from Unit 2. It still performs the same functions, allowing us to load images and sounds into memory to be used throughout the game. We can no longer use the same methods for file loading, however, as Android handles file management a little differently.

Memory vs. File System

Memory management in game development is similar to being hungry at a buffet—you want to maximize the amount of time spent eating and minimize the amount of time spent retrieving food.

Think of RAM as a plate of food on your dining table. You have easy access to it and can grab things from it immediately if needed. The file system, on the other hand, is more like the buffet table across the room with a long line of people who don't share your sense of urgency.

When our Android game starts for the first time, all of our assets will initially be stored in the file system. For easy access to these assets during gameplay, we must retrieve these assets from the file system and load them into our RAM, much as we would grab a plate of food from the buffet table to bring back to our dining table.

RAM is limited, and you must be careful in order to avoid running out of space. Rather than choosing to load one high quality image, you may opt for two medium quality images. Rather than loading every asset into the memory at once, you may choose to only keep the most frequently needed assets in memory and make a trip to the file system for the less frequently needed files.

Loading Images from assets Folder

Have a look at the `loadBitmap()` method, which performs an image load in three steps. It first creates an **InputStream** object (used to read data from the device's file system) by opening an image file from the **assets** folder. It then creates an **Options** object that specifies how that image should be stored in memory, and finally creates a new Bitmap using the **BitmapFactory** class, passing in the **InputStream** and the **Options** objects as argumetns.

Let's talk a little more about the **Options** object. When loading a Bitmap in Android, you need to be aware of its memory footprint—i.e. how much RAM that Bitmap will take up. Memory usage increases with an image's size and quality. Supporting transparency for your image also increases memory consumption.

When loading an image into memory, we simply create a Bitmap variable and call the `loadBitmap()` method, passing in the name of the image to be loaded. The `loadBitmap()` method accepts boolean argument, which allows you to specify whether you want transparency or not. This value is used to determine whether the Bitmap configuration should be `RGB_565` (no transparency, less memory consumption) or `ARGB_8888` (transparent images, greater memory consumption).

For more on Bitmap configurations and to learn how to calculate the amount of memory each Bitmap will take up at runtime, please see the following page:

`http://developer.android.com/reference/android/graphics/Bitmap.Config.html`

Loading Sounds from assets Folder

Short sound files should be loaded into the RAM. This allows you to access them quickly so that you can play sound effects without waiting for the sound to be retrieved from the file system.

To make this happen, we create a single **SoundPool** object that will act as a manager of every sound file loaded into memory. The Assets class's `loadSound()` method will accept a filename, open the requested sound file and load it into the **SoundPool**. At this point, the requested sound file receives an integer ID which we can use to play that sound using the `playSound()` method in the **Assets** class. You will see an example of this in the next chapter.

For more information about the **SoundPool** and the various arguments that I have provided when calling its methods, please see:

`http://developer.android.com/reference/android/media/SoundPool.html`

Note: Larger sound files, which tend to be music files, may take up too much space in RAM and should be streamed directly from the file system. We will discuss how to implement this in Unit 4.

Creating the State Classes

Now that we have our welcome image loaded, we can begin creating our state classes. Begin by creating the **LoadState** class inside com.jamescho.game.state, extending the **State** class (com.jamescho.game.State) and adding the unimplemented methods, as shown in Figure 8-15.

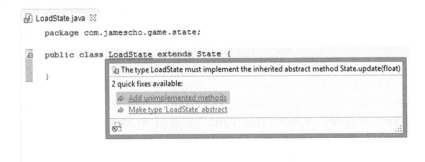

Figure 8-15   Creating the **LoadState** Class

Then, fill in the method bodies as shown in listing 8.09, double-checking the import statements.

Listing 8.09   LoadState (Completed)

```
package com.jamescho.game.state;

import android.view.MotionEvent;

import com.jamescho.framework.util.Painter;
import com.jamescho.simpleandroidgdf.Assets;

public class LoadState extends State {

        @Override
        public void init() {
                Assets.load();
        }

        @Override
        public void update(float delta) {
                setCurrentState(new MenuState());
        }
```

```
    @Override
    public void render(Painter g) {
    }

    @Override
    public boolean onTouch(MotionEvent e, int scaledX, int scaledY) {
            return false;
    }

}
```

The **LoadState** asks the **Assets** class to load our assets, and sets the current state to **MenuState**, which we will create next.

Following the same steps as before, create the **MenuState** class inside com.jamescho.game.state, extending **State**, adding the unimplemented methods and filling in the render() method as shown in listing 8.10:

Listing 8.10   MenuState (Completed)

```
package com.jamescho.game.state;

import android.view.MotionEvent;

import com.jamescho.framework.util.Painter;
import com.jamescho.simpleandroidgdf.Assets;

public class MenuState extends State {

        @Override
        public void init() {
        }

        @Override
        public void update(float delta) {
        }

        @Override
        public void render(Painter g) {
                g.drawImage(Assets.welcome, 0, 0);
        }

        @Override
        public boolean onTouch(MotionEvent e, int scaledX, int scaledY) {
                return false;
        }

}
```

The **MenuState** simply displays the Assets.welcome image for now.

Note: If you are having problems with any of the classes at this point, you can download the source code at jamescho7.com/book/chapter8/checkpoint3.

Creating the GameView Class

All of our individual components are ready, and we can now start implementing our **GameView**. This class will be very similar to the **Game** class from Unit 2, except for the inclusion of some Android-specific code.

Declaring the Variables
Start by declaring the following variables:

```
private Bitmap gameImage;
private Rect gameImageSrc;
private Rect gameImageDst;
private Canvas gameCanvas;
private Painter graphics;

private Thread gameThread;
private volatile boolean running = false;
private volatile State currentState;

private InputHandler inputHandler;
```

Update your import statements as shown below:

```
import android.content.Context;
import android.graphics.Bitmap;
import android.graphics.Canvas;
import android.graphics.Rect;
import android.view.SurfaceView;

import com.jamescho.framework.util.InputHandler;
import com.jamescho.framework.util.Painter;
import com.jamescho.game.state.State;
```

You have seen most of these variables before from our Java game development framework, but a few additions and changes are noteworthy. Recall that our drawing strategy is to create an off-screen image and render it to the screen when ready. For this purpose, `gameImage` makes a return, this time as type Bitmap. We also create a variable that will represent this `gameImage`'s Canvas object, which we will pass on to our Painter called `graphics`. The Painter will handle the `currentState`'s draw calls by drawing the requested images to the `gameCanvas`. I elaborate on this process later.

Initializing the Graphics Variables
Inside our constructor, initialize the five graphics-related variables as shown below:

```
...
public GameView(Context context, int gameWidth, int gameHeight) {
        super(context);
        gameImage = Bitmap.createBitmap(gameWidth, gameHeight, Bitmap.Config.RGB_565);
        gameImageSrc = new Rect(0, 0, gameImage.getWidth(), gameImage.getHeight());
        gameImageDst = new Rect();
        gameCanvas = new Canvas(gameImage);
        graphics = new Painter(gameCanvas);
}
...
```

The gameImage is initialized using the **Bitmap** class's createBitmap method, which accepts an image width, height and configuration. We set the width and height equal to the gameWidth and gameHeight variables and configure the image as RGB_565. gameImage will cover the entire screen and will not need to be transparent.

The **Rect** gameImageSrc will be used to specify which region of the gameImage should be drawn to the screen. In our case, we want the entire gameImage drawn, so we pass in the appropriate arguments.

The **Rect** gameImageDst will be used to specify how the gameImage should be scaled when drawn to the screen. We will come back to modify this value later.

The Canvas gameCanvas is the Canvas of our gameImage. To draw an image onto our gameImage, we must draw onto its Canvas. Rather than doing this directly, we go through the **Painter** class, who will accept the gameCanvas and perform drawing calls as requested by the current state.

At this point, your **GameView** class should match that shown in listing 8.11.

Listing 8.11   GameView (Incomplete)

```
package com.jamescho.simpleandroidgdf;

import android.content.Context;
import android.graphics.Bitmap;
import android.graphics.Canvas;
import android.graphics.Rect;
import android.view.SurfaceView;

import com.jamescho.framework.util.InputHandler;
import com.jamescho.framework.util.Painter;
import com.jamescho.game.state.State;

public class GameView extends SurfaceView {

  private Bitmap gameImage;
  private Rect gameImageSrc;
  private Rect gameImageDst;
  private Canvas gameCanvas;
  private Painter graphics;

  private Thread gameThread;
  private volatile boolean running = false;
  private volatile State currentState;
```

```java
    private InputHandler inputHandler;

    public GameView(Context context, int gameWidth, int gameHeight) {
        super(context);
        gameImage = Bitmap.createBitmap(gameWidth, gameHeight, Bitmap.Config.RGB_565);
        gameImageSrc = new Rect(0, 0, gameImage.getWidth(), gameImage.getHeight());
        gameImageDst = new Rect();
        gameCanvas = new Canvas(gameImage);
        graphics = new Painter(gameCanvas);
    }

    public GameView(Context context) {
        super(context);
    }

    public void setCurrentState(State newState) {
        // TODO Auto-generated method stub

    }

}
```

Adding the SurfaceHolder Callback

When working with a surface such as SurfaceView, we must be careful not to start rendering too early and stop rendering too late. An Android application switches from one Activity to another, meaning that our SurfaceView may be created and destroyed at our player's whim.

We can choose to be informed when the surface has been created and when the surface has been destroyed by implementing a SurfaceHolder Callback. To do so, we must first update our import statements by adding the lines shown below:

```java
import android.util.Log;
import android.view.SurfaceHolder;
import android.view.SurfaceHolder.Callback;
```

Next, add the lines of code shown below in bold at the bottom of your constructor:

```java
public GameView(Context context, int gameWidth, int gameHeight) {
                super(context);
                ...
                graphics = new Painter(gameCanvas);

                SurfaceHolder holder = getHolder();
                holder.addCallback(new Callback() {

                });

}
```

This retrieves the SurfaceHolder of our SurfaceView (an interface that grants us access to the SurfaceView's surface) and attaches a new instance of **Callback** to it.

Note: The lines of code colored red above make up an anonymous inner class implementing the **Callback** Interface. This is the same syntax we used in Chapter 7 to implement an OnClickListener for our buttons.

As **Callback** is an interface, we must add its unimplemented methods as shown in Figure 8-16.

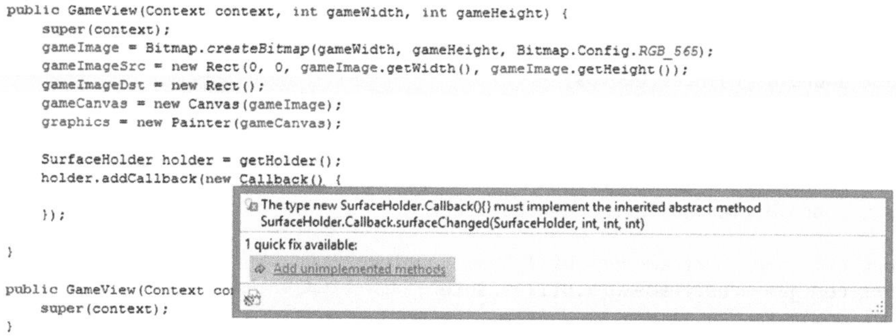

```
public GameView(Context context, int gameWidth, int gameHeight) {
    super(context);
    gameImage = Bitmap.createBitmap(gameWidth, gameHeight, Bitmap.Config.RGB_565);
    gameImageSrc = new Rect(0, 0, gameImage.getWidth(), gameImage.getHeight());
    gameImageDst = new Rect();
    gameCanvas = new Canvas(gameImage);
    graphics = new Painter(gameCanvas);

    SurfaceHolder holder = getHolder();
    holder.addCallback(new Callback() {
                      ┌──────────────────────────────────────────────────────────────┐
    });              │ ⓘ The type new SurfaceHolder.Callback(){} must implement the inherited abstract method │
                     │   SurfaceHolder.Callback.surfaceChanged(SurfaceHolder, int, int, int)                 │
}                    │ 1 quick fix available:                                                                 │
                     │ ⊹ Add unimplemented methods                                                            │
public GameView(Context co│                                                                              │
    super(context);       │ ⊞                                                                             │
}                     └──────────────────────────────────────────────────────────────┘
```

Figure 8-16   Implementing the **Callback** Interface

Let's see if our Callbacks are working properly. Fill in the method bodies for surfaceCreated() and surfaceDestroyed() as shown below:

```java
SurfaceHolder holder = getHolder();
holder.addCallback(new Callback() {

        @Override
        public void surfaceCreated(SurfaceHolder holder) {
                Log.d("GameView", "Surface Created");
        }

        @Override
        public void surfaceChanged(SurfaceHolder holder, int format,
                int width, int height) {
                // TODO Auto-generated method stub
        }

        @Override
        public void surfaceDestroyed(SurfaceHolder holder) {
                Log.d("GameView", "Surface Destroyed");
        }

});
```

Note: Log.d() is used for printing debug messages to LogCat. By convention, you pass in the name of the class calling the method and a **String** message. The method behaves like System.out.println().

If you are having any errors in **GameView**, compare your import statements, variable names and methods to listing 8.12.

Listing 8.12   GameView (Incomplete)

```
01 package com.jamescho.simpleandroidgdf;
02
03 import android.content.Context;
04 import android.graphics.Bitmap;
05 import android.graphics.Canvas;
06 import android.graphics.Rect;
07 import android.view.SurfaceView;
08 import android.util.Log;
09 import android.view.SurfaceHolder;
10 import android.view.SurfaceHolder.Callback;
11
12 import com.jamescho.framework.util.InputHandler;
13 import com.jamescho.framework.util.Painter;
14 import com.jamescho.game.state.State;
15
16 public class GameView extends SurfaceView {
17
18      private Bitmap gameImage;
19      private Rect gameImageSrc;
20      private Rect gameImageDst;
21      private Canvas gameCanvas;
22      private Painter graphics;
23
24      private Thread gameThread;
25      private volatile boolean running = false;
26      private volatile State currentState;
27
28      private InputHandler inputHandler;
29
30      public GameView(Context context, int gameWidth, int gameHeight) {
31          super(context);
32          gameImage = Bitmap.createBitmap(gameWidth, gameHeight, Bitmap.Config.RGB_565);
33          gameImageSrc = new Rect(0, 0, gameImage.getWidth(), gameImage.getHeight());
34          gameImageDst = new Rect();
35          gameCanvas = new Canvas(gameImage);
36          graphics = new Painter(gameCanvas);
37
38          SurfaceHolder holder = getHolder();
39          holder.addCallback(new Callback() {
40
41              @Override
42              public void surfaceCreated(SurfaceHolder holder) {
43                      Log.d("GameView", "Surface Created");
44              }
45
46              @Override
47              public void surfaceChanged(SurfaceHolder holder, int format,
```

```
                                      int width, int height) {
48              // TODO Auto-generated method stub
49              }
50
51              @Override
52              public void surfaceDestroyed(SurfaceHolder holder) {
53                      Log.d("GameView", "Surface Destroyed");
54              }
55
56          });
57
58      }
59
60      public GameView(Context context) {
61              super(context);
62      }
63
64      public void setCurrentState(State newState) {
65              // TODO Auto-generated method stub
66      }
67
68 }
```

Testing the Application in DDMS Perspective

We will now switch to a new Eclipse Perspective—a pre-configured set of view tabs that helps you accomplish a certain task. Thus far, we've been working exclusively from the Java perspective, as indicated in the top-right corner of the application (shown in Figure 8-17).

Figure 8-17   The Current Perspective (Top Right Corner of Eclipse Window)

To switch into the DDMS perspective, click the DDMS button in shown in Figure 8-17. If this button is not present, click the Open Perspective Button (The button shown to the left of the "Java" perspective in Figure 8-17). You should see the window shown in Figure 8-18 appear:

Figure 8-18   The Open Perspective Window

Select the DDMS option, and hit OK. You will see the DDMS Perspective as shown in Figure 8-19.

Figure 8-19   The DDMS Perspective

Now connect a physical Android device or run an emulator. You should see your device listed as Online in the Devices window to the top-left, as shown in Figure 8-20.

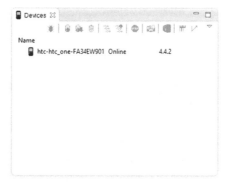

Figure 8-20   Devices View

Note: If your physical device says Offline, try reconnecting the phone and verify that you have the latest USB drivers installed for the device. If an emulator says Offline, let it boot completely and check again.

Now run your application. Your Devices view will update, listing the application under your device as shown in Figure 8-21.

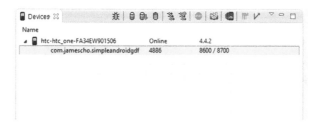

Figure 8-21   Application Running

You will notice that your LogCat view to the bottom of the screen will begin to update, listing various events that are happening on your device. This can be a bit overwhelming, because a lot of things are happening behind the scenes on your device.

As we only care about our application at the moment, let's add a filter. Click the + button next to Saved Filters in your LogCat view, as shown in Figure 8-22.

Figure 8-22   Creating a Filter

Choose a Filter Name and enter the Application Name as shown in Figure 8-23. This should match the application listed under your Devices view.

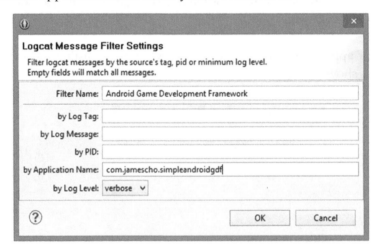

Figure 8-23   Logcat Filter Settings

Once you have created and selected the filter, LogCat will display all of the messages that are arising from your application. Look for the message "Surface Created" with the tag "GameView" as shown in Figure 8-24 (this should have appeared when your application was executed for the first time).

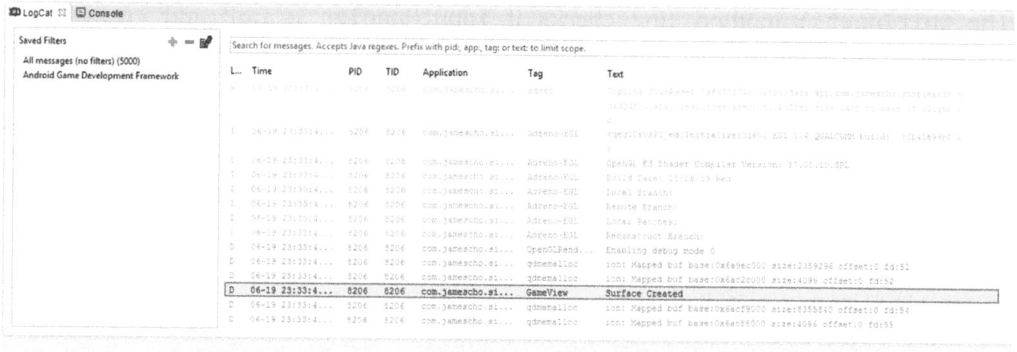

Figure 8-24   Logcat (Filtered)

As you switch in and out of the application, you will notice the following messages appear accordingly:

```
Tag:            Text:
GameView        Surface Created
....
GameView        Surface Destroyed
```

This verifies that our SurfaceHolder Callback is indeed working, and the messages tells us that whenever we switch out of our application, our surface will be destroyed. On the other hand, when we open our application for the first time or switch back into our application, our surface will be created. We will use this knowledge to continue building our **GameView**.

Note: You can use the DDMS perspective to take screenshots of your device, simulate phone calls or even check its memory usage. For more information on the DDMS perspective, please see the official documentation:
http://developer.android.com/tools/debugging/ddms.html

Setting up Input

Let's now attach an instance of **InputHandler** as the **GameView's** OnTouchListener. Return to the Java perspective and add the following method into your **GameView** class:

```java
private void initInput() {
        if (inputHandler == null) {
                inputHandler = new InputHandler();
        }
        setOnTouchListener(inputHandler);
}
```

The `initInput()` method first checks if `inputHandler` is null and creates one if necessary (this step is necessary because `initInput()` will be called every time our surface is created—i.e. when the app is running for the first time or resuming after being paused. See next paragraph). The method then sets the `inputHandler` as the `OnTouchListener` of the **GameView**.

Call the newly-created method inside the `surfaceCreated()` method of our SurfaceHolder's Callback, as shown in bold below:

```
holder.addCallback(new Callback() {

        @Override
        public void surfaceCreated(SurfaceHolder holder) {
                Log.d("GameView", "Surface Created");
                initInput();
        }

        @Override
        public void surfaceChanged(SurfaceHolder holder, int format,
                        int width, int height) {
                // TODO Auto-generated method stub
        }

        @Override
        public void surfaceDestroyed(SurfaceHolder holder) {
                Log.d("GameView", "Surface Destroyed");
        }
});
```

Note: In the Android game framework, the surfaceCreated() method will behave as the `addNotify()` method from the Game class in Unit 2.

Setting the Initial State

Next, complete the empty `setCurrentState()` method as shown below:

```
public void setCurrentState(State newState) {
        System.gc();
        newState.init();
        currentState = newState;
        inputHandler.setCurrentState(currentState);
}
```

We will call this method after initializing the input. Import the **LoadState** class (`com.jamescho.game.state.LoadState`), and add the lines shown in bold to the `surfaceCreated()` method in callback.

```
public void surfaceCreated(SurfaceHolder holder) {
        initInput();
        if (currentState == null) {
                setCurrentState(new LoadState());
        }
}
```

As with `inputHandler`, we first make sure `currentState` is null before creating a new **LoadState**. This has the effect of retaining the `currentState` even when the application is paused. For example, if the user switches out of our application during the **PlayState** and returns to the application later, the `currentState` will remain as **PlayState**.

Implementing the Game Loop Thread

We will now setup our game loop using the same pattern from Unit 2. This means that we will be executing the game loop in a separate Thread (`gameThread`). Let's take this one step at a time.

1. Implement the **Runnable** interface. Your class declaration should change to include "implements Runnable" as shown below:

```
public class GameView extends SurfaceView implements Runnable {
```

2. Add the unimplemented `run()` method.
3. Create the methods `initGame()` and `pauseGame()` as shown below:

```
private void initGame() {
        running = true;
        gameThread = new Thread(this, "Game Thread");
        gameThread.start();
}

private void pauseGame() {
        running = false;
        while (gameThread.isAlive()) {
                try {
                        gameThread.join();
                        break;
                } catch (InterruptedException e) {
                }
        }
}
```

The `initGame()` method remains unchanged from the Java game development framework. The `pauseGame()` method is a new addition. Inside it, the `Thread.join()` method is used to tell `gameThread` to stop executing when the application should pause. We will call this method when our game is about to pause—specifically inside the `surfaceDestroyed()` method of the Callback.

4. Call the `initGame()` and `pauseGame()` methods as shown in `surfaceCreated()` and `surfaceDestroyed()` in the following example, removing the `Log.d(...)` statements and importing `com.jamescho.game.state.LoadState`.

```
...
SurfaceHolder holder = getHolder();
holder.addCallback(new Callback() {
```

```
@Override
public void surfaceCreated(SurfaceHolder holder) {
    initInput();
    if (currentState == null) {
        setCurrentState(new LoadState());
    }
    initGame();
}

@Override
public void surfaceChanged(SurfaceHolder holder, int format,int width,
                    int height) {
    // TODO Auto-generated method stub
}

@Override
public void surfaceDestroyed(SurfaceHolder holder) {
    pauseGame();
}

});
...
```

Before we implement the run() method, let's add the methods to update and render the current state and draw the gameImage to the screen

5. Add the following methods to your class:

```
private void updateAndRender(long delta) {
    currentState.update(delta / 1000f);
    currentState.render(graphics);
    renderGameImage();
}

private void renderGameImage() {
    Canvas screen = getHolder().lockCanvas();
    if (screen != null) {
        screen.getClipBounds(gameImageDst);
        screen.drawBitmap(gameImage, gameImageSrc, gameImageDst, null);
        getHolder().unlockCanvasAndPost(screen);
    }
}
```

The updateAndRender() method remains unchanged from the Java game framework, except for the fact that we no longer call prepareGameImage() in every frame. The renderGameImage() method has some significant changes, but serves the same function. Let's talk about renderGameImage() in more detail.

All Canvas drawing should occur between the following methods:

```
Canvas screen = getHolder().lockCanvas();
// Draw Here
getHolder().unlockCanvasAndPost(screen);
```

The getHolder().lockCanvas() method locks the Canvas for drawing. This allows only one Thread to draw at a time. The method getHolder().unlock CanvasAndPost(screen) will unlock the Canvas and end the drawing.

In between these two methods, we verify that the Canvas screen is not null. We then check the boundaries of the screen using the method screen.getClipBounds(), passing in gameImageDst, a **Rect** object we created earlier. This informs the **Rect** object how big the screen is (gameImageDst's left, top, right and bottom values are updated to match the screen's). With this information, we draw the gameImage to the screen (using gameImageSrc to retrieve the entire gameImage and using gameImageDst to scale it to fit the screen—see the **Painter** class for a reminder on how this is handled).

6. Update the run() method as shown below. It remains unchanged from Unit 2 with the exception of the omission of the System.exit(0) call:

```java
@Override
public void run() {
    long updateDurationMillis = 0;
    long sleepDurationMillis = 0;

    while (running) {
        long beforeUpdateRender = System.nanoTime();
        long deltaMillis = sleepDurationMillis + updateDurationMillis;
        updateAndRender(deltaMillis);

        updateDurationMillis = (System.nanoTime() - beforeUpdateRender) / 1000000L;
        sleepDurationMillis = Math.max(2, 17 - updateDurationMillis);

        try {
                Thread.sleep(sleepDurationMillis);
        } catch (Exception e) {
                e.printStackTrace();
        }
    }
}
```

And now our game loop is finished, and our **GameView** is fully implemented. If you have errors, compare your class to the full class provided in listing 8.13.

Listing 8.13   **GameView** (Completed)

```java
001 package com.jamescho.simpleandroidgdf;
002
003 import android.content.Context;
004 import android.graphics.Bitmap;
005 import android.graphics.Canvas;
006 import android.graphics.Rect;
007 import android.view.SurfaceView;
008 import android.view.SurfaceHolder;
```

```
009 import android.view.SurfaceHolder.Callback;
010
011 import com.jamescho.framework.util.InputHandler;
012 import com.jamescho.framework.util.Painter;
013 import com.jamescho.game.state.LoadState;
014 import com.jamescho.game.state.State;
015
016 public class GameView extends SurfaceView implements Runnable {
017
018     private Bitmap gameImage;
019     private Rect gameImageSrc;
020     private Rect gameImageDst;
021     private Canvas gameCanvas;
022     private Painter graphics;
023
024     private Thread gameThread;
025     private volatile boolean running = false;
026     private volatile State currentState;
027
028     private InputHandler inputHandler;
029
030     public GameView(Context context, int gameWidth, int gameHeight) {
031         super(context);
032         gameImage = Bitmap.createBitmap(gameWidth, gameHeight, Bitmap.Config.RGB_565);
033         gameImageSrc = new Rect(0, 0, gameImage.getWidth(), gameImage.getHeight());
034         gameImageDst = new Rect();
035         gameCanvas = new Canvas(gameImage);
036         graphics = new Painter(gameCanvas);
037
038         SurfaceHolder holder = getHolder();
039         holder.addCallback(new Callback() {
040
041             @Override
042             public void surfaceCreated(SurfaceHolder holder) {
043                 initInput();
044                 if (currentState == null) {
045                     setCurrentState(new LoadState());
046                 }
047                 initGame();
048             }
049
050             @Override
051             public void surfaceChanged(SurfaceHolder holder, int format,int width,
                                        int height) {
052                 // TODO Auto-generated method stub
053             }
054
055             @Override
056             public void surfaceDestroyed(SurfaceHolder holder) {
057                 pauseGame();
058             }
059
060         });
061
062     }
063
064     public GameView(Context context) {
065         super(context);
066     }
```

332

```
067
068    public void setCurrentState(State newState) {
069        System.gc();
070        newState.init();
071        currentState = newState;
072        inputHandler.setCurrentState(currentState);
073    }
074
075    private void initInput() {
076        if (inputHandler == null) {
077                inputHandler = new InputHandler();
078        }
079        setOnTouchListener(inputHandler);
080    }
081
082    private void initGame() {
083        running = true;
084        gameThread = new Thread(this, "Game Thread");
085        gameThread.start();
086    }
087
088    private void pauseGame() {
089        running = false;
090        while (gameThread.isAlive()) {
091                try {
092                        gameThread.join();
093                        break;
094                } catch (InterruptedException e) {
095                }
096        }
097    }
098
099    private void updateAndRender(long delta) {
100        currentState.update(delta / 1000f);
101        currentState.render(graphics);
102        renderGameImage();
103    }
104
105    private void renderGameImage() {
106        Canvas screen = getHolder().lockCanvas();
107        if (screen != null) {
108                screen.getClipBounds(gameImageDst);
109                screen.drawBitmap(gameImage, gameImageSrc, gameImageDst, null);
110                getHolder().unlockCanvasAndPost(screen);
111        }
112    }
113
114    @Override
115    public void run() {
116        long updateDurationMillis = 0;
117        long sleepDurationMillis = 0;
118
119        while (running) {
120                long beforeUpdateRender = System.nanoTime();
121                long deltaMillis = sleepDurationMillis + updateDurationMillis;
122                updateAndRender(deltaMillis);
123
124                updateDurationMillis = (System.nanoTime() - beforeUpdateRender) / 1000000L;
125                sleepDurationMillis = Math.max(2, 17 - updateDurationMillis);
```

```
126
127          try {
128              Thread.sleep(sleepDurationMillis);
129          } catch (Exception e) {
130              e.printStackTrace();
131          }
132     }
133   }
134
135 }
```

Note: If you are having problems with any of the classes at this point, you can download the source code at `jamescho7.com/book/chapter8/checkpoint4`.

Running the Application

Our **GameView** is finally up and running, and it should now render the current state. Run your application once more, and you should be greeted as shown in Figure 8-25.

Figure 8-25   The Welcome Screen

Create Animation, Frame, RandomNumberGenerator Classes

To complete our framework, we need to bring in the utility and animation classes from the Java framework. Listings 8.14 through 8.16 contain the full source for the **Animation**, **Frame** and **RandomNumberGenerator** classes. The **Animation** and **Frame** classes should be added to the package `com.jamescho.framework.animation`. The **RandomNumberGenerator** class should be added to the `com.jamescho.framework.util` package.

Listing 8.14   The **Animation** (Completed)

```
package com.jamescho.framework.animation;

import com.jamescho.framework.util.Painter;
```

```java
public class Animation {
        private Frame[] frames;
        private double[] frameEndTimes;
        private int currentFrameIndex = 0;

        private double totalDuration = 0;
        private double currentTime = 0;

        public Animation(Frame... frames) {
                this.frames = frames;
                frameEndTimes = new double[frames.length];

                for (int i = 0; i < frames.length; i++) {
                        Frame f = frames[i];
                        totalDuration += f.getDuration();
                        frameEndTimes[i] = totalDuration;
                }
        }

        public synchronized void update(float increment) {
                currentTime += increment;

                if (currentTime > totalDuration) {
                        wrapAnimation();
                }

                while (currentTime > frameEndTimes[currentFrameIndex]) {
                        currentFrameIndex++;
                }
        }

        private synchronized void wrapAnimation() {
                currentFrameIndex = 0;
                currentTime %= totalDuration;
        }

        public synchronized void render(Painter g, int x, int y) {
                g.drawImage(frames[currentFrameIndex].getImage(), x, y);
        }

        public synchronized void render(Painter g, int x, int y, int width,
                        int height) {
                g.drawImage(frames[currentFrameIndex].getImage(), x, y, width, height);
        }

}
```

The **Animation** class requires minor adjustments to its two render() methods. We no longer use the java.awt.Graphics object. Instead, we use the Painter object that we have created earlier.

Listing 8.15   The **Frame** Class (Completed)

```java
package com.jamescho.framework.animation;
```

```
import android.graphics.Bitmap;

public class Frame {
        private Bitmap image;
        private double duration;

        public Frame(Bitmap image, double duration) {
                this.image = image;
                this.duration = duration;
        }

        public double getDuration() {
                return duration;
        }

        public Bitmap getImage() {
                return image;
        }

}
```

Frame no longer stores an **Image**. Instead, we store an Android-specific **Bitmap**. No other changes are required.

Listing 8.16   **RandomNumberGenerator** (Completed)

```
package com.jamescho.framework.util;

import java.util.Random;

public class RandomNumberGenerator {
        private static Random rand = new Random();

        public static int getRandIntBetween(int lowerBound, int upperBound) {
                return rand.nextInt(upperBound - lowerBound) + lowerBound;
        }

        public static int getRandInt(int upperBound) {
                return rand.nextInt(upperBound);
        }
}
```

No changes to the **RandomNumberGenerator** are required.

Wrapping Up

Our Android game development framework is almost finished! It now has the same features that our Java game development framework had. Before we move on to Chapter 9, we will make one final addition to our code.

By default, an Android device turns off its screen when it has not been touched for several seconds. Certain applications, such as video players and games should not behave this way—they should keep the screen on at all times, because the user may be actively consuming media without touching the screen. To add this feature to our framework, we make a simple change to our **GameMainActivity** as shown in bold below (importing `android.view.WindowManager`):

```java
package com.jamescho.simpleandroidgdf;

import android.app.Activity;
import android.content.res.AssetManager;
import android.os.Bundle;
import android.view.WindowManager;

public class GameMainActivity extends Activity {

        public static final int GAME_WIDTH = 800;
        public static final int GAME_HEIGHT = 450;
        public static GameView sGame;
        public static AssetManager assets;

        @Override
        protected void onCreate(Bundle savedInstanceState) {
                super.onCreate(savedInstanceState);
                assets = getAssets();
                sGame = new GameView(this, GAME_WIDTH, GAME_HEIGHT);
                setContentView(sGame);
                getWindow().addFlags(WindowManager.LayoutParams.FLAG_KEEP_SCREEN_ON);
        }

}
```

> **Note:** If you are having problems with any of the classes at this point, you can download the source code at `jamescho7.com/book/chapter8/complete`.

In this chapter, you've applied your knowledge of Java game development and Android application development to build an Android game framework from scratch. You are another step closer to becoming an Android game developer. Join me in Chapter 9, where we will put this framework to the test by building a full Android game.

CHAPTER 9: BUILDING THE GAME

Our Android game development framework is ready, and you are one step closer to bringing your ideas to the market for the masses to enjoy. This chapter is all about creating an Android game, exploring principles of optimization and getting your application ready for publication.

We will begin the chapter by porting to Android an existing Java game—Ellio. As our Android game framework is modeled after our Java game framework, you will find this process to be very straightforward. In many of our game-specific classes, you will only be changing a few lines of code, typically lines of code that make use of classes that do not exist inside the Android libraries.

In the middle portion of the chapter, we will learn about some pitfalls of Android game development and discuss principles to follow in order to optimize our game. At the end of this discussion, you will be better equipped to make your own games and ensure that they run well on a variety of Android devices.

To wrap up our discussion of Android game development, we will learn how we can implement features such as a high score system to keep your players coming back to your game.

Preparing the Project

Copying the Framework

Let's make a copy of the Android game framework from Chapter 8. Give the copy the name *EllioAndroid*. Your project should appear in your Package Explorer as shown in Figure 9-1.

Note: If you do not have access to the framework on your computer, the appropriate version can be downloaded in .zip format at jamescho7.com/book/chapter8/complete. To import the downloaded framework into your workspace, follow the instructions provided on page 148.

Let's change the name that our application will be displayed with on an Android device. To do so, open up the AndroidManifest.

Under the application tag, you will see the android:label option, which currently has the value "@string/app_name" (this references an existing String literal inside res/values/string.xml). This is the value that we need to modify in order to change the name of our application. The fastest way to do this is to enter a String literal such as "Ellio" in place of "@string/app_name", but this is discouraged by Android. The better way to do this is to go inside the **values** folder inside our project's **res** folder and modify the value of the element app_name inside strings.xml.

Open up res/values/string.xml, and switch to the text-based editor by selecting the strings.xml tab (shown in Figure 9-2).

Figure 9-1   EllioAndroid Project Structure

Figure 9-2   Editing strings.xml

Now replace the text *SimpleAndroidGDF* with *Ellio,* as shown in listing 9.01.

Listing 9.01   Editing strings.xml

```
<resources>

    <string name="app_name">SimpleAndroidGDF</string>
    <string name="app_name">Ellio</string>

</resources>
```

This may seem like a roundabout way of changing the app name. Why not just change it to "Ellio" inside the AndroidManifest? The answer is two-fold.

The first reason has to do with localization. As mentioned earlier in Unit 3, the **res** folder allows us to provide multiple versions of the same file. This means that we can provide a second **strings.xml** for a different language and display the name of our game in the default language of our user.

Note: For more on localization in Android, please see:
http://developer.android.com/guide/topics/resources/localization.html

The second reason is for reducing dependencies. Let's say that you are very proud of your app name, and you display it everywhere inside of your application (and even use it inside of your source code). A week later, you discover that your app name is someone else's trademark and realize that you must change the name.

If you've used a String literal of your name across your application, you will have to track down each usage and modify it to reflect the new app name. If instead you chose to use @string/app_name, you only have to change one line of XML inside a single file— strings.xml.

Download and Setting the Icons
We will be using a custom icon for Ellio on Android. Download the following images available at jamescho7.com/book/chapter9.

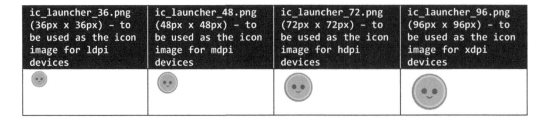

ic_launcher_36.png (36px x 36px) – to be used as the icon image for ldpi devices	ic_launcher_48.png (48px x 48px) – to be used as the icon image for mdpi devices	ic_launcher_72.png (72px x 72px) – to be used as the icon image for hdpi devices	ic_launcher_96.png (96px x 96px) – to be used as the icon image for xdpi devices

Place the downloaded icons into the appropriate **drawable** folder folders. You must rename all of the downloaded files to ic_launcher.png (without a size suffix). Refer to

Figure 8-10 through 8-12 if you need help with this process. At the end of the process, you should have the following:

- An image named ic_launcher.png with a width and height of 36px inside **drawable-ldpi.**
- An image named ic_launcher.png with a width and height of 48px inside **drawable-mdpi.**
- An image named ic_launcher.png with a width and height of 72px inside **drawable-hdpi.**
- An image named ic_launcher.png with a width and height of 96px inside **drawable-xhdpi.**

Download the Assets

We will be reusing many of the assets from Chapter 6 and adding some new ones. Download the following assets (images and sound files) available at jamescho7.com/book/chapter9. You may also use your own by creating images and sound files of the appropriate dimensions and type.

`welcome.png` (800px x 450px) - to be used as the new welcome screen for Ellio.

`start_button.png` (168px x 59px) - to be used as the default start button.

START

`start_button_down.png` (168px x 59px) - to be shown when the user is pressing the start button.

START

`score_button.png` (168px x 59px) - to be used as the default score button.

SCORE

`score_button_down.png` (168px x 59px) - to be shown when the user is pressing the score button.

SCORE

cloud1.png (128px x 71px) – to be used in the background.

cloud2.png (129px x 71px) – also to be used in the background.

runanim1.png (72px x 97px) – used as part of running animation for Ellio.

runanim2.png (72px x 97px) – used as part of running animation for Ellio.

runanim3.png (72px x 97px) – used as part of running animation for Ellio.

runanim4.png (72px x 97px) – used as part of running animation for Ellio.

runanim5.png (72px x 97px) – used as part of running animation for Ellio.

duck.png (72px x 97px) – used to show a ducking Ellio.

jump.png (72px x 97px) – used to show a jumping Ellio.

grass.png (800px x 45px) – used to draw the grass in PlayState.

block.png (20px x 50px) – used to draw obstacles in PlayState.

onjump.wav (Duration: <1 sec) – to be played when Ellio jumps. Created using bfxr.

hit.wav (Duration: <1 sec) – to be played when the player gets hit by the blocks. Created using bfxr.

Place these assets into your **assets** folder, overwriting any existing files (such as welcome.png). At the end of this step, your **assets** folder should match that shown in Figure 9-3.

Figure 9-3   Adding the Assets

Loading the Assets

Now that our assets are downloaded and ready, let's open up our **Assets** folder and start loading them into our game. In the **Assets** class declare the following static variables to represent our image files:

```
public static Bitmap welcome, block, cloud1, cloud2, duck, grass, jump, run1, run2, run3,
        run4, run5, scoreDown, score, startDown, start;
```

We will also need the following variable for our run animation (make sure to import com.jamescho.framework.animation):

```
public static Animation runAnim;
```

Loading sound files will work a little bit differently in our Android framework. Rather than creating Java's **AudioClip** objects, we will *register* sound files with our **SoundPool** object, and ask it to play a sound using an integer ID. Declare the following static variables for our sound files:

```
public static int hitID, onJumpID;
```

Now initialize these variables inside the load() method as shown below, importing com.jamescho.framework.animation.Frame. Note that we only enable transparency when necessary:

```
public static void load() {
        welcome = LoadBitmap("welcome.png", false);
        block = LoadBitmap("block.png", false);
        cloud1 = LoadBitmap("cloud1.png", true);
        cloud2 = LoadBitmap("cloud2.png", true);
```

```
    duck = LoadBitmap("duck.png", true);
    grass = LoadBitmap("grass.png", false);
    jump = LoadBitmap("jump.png", true);
    run1 = LoadBitmap("run_anim1.png", true);
    run2 = LoadBitmap("run_anim2.png", true);
    run3 = LoadBitmap("run_anim3.png", true);
    run4 = LoadBitmap("run_anim4.png", true);
    run5 = LoadBitmap("run_anim5.png", true);
    scoreDown = LoadBitmap("score_button_down.png", true);
    score = LoadBitmap("score_button.png", true);
    startDown = LoadBitmap("start_button_down.png", true);
    start = LoadBitmap("start_button.png", true);

    Frame f1 = new Frame(run1, .1f);
    Frame f2 = new Frame(run2, .1f);
    Frame f3 = new Frame(run3, .1f);
    Frame f4 = new Frame(run4, .1f);
    Frame f5 = new Frame(run5, .1f);
    runAnim = new Animation(f1, f2, f3, f4, f5, f3, f2);

    hitID = LoadSound("hit.wav");
    onJumpID = LoadSound("onjump.wav");
}
```

Double check your code for any typos, and run your project by right clicking on **SimpleAndroidGDF** and running it as an Android Application. You will be greeted by the *Ellio* welcome screen!

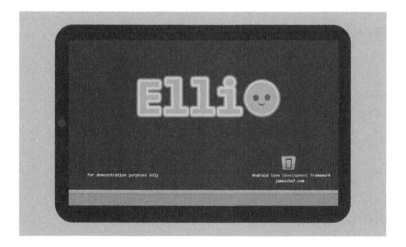

Figure 9-4   Welcome to Ellio!

Our project is setup properly, and we can now start implementing our game.

Note: If you are having problems with any of the classes at this point, you can download the source code at jamescho7.com/book/chapter9/checkpoint1.

345

Implementing the Model Classes

Let's start implementing *Ellio*'s three model classes: **Block**, **Cloud** and **Player**. Because of the way we've designed our game's architecture, our model classes can be reused without any substantial modifications. The one change we *must* make is to replace all usage of the java.awt.Rectangle with Android's own **Rect** class (updating some logic in the process).

Add a new package called com.jamescho.game.model into your project, and create the classes **Block**, **Cloud** and **Player**. We will be implementing these one at a time.

Implementing the Cloud Class

The **Cloud** class can be reused without any changes from the Java version. Implement it as shown in listing 9.02.

Listing 9.02   The **Cloud** Class (unchanged)

```
package com.jamescho.game.model;

import com.jamescho.framework.util.RandomNumberGenerator;

public class Cloud {

        private float x,y;
                private static final int VEL_X = -15;

        public Cloud(float x, float y) {
                this.x = x;
                this.y = y;
        }

        public void update(float delta) {
                x += VEL_X * delta;

                if (x <= -200) {
                        // Reset to the right
                        x += 1000;
                        y = RandomNumberGenerator.getRandIntBetween(20, 100);
                }
        }

        public float getX() {
                return x;
        }

        public float getY() {
                return y;
        }
}
```

Implementing the Block Class

The **Block** class makes use of the `java.awt.Rectangle`, so a few changes are made. Listing 9.03 shows you which lines of code need to be modified from the original:

Listing 9.03   The **Block** Class (Updated)

```
package com.jamescho.game.model;

import java.awt.Rectangle;
import android.graphics.Rect;

import com.jamescho.framework.util.RandomNumberGenerator;

public class Block {
        private float x, y;
        private int width, height;
        private Rectangle rect;
        private Rect rect;
        private boolean visible;

        private static final int UPPER_Y = 275;
        private static final int LOWER_Y = 355;

        public Block(float x, float y, int width, int height) {
                this.x = x;
                this.y = y;
                this.width = width;
                this.height = height;
                rect = new Rectangle((int) x, (int) y, width, height);
                rect = new Rect((int) x, (int) y, (int) x + width, (int) y + height);
                visible = false;
        }

        public void update(float delta, float velX) {
                x += velX * delta;
                updateRect();
                if (x <= -50) {
                        reset();
                }
        }

        public void updateRect() {
                rect.setBounds((int) x, (int) y, width, height);
                rect.set((int) x, (int) y, (int) x + width, (int) y + height);
        }

        public void reset() {
                visible = true;

                // 1 in 3 chance of becoming an Upper Block
                if (RandomNumberGenerator.getRandInt(3) == 0) {
                        y = UPPER_Y;
                } else {
                        y = LOWER_Y;
                }
                x += 1000;
                updateRect();
```

```
        }

        public void onCollide(Player p) {
                visible = false;
                p.pushBack(30);
        }

        public float getX() {
                return x;
        }

        public float getY() {
                return y;
        }

        public boolean isVisible() {
                return visible;
        }

        public Rectangle getRect() {
        public Rect getRect() {
                return rect;
        }

}
```

With those few changes, our **Block** class will behave exactly as it did in Chapter 6.

Implementing the Player Class
The **Player** class also makes use of `java.awt.Rectangle` and requires the same set of changes. Listing 9.04 shows the updated **Player** class.

Listing 9.04   The Player Class (Updated)

```
package com.jamescho.game.model;

import com.jamescho.simpleandroidgdf.Assets;

import android.graphics.Rect;

public class Player {
        private float x, y;
        private int width, height, velY;
        private Rect rect, duckRect, ground;

        private boolean isAlive;
        private boolean isDucked;
        private float duckDuration = .6f;

        private static final int JUMP_VELOCITY = -600;
        private static final int ACCEL_GRAVITY = 1800;

        public Player(float x, float y, int width, int height) {
                this.x = x;
                this.y = y;
```

```
                this.width = width;
                this.height = height;

                ground = new Rect(0, 405, 0 + 800, 405 + 45);
                rect = new Rect();
                duckRect = new Rect();
                isAlive = true;
                isDucked = false;
        }

        public void update(float delta) {

                if (duckDuration > 0 && isDucked) {
                        duckDuration -= delta;
                } else {
                        isDucked = false;
                        duckDuration = .6f;
                }

                if (!isGrounded()) {
                        velY += ACCEL_GRAVITY * delta;
                } else {
                        y = 406 - height;
                        velY = 0;
                }

                y += velY * delta;
                updateRects();
        }

        public void updateRects() {
                rect.set((int) x + 10, (int) y, (int) x + (width - 20), (int) y
                                + height);
                duckRect.set((int) x, (int) y + 20, (int) x + width, (int) y + 20
                                + (height - 20));
        }

        public void jump() {
                if (isGrounded()) {
                        Assets.playSound(Assets.onJumpID);
                        isDucked = false;
                        duckDuration = .6f;
                        y -= 10;
                        velY = JUMP_VELOCITY;
                        updateRects();
                }
        }

        public void duck() {
                if (isGrounded()) {
                        isDucked = true;
                }
        }

        public void pushBack(int dX) {
                x -= dX;
                Assets.playSound(Assets.hitID);
                if (x < -width / 2) {
                        isAlive = false;
```

```
                }
                rect.set((int) x, (int) y, (int) x + width, (int) y + height);
        }

        public boolean isGrounded() {
                return Rect.intersects(rect, ground);
        }

        public boolean isDucked() {
                return isDucked;
        }

        public float getX() {
                return x;
        }

        public float getY() {
                return y;
        }

        public int getWidth() {
                return width;
        }

        public int getHeight() {
                return height;
        }

        public int getVelY() {
                return velY;
        }

        public Rect getRect() {
                return rect;
        }

        public Rect getDuckRect() {
                return duckRect;
        }

        public Rect getGround() {
                return ground;
        }

        public boolean isAlive() {
                return isAlive;
        }

        public float getDuckDuration() {
                return duckDuration;
        }
}
```

One notable change is the implementation for isGrounded(). The method still performs the same task, but now uses the static Rect.intersects(Rect a, Rect b) method for the intersection logic. Note also that we play sound files from **Assets** using sound IDs. Refer to `Assets.playSound()` if necessary.

That's it! Porting our model classes from Java to Android is that easy. Now, we can start implementing our state classes, which will require a little more change.

> **Note:** If you are having problems with any of the classes at this point, you can download the source code at `jamescho7.com/book/chapter9/checkpoint2`.

Implementing the State Classes

Our state classes can be mostly reused, but do require a few changes. The Java version of *Ellio* allowed players to navigate and control the game using a keyboard. In the Android version, we will only allow touch-based input, so we need to make adjustments to the game's UI and controls.

Changing the MenuState

Let's begin by making changes to our **MenuState**. We will be adding two interactive buttons to the regions marked red in Figure 9-5.

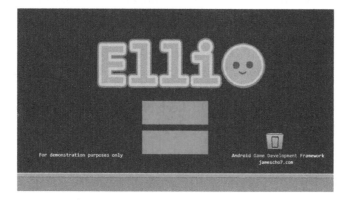

Figure 9-5   Button Placement

The two buttons will be implemented using **Rect** objects. On every touch event, we will be checking if the Player's finger is touching one of the two **Rect** objects in order to determine the proper action.

There are three ways of implementing a touch-based button.

- Method #1: The button can act on a touch down event (when the finger first touches the screen).
- Method #2: The button can act on a touch up event (when the finger is lifted from the screen).

- Method #3: The button can use a combination of steps 1 and 2. The button would only be triggered if a touch down event and touch up event occur together inside the same button Rect.

Method #1 is not my favorite solution. In some situations, an interactive element *should* perform an action on a touch down event (such as when you tap an empty checkbox), but buttons should not behave this way for two reasons.

Firstly, a player might change his or her mind during a touch event. After putting a finger on the Play button, the player might decide to cancel that event by swiping his or her finger outside of the button. If we implement our buttons using method #1, this would not be possible.

Implementing method #1 would also mean that the subsequent touch up event (when the player lifts the finger after pressing the button) will be received by the **PlayState**. This is probably not good behavior as the player is not expecting any of his or her touch events from the **MenuState** to perform an action in the **PlayState**.

Method #2 is better, as it does allow a player to change his or her mind. The player can easily tap a button and swipe away and release elsewhere to prevent invoking the button's action. The main problem with Method #2 arises when the player touches down on one button then slides and releases the finger on top of another button. When an ambiguous action such as this happens, we should probably cancel the touch event; however, method #2 will just treat this as a regular press of the second button.

Method #3 is the best solution because it has the benefits of both Methods #1 and 2 without having their limitations. Method #3 can allow the player to cancel a touch event without worrying about releasing his or her finger inside another button. More importantly, method #3 allows us to keep track of when a button is pressed and released—this property can be used to display a standard button image and a button-pressed image.

Let's implement method #3 for our **MenuState**. Try updating your **MenuState** as shown in listing 9.05.

Listing 9.05   MenuState (Working Buttons)

```
package com.jamescho.game.state;

import android.graphics.Rect;
import android.util.Log;
import android.view.MotionEvent;

import com.jamescho.framework.util.Painter;
import com.jamescho.simpleandroidgdf.Assets;

public class MenuState extends State {

    // Declare a Rect object for each button.
    private Rect playRect;
    private Rect scoreRect;
```

```
// Declare booleans to determine whether a button is pressed down.
private boolean playDown = false;
private boolean scoreDown = false;

@Override
public void init() {
    // Initialize the button Rects at the proper coordinates.
    playRect = new Rect(316, 227, 484, 286);
    scoreRect = new Rect(316, 300, 484, 359);
}

@Override
public void update(float delta) {
}

@Override
public void render(Painter g) {
    g.drawImage(Assets.welcome, 0, 0);

    if (playDown) {
            g.drawImage(Assets.startDown, playRect.left, playRect.top);
    } else {
            g.drawImage(Assets.start, playRect.left, playRect.top);
    }

    if (scoreDown) {
            g.drawImage(Assets.scoreDown, scoreRect.left, scoreRect.top);
    } else {
            g.drawImage(Assets.score, scoreRect.left, scoreRect.top);
    }
}

@Override
public boolean onTouch(MotionEvent e, int scaledX, int scaledY) {

    if (e.getAction() == MotionEvent.ACTION_DOWN) {
        if (playRect.contains(scaledX, scaledY)) {
            playDown = true;
            scoreDown = false; // Only one button should be active (down) at a time.
        } else if (scoreRect.contains(scaledX, scaledY)) {
            scoreDown = true;
            playDown = false; // Only one button should be active (down) at a time.

        }
    }

    if (e.getAction() == MotionEvent.ACTION_UP) {
        // If the play button is active and the release was within the play button:
        if (playDown && playRect.contains(scaledX, scaledY)) {
            // Button has been released.
            playDown = false;
            // Perform an action here!
            Log.d("MenuState", "Play Button Pressed!");

            // If score button is active and the release was within the score button:
        } else if (scoreDown && scoreRect.contains(scaledX, scaledY)){
            // Button has been released.
            scoreDown = false;
```

```
            // Perform an action here!
            Log.d("MenuState", "Score Button Pressed!");

        // If the finger was released anywhere else:
        } else {
            // Cancel all actions.
            scoreDown = false;
            playDown = false;
        }
    }

    return true;
}

}
```

Now run your application in the DDMS perspective and you should see the following screen:

Figure 9-6   Start and Score Buttons

Now check the LogCat output as you push the two buttons. You will find that the buttons behave very intuitively, printing the Log statements exactly when you would expect them to.

The solution in listing 9.05 is works perfectly fine. Here's the issue, however. To implement an interactive button, we have to create a new **Rect** object, a corresponding **boolean**, and a series of if-statements for rendering and logic handling. That is a lot of work to do for one button, no matter how shiny it is.

Good programmers should be lazy—not in the sense that they should refuse to get any work done, but in the sense that they should seek minimize their effort and maximize their output. If you write code for this purpose, you will end up with a much cleaner, intuitive and easy to maintain project.

Let's try being lazy with buttons. How can we make it easier to create buttons in the future—not just in this **MenuState**, but in the **PlayState** and other states to come? We can create a class to represent a button that handles all of the logic by itself!

Making a UIButton Class

Inside com.jamescho.framework.util, create a class named **UIButton** and implement it as shown in listing 9.06.

Listing 9.06   **UIButton** Class (Complete)

```
package com.jamescho.framework.util;

import android.graphics.Bitmap;
import android.graphics.Rect;

public class UIButton {
        private Rect buttonRect;
        private boolean buttonDown = false;
        private Bitmap buttonImage, buttonDownImage;

        public UIButton(int left, int top, int right, int bottom, Bitmap buttonImage,
                            Bitmap buttonPressedImage) {
            buttonRect = new Rect(left, top, right, bottom);
            this.buttonImage = buttonImage;
            this.buttonDownImage = buttonPressedImage;
        }

        public void render(Painter g) {
            Bitmap currentButtonImage = buttonDown ? buttonDownImage : buttonImage;
            g.drawImage(currentButtonImage, buttonRect.left, buttonRect.top,
                            buttonRect.width(), buttonRect.height());
        }

        public void onTouchDown(int touchX, int touchY) {
            if (buttonRect.contains(touchX, touchY)) {
                    buttonDown = true;
            } else {
                    buttonDown = false;
            }
        }

        public void cancel() {
            buttonDown = false;
        }

        public boolean isPressed(int touchX, int touchY) {
            return buttonDown && buttonRect.contains(touchX, touchY);
        }
}
```

> **Note:** The following syntax from the `render()` method may be unfamiliar to you:
>
> ```
> Bitmap currentButtonImage = buttonDown ? buttonDownImage : buttonImage;
> ```
>
> In Java the **?:** is called a ternary operator. It is used to replace the simple if-else blocks. The syntax for using the ternary operator is always as follows:
>
> ```
> someVariable = someBooleanCondition ? a : b;
> ```
>
> In the example above, `someVariable` will take the value of a if `someBooleanCondition` is true and take the value of b if `someBooleanCondition` is false. This means that the above example is equivalent to the following:
>
> ```
> if (someBooleanCondition) {
>     someVariable = a;
> } else {
>     someVariable = b;
> }
> ```
>
> As you can see, the ternary operator is much easier to write (and, admit it, quite elegant)! We lazy programmers gravitate towards such things.

We have created a **UIButton** class that encapsulates all of the logic needed to create a button and handle button presses and button rendering. Now let's use the **UIButton** class inside our **MenuState** to clean up our code! Rewrite your **MenuState** as shown in listing 9.07. Double-check your import statements.

Listing 9.07   MenuState (Updated)

```
package com.jamescho.game.state;

import android.util.Log;
import android.view.MotionEvent;

import com.jamescho.framework.util.Painter;
import com.jamescho.framework.util.UIButton;
import com.jamescho.simpleandroidgdf.Assets;

public class MenuState extends State {

        private UIButton playButton, scoreButton;

        @Override
        public void init() {
                playButton = new UIButton(316, 227, 484, 286, Assets.start,
                        Assets.startDown);
                scoreButton = new UIButton(316, 300, 484, 359, Assets.score,
                        Assets.scoreDown);
        }
```

```
@Override
public void update(float delta) {
}

@Override
public void render(Painter g) {
        g.drawImage(Assets.welcome, 0, 0);
        playButton.render(g);
        scoreButton.render(g);
}

@Override
public boolean onTouch(MotionEvent e, int scaledX, int scaledY) {

        if (e.getAction() == MotionEvent.ACTION_DOWN) {
                playButton.onTouchDown(scaledX, scaledY);
                scoreButton.onTouchDown(scaledX, scaledY);
        }

        if (e.getAction() == MotionEvent.ACTION_UP) {
                if (playButton.isPressed(scaledX, scaledY)) {
                        playButton.cancel();
                        Log.d("MenuState", "Play Button Pressed!");

                } else if (scoreButton.isPressed(scaledX, scaledY)) {
                        scoreButton.cancel();
                        Log.d("MenuState", "Score Button Pressed!");

                } else {
                        playButton.cancel();
                        scoreButton.cancel();
                }
        }

        return true;
}

}
```

With that change, we made it much easier to create, render and handle buttons. We could simplify **MenuState** even further and remove all button-related logic from the onTouch() method, but we will keep this for now! Try running your application and verify that your buttons still behave the same way as before.

We will now make some final change to our onTouch() method to allow a transition to the **PlayState**, as shown highlighted below:

```
@Override
public boolean onTouch(MotionEvent e, int scaledX, int scaledY) {

        if (e.getAction() == MotionEvent.ACTION_DOWN) {
                playButton.onTouchDown(scaledX, scaledY);
                scoreButton.onTouchDown(scaledX, scaledY);
        }
```

```
if (e.getAction() == MotionEvent.ACTION_UP) {
        if (playButton.isPressed(scaledX, scaledY)) {
                playButton.cancel();
                Log.d("MenuState", "Play Button Pressed!");
                setCurrentState(new PlayState());
        } else if (scoreButton.isPressed(scaledX, scaledY)) {
                scoreButton.cancel();
                Log.d("MenuState", "Score Button Pressed!");

        } else {
                playButton.cancel();
                scoreButton.cancel();
        }
}
return true;
}
```

Implementing the PlayState

Create a new class called **PlayState** inside com.jamescho.game.state, and extend **State**. As with the Java version of *Ellio*, the **PlayState** will handle all of the gameplay for our Android game.

The **PlayState** can be implemented with some minor changes from its Java counterpart:

- All references to **Graphics** class will be replaced by a reference to **Painter**.
- All references to the **Resources** class will be replaced by a reference to **Assets**.
- All references to the **Rectangle** class will be replaced by a reference to **Rect**. Rectangle collision logic will similarly need to change.
- All references to **GameMain** will be replaced by a reference to **GameMainActivity**.
- All references to **java.awt.Color** will be replaced by a reference to **android.graphics.Color**. We can also use the static Color.rgb(int r, int g, int b) method to select colors as needed before drawing shapes and Strings.
- The **Font** class is no longer necessary. We will use **TypeFace** instead.
- The keyboard and mouse input methods will be replaced by the onTouch() method.

Listing 9.08 contains the **PlayState** class as it should appear after making these changes. Note that the touch-based controls are not implemented yet.

Listing 9.08   PlayState (Incomplete)

```
package com.jamescho.game.state;

import java.util.ArrayList;

import android.graphics.Color;
import android.graphics.Rect;
import android.graphics.Typeface;
import android.view.MotionEvent;

import com.jamescho.framework.util.Painter;
import com.jamescho.game.model.Block;
import com.jamescho.game.model.Cloud;
import com.jamescho.game.model.Player;
```

```java
import com.jamescho.simpleandroidgdf.Assets;
import com.jamescho.simpleandroidgdf.GameMainActivity;

public class PlayState extends State {

  private Player player;
  private ArrayList<Block> blocks;
  private Cloud cloud, cloud2;

  private int playerScore = 0;

  private static final int BLOCK_HEIGHT = 50;
  private static final int BLOCK_WIDTH = 20;
  private int blockSpeed = -200;

  private static final int PLAYER_WIDTH = 66;
  private static final int PLAYER_HEIGHT = 92;

  @Override
  public void init() {
        player = new Player(160, GameMainActivity.GAME_HEIGHT - 45 -
                PLAYER_HEIGHT, PLAYER_WIDTH, PLAYER_HEIGHT);
        blocks = new ArrayList<Block>();
        cloud = new Cloud(100, 100);
        cloud2 = new Cloud(500, 50);

        for (int i = 0; i < 5; i++) {
                Block b = new Block(i * 200, GameMainActivity.GAME_HEIGHT - 95,
                        BLOCK_WIDTH, BLOCK_HEIGHT);
                blocks.add(b);
        }
  }

  @Override
  public void update(float delta) {
        if (!player.isAlive()) {
                setCurrentState(new GameOverState(playerScore / 100));
        }

        playerScore += 1;

        if (playerScore % 500 == 0 && blockSpeed > -280) {
                blockSpeed -= 10;
        }

        cloud.update(delta);
        cloud2.update(delta);
        Assets.runAnim.update(delta);
        player.update(delta);
        updateBlocks(delta);
  }

  private void updateBlocks(float delta) {
    for (Block b : blocks) {
        b.update(delta, blockSpeed);

        if (b.isVisible()) {
           if (player.isDucked() && Rect.intersects(b.getRect(),
                            player.getDuckRect())) {
```

359

```
                    b.onCollide(player);
                } else if (!player.isDucked() && Rect.intersects(b.getRect(),
                        player.getRect())) {
                    b.onCollide(player);
                }

            }
        }
    }

    @Override
    public void render(Painter g) {
        g.setColor(Color.rgb(208, 244, 247));
        g.fillRect(0, 0, GameMainActivity.GAME_WIDTH, GameMainActivity.GAME_HEIGHT);

        renderPlayer(g);
        renderBlocks(g);
        renderSun(g);
        renderClouds(g);
        g.drawImage(Assets.grass, 0, 405);
        renderScore(g);

    }

    private void renderScore(Painter g) {
        g.setFont(Typeface.SANS_SERIF, 25);
        g.setColor(Color.GRAY);
        g.drawString("" + playerScore / 100, 20, 30);
    }

    private void renderPlayer(Painter g) {
      if (player.isGrounded()) {
        if (player.isDucked()) {
                g.drawImage(Assets.duck, (int) player.getX(), (int) player.getY());
        } else {
                Assets.runAnim.render(g, (int) player.getX(), (int) player.getY(),
                        player.getWidth(), player.getHeight());

        }
        } else {
                g.drawImage(Assets.jump, (int) player.getX(), (int) player.getY(),
                        player.getWidth(), player.getHeight());
      }

    }

    private void renderBlocks(Painter g) {
        for (Block b : blocks) {
                if (b.isVisible()) {
                        g.drawImage(Assets.block, (int) b.getX(), (int) b.getY(),
                                BLOCK_WIDTH, BLOCK_HEIGHT);
                }
        }
    }

    private void renderSun(Painter g) {
        g.setColor(Color.rgb(255, 165, 0));
        g.fillOval(715, -85, 170, 170);
        g.setColor(Color.YELLOW);
```

```
        g.fillOval(725, -75, 150, 150);
    }

    private void renderClouds(Painter g) {
        g.drawImage(Assets.cloud1, (int) cloud.getX(), (int) cloud.getY(), 100, 60);
        g.drawImage(Assets.cloud2, (int) cloud2.getX(), (int) cloud2.getY(), 100, 60);
    }

    @Override
    public boolean onTouch(MotionEvent e, int scaledX, int scaledY) {
        // TO-DO: Implement touch-based Controls Here
        return false;
    }

}
```

Implementing Touch Controls

There are many ways we could implement touch controls in our game. We could create two buttons: one for jumping and one for ducking. This would be easy because we made a **UIButton** class earlier in the chapter. For a game like *Ellio*, however, swipe controls are even better! We will allow our player to jump by swiping a finger upwards and duck by swiping a finger downwards.

A swipe is just a combination of a touch down and touch up event, so the logic for implementing swipe controls is quite simple. Inside our onTouch() method, we will store the Y-coordinate of the most recent touch down event. Later on, when a touch up event is detected, we compare its Y-coordinate to the stored Y-coordinate of the most recent touch down event—the difference of the two values is the swipe distance. If the swipe distance is greater than 50 pixels (arbitrarily chosen), we will tell *Ellio* to jump or duck depending on the direction of the swipe.

Add the following instance variable to your **PlayState**:

```
private float recentTouchY;
```

This float value will store the Y-coordinate of the most recent touch down event. Next, implement your onTouch() method as follows:

```
@Override
public boolean onTouch(MotionEvent e, int scaledX, int scaledY) {
        if (e.getAction() == MotionEvent.ACTION_DOWN) {
                recentTouchY = scaledY;
        } else if (e.getAction() == MotionEvent.ACTION_UP) {
                if (scaledY - recentTouchY < -50) {
                        player.jump();
                } else if (scaledY - recentTouchY > 50) {
                        player.duck();
                }
        }
        return true;
}
```

Note: Be sure to return `true` whenever you handle input. This should be done inside the if-statements for completeness (returning false below the else-if statement), but I have chosen to do it outside for simplicity.

Try commenting out the following line in bold inside your `update()` method:

```
...
if (!player.isAlive()) {
            setCurrentState(new GameOverState(playerScore / 100));
}
...
```

Now run your application and try playing the game! You should be able to use swipe controls to dodge the obstacles, as shown in Figure 9-7

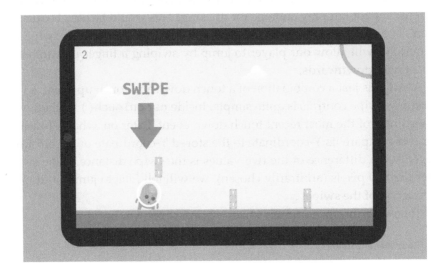

Figure 9-7   Better with Swipe!

Feel free to experiment with the touch controls and tweak them to your liking.

Note: If you are having problems with any of the classes at this point, you can download the source code at `jamescho7.com/book/chapter9/checkpoint3`.

Implementing the GameOverState
Now uncomment this line of code from **PlayState**'s `update()` method:

```
...
if (!player.isAlive()) {
            setCurrentState(new GameOverState(playerScore / 100));
```

```
}
...
```

Now create the **GameOverState** class inside `com.jamescho.game.state`, extending **State** and adding unimplemented methods. Recall that we need to have a custom constructor to accept an integer representing the player's score, which we will need a variable for. Add these as shown below:

```
private String playerScore;

public GameOverState(int playerScore) {
        this.playerScore = playerScore + ""; // Convert int to String
}
```

Now add the following import statements:

```
import android.graphics.Color;
import android.graphics.Typeface;
import android.view.MotionEvent;

import com.jamescho.framework.util.Painter;
import com.jamescho.simpleandroidgdf.GameMainActivity;
```

We will implement our render method very similarly to that of our **GameOverState** from Chapter 6, as shown below:

```
@Override
public void render(Painter g) {
        g.setColor(Color.rgb(255, 145, 0));
        g.fillRect(0, 0, GameMainActivity.GAME_WIDTH, GameMainActivity.GAME_HEIGHT);
        g.setColor(Color.DKGRAY);
        g.setFont(Typeface.DEFAULT_BOLD, 50);
        g.drawString("GAME OVER", 257, 175);
        g.drawString(playerScore, 385, 250);
        g.drawString("Touch the screen.", 220, 350);
}
```

Finally, we just have to listen for a touch up event and transition to the **MenuState**!

```
@Override
public boolean onTouch(MotionEvent e, int scaledX, int scaledY) {
        if (e.getAction() == MotionEvent.ACTION_UP) {
                setCurrentState(new MenuState());
        }
        return true;
}
```

The full **GameOverState** class is shown in listing 9.09.

Listing 9.09   **GameOverState** (Complete)

```java
package com.jamescho.game.state;

import android.graphics.Color;
import android.graphics.Typeface;
import android.view.MotionEvent;

import com.jamescho.framework.util.Painter;
import com.jamescho.simpleandroidgdf.GameMainActivity;

public class GameOverState extends State {
    private String playerScore;

    public GameOverState(int playerScore) {
        this.playerScore = playerScore + ""; // Convert int to String
    }

    @Override
    public void init() {
    }

    @Override
    public void update(float delta) {
    }

    @Override
    public void render(Painter g) {
        g.setColor(Color.rgb(255, 145, 0));
        g.fillRect(0, 0, GameMainActivity.GAME_WIDTH, GameMainActivity.GAME_HEIGHT);
        g.setColor(Color.DKGRAY);
        g.setFont(Typeface.DEFAULT_BOLD, 50);
        g.drawString("GAME OVER", 257, 175);
        g.drawString(playerScore, 385, 250);
        g.drawString("Touch the screen.", 220, 350);
    }

    @Override
    public boolean onTouch(MotionEvent e, int scaledX, int scaledY) {
        if (e.getAction() == MotionEvent.ACTION_UP) {
                setCurrentState(new MenuState());
        }
        return true;
    }
}
```

Now, upon death, the player will see the screen shown in Figure 9-8.

Another Milestone

We still have some work to do in order to polish our game and implement a high score system (remember that score button from **MenuState**?), but you've completed the core implementation of *Ellio* in Android! Congratulations on reaching another milestone. If you've set out to make your own Android game, you can now say that you've done just that.

Our work is not over, and you still have much to learn before you can make awesome games. We will next spend some time talking about optimization principles—how we can make our game run better on more devices. Before that, however, take a well-deserved break. You've done a lot of hard work, and you will be better off reading the next sections with a fresh mind!

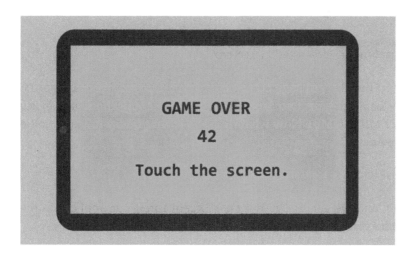

Figure 9-8   Don't Panic!

Note: If you are having problems with any of the classes at this point, you can download the source code at `jamescho7.com/book/chapter9/checkpoint4`.

Make It Faster: Optimizing Your Game

Ellio is not the most resource demanding game for an Android device–we perform only a few 2D rendering operations in every frame, and we keep our CPU's load light by performing a small number of physics and collision-related calculations. As such, there is little we can do to optimize the game and improve performance.

After reading this chapter, however, you will inevitably go on to build games that are bigger than *Ellio* and these games will probably be more graphically and computationally-intensive. Let's make sure that your game's performance does not become a bottleneck for you by discussing some principles to follow in order to optimize your game. This will be a conceptual exercise. You do not need to follow along with your own code (except at the very end).

Loading the Game: Conserve Memory

As you know, memory (RAM) is finite. If you keep filling your memory with data, you will eventually run out of memory. Let me illustrate this with an example and discuss ways of preventing this.

Pretend that you are running a game on an Android device that has 1 GB of total RAM. The Android Operating System, being a multi-application environment, may allocate as little as 16 MB to your application to use. We start filling our 16 MB heap (where objects are stored) with two images, as shown:

```
Bitmap largeImage = loadImage("large.png"); // +4 MB
Bitmap largerImage = loadImage("larger.png"); // +8 MB
```

Let's pretend that `largeImage` takes up 4 MB of RAM and that `largerImage` takes up 8 MB. After loading these two large images, your application has allocated 75% of its memory (12 MB / 16 MB). Now what happens when you try to load another image of size 8 MB into memory?

```
Bitmap puppyPicture = loadImage("puppy.png"); // + 8 MB
```

It cannot fit, and we get an `OutOfMemoryException`. Your application then crashes, and your game becomes unplayable.

Note: At this point, memory is not *full*. It is still at 75% capacity. `OutOfMemoryException` just informs you that the requisite amount of memory needed to allocate room for another object is not there.

How do we prevent an `OutOfMemoryException` arising from Bitmaps? We need to conserve memory. There are a three ways that we will discuss (starting from the least time consuming method to the most time consuming).

The easiest way to conserve memory is to make some of your images smaller—especially those that could get away with being a little blurry, such as the background image. Resizing can be done inside an external application such as Gimp or Photoshop, or you could use the `BitmapFactory.Options.inSampleSize` to do this in code (example below).

Recall that we instantiate a **BitmapFactory.Options** object when loading Bitmaps in the **Assets** class. We use it to configure an image as RGB_565 of ARGB_8888 as it is being loaded. The `inSampleSize` value is an integer inside the **Options** class used to resize images when loading them into memory. Having an `inSampleSize` value of 2 would load the image with half the width and half the height of the original.

The example below shows a modified `Assets.loadBitmap()` method that allows you to subsample an image and reduce its size in half using a third parameter called `shouldSubsample`. You should NOT make this change to your *Ellio* project.

```
private static Bitmap loadBitmap(String filename, boolean transparency, boolean shouldSubsample) {
        InputStream inputStream = null;
        try {
                inputStream = GameMainActivity.assets.open(filename);
        } catch (IOException e) {
                e.printStackTrace();
        }
        Options options = new Options();

        if (shouldSubsample) {
                options.inSampleSize = 2;
        }

        if (transparency) {
                options.inPreferredConfig = Config.ARGB_8888;
        } else {
                options.inPreferredConfig = Config.RGB_565;
        }
        Bitmap bitmap = BitmapFactory.decodeStream(inputStream, null, options);
        return bitmap;
}
```

Note: `inSampleSize` must be a multiple of 2.

A second way of conserving memory is to replace your images (or parts of your images) with the **Canvas** class's geometry drawing calls. For example, take the image shown in Figure 9-9 (art by `Kenney.nl`).

Figure 9-9   Grumpy and the Floating House

Rather than storing this entire image inside memory, we could slice it into multiple pieces as shown in Figure 9-10.

Now, we can take these individual images, save them into our **assets** folder, and draw them separately, using `Painter.setColor(Color.rgb(...))` and `Painter.fillRect (0, 0, gameWidth, gameHeight)` to draw the background. Notice that we would only need a small portion of the water because we can redraw the same image multiple times across the screen.

Figure 9-10   Slicing an Image

A third method for conserving memory would be to create *multiple* loading screens to load and unload images within each state-to-state transition. Let's talk about this using an example.

In *Ellio*, we load all of our images into memory at once. We take every image file inside our **assets** folder and create Bitmap objects for them using the **Assets** class. This allows us to have just one loading screen (which just shows a black screen) that only has to run once throughout the game session.

In theory, we could handle asset loading on a state by state basis. The **LoadState** could simply load all of the images needed for **MenuState** (ignoring the images needed by the **PlayState**). We could then create a second loading screen called **LoadPlayState**, in which we would do three things:

1. Unload all of the images used by the **MenuState** using the method `Bitmap.recycle()`.
2. Ask the garbage collector to clean up the memory: `System.gc();`
3. Load all of the images needed by the **PlayState**, and transition to **PlayState**.

Note: For a real example on implementing multiple loading screens, please see: `jamescho7.com/book/samples`.

As you can see, there are many ways of conserving memory when setting up our game. Let's now talk about how to prevent lag during gameplay.

During Gameplay: Avoid Garbage Collection

During gameplay, you may switch to the DDMS perspective and see a series of LogCat messages like the following:

```
dalvikvm  D  GC_FOR_MALLOC freed 33 objects / 21013 bytes in 8ms
dalvikvm  D  GC_EXPLICIT freed 281 objects / 1853 bytes in 7ms
```

The `GC_FOR_MALLOC` and `GC_EXPLICIT` messages above mean that garbage collection has been triggered inside your application. The above two executions took 8 and 7ms to complete.

These are messages that you should watch out for during gameplay, as they may indicate that you are *leaking memory* (allocating space for a lot of new objects rather than reusing existing objects).

Note: We do explicitly ask for garbage collection using `System.gc()` as we switch from one state to another, so do not be alarmed if you see `GC_EXPLICIT` during these transitions.

The Problem with Garbage Collection

As we've discussed briefly in Chapter 6, garbage collection is considered bad during gameplay because it takes time to complete. In our game development framework, we aim for 60 FPS, or roughly 17 milliseconds per frame. Let's suppose that *Ellio* takes an average of 13 milliseconds to update and render (this would mean 4 milliseconds of sleep time).

What happens if the garbage collector were to run for some 15 milliseconds during a particular frame? That leaves us with 2 milliseconds (`17 - 15`) during which we must try to squeeze in 13 milliseconds worth of update and render calls. In this scenario, this iteration of the game loop may take not 17 milliseconds but something like 30 milliseconds. This excess time elapsed is what players would call *lag*.

Avoiding Memory Allocation

To avoid leaking memory and invoking the garbage collector, refrain from using the `new` keyword inside the game loop. Stay away from methods such as the following:

....

```
// Update method called by game loop. Called on every frame.
public void update() {
```

```
        x += 10;
        y += 5;

        Rect boundingBox = new Rect(x, y, x + width, y + height);
        checkCollision(boundingBox, monster);
}
....
```

Assuming 60 FPS, the above `update()` method would create 60 new **Rect** objects per second, filling up your memory quickly, prompting the garbage collector to come in and do time-consuming work. The better solution would be the following:

```
...
// Class and Variable Declarations

private Rect boundingBox = new Rect(x, y, x + width, y + height);

...

// Update method called by game loop. Called on every frame.
public void update() {
        x += 10;
        y += 5;
        boundingBox.set(x, y, x + width, y + height);
        checkCollision(boundingBox, monster);
}
```

In the previous example, we only create the `boundingBox` **Rect** one time. We avoid creating new objects in every frame by opting to update the existing **Rect** object. Garbage collection is no longer needed.

Finding Memory Leaks and Tracking Allocations

Now, when you notice a lot of lag in your gameplay and see the garbage collection messages in your LogCat, you should be able to find the memory leak by searching for the new keyword inside the game loop. Sometimes, however, finding a leak can be a little more difficult. Have a look at the `renderScore()` method from *Ellio*'s **PlayState** class, reproduced below:

```
private void renderScore(Painter g) {
        g.setFont(Typeface.SANS_SERIF, 25);
        g.setColor(Color.GRAY);
        g.drawString("" + playerScore / 100, 20, 30);
}
```

At first, this method seems completely innocuous. After all, we are not allocating any *new* objects—or are we?

Strings are objects. Every time we create a new String using "", we are allocating space for an object in memory. This means that `"" + playerScore / 100` is leaking memory! To verify this, I will run *Ellio* in the DDMS perspective and select the *Ellio* application under Devices as shown in Figure 9-11.

Figure 9-11   *Ellio* in DDMS Perspective

Notice that there is a tab labeled Allocation Tracker in the DDMS perspective, as shown in Figure 9-12. This tool will keep track of all object allocations in the selected application.

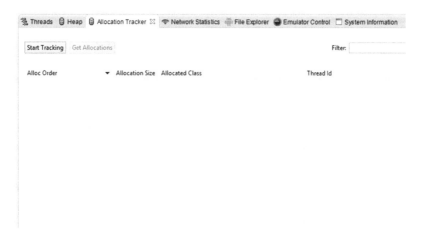

Figure 9-12   Allocation Tracker

Let's start the **PlayState** by hitting the start button inside *Ellio*, and then click on the **Start Tracking** button inside the Allocation Tracker. After playing *Ellio* for a while, we can click on **Get Allocations** and then **Stop Tracking**. The result of these actions in shown in Figure 9-13.

Figure 9-13 shows that there have been multiple allocations of significant size of the class   `java.lang.StringBuilder`.   Note   that   this   is   allocated   in com.jamescho.game.state.PlayState.renderScore. This makes it clear that during gameplay, we are leaking memory inside renderScore() by creating a new String. If we were to comment out the renderScore() method and run the game, we would no longer see these allocations.

Alloc Order	▲ Allocation Size	Allocated Class	Thread Id	Allocated in	Allocated in
2785	17	byte[]	4	android.ddm.DdmHandleHeap	handleREAQ
2781	20	java.lang.StringBuilder	13	com.jamescho.game.state.PlayState	renderScore
2776	20	java.lang.StringBuilder	13	com.jamescho.game.state.PlayState	renderScore
2771	20	java.lang.StringBuilder	13	com.jamescho.game.state.PlayState	renderScore
2766	20	java.lang.StringBuilder	13	com.jamescho.game.state.PlayState	renderScore
2761	20	java.lang.StringBuilder	13	com.jamescho.game.state.PlayState	renderScore
2756	20	java.lang.StringBuilder	13	com.jamescho.game.state.PlayState	renderScore
2751	20	java.lang.StringBuilder	13	com.jamescho.game.state.PlayState	renderScore
2746	20	java.lang.StringBuilder	13	com.jamescho.game.state.PlayState	renderScore
2741	20	java.lang.StringBuilder	13	com.jamescho.game.state.PlayState	renderScore
2736	20	java.lang.StringBuilder	13	com.jamescho.game.state.PlayState	renderScore
2731	20	java.lang.StringBuilder	11	com.jamescho.game.state.PlayState	renderScore
2726	20	java.lang.StringBuilder	13	com.jamescho.game.state.PlayState	renderScore
2721	20	java.lang.StringBuilder	13	com.jamescho.game.state.PlayState	renderScore
2716	20	java.lang.StringBuilder	13	com.jamescho.game.state.PlayState	renderScore
2711	20	java.lang.StringBuilder	13	com.jamescho.game.state.PlayState	renderScore
2706	20	java.lang.StringBuilder	13	com.jamescho.game.state.PlayState	renderScore
2701	20	java.lang.StringBuilder	13	com.jamescho.game.state.PlayState	renderScore
2696	20	java.lang.StringBuilder	13	com.jamescho.game.state.PlayState	renderScore
2691	20	java.lang.StringBuilder	13	com.jamescho.game.state.PlayState	renderScore
2686	20	java.lang.StringBuilder	13	com.jamescho.game.state.PlayState	renderScore
2681	20	java.lang.StringBuilder	13	com.jamescho.game.state.PlayState	renderScore
2676	20	java.lang.StringBuilder	13	com.jamescho.game.state.PlayState	renderScore
2671	20	java.lang.StringBuilder	13	com.jamescho.game.state.PlayState	renderScore
2666	20	java.lang.StringBuilder	13	com.jamescho.game.state.PlayState	renderScore
2661	20	java.lang.StringBuilder	13	com.jamescho.game.state.PlayState	renderScore
2656	20	java.lang.StringBuilder	13	com.jamescho.game.state.PlayState	renderScore
2651	20	java.lang.StringBuilder	13	com.jamescho.game.state.PlayState	renderScore
2646	20	java.lang.StringBuilder	13	com.jamescho.game.state.PlayState	renderScore
2641	20	java.lang.StringBuilder	13	com.jamescho.game.state.PlayState	renderScore
2636	20	java.lang.StringBuilder	13	com.jamescho.game.state.PlayState	renderScore
2631	20	java.lang.StringBuilder	13	com.jamescho.game.state.PlayState	renderScore
2626	20	java.lang.StringBuilder	13	com.jamescho.game.state.PlayState	renderScore

Figure 9-13   Allocated Class: java.lang.StringBuilder

I will be keeping the renderScore() method intact for the purposes of this chapter, but keep in mind that this method is indeed leaking memory.

Note: For an example of how you might print the score without using String objects, please see: **jamescho7.com/book/samples**

There is one more source of garbage collection that you should be aware of. When iterating through an **ArrayList** of objects, you may allocate something called an **ArrayListIterator**, as shown in Figure 9-14.

The cause of this allocation is not revealed directly in LogCat, except for the fact that **ArrayLists** are involved. The actual reason behind these allocations is our use a for each loop in our updateBlocks() and renderBlocks() methods:

```
....
// For each loop leaks memory:
for (Block b : blocks) {
    ....
}
```

Alloc Order	▲ Allocation Size	Allocated Class	Thread Id	Allocated in	Allocated in
715	12	java.lang.Integer	4	java.lang.Integer	valueOf
2	12	java.lang.Integer	4	java.lang.Integer	valueOf
713	17	byte[]	4	android.ddm.DdmHandleHeap	handleREAQ
716	24	byte[]	4	dalvik.system.NativeStart	run
714	24	org.apache.harmony.dalvik.ddmc.Chunk	4	org.apache.harmony.dalvik.ddmc.DdmServer	dispatch
712	24	org.apache.harmony.dalvik.ddmc.Chunk	4	android.ddm.DdmHandleHeap	handleREAQ
711	24	java.util.ArrayList$ArrayListIterator	12	java.util.ArrayList	iterator
710	24	java.util.ArrayList$ArrayListIterator	12	java.util.ArrayList	iterator
709	24	java.util.ArrayList$ArrayListIterator	12	java.util.ArrayList	iterator
708	24	java.util.ArrayList$ArrayListIterator	12	java.util.ArrayList	iterator
707	24	java.util.ArrayList$ArrayListIterator	12	java.util.ArrayList	iterator
706	24	java.util.ArrayList$ArrayListIterator	12	java.util.ArrayList	iterator
705	24	java.util.ArrayList$ArrayListIterator	12	java.util.ArrayList	iterator
704	24	java.util.ArrayList$ArrayListIterator	12	java.util.ArrayList	iterator
703	24	java.util.ArrayList$ArrayListIterator	12	java.util.ArrayList	iterator
702	24	java.util.ArrayList$ArrayListIterator	12	java.util.ArrayList	iterator
701	24	java.util.ArrayList$ArrayListIterator	12	java.util.ArrayList	iterator
700	24	java.util.ArrayList$ArrayListIterator	12	java.util.ArrayList	iterator
699	24	java.util.ArrayList$ArrayListIterator	12	java.util.ArrayList	iterator
698	24	java.util.ArrayList$ArrayListIterator	12	java.util.ArrayList	iterator
697	24	java.util.ArrayList$ArrayListIterator	12	java.util.ArrayList	iterator
696	24	java.util.ArrayList$ArrayListIterator	12	java.util.ArrayList	iterator
695	24	java.util.ArrayList$ArrayListIterator	12	java.util.ArrayList	iterator
694	24	java.util.ArrayList$ArrayListIterator	12	java.util.ArrayList	iterator
693	24	java.util.ArrayList$ArrayListIterator	12	java.util.ArrayList	iterator
692	24	java.util.ArrayList$ArrayListIterator	12	java.util.ArrayList	iterator

Figure 9-14   More Leaking

The for each loop makes use of an **ArrayListIterator** object to iterate through each child element, leaking memory. There is a simple solution to this, and that is to use a regular, index-based for loop as shown in the modified updateBlocks() and renderBlocks() methods provided in listings 9.10 and 9.11:

Listing 9.10   updateBlocks() (Updated)

```
private void updateBlocks(float delta) {
  for (int i = 0; i < blocks.size(); i++) {
    Block b = blocks.get(i);
    b.update(delta, blockSpeed);

    if (b.isVisible()) {

        if (player.isDucked() && Rect.intersects(b.getRect(), player.getDuckRect())) {
            b.onCollide(player);
        } else if (!player.isDucked() && Rect.intersects(b.getRect(), player.getRect())) {
            b.onCollide(player);
        }

    }
  }
}
```

Listing 9.11   renderBlocks() (Updated)

```
private void renderBlocks(Painter g) {
 for (int i = 0; i < blocks.size(); i++) {
    Block b = blocks.get(i);
```

```
    if (b.isVisible()) {
      g.drawImage(Assets.block, (int) b.getX(), (int) b.getY(), BLOCK_WIDTH, BLOCK_HEIGHT);
    }
  }
}
}
```

I recommend that you make these two changes to your **PlayState** class to maximize performance.

We've now sufficiently discussed how we can optimize our framework. If you keep the aforementioned principles in mind, you will be able to make high-performance games that run well on a wide variety of devices. Let's now go back to *Ellio* and add a final new feature—a high score system.

Note: If you are having problems with any of the classes at this point, you can download the source code at jamescho7.com/book/chapter9/checkpoint5.

Implementing a High Score System

In many mobile games, you are going to want to keep track of the all-time best score reached on a device. The easiest way to accomplish this is by using Android's shared preferences feature.

You can think of shared preferences as a repository of data. You can use it to save information relevant to your application. The saved data will persist in the device's file storage until your application has been uninstalled from the device.

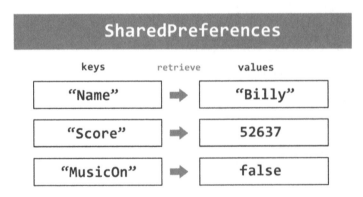

Figure 9-15   Storing SharedPreferences

As shown in Figure 9-15, you must save data in key-value pairs, and you can have as many pairs as you want. This means that, to store a value inside the shared preferences, you must provide a key associated with that value, such as "Name." Later, this key is used to retrieve the saved value.

Planning the High Score System

To implement the high score system, we will be saving the all-time best score as an integer inside our application's shared preferences. When our **GameMainActivity** is launched, we will retrieve the saved high score from shared preferences and store it as a regular integer. When the player finishes the game and reaches the **GameOverState**, we will check if the current score is greater than the saved high score. If so, we will replace the high score with the current score and save it to the shared preferences.

Providing the Accessor Methods

Open up the **GameMainActivity** class for *Ellio* and add the following variables:

```
private static SharedPreferences prefs;
private static final String highScoreKey = "highScoreKey";
private static int highScore;
```

Add the corresponding import statements:

```
import android.content.SharedPreferences;
import android.content.SharedPreferences.Editor;
```

The prefs variable will be the reference to our application's **SharedPreferences** object. Inside prefs, we will be storing a highScore using the key highScoreKey.

Initialize the prefs and highScore variables as shown below in the onCreate() method. Ignore the error shown for retrieveHighScore() for now.

```
@Override
protected void onCreate(Bundle savedInstanceState) {
        super.onCreate(savedInstanceState);
        prefs = getPreferences(Activity.MODE_PRIVATE);   // New line!
        highScore = retrieveHighScore();                 // New Line!
        assets = getAssets();
        sGame = new GameView(this, GAME_WIDTH, GAME_HEIGHT);
        setContentView(sGame);
        getWindow().addFlags(WindowManager.LayoutParams.FLAG_KEEP_SCREEN_ON);
}
```

As you can see, we can retrieve our application's shared preferences by calling the getPreferences() method, passing in the constant Activity.MODE_PRIVATE so that only our application can access the preferences' contents.

Finally, declare the following methods which will provide the access to the shared preferences:

```
public static void setHighScore(int highScore) {
        GameMainActivity.highScore = highScore;
        Editor editor = prefs.edit();
        editor.putInt(highScoreKey, highScore);
        editor.commit();
}
```

```
private int retrieveHighScore() {
        return prefs.getInt(highScoreKey, 0);
}

public static int getHighScore() {
        return highScore;
}
```

The setHighScore() method will be called when the player's score is greater than the saved high score. To actually edit the shared preferences, we must get its **SharedPreferences.Editor** object by calling prefs.edit(). We store the resulting **Editor** into the editor variable and stash the integer highScore with the key highScoreKey into the editor. Once we call editor.commit(), the **Editor** object will commit the changes to the shared preferences, overwriting any existing values.

The retrieveHighScore() method is called once when the application is started. Its value is stored into memory as highScore for quicker access later. This method simply retrieves the integer associated with highScoreKey. If there is no associated value, we use the default value of zero.

The getHighScore() method is a simple static getter that will retrieve the current high score. This method exists to allow us to retrieve the high score without going into the file system, which takes a bit longer.

Listing 9.12 shows the completed **GameMainActivity** Class.

Listing 9.12   GameMainActivity (Completed)

```
package com.jamescho.simpleandroidgdf;

import android.app.Activity;
import android.content.SharedPreferences;
import android.content.SharedPreferences.Editor;
import android.content.res.AssetManager;
import android.os.Bundle;
import android.view.WindowManager;

public class GameMainActivity extends Activity {

        public static final int GAME_WIDTH = 800;
        public static final int GAME_HEIGHT = 450;
        public static GameView sGame;
        public static AssetManager assets;

        private static SharedPreferences prefs;
        private static final String highScoreKey = "highScoreKey";
        private static int highScore;

        @Override
        protected void onCreate(Bundle savedInstanceState) {
                super.onCreate(savedInstanceState);
                prefs = getPreferences(Activity.MODE_PRIVATE);
                highScore = retrieveHighScore();
                assets = getAssets();
```

```
        sGame = new GameView(this, GAME_WIDTH, GAME_HEIGHT);
        setContentView(sGame);
        getWindow().addFlags(WindowManager.LayoutParams.FLAG_KEEP_SCREEN_ON);
    }

    public static void setHighScore(int highScore) {
        GameMainActivity.highScore = highScore;
        Editor editor = prefs.edit();
        editor.putInt(highScoreKey, highScore);
        editor.commit();
    }

    private int retrieveHighScore() {
        return prefs.getInt(highScoreKey, 0);
    }

    public static int getHighScore() {
        return highScore;
    }

}
```

Setting the High Score

Now that we have created the accessor methods, saving the high score is very easy. Open **GameOverState** and make the following changes to its constructor:

```
public GameOverState(int playerScore) {
        this.playerScore = playerScore + ""; // Convert int to String
        if (playerScore > GameMainActivity.getHighScore()) {
                GameMainActivity.setHighScore(playerScore);
        }
}
```

Those are all the changes needed to save the high score into the shared preferences. Make sure you understand these three lines of code.

We will make one additional change to make the **GameOverState** display "HIGH SCORE" rather than "GAME OVER" in the event of a high score. Create the following String variable with the default value of "GAME OVER":

```
private String gameOverMessage = "GAME OVER";
```

Next, inside the constructor, add the new line of code shown below:

```
public GameOverState(int playerScore) {
        this.playerScore = playerScore + ""; // Convert int to String
        if (playerScore > GameMainActivity.getHighScore()) {
                GameMainActivity.setHighScore(playerScore);
                gameOverMessage = "HIGH SCORE";        // This is the new line!
        }
}
```

Finally, make the following change to the render() method.

```
@Override
public void render(Painter g) {
        g.setColor(Color.rgb(255, 145, 0));
        g.fillRect(0, 0, GameMainActivity.GAME_WIDTH, GameMainActivity.GAME_HEIGHT);
        g.setColor(Color.DKGRAY);
        g.setFont(Typeface.DEFAULT_BOLD, 50);
        g.drawString("GAME OVER", 257, 175);
        g.drawString(gameOverMessage, 257, 175);
        g.drawString(playerScore, 385, 250);
        g.drawString("Touch the screen.", 220, 350);
}
```

The full updated class listing for **GameOverState** is shown in listing 9.13:

Listing 9.13   **GameOverState** (Completed)

```
package com.jamescho.game.state;

import android.graphics.Color;
import android.graphics.Typeface;
import android.view.MotionEvent;

import com.jamescho.framework.util.Painter;
import com.jamescho.simpleandroidgdf.GameMainActivity;

public class GameOverState extends State {

        private String playerScore;
        private String gameOverMessage = "GAME OVER";

        public GameOverState(int playerScore) {
                this.playerScore = playerScore + ""; // Convert int to String
                if (playerScore > GameMainActivity.getHighScore()) {
                        GameMainActivity.setHighScore(playerScore);
                        gameOverMessage = "HIGH SCORE"; // This is the new line!
                }
        }

        @Override
        public void init() {
                // TODO Auto-generated method stub

        }

        @Override
        public void update(float delta) {
                // TODO Auto-generated method stub

        }

        @Override
        public void render(Painter g) {
                g.setColor(Color.rgb(255, 145, 0));
                g.fillRect(0, 0, GameMainActivity.GAME_WIDTH,
                                GameMainActivity.GAME_HEIGHT);
```

```
            g.setColor(Color.DKGRAY);
            g.setFont(Typeface.DEFAULT_BOLD, 50);
            g.drawString(gameOverMessage, 257, 175);
            g.drawString(playerScore, 385, 250);
            g.drawString("Touch the screen.", 220, 350);
    }

    @Override
    public boolean onTouch(MotionEvent e, int scaledX, int scaledY) {
            if (e.getAction() == MotionEvent.ACTION_UP) {
                    setCurrentState(new MenuState());
            }
            return true;
    }

}
```

Now try running your application and verify that you are able to set a high score, as shown in Figure 9-16:

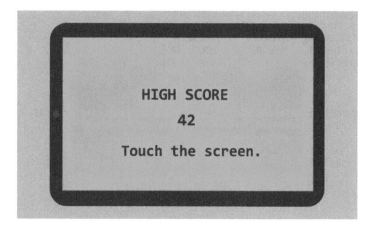

Figure 9-16   High Score!

Implementing the ScoreState

The final thing we will do is implement the **ScoreState** class. Create this inside `com.jamescho.game.state` and extend **State**. We will make it behave just like the **GameOverState**, except that it will always show the high score. As an exercise, try to implement this class yourself. If you need help, listing 9.14 contains my implementation.

Listing 9.14   ScoreState (Completed)

```
package com.jamescho.game.state;

import android.graphics.Color;
import android.graphics.Typeface;
```

379

```
import android.view.MotionEvent;

import com.jamescho.framework.util.Painter;
import com.jamescho.simpleandroidgdf.GameMainActivity;

public class ScoreState extends State {

        private String highScore;
        @Override
        public void init() {
                highScore = GameMainActivity.getHighScore() + "";
        }

        @Override
        public void update(float delta) {
        }

        @Override
        public void render(Painter g) {
           g.setColor(Color.rgb(53, 156, 253));
           g.fillRect(0, 0, GameMainActivity.GAME_WIDTH, GameMainActivity.GAME_HEIGHT);
           g.setColor(Color.WHITE);
           g.setFont(Typeface.DEFAULT_BOLD, 50);
           g.drawString("The All-Time High Score", 120, 175);
           g.setFont(Typeface.DEFAULT_BOLD, 70);
           g.drawString(highScore, 370, 260);
           g.setFont(Typeface.DEFAULT_BOLD, 50);
           g.drawString("Touch the screen.", 220, 350);
        }

        @Override
        public boolean onTouch(MotionEvent e, int scaledX, int scaledY) {
                if (e.getAction() == MotionEvent.ACTION_UP) {
                        setCurrentState(new MenuState());
                }
                return true;
        }

}
```

Now open **MenuState** and update its onTouch() method to start the **ScoreState** when the score button is pressed:

```
@Override
public boolean onTouch(MotionEvent e, int scaledX, int scaledY) {

    if (e.getAction() == MotionEvent.ACTION_DOWN) {
            playButton.onTouchDown(scaledX, scaledY);
            scoreButton.onTouchDown(scaledX, scaledY);
    }

    if (e.getAction() == MotionEvent.ACTION_UP) {
            if (playButton.isPressed(scaledX, scaledY)) {
                    playButton.cancel();
                    Log.d("MenuState", "Play Button Pressed!");
                    setCurrentState(new PlayState());
```

```
        } else if (scoreButton.isPressed(scaledX, scaledY)) {
                scoreButton.cancel();
                Log.d("MenuState", "Score Button Pressed!");
                setCurrentState(new ScoreState());        // This is the new line!
        } else {
                playButton.cancel();
                scoreButton.cancel();
        }
    }

    return true;
}
```

Run the application one more time and press the score button. You should see a screen like that shown in Figure 9-17.

Figure 9-17   Displaying **ScoreState**

Note: If you are having problems with any of the classes at this point, you can download the source code at **jamescho7.com/book/chapter9/complete**

And we are done! We've implemented an Android game using our framework, studied optimization principles and created shared preferences for data persistence. It's your turn to get some practice. Try to create a game from scratch using your own ideas! If you need inspiration, I'd like to point you to the book's companion site, where you can see various samples of the framework in action!

jamescho7.com/book/samples/

We are nearing the end of our journey. In Unit 4, we will learn how we can publish an Android game onto the Google Play Store and talk about integrating some cool Google services to make your app even more fun.

UNIT 4

FINISHING TOUCHES

CHAPTER 10: RELEASING YOUR GAME

You've now developed an Android game, and you are probably eager to get it into as many people's hands as possible. With the help of Eclipse and ADT, you can publish your application in a matter of minutes; however, you will probably not get the results you want unless you do some homework first.

When building an Android game or application, you will go through three primary stages: designing, developing and distributing. Google provides detailed steps and guidelines for each of these stages on the official Android developer site at the following URL, and I highly suggest that you take some time looking at the following site before moving any further:

`http://developer.android.com/distribute/index.html`

Getting Your Game Ready

For you to begin sharing your Android project with your audience, you must create an Android Package file (APK for short). Using Eclipse makes this very easy! We will be using the Android version of *Ellio* from Chapter 9 as an example. Before we get started, let's make sure that your game is ready to be published.

Note: If necessary, you can download the *Ellio* project from `jamescho7.com/book/chapter9/complete`

Changing the Package Name
Open your `AndroidManifest.xml` and check your `manifest` element (shown in listing 10.01).

Listing 10.01   manifest Element

```
<manifest xmlns:android="http://schemas.android.com/apk/res/android"
    package="com.jamescho.simpleandroidgdf"
    android:versionCode="1"
    android:versionName="1.0" >
...
```

Note that the package name is currently set to `com.jamescho.simpleandroidgdf`. We must change this package name to a unique value in order for us to publish the game on Google Play.

Assign a new package name, such as com.*yourname*.ellio. This package name will be publicly visible on your game's Google Play listing, so choose wisely. Once you have selected a new name, update your activity element as shown in listing 10.02:

Listing 10.02   Updating the activity element.

```
<activity
        android:screenOrientation="sensorLandscape"
        android:name="com.jamescho.simpleandroidgdf.GameMainActivity"
        android:name="com.jamescho.ellio.GameMainActivity"
        android:label="@string/app_name"
        android:theme="@android:style/Theme.NoTitleBar.Fullscreen" >
        <intent-filter>
                <action android:name="android.intent.action.MAIN" />
                <category android:name="android.intent.category.LAUNCHER" />
        </intent-filter>
</activity>
```

Next, you must rename the com.jamescho.simpleandroidgdf package in the Package Explorer, by giving it the same, updated package name from the manifest element.

Note: Make sure to use your *own* name, not com.jamescho.ellio. Otherwise, you will not be able to publish this application.

Creating the APK
Select your Android project inside the Package Explorer and select **File > Export**. You will see the Export dialog, as shown in Figure 10-1.

Figure 10-1   Export Android Application

Open the **Android** folder, select **Export Android Application** and click **Next**. You should see EllioAndroid as the selected project. Click **Next** again, and you will see the dialog shown in Figure 10-2.

Figure 10-2   Keystore Selection

All Android applications must be digitally signed before they can be shared. To begin this process, simply select the **Create new keystore** option in the Keystore selection dialog. I will create the keystore on my Desktop with the name EllioAndroid.keystore.

Note: A keystore is a collection of keys, which are used when signing application. Make sure to keep this file backed up and secure, as you must use it each time you want to update your application. If you lose your keystore, you cannot make changes to a published application.

After hitting **Next**, you will see the dialog shown in Figure 10-3. You must now create a key using the provided form. Think of a key as a seal of authentication. Signing digitally using a key allows others to verify your authorship of an app.

- The **alias** is the name of the key. In this case, I will use release.
- The **password** is the corresponding password. Note that this password is not the same as the password for the keystore. Choose a password you will remember!
- The **validity** refers to your key's lifetime. The recommended value is 30 years.

You must also complete at least one of the six certificate issuer fields to complete the key creation process, as shown in Figure 10-4.

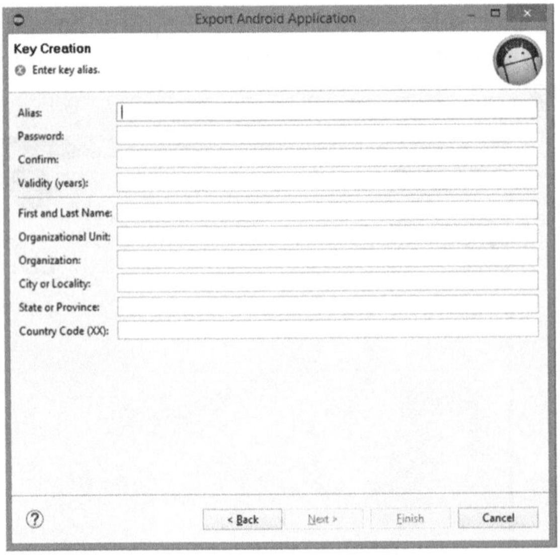

Figure 10-3   Key Creation

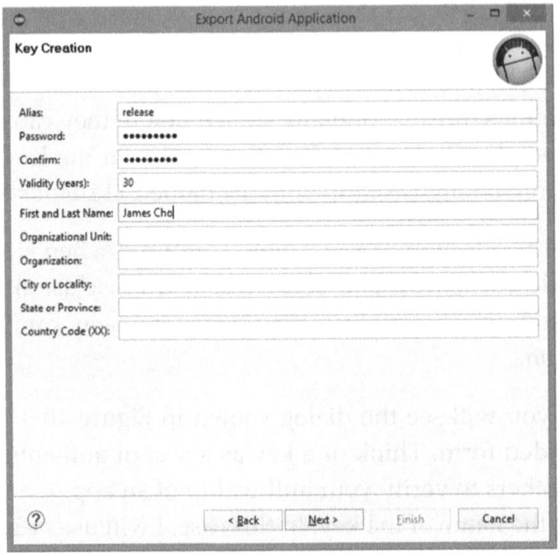

Figure 10-4   Key Creation (Updated)

Once you have entered the required values, click **Next** and you will then see the screen shown in Figure 10-5 where you are asked for the destination APK file. Select a location where you would like to save your APK file to, and click **Finish**. And you are done! You have successfully created an APK file and signed it with a digital key. You can now share the APK file with your buddies, and they will be able to install your game on their devices.

Figure 10-5   Destination APK

Choosing a Marketplace

You will probably not reach that big of an audience using email to distribute your apps. Once you publish your game to an application market place such as the Amazon Appstore or Google Play, however, your game will be available to millions of people around the world.

As Google Play comes pre-installed on a vast majority of Android devices (and because of the services that Google offers such as leaderboard and achievements integration), a developer license on Google Play is a must-have. If you want to target users who rely on proprietary marketplaces such as Samsung Apps and Amazon Appstore, you will have to publish your app on them on an individual basis.

Publishing the Game on Google Play

Creating a Developer Account

I will now show you how to create a developer account on Google Play. For this, you will need to pay a one-time fee of $25 USD. If you do not want to pay at this time, continue reading for future reference and return to this section at your convenience.

Navigate to the following URL on your web browser `https://play.google.com` `/apps/publish/`. Log into the Google Play Developer Console by using the Google account you would like to associate your developer account with. Google recommends using a new account rather than a personal account if you would like to publish as an organization. Upon logging in, you will see the following page:

Figure 10-6   Accept the Developer Agreement

Read through the text, review the Google Play Developer distribution agreement, agree to the terms, and click **Continue to payment**. Choose a method of payment and complete your account details. Once you are finished, you should be in your Developer Console. If not, navigate to the Console manually using the provided URL:

```
https://play.google.com/apps/publish/
```

You should see the page shown in Figure 10-7.

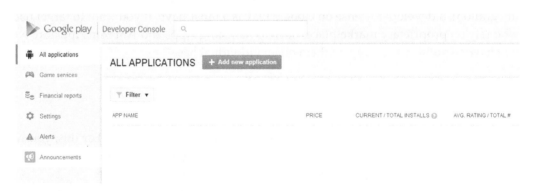

Figure 10-7   The Google Play Developer Console

Creating a new Application

Click **Add new application**, enter a name for your application then click **Upload APK**, and you will be able to begin uploading the APK file we created in the previous section. When the screen shown in Figure 10-8 displays, click **Upload your first APK to Production.**

Figure 10-8   Ellio – Demo APK

Follow the provided instructions to upload your APK file. Once that step is complete, you will get a message telling you how many devices your application is compatible with. As you will notice, thousands of device can support *Ellio* (this number is primarily dependent on the Minimum SDK value we have chosen in our AndroidManifest). Next, click on the Store Listing button as shown in Figure 10-9.

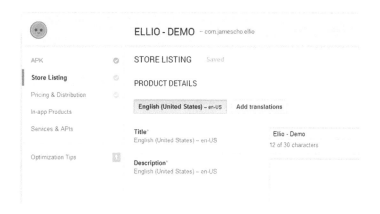

Figure 10-9   Store Listing for *Ellio*

Here, you can enter details about your application that will be used throughout Google Play to help users learn more about your game before downloading. To learn more about the purpose of each field and to maximize your game's visibility, please see the following page:

https://support.google.com/googleplay/android-developer/answer/4448378?hl=en

The product details information can be changed at a later time. Some developers will update it with each new release so that their users can learn about ongoing promotions or changes. Enter any information that you wish for your *Ellio* listing.

Next, you must provide some graphic assets in order for Google to display your application in various areas of the Play Store. These include a high resolution icon, various screenshots and a feature graphic for apps chosen to be featured by the Google Play Team. You can download the appropriate assets from the book's companion site:

jamescho7.com/book/chapter10/

Finally, select an application type (game vs app), category and content rating (intended audience), and provide contact details through which users can reach you. You must also provide a URL to your privacy policy, or mark "Not submitting a privacy policy URL at this time."

Once you've completed the store listing information, move on to the Pricing & Distribution as shown in Figure 10-10.

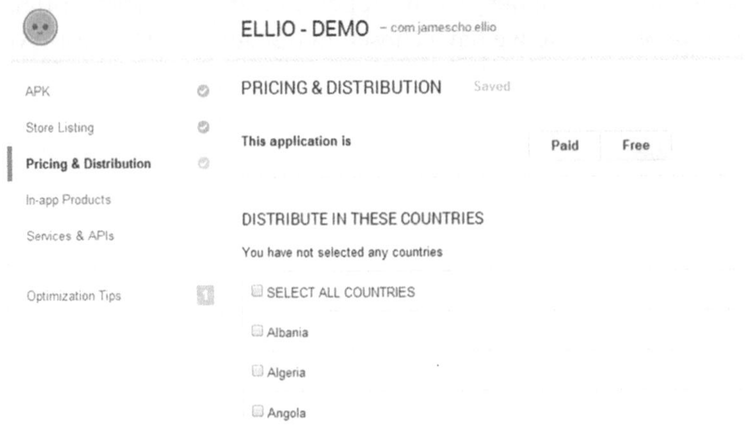

Figure 10-10   Pricing & Distribution

Here, you can set the price of the application and specify which countries you want your application to be available in. You must then declare that your application meets the Android Content Guidelines and acknowledge that your application will be subject to various laws. Read through this section and complete it as you desire.

If you've successfully completed the APK, Store Listing and Pricing & Distribution information for your application, you will see the following button at the top right corner of your screen:

Figure 10-11   The "Ready to Publish" Button

To publish your application, click on the button and select "Publish this app." You will then see your app listed under All Applications with the status of "Published," along with some pricing and install information as shown in Figure 10-12.

Figure 10-12   Ellio Published!

After several hours (in some cases more than ten hours), your application will be visible on Google Play via `play.google.com` and the Play Store application.

Updating the Game

Now that your game is available on the web, millions of people will be able to access your application! Once they have downloaded the game, the real test begins.

Chances are, your game will have some bugs that will cause crashes for certain users. In addition, you might decide that your app is missing a crucial feature and decide to implement it. In this section, you will learn how to make changes to your application and upload a new APK file to Google Play, so that your game's users can have access to the latest updates and bug fixes.

The Resource Management Bug

We've carefully analyzed our code in order to minimize memory leaks, but our game is still leaking some resources, meaning that our app is leaving objects floating around in memory even when the user is done with our application. Some of these objects, such as our Bitmaps, will be disposed of by the garbage collector once our app is finished. Others, such as the **SoundPool** object that we use to play sound effects with, will still consume native resources after our app is closed. We should explicitly dispose of the **SoundPool** object once we are finished.

Note: Prior to Android 3.0, Bitmaps were not always automatically garbage collected. Instead, you had to call the `Bitmap.recycle()` method explicitly, as we will with our **SoundPool** object in the coming discussion. For more information, see this DevBytes video on Bitmap Allocation created by Android Engineers: https://www.youtube.com/watch?v=rsQet4nBVi8

As responsible Android developers, we want to minimize our game's toll on our players' devices (to maximize battery life and performance), and it is vital that we provide a means of disposing of assets once they are no longer in use.

Recall that our game runs as a single Activity. This allows us to easily manage resources using our knowledge of the Activity Lifecycle (refer to Figure 7-30 for a refresher). You will find that a good place to dispose of resources is in the `onPause()` method when another Activity comes into the foreground. As the user may choose not to return to our game after switching to a new application, our game should get out of the way by disposing of its assets.

In some cases, the user *may* navigate back to our game, and the disposed assets will be needed again. In that case, we will rely on `onResume()` method to reinitialize the disposed assets. Conveniently, `onResume()` is also called when the app is first started, and so we will not need to initialize these assets in two different places. You will see what this means when we make our changes to the **Assets** class.

Pausing the Game

When the player switches to another Activity, it is good practice to pause the gameplay. If the player chooses to navigate back, he or she should see a Paused screen waiting for the player to get ready. Using onPause() and onResume(), we can easily implement this feature as well.

Adding `onResume()` and `onPause()` to Assets and State

Let's add the methods `onResume()` and `onPause()` to our **Assets** and **State** classes. As **Assets** and **State** are not subclasses of **Activity**, these new methods will NOT be called automatically by the Android system. Instead, we will manually call `Assets.onResume()` and `currentState.onResume()` when our Activity's `onResume()` method is called. This allows us to inform the **Assets** class and the **currentState** that there was a resume or pause event in the Activity's lifecycle. We will do the same with `onPause()`

Begin by removing the following lines from your `Assets.load()` method. You will no longer be loading any sounds inside the `load()` method.

```
hitID = loadSound("hit.wav");
onJumpID = loadSound("onjump.wav");
```

Next, add the following two methods to the same class:

```
public static void onResume() {
        hitID = loadSound("hit.wav");
        onJumpID = loadSound("onjump.wav");
}

public static void onPause() {
        if (soundPool != null) {
                soundPool.release();
                soundPool = null;
        }
}
```

The `onPause()` method will be called by `GameMainActivity.onPause()` when the Activity is pausing. As there is no guarantee that `soundPool` will be needed again, we explicitly release it (to release native resources) and set it equal to `null` (to make the job easier for the garbage collector).

We will call the `onResume()` method each time that the method `GameMainActivity.onResume()` is called by the Android system. This happens when our Activity is resuming from a paused state or when our Activity is starting for the first time, so we no longer need to load sounds in the `load()` method. Note that we do not have to reinitialize `soundPool`, because the logic in our `loadSound()` method will do that for us automatically.

With those changes made, we need to prevent the player from calling `playSound()` when `soundPool` is null. Make the following change to the `playSound()` method:

```
public static void playSound(int soundID) {
        if (soundPool != null) {
                soundPool.play(soundID, 1, 1, 1, 0, 1);
        }
}
```

The updated **Assets** class is provided in listing 10.03.

Warning: Your package name may differ from all subsequent code listings because of the changes made to the Manifest earlier in the chapter.

Listing 10.03   Assets (Updated)

```
01 package com.jamescho.ellio;
02
03 import java.io.IOException;
04 import java.io.InputStream;
05
06 import android.graphics.Bitmap;
07 import android.graphics.Bitmap.Config;
08 import android.graphics.BitmapFactory;
09 import android.graphics.BitmapFactory.Options;
10 import android.media.AudioManager;
11 import android.media.SoundPool;
12
13 import com.jamescho.framework.animation.Animation;
14 import com.jamescho.framework.animation.Frame;
15
16 public class Assets {
17
18     private static SoundPool soundPool;
19     public static Bitmap welcome, block, cloud1, cloud2, duck, grass, jump, run1,
                 run2, run3, run4, run5, scoreDown, score, startDown, start;
20     public static int hitID, onJumpID;
21     public static Animation runAnim;
22
23     public static void load() {
24             welcome = loadBitmap("welcome.png", false);
25             block = loadBitmap("block.png", false);
26             cloud1 = loadBitmap("cloud1.png", true);
27             cloud2 = loadBitmap("cloud2.png", true);
28             duck = loadBitmap("duck.png", true);
29             grass = loadBitmap("grass.png", false);
30             jump = loadBitmap("jump.png", true);
31             run1 = loadBitmap("run_anim1.png", true);
32             run2 = loadBitmap("run_anim2.png", true);
33             run3 = loadBitmap("run_anim3.png",  true);
34             run4 = loadBitmap("run_anim4.png", true);
35             run5 = loadBitmap("run_anim5.png", true);
36             scoreDown = loadBitmap("score_button_down.png", true);
37             score = loadBitmap("score_button.png", true);
38             startDown = loadBitmap("start_button_down.png", true);
39             start = loadBitmap("start_button.png", true);
40
41             Frame f1 = new Frame(run1, .1f);
42             Frame f2 = new Frame(run2, .1f);
43             Frame f3 = new Frame(run3, .1f);
44             Frame f4 = new Frame(run4, .1f);
45             Frame f5 = new Frame(run5, .1f);
46             runAnim = new Animation(f1, f2, f3, f4, f5, f3, f2);
47     }
48
49     public static void onResume() {
50             hitID = loadSound("hit.wav");
51             onJumpID = loadSound("onjump.wav");
52     }
53
54     public static void onPause() {
55             if (soundPool != null) {
56                     soundPool.release();
```

```
57                          soundPool = null;
58                  }
59          }
60
61      private static Bitmap loadBitmap(String filename, boolean transparency) {
62              InputStream inputStream = null;
63              try {
64                      inputStream = GameMainActivity.assets.open(filename);
65              } catch (IOException e) {
66                      e.printStackTrace();
67              }
68
69              Options options = new Options();
70
71              if (transparency) {
72                      options.inPreferredConfig = Config.ARGB_8888;
73              } else {
74                      options.inPreferredConfig = Config.RGB_565;
75              }
76              Bitmap bitmap = BitmapFactory.decodeStream(inputStream, null, options);
77              return bitmap;
78      }
79
80      private static int loadSound(String filename) {
81              int soundID = 0;
82              if (soundPool == null) {
83                      soundPool = new SoundPool(25, AudioManager.STREAM_MUSIC, 0);
84              }
85              try {
86                  soundID = soundPool.load(GameMainActivity.assets.openFd(filename), 1);
87              } catch (IOException e) {
88                  e.printStackTrace();
89              }
90              return soundID;
91      }
92
93      public static void playSound(int soundID) {
94              if (soundPool != null) {
95                      soundPool.play(soundID, 1, 1, 1, 0, 1);
96              }
97      }
98 }
```

The **State** class also needs the onResume() and onPause() methods in order to respond to the Activity's resume and pause events. Remember that the **State** class is an abstract superclass, so creating non-abstract onResume() and onPause() methods allows all **State** subclasses to *optionally* override onResume() and onPause() to provide some functionality. Add the empty onResume() and onPause() methods as shown in listing 10.04.

Listing 10.04   State (Updated)

```
package com.jamescho.game.state;
```

```
import android.view.MotionEvent;

import com.jamescho.ellio.GameMainActivity;
import com.jamescho.framework.util.Painter;

public abstract class State {

        public void setCurrentState(State newState) {
                GameMainActivity.sGame.setCurrentState(newState);
        }

        public abstract void init();

        public abstract void update(float delta);

        public abstract void render(Painter g);

        public abstract boolean onTouch(MotionEvent e, int scaledX, int scaledY);

        public void onResume() {}

        public void onPause() {}

}
```

Note: We intentionally keep the `State.onResume()` and `State.onPause()` empty (these methods should be overridden by a particular state wanting to be informed of the Activity's lifecycle changes), but you could provide some default functionality for every state class by adding to the method bodies.

Adding `onResume()` *and* `onPause()` *to* `GameView` *and* `GameMainActivity`

The **GameMainActivity** does not have access to the current state. Therefore, it must ask the **GameView** to call the current state's `onResume()` and `onPause()` methods on the Activity's behalf. Add the following two methods to your **GameView** class.

```
public void onResume() {
        if (currentState != null) {
                currentState.onResume();
        }
}
public void onPause() {
        if (currentState != null) {
                currentState.onPause();
        }
}
```

Finally, let's make the most important change. Add these two methods to the **GameMainActivity** class.

```
@Override
protected void onResume() {
```

```
        super.onResume();
        Assets.onResume();
        sGame.onResume();
}

@Override
protected void onPause() {
        super.onPause();
        Assets.onPause();
        sGame.onPause();
}
```

Let's summarize the changes. We've allowed our **Assets** class and the currentState to respond to the Activity's onResume() and onPause() method by giving each of them two methods of the same name and calling these methods inside our GameMainActivity.onResume() and GameMainActivity.onPause() methods.

The **Assets** class can now use its onResume() and onPause() methods to load and dispose of certain resources. The currentState can now override onResume() and onPause() in order to provide some functionality. We will explore this feature next.

Note: If you are having problems with any of the classes at this point, you can download the source code at jamescho7.com/book/chapter10/checkpoint1

Implementing Pause to the PlayState

Thanks to the changes we have just made, your **PlayState** can pause and resume as the player switches in and out of your game. Implementing this entails adding a few new variables and making a few changes to the update() and render() methods. The full, updated **PlayState** class is provided in listing 10.05. As all of the changes are self-explanatory, I will allow you to review the changes highlighted on your own. I have added some comments to help you with this process.

Note: An ARGB color allows you to set an RGB color with an alpha (transparency) channel. Each value is provided as an integer out of 255. The value 153/255, then, would mean 60% opacity.

Listing 10.05   PlayState (Updated)

```
package com.jamescho.game.state;

import java.util.ArrayList;

import android.graphics.Color;
import android.graphics.Rect;
import android.graphics.Typeface;
import android.view.MotionEvent;

import com.jamescho.framework.util.Painter;
import com.jamescho.game.model.Block;
import com.jamescho.game.model.Cloud;
```

```java
import com.jamescho.game.model.Player;
import com.jamescho.simpleandroidgdf.Assets;
import com.jamescho.simpleandroidgdf.GameMainActivity;

public class PlayState extends State {

    private Player player;
    private ArrayList<Block> blocks;
    private Cloud cloud, cloud2;

    private int playerScore = 0;

    private static final int BLOCK_HEIGHT = 50;
    private static final int BLOCK_WIDTH = 20;
    private int blockSpeed = -200;

    private static final int PLAYER_WIDTH = 66;
    private static final int PLAYER_HEIGHT = 92;

    private float recentTouchY;

    // Boolean to keep track of game pauses.
    private boolean gamePaused = false;
    // String displayed when paused.
    private String pausedString = "Game Paused. Tap to resume.";

    @Override
    public void init() {
        player = new Player(160, GameMainActivity.GAME_HEIGHT - 45 - PLAYER_HEIGHT,
                PLAYER_WIDTH, PLAYER_HEIGHT);
        blocks = new ArrayList<Block>();
        cloud = new Cloud(100, 100);
        cloud2 = new Cloud(500, 50);

        for (int i = 0; i < 5; i++) {
            Block b = new Block(i * 200, GameMainActivity.GAME_HEIGHT - 95,
                    BLOCK_WIDTH, BLOCK_HEIGHT);
            blocks.add(b);
        }
    }

    // Overrides onPause() from State.
    // Called when Activity is pausing.
    @Override
    public void onPause() {
        gamePaused = true;
    }

    @Override
    public void update(float delta) {
        // If game is paused, do not update anything.
        if (gamePaused) {
            return;
        }

        if (!player.isAlive()) {
            setCurrentState(new GameOverState(playerScore / 100));
        }
```

```
        playerScore += 1;

        if (playerScore % 500 == 0 && blockSpeed > -280) {
                blockSpeed -= 10;
        }

        cloud.update(delta);
        cloud2.update(delta);
        Assets.runAnim.update(delta);
        player.update(delta);
        updateBlocks(delta);
}

private void updateBlocks(float delta) {
        for (int i = 0; i < blocks.size(); i++) {
                Block b = blocks.get(i);
                b.update(delta, blockSpeed);

                if (b.isVisible()) {
                        if (player.isDucked() && Rect.intersects(b.getRect(),
                                        player.getDuckRect())) {
                                b.onCollide(player);
                        } else if (!player.isDucked() && Rect.intersects(b.getRect(),
                                        player.getRect())) {
                                b.onCollide(player);
                        }

                }
        }
}

@Override
public void render(Painter g) {
        g.setColor(Color.rgb(208, 244, 247));
        g.fillRect(0, 0, GameMainActivity.GAME_WIDTH, GameMainActivity.GAME_HEIGHT);

        renderPlayer(g);
        renderBlocks(g);
        renderSun(g);
        renderClouds(g);
        g.drawImage(Assets.grass, 0, 405);
        renderScore(g);

        // If game is Paused, draw additional UI elements:
        if (gamePaused) {
                // ARGB is used to set an ARGB color.
                // See note accompanying listing 10.05.
                g.setColor(Color.argb(153, 0, 0, 0));
                g.fillRect(0, 0, GameMainActivity.GAME_WIDTH,
                                        GameMainActivity.GAME_HEIGHT);
                g.drawString(pausedString, 235, 240);
        }

}

private void renderScore(Painter g) {
        g.setFont(Typeface.SANS_SERIF, 25);
        g.setColor(Color.GRAY);
        g.drawString("" + playerScore / 100, 20, 30);
```

```
        }

    private void renderPlayer(Painter g) {
        if (player.isGrounded()) {
            if (player.isDucked()) {
                g.drawImage(Assets.duck, (int) player.getX(), (int) player.getY());
            } else {
                Assets.runAnim.render(g, (int) player.getX(), (int) player.getY(),
                        player.getWidth(), player.getHeight());
            }
        } else {
            g.drawImage(Assets.jump, (int) player.getX(), (int) player.getY(),
                    player.getWidth(), player.getHeight());
        }
    }

    private void renderBlocks(Painter g) {
        for (int i = 0; i < blocks.size(); i++) {
            Block b = blocks.get(i);
            if (b.isVisible()) {
                g.drawImage(Assets.block, (int) b.getX(), (int) b.getY(),
                        BLOCK_WIDTH, BLOCK_HEIGHT);
            }
        }
    }

    private void renderSun(Painter g) {
        g.setColor(Color.rgb(255, 165, 0));
        g.fillOval(715, -85, 170, 170);
        g.setColor(Color.YELLOW);
        g.fillOval(725, -75, 150, 150);
    }

    private void renderClouds(Painter g) {
        g.drawImage(Assets.cloud1, (int) cloud.getX(), (int) cloud.getY(), 100, 60);
        g.drawImage(Assets.cloud2, (int) cloud2.getX(), (int) cloud2.getY(), 100, 60);
    }

    @Override
    public boolean onTouch(MotionEvent e, int scaledX, int scaledY) {
        if (e.getAction() == MotionEvent.ACTION_DOWN) {
            recentTouchY = scaledY;
        } else if (e.getAction() == MotionEvent.ACTION_UP) {
            // Resume game if paused.
            if (gamePaused) {
                gamePaused = false;
                return true;
            }
            if (scaledY - recentTouchY < -50) {
                player.jump();
            } else if (scaledY - recentTouchY > 50) {
                player.duck();
            }
        }
        return true;
    }

}
```

With those changes made to the **GameState** class, your game should now pause when you press the home button or switch to a new application, as shown in Figure 10-13.

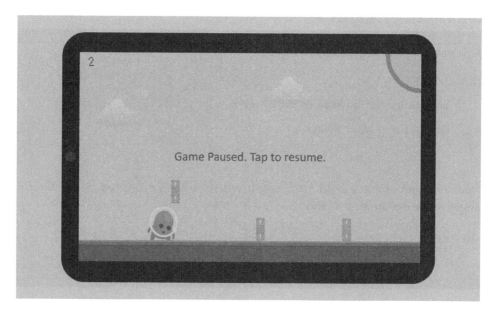

Game Paused. Tap to resume.

Figure 10-13 *Ellio* Paused

Now, players won't be punished when they need to take a phone call. Ellio will patiently wait mid-action.

Feeling adventurous? As an exercise, try adding a new button to allow the player to pause the game without switching to a new Activity. Hint: the **UIButton** class may come in handy.

Note: The back button will exit an Activity completely, and our game will not be able to resume after a back button press. You could listen for the back button and make it behave as a pause button or have it navigate the game to the previous state, but I will not be doing that for *Ellio*.

Adding Music

Ellio is jumping around and making a lot of noise, but the air is awfully silent. Let's make things a little livelier by adding in some background music!

To add music, we need to make use of the **MediaPlayer** class (android.media.MediaPlayer). A **MediaPlayer** object behaves very much like a **SoundPool** object, accepting a desired file and playing it when asked.

Recall that music is distinct from sound because it tends to be longer and thus requires a larger file. Rather than putting an entire track into RAM, we will stream music directly from the file system.

Open your **Assets** class once more, and importing the following:

```
import android.content.res.AssetFileDescriptor;
import android.media.MediaPlayer;
```

Next, declare a new **MediaPlayer** object:

```
....
public class Assets {
....

        private static MediaPlayer mediaPlayer;

        public static void load() {

....
```

A **MediaPlayer** object should be released when no longer needed. Make the following changes to the onPause() method.

```
public static void onPause() {
        if (soundPool != null) {
                soundPool.release();
                soundPool = null;
        }

        if (mediaPlayer != null) {
                mediaPlayer.stop();
                mediaPlayer.release();
                mediaPlayer = null;
        }
}
```

Lastly, let's create a method that will allow us to easily play music by providing a name of a music file inside the **assets** folder. Add the playMusic() method shown in listing 10.06:

Listing 10.06   playMusic()

```
public static void playMusic(String filename, boolean looping) {
    if (mediaPlayer == null) {
        mediaPlayer = new MediaPlayer();
    }
    try {
        AssetFileDescriptor afd = GameMainActivity.assets.openFd(filename);
        mediaPlayer.setDataSource(afd.getFileDescriptor(), afd.getStartOffset(),
                        afd.getLength());
        mediaPlayer.setAudioStreamType(AudioManager.STREAM_MUSIC);
        mediaPlayer.prepare();
        mediaPlayer.setLooping(looping);
        mediaPlayer.start();
    } catch (Exception e) {
        e.printStackTrace();
    }
}
```

The `playMusic()` method looks intimidating (and the underlying implementation can be), but let's try to understand it, a few lines at a time. Before I explain the code, keep these points in mind:

- A **MediaPlayer** object, like an Activity, has a lifecycle. It begins its life in the idle state and cannot play music until it has been initialized and prepared.
- To initialize a **MediaPlayer**, we must provide it with a data source. We cannot simply give it a filename. We must provide a music file's file descriptor (this concept is beyond the scope of this book, but think of it as some integer representation of a file inside the OS), and tell it how many bytes of data to read.
- A **MediaPlayer** can be used for many purposes (such as playing notification sounds or alarm sounds). We will be using it to stream music, and will explicitly say so.

Let's talk about `playMusic()` in detail, starting with the method header. Notice that the method accepts two arguments: `String filename` and `boolean looping`. We will come back to these arguments later.

In the method body, we first check if `mediaPlayer` is `null`, instantiating one if necessary. At instantiation, the `mediaPlayer` will be in the idle state. Next, we retrieve the file descriptor for the music file and provide it as the data source for the **MediaPlayer** object, telling it to play from the beginning to end using `afd.getStartOffset()` and `afd.getLength()`. Now, `mediaPlayer` is in the initialized state. Next, we tell the `mediaPlayer` that it will be streaming music. Before it can play anything, however, we must tell it to get ready by calling `prepare()` to put it in the prepared state. Lastly, we set looping to the value of `boolean looping` and tell it to start playing.

A catch block is required as many of these methods may fail if you call them at the wrong time or provide an invalid argument.

Note: If you are confused, it may help to see the official documentation on the **MediaPlayer** class at the following URL: `http://developer.android.com/reference/android/media/MediaPlayer.html`

Let's make sure everything is working properly by downloading an mp3 file to play as our background music. I recently discovered Matt McFarland (**mattmcfarland.com**)–a very talented composer who makes high-quality royalty free music available on his website. Matt's music can be used without licensing fees in your projects, as long as you give him credit and link to his site!

We will be using the *Nintendo was Cool* track (listen to it at `mattmcfarland.com/song/nintendo-was-cool/`) as it captures the light-hearted, rhythmic feel of *Ellio* perfectly. Download the track for free at Matt's website (along with the license information), rename it to `bgmusic.mp3` and add it to the **assets** folder as shown in Figure 10-14.

Figure 10-14 Adding the Music File

Let's also download a new `welcome.png` with proper attribution for the music. You can download the image shown in Figure 10-15 at the link following URL: `jamescho7.com/book/chapter10/`

Figure 10-15 New welcome.png

Since we will be streaming music directly from the file system, we do not need to create a new variable for the newly-added `bgmusic.mp3`. Instead, add the following line of code shown in bold to your `Assets.onResume()` method:

```
public static void onResume() {
        hitID = loadSound("hit.wav");
        onJumpID = loadSound("onjump.wav");
        playMusic("bgmusic.mp3", true);
}
```

Now, every time your **GameMainActivity**'s onResume() method is called, *Nintendo was Cool* will start playing. This music will continue to loop until another Activity takes our game's place on the screen. Run your game and make sure this is working!

Note: If you are having problems with any of the classes at this point, you can download the source code at jamescho7.com/book/chapter10/checkpoint2

Here's an exercise for you. Make a copy of your project and try creating a button in the **MenuState** that allows users to mute all sounds (you will probably want to use the **UIButton** class). For an additional challenge, see if you can save the state of the button (muted or unmuted) using **GameMainActivity**'s shared preferences. If you get stuck, a solution is available on jamescho7.com/book/chapter10.

Uploading an Updated APK to Google Play

Now that we have added some new features to *Ellio*, let's upload the newest APK to the store. Before we do that, however, we must change the version information in our AndroidManifest.xml as shown below.

```
<manifest xmlns:android="http://schemas.android.com/apk/res/android"
    package="com.jamescho.ellio"
    android:versionCode="1"
    android:versionName="1.0" >
    android:versionCode="2"
    android:versionName="1.1" >
....
```

As mentioned in Chapter 7, you should increment android:versionCode by 1 each time you update our application. This value will be used to determine whether one version of the app is an upgrade or a downgrade with respect to another. The android:versionName option can follow any convention you wish. For this example, I have chosen **1.1,** but **2.0** or even **1.0001** would be valid.

Now that the Manifest has been updated, you must export the Android project as an APK file again. Repeat the steps from Make sure you use the same keystore from earlier in the chapter by choosing the **Use existing keystore** option rather than **Create new keystore**. Otherwise you will be unable to update the existing listing in your Developer Console.

Once your APK is ready, log back into your Developer Console, select the *Ellio* application listing, go to the APK page, and click **Upload new APK to Production**. Once the upload is complete, you should see a confirmation dialog as shown in Figure 10-16.

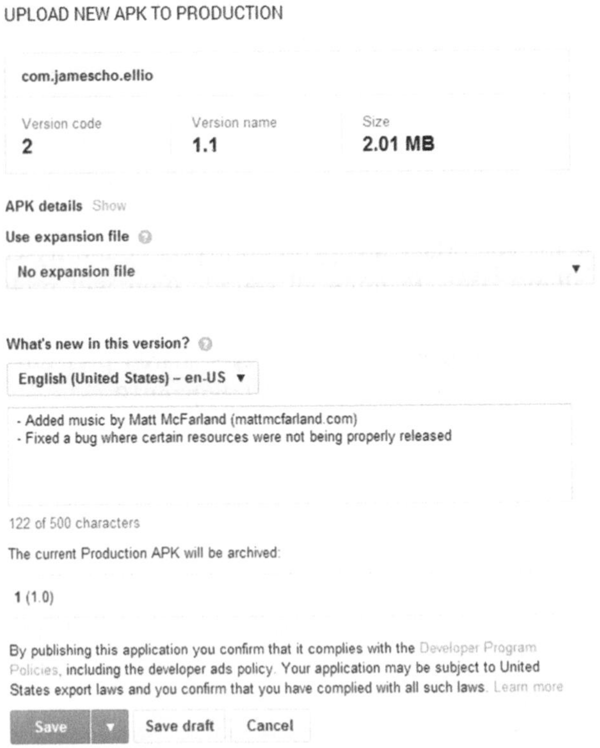

UPLOAD NEW APK TO PRODUCTION

com.jamescho.ellio

Version code	Version name	Size
2	**1.1**	**2.01 MB**

APK details Show

Use expansion file

No expansion file ▼

What's new in this version?

English (United States) – en-US ▼

- Added music by Matt McFarland (mattmcfarland.com)
- Fixed a bug where certain resources were not being properly released

122 of 500 characters

The current Production APK will be archived:

1 (1.0)

By publishing this application you confirm that it complies with the Developer Program Policies, including the developer ads policy. Your application may be subject to United States export laws and you confirm that you have complied with all such laws. Learn more

Save ▼   Save draft   Cancel

Figure 10-16   Saving the APK

Press **Save**, and the newest version of your game will be available through the Play Store. For those who have enabled auto-update, the new version will automatically begin downloading on their devices the next time their device checks for updates!

Integrating Google Play Game Services

In 2013, Google announced the Google Play game services—a tool that is designed to help developers enhance their games by adding social features using Google's API and infrastructure. Thanks to this new service, developers can now add global leaderboards, achievements, real-time multiplayer, quests and more into their games without worrying about maintaining their own servers and writing code to support networking.

Google Play game services are extremely powerful. With a few lines of code, you can allow users to sign into their Google accounts and store achievements, high-scores and game saves to the cloud. Under this cross-platform service, user data synchronizes across players' devices, meaning that players do not have to worry about losing progress as they switch from one device to another. As of this writing, Google Play games services support Android, iOS, and web-based games.

I will not be providing step-by-step instructions for integrating Google Play game services into *Ellio*, as Google has some top-notch instructions on their Developers website. Instead, I will give you a general overview of the concepts, allow you to experiment on your own with some sample projects, and share the full source code demonstrating a leaderboard implementation in *Ellio*.

The Player's Perspective

Before you learn how to integrate the game services, let's see an example of it in action. I have implemented a leaderboard using the Google Play game services in *Ellio*. Upon opening *Ellio* for the first time, players will see the pop-up shown in Figure 10-17.

Figure 10-17   Connecting to Google Play

Once the player successfully signs in, the game will automatically display a welcome message. In addition, a sign out button will appear on the top-left corner of the screen, and the Score button will display a Google Play Games icon to indicate that it is now social. This is shown in Figure 10-18.

With this simple change, players' local high scores are now submitted to Google's servers and shared with the world. Of course, *Ellio* is a demo game that people will not be competing over, but this could be an exciting way to encourage players to spend more time fighting monsters or setting records in your future games.

Feel free to download *Ellio* at `play.google.com/store/apps/details?id=com.jamescho.ellio` to see the leaderboard for yourself!

Figure 10-18   Welcome Player!

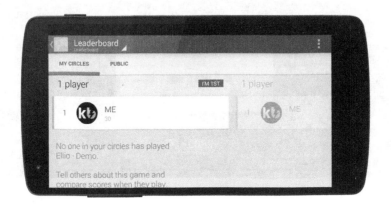

Figure 10-19   *Ellio* Leaderboard

The Developer's Perspective

As mentioned earlier, Google provides step-by-step instructions on getting an app integrated with Google Play game services. In order to provide some context, let me give you a brief overview of the different components involved and discuss how these pieces fit together. Remember that the following points are just for conceptual understanding. More details are provided in the official instructions.

1. Google Play game services are powered by Google's servers. In order for us to use the services, we must first download the **Google Play Services SDK**, which includes classes that will enable us to communicate with the servers.

2. We are specifically interested in the **Google Play game services API** included with **Google Play Services SDK**.

3. To make it as easy as possible to use the **Google Play game services API**, Google provides a **BaseGameUtils** library. One of the classes in this library is called **BaseGameActivity**. This class should be used as the superclass of **GameMainActivity**, replacing the existing **Activity** superclass.

4. Google handles a game application and its game service separately. In the Developer Console, we must register a new game service and link it to our game application. This allows our game service to authenticate our game when it attempts to connect.

5. The newly-created game service mentioned in step 4 will receive an ID (called an OAuth 2.0 client ID). We must add this to our Android project's Manifest so that our application can connect to the correct game service.

6. The game service entry in the Developer Console mentioned in steps 4 and 5 is used to configure leaderboards, achievements and events. For example, if you wanted to add an achievement for *Ellio* that should be unlocked when the player reaches the score of a hundred, you would add it to the game service in the Developer Console. An example is shown in Figure 10-20.

Figure 10-20   Adding a New Achievement

7.   For each new quest, achievement or leaderboard you add to the game service, you will receive an ID such as Ck5azno11kn631km43. This ID is used within

your app to reference a specific quest, achievement or leaderboard. For example, when the player of *Ellio* reaches a score of 100, we could run the following line of code (the ID is just an example):

```
Games.Achievements.unlock(getApiClient(), "Ck5azno1lkn631km43");
```

The ID is used to specify which achievement inside your game service should be unlocked for the current user.

On Your Own: Integrating Google Play Game Services
Now that you have a general idea of the steps you need to take in order to integrate game services, follow Google's guides to experiment with a sample project.

1. **Getting Started for Android Game Development:** developers.google.com/games/services/android/quickstart

> **Note:** When registering a new game service entry, (developers.google.com/games/services/console/enabling) you will be asked to provide a SHA1 signing certificate fingerprint. This is a unique ID associated with a keystore used when signing an application.
>
> Your app will only be able to communicate with a game service entry if it has been signed with the keystore whose SHA1 signing certificate fingerprint has been registered in the developer console for that game service entry.
>
> You need to be aware that when you run an application using Eclipse, it will be signed using a debug keystore. An exported APK will be signed using the keystore that you specify.
>
> The signing certificate for the **debug keystore** can be located in Eclipse at **Window > Preferences > Android > Build** as shown:

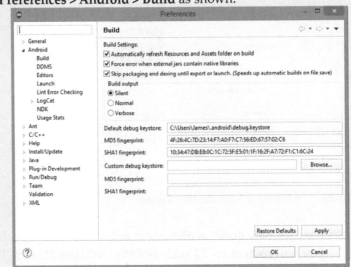

The signing certificate for a **release keystore** is displayed when exporting an application with that keystore, as shown below:

2. Leaderboards in Android: `developers.google.com/games/services/android /leaderboards`

You should also reference the **Quality Checklist for Google Play Game Services** (`developers.google.com/games/services/checklist`) for rules to follow when implementing game services.

Download the Source Code

The full source code for *Ellio* with a leaderboard implementation, along with step-by-step instructions on configuring the game project and game service for testing, can be found at `jamescho7.com/book/chapter10/complete`. Remember that if you are having any trouble getting things working, let me know in the forums at the book's companion site `jamescho7.com`. I will try to help as best as I can.

If you've successfully integrated Google Play games services into your *Ellio* project, congratulations! Now you know how to publish a game on the Play Store, release updates and even integrate cloud-based features. You have all the skills and knowledge necessary to start creating some exciting games for people to enjoy. Of course, you will need to spend a lot of time practicing and experimenting in order to make games that people will play regularly. In Chapter 11, we will talk about how you can continue to improve your skill and your games.

Note: Appendix C summarizes all the steps you will need to take in order to build and publish a game using our Android game development framework, covering all of the material from Units 3 and 4.

.

CHAPTER 11: CONTINUING THE JOURNEY

You've made it to the end of the book. That means you've built an Android game from scratch just like you've set out to do and picked up the Java programming language in the process; however, if you plan to continue pursuing game development (as I hope you will) the journey is far from over.

As you know, game development is wide ranging and extensive area. Despite my best efforts to make this book comprehensive, there were a lot of topics that I could not cover. In spite of this, my hope is that—in reading this book from start to finish—you have built a solid foundation upon which you can continue your quest to build great games. If I have done my job correctly, you will now be able to use the wealth of resources available online in order to continue getting better, so that you can start building those games with 3D graphics, networking, artificial intelligence, particle effects, controller support, and other exciting features that will immerse your players.

Publish a Game!

Before moving on to bigger, newer topics, I recommend that you first try making a complete Android game of your own to publish and share with the world by using the game framework (see Appendix C for a step-by-step overview). The book's companion site `jamescho7.com` will be a great resource for learning how to implement certain features and building a better game; you will be able to access all of the source code from this book, download sample game projects for you to reverse-engineer, and learn even more about game development. By applying the concepts you've learned in this book to build your own products, you will be able to solidify your understanding and prepare yourself for further learning.

Additional Resources

If you are looking for inspiration, join a community of game developers such as the one at `java-gaming.org`. You will find thousands of fellow developers who are committed to building high-performance Java games, and you will realize that there is no limit to what you can accomplish using Java!

To learn more about Android, Play Services and more, subscribe to the Android Developers channel on YouTube at the following URL:

`youtube.com/channel/UCVHFbqXqoYvEWM1Ddxl0QDg`

You will regularly find relevant, interesting videos and learn new information you can use in order to improve our Android game development framework.

I'd also like to share the tutorial website created by my indie game development company. At `tuts.kilobolt.com`, we offer tutorials on topics such as Android, libGDX (more on this in the next section) and team collaboration.

Figure 11-1   `tuts.kilobolt.com`

We also maintain a friendly community forum at `forum.kilobolt.com` to help out when people are having issues with their projects. In addition, if you are interested, you will be able to find a team of developers to work on large-scale projects with! So go ahead and register and introduce yourself to the community. It would be awesome for me to get to know you!

Going Beyond

Eventually, you will want to move on from simple 2D Android games in search of greater games, and you will outgrow our basic Android game development framework. There are two broad pathways that you might take in order to take things to a higher level. Of course, these are generalizations, and you will likely find an intermediate path that works for you.

Pathway I: Learning to use a Game Engine or Game Framework

If you want to make highly-polished games packed with awesome features without learning how every detail is implemented in code, learning how to use a game engine or a popular game framework is your best bet. Doing so will mean that you can spend the majority of your development time on building your game, not preparing a framework to build a game.

My favorite game engine is Unity—a cross-platform engine that will allow you to build 2D and 3D games using an intuitive user interface. It lets you drag and drop characters, add fancy lighting effects, and build big game levels without writing a single line of code (of course you can add your own code to make the game behave exactly as you want it). Unity also comes with an Asset Store where you can download pre-made content such as animated characters, particle effects or environments to use in your own game.

Figure 11-2   Unity 2D Platformer Demo

Perhaps the greatest feature of Unity is its cross-platform nature. You can build a game once in the engine and deploy it to variety of platforms including iOS, Android, PC, Mac, and consoles. Unity *does* require a knowledge of C# (or Boo or JavaScript); however, C# is very similar to Java, and you will have little trouble learning it with the help of the official Unity site, which offers dozens of video tutorials and extensive documentation that will help you get started. For this, please see the following `unity3d.com/learn/tutorials /modules/beginner/scripting`.

An alternative to a full-fledged game engine is a game development framework such as libGDX (`libgdx.com`). Taking this route will mean that you will need to do a little more work to get the results you want, but this can be helpful when learning how games are built. If you want to stick with Java and you are happy with coding your game from start to finish rather than using a GUI game editor, libGDX is the perfect solution.

libGDX is an open source, cross-platform game development framework that allows you to build Java games that run on a variety of platforms, such as Windows, Mac, HTML5, Android and IOS. It is a constantly growing project that offers hundreds of classes for you to use in your projects, meaning that you do not have to waste time and resources on writing utility classes to solve problems that every other game developer has encountered in his or her career. To get started with libGDX, check out the official wiki: `github.com/libgdx/libgdx/wiki`

Pathway II: Studying the Technology of Game Development

Perhaps you care less about creating game content and care more about growing as a game programmer. If you are interested in the technical aspects of game development and want to learn more about the technologies that power modern games, here are some you might want to consider:

- OpenGL (Open Graphics Library): To make the leap into high performance 2D and 3D mobile games without relying on a game development framework, the natural first step is to learn OpenGL. See the Android API Guides on OpenGL ES (OpenGL for Embedded Systems) at the following URL for an introduction: `developer.android.com/guide/topics/graphics/opengl.html`
- Box2D: You might want to start implementing realistic physics into your games, so that your game objects react more realistically on the screen. You *could* build a brand new physics engine from scratch, but there is already a free, open source solution that has been featured in games such as *Angry Birds* and *Limbo*. Box2D is written in the C++ programming language, meaning that you must learn C/C++ to start tackling Box2D in its native language. For this, a great starting point is the official manual: `box2d.org/manual.pdf`

  Alternatively, you can begin using Box2D through game development frameworks such as libGDX, which can act as a bridge between your Java code and C++ Box2D code. For more on this, please see the following URL (Note: a basic knowledge of libGDX is recommended before you read this tutorial): `github.com/libgdx/libgdx/wiki/Box2d`

Of course, to be a better game programmer, you need to be a better programmer in general. Here are some tips on improving your skill.

1. Practice problem solving. Coders need to solve problems on a daily basis. As such, it is essential that you practice problem solving in order to become a versatile coder. Visit `codingbat.com` and `projecteuler.net` to start practicing.
2. Read lots of code. There is always someone better than you (and there's always someone worse). Find open source projects you are interested in and study how

other people approach certain problems. Learn from other people's successes and mistakes and incorporate this knowledge into your own work.

3. Write lots of code. You can read Shakespeare all day long, but you won't be able to write anywhere close to his level without practice. Create many mini-projects and try something new every day.

4. Study how computers work. If you understand the lower-level details of a computer's operation, you will be better equipped to write higher-level code. This means that you will be able to write more efficient code, which is crucial in game development.

Choosing to study the technology may be the more difficult path. It promises fewer immediate rewards and lots of hard work. In the long run, however, you will have a much more intimate understanding of game development. That means you will one day be able to write your own game engines, modify existing ones to suit your needs and, when the time comes, make your games much better.

Final Words

Thank you for reading! I hope this book was helpful in getting you up and running with game development. Now for your next quest, build on! I look forward to playing your games one day. Remember to tweet all the cheat codes to @jamescho7.

Appendix A: More on Static

To understand `static`, we will talk about a usage of the `static` keyword we have encountered and ignored throughout Unit 1: the main method. But first, as review, ask yourself what steps you must take to call a non-static method belonging to some class, such as those shown in listing A.01.

Listing A.01   A Very Simple Class

```java
public class SimpleClass {
    private int age;

    public void sayHello() {
        System.out.println("Hello");
    }

    public void sayAge() {
        System.out.println("My age is " + age);
    }

    public static void main(String[] args) {
        // What goes here?
    }

}
```

What would go inside the main method if you wanted to call the `sayHello()` method? Think about it for a second and write down an answer.

If you thought the following, you would be wrong:

```java
public static void main(String[] args) {
        sayHello();
}
```

Remember that if you want to use a method belonging to the **SimpleClass**, you must first instantiate the class. The correct answer is as follows:

```java
public static void main(String[] args) {
        SimpleClass simple = new SimpleClass();
        simple.sayHello();
}
```

In the case of listing A.01, it was very easy to instantiate **SimpleClass** to call its method; however, in some situations, this is not the case.

Uses of Static

The keyword `static` exists for situations in which you cannot instantiate an object prior to using its variables and methods. The main method in listing A.01 is a good example. If the main method were not `static`, where would you instantiate **SimpleClass** to call its main method? You couldn't.

The keyword `static` is also useful when a method or a variable is not dependent on some property of an instance of some class. In listing A.01, for example, the `sayHello()` method will perform the exact same behavior for ALL instances of **SimpleClass**. In such a situation, you may be better off making the method `static` so that you do not have to create an instance of the object to use the method.

In contrast, the implementation of `sayAge()` depends on the individual object's modifiable `age` variable. It would not make sense for it to be `static`, as EACH instance of **SimpleClass** should have its own `age` and therefore `sayAge()`.

APPENDIX B: SIMPLE PHYSICS OF MOTION

Let's review some elementary physics concepts and discuss how they fit into game development. We will specifically be focusing on the two-dimensional motion of simple bodies.

Position is the location of a body at a given time. We can express this using an x value and a y value. In our game development frameworks, the position will be the top-left corner of a character's sprite, as shown in Figure B-1.

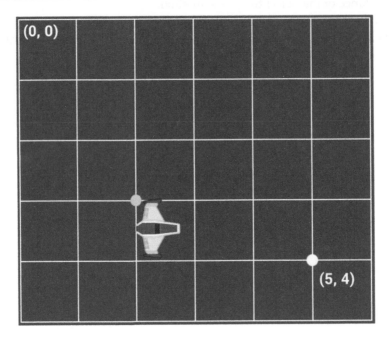

Figure B-1   Position Example (Spaceship Art by **Kenney.nl**)

In the example shown in Figure B-1, the spaceship has an x-position of 2 and a y-position of 3. Note that we use the top-left corner as the origin and that x and y increase to the bottom right direction. Coordinate systems in computer graphics are typically handled this way.

Velocity is the signed (+ or -) speed of a body. A given velocity describes how the position of an object will change with respect to time.

To illustrate this, assume that the spaceship shown in Figure B-1 has an x-velocity of 3 per frame and a y-velocity of 1 per frame. In the frame following Figure B-1 (approximately

17 milliseconds later at 60 FPS), the spaceship will have a *new* position of (x = 5, y = 4). Note that x-velocity and y-velocity do not interact with each other.

Acceleration describes the change in velocity of a body per given time. As with velocity, acceleration in the x-axis is independent from acceleration in the y-axis.

Acceleration is most commonly used to implement gravity in games and to provide smooth changes in a character's velocity. If you want a character to begin moving, consider adding to the acceleration values rather than the velocity values. This will give you a more natural result.

Listing B.01 provides a simple example of how acceleration, velocity and position can be handled in a game object's update() method.

Listing B.01   A Very Simple Class

```
public class Spaceship {
    private float x,y;
    private float velX, velY;
    private float accelX, accelY;

    private Spaceship (float x, float y, float velX, float velY, float accelX,
                    float accelY) {
        this.x = x;
        this.y = y;
        this.velX = velX;
        this.velY = velY;
        this.accelX = accelX;
        this.accelY = accelY;
    }

    Private void update(float delta) {
        // Accelerate Object
        velX += accelX * delta;
        velY += accelY * delta;

        // Reposition Object
        x += velX * delta;
        y += velY * delta;
    }
}
```

APPENDIX C: BUILDING ANDROID GAMES IN 7 STEPS

This Appendix condenses the material covered in Units 3 and 4 into a simple, actionable guide. Some of the steps may be taken out of sequence at your convenience.

Step 1: Design Your Game

The best place to begin developing a game is away from a computer. I always start with a simple gameplay idea—something that will be fun to do as a player. I then jot down ideas and draw a bunch of pictures until I have a design that I am happy with. I *then* start outlining the Java classes that I will be requiring, and begin coding. When designing and building a game, use an iterative process where you continuously design and redesign your game as you experiment with various features.

This is a good stage for you to consider if and how you will monetize your game. A good resource for this is provided below:

`developer.android.com/training/distribute.html`

You should also decide whether you will be making use of Google Play game services.

Step 2: Download the Most Recent Android Game Development Framework

Visit `jamescho7.com/book/downloads` to download the Eclipse project for the game development framework. Import it into your Eclipse workspace and rename it as needed.

Upon doing so, you may see a bunch of Java errors. This typically occurs when you do not have the version of the Android platform that was used to build the project. The simple fix is to right-click on your project (Ctrl + click on Mac) and select **Properties**. Next, select **Android** as shown in Figure C-1 and choose the most recent target. Hit **Apply** and press **OK**.

Figure C-1   Selecting a Build Target

Step 3: Update the Icons

Open the **res/drawable** folders and replace the icon images. The appropriate image resolutions are provided below:
- LDPI: 36 x 36px
- MDPI: 48 x 48px
- HDPI: 72 x 72px
- XHDPI: 96 x 96px

Step 4: Update the Package Name

You must change the package name of your application in three different places. Firstly, you should change the package name of com.jamescho.simpleandroidgdf in the workspace to a desired value. Next, open AndroidManifest.xml and update the manifest and activity tags to mirror the change (lines needing change are highlighted in bold below).

```
<manifest xmlns:android="http://schemas.android.com/apk/res/android"
        package="com.jamescho.simpleandroidgdf"
        ....
                <activity
                        android:screenOrientation="sensorLandscape"
                        android:name="com.jamescho.simpleandroidgdf.GameMainActivity"
                        ....
```

You can also set the name of your Android game using the android:label attribute in the Manifest.

Step 5: Build the Game

At this point, you need to build your game, using state and model classes as your building blocks.

Choosing a game resolution: For simplicity and an easy transition from Java to Android, *Ellio* has used a fixed 800 x 450 game resolution. For your games, you may want a more flexible solution so that each device has a game resolution equal to its screen size. To see an example of how you might implement this, please see jamescho7.com/book/samples.

If you do not want to create your own assets, the following resources may be of use:

Art: kenney.nl
Music: mattmcfarland.com
Sounds: bfxr.net

Step 6: Integrate Google Play Game Services (Optional)

Please see the samples (jamescho7.com/book/samples) and the official Google guides for help with this process.

Introduction
developer.android.com/google/play-services/games.html

Getting Started
developers.google.com/games/services/android/quickstart

Quality Checklist for Google Play Game Services
developers.google.com/games/services/checklist

Step 7: Deploy Your Game and Market It!
Export your game as an APK and upload it to the Developer Console
(play.google.com/apps/publish/). Next, use the power of social media to tell the
world about your game! At this point, you should be actively listening to user feedback
and updating your game as necessary.

Lightning Source UK Ltd.
Milton Keynes UK
UKOW07f1248080715

254740UK00005B/35/P